BRIDGER

T0308777

Brad and Michele Moore Roots Music Series

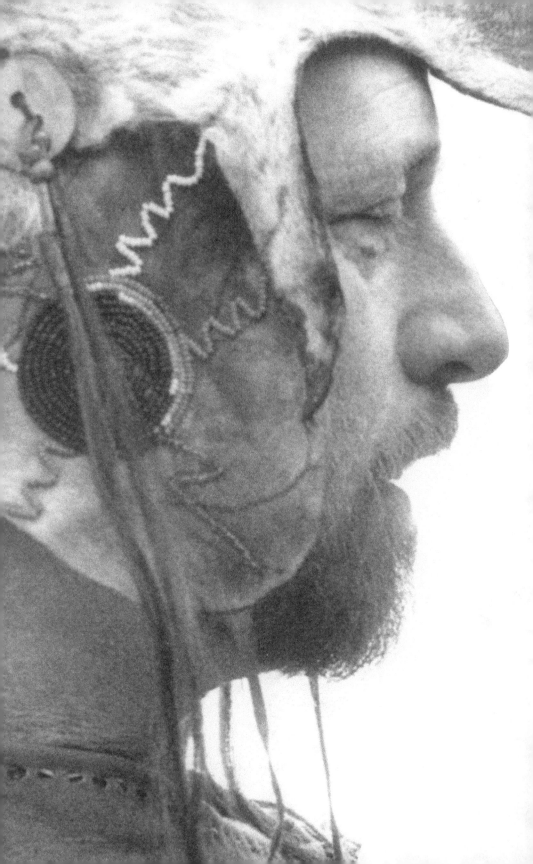

B R I D G E R

Bobby Bridger

University of Texas Press  Austin

Requests for permission to reproduce material from this work should be sent to:

Permissions
University of Texas Press
P.O. Box 7819
Austin, TX 78713-7819
utpress.utexas.edu/rp-form

♾ The paper used in this book meets the minimum requirements of ANSI/NISO Z39.48-1992 (R1997) (Permanence of Paper).

Library of Congress Cataloging-in-Publication Data

Bridger, Bobby.
Bridger / Bobby Bridger. — 1st ed.
    p. cm. — (Brad and Michele Moore roots music series)
Includes index.
ISBN 978-1-4773-2699-5 (paperback: alk. paper)
  1. Bridger, Bobby. 2. Musicians—United States—Biography. I. Title.
ML420.B7775A3 2009
781.642092—dc22
[B]
                                         2008033286

For Hill and Roberta

Contents

BRIDGER

Acknowledgments

MY UNUSUAL CAREER WOULD HAVE WITHERED in the 1970s without the steadfast support of Vine Deloria Jr. My closest friend for over thirty years, Vine adopted me into his family and introduced my historical ballads to important individuals, organizations, and institutions throughout America. On those numerous occasions when my work slipped through the cracks, Vine *always* stood beside me with encouragement and intelligent suggestions for alternative plans. He wrote introductions and forewords for print publications of *A Ballad of the West* and liner notes for record releases of the trilogy. At the time of his passing in November 2005 he was helping with editorial notes for this text. In 1996, when I completed the first draft of a manuscript based on Buffalo Bill's relationship with Plains Indians, Vine suggested I submit it to the University of Texas Press. Theresa May, assistant director and editor-in-chief at UT Press, proved such a talented guide through every aspect of publishing *Buffalo Bill and Sitting Bull: Inventing the Wild West* that I wanted very much to work with her again. So when we had a moment to visit during the 2003 Texas Book Festival in Austin, I mentioned that I was working on an autobiography. I was thrilled when Theresa immediately asked to have a look at it. Over the past four years, through multiple drafts, Theresa once again offered straightforward criticism and clever editorial insight that helped prune and shape my text. Finally, I was fortunate to have copy editors Lynne Chapman and Jan McInroy go through my manuscript with a fine-tooth comb. Their corrections and insightful comments made a much-improved final draft.

BRIDGER

PROLOGUE

The Remuda

I SPURRED MY HORSE AND SLAPPED HIS WITHERS HARD with my reins as we galloped over open prairie. In a cloud of dust a half mile ahead, the remuda held its lead, but. not for long. Leaping arroyos and dodging sagebrush, ten rowdy riders sprinted alongside me in fierce pursuit of the thundering herd. I let my horse have his head as we rapidly approached a particularly wide arroyo. We galloped and leapt. A moment of midair suspension on horseback is one of the most thrilling experiences a human can have; in an instant time slips into timelessness and you glimpse that horses and men were meant to be together throughout the ages. An electric feeling of triumph surged through me upon return to terra firma, and I leaned forward in the saddle and spurred my horse again. Soon we were galloping within the remuda.

A year earlier, in another remuda, my horse zigged when I zagged and, departing the saddle, I broke three ribs while cartwheeling through cactus. So, echoing my wife Melissa's admonition before I headed into the Wind River Mountains on one last cattle drive, our eleven-year-old son, Gabriel, cautioned, "Remember, Dad, you aren't thirty anymore." Indeed. I was fifty-six.

In spite of his concerns, Gabe certainly understood why I had to run one last remuda. He had toured America with me his entire life. The day Gabe was born, Melissa and I promised each other that we would never surrender the responsibility of rearing our child to day care facilities. After Melissa took a regular job, however, our time together touring as a family came to an end. Faced with putting Gabe in day care when he was four, I took him with me to Wyoming and the Dakotas for sixty-five days on a summer tour. We lived in the back of our pickup truck for the entire two months. After that, Gabe and I headed out west together each summer, while Melissa remained in Texas. Along the way, Gabe became a musician himself, and by age ten he began opening my one-man shows, playing fiddle. By eleven Gabe was mature enough to "man" our box office while I was onstage. During the summer of 2000 I began performing my epic trilogy, *A Ballad of the West*, in repertory at Old Trail Town in Cody, Wyoming, and Gabe and I had just enjoyed our second season of performing together there and living in our tipi. Ironically, at eleven, an age when many cowboys traditionally started working on ranches, he was too young for the High Island Cattle Company's insurance to allow him to join me on my annual cattle drives.

So elevated that clouds often encircled it like an ocean, the sixty-thousand-acre High Island Ranch was poetically named. Even though the ranch advertised "horseback adventures," High Island was anything but a dude ranch. Extending along the northern border of the Wind River Indian Reservation in Wyoming, it was one of the last American ranches with enough open range to replicate starkly authentic, weeklong, "1800s-period" cattle drives. From food to costume, every detail of the 1880s cowboy experience was meticulously replicated at High Island. Since falling in love with the cowboy life after my first cattle drive in 1992, I structured my itinerary so that I could return there for several weeks each year. Melissa had joined Gabe and me in the tipi for the last week of my summer performances of *A Ballad of the West* in Cody. Then the two of them flew back to Texas to enroll Gabe in school, and I headed into the mountains on horseback.

My wife and son understood why I was leaping arroyos on horseback. But as I raced across the high desert prairie surrounded by a wild herd of horses and riders, I wondered how I might explain to anyone else why I became a cowboy so late in life.

An answer to that question became crystal clear to me in late summer 1998, as we brought a herd of cattle down from high country to winter pastures. Returning from two weeks in the mountains, we learned that the "King of the Cowboys," Roy Rogers, had died. News of the singing celluloid hero's death summoned profound grief from the group that could only be compared to that experienced upon the loss of a close relative. Nevertheless, having spent decades exploring the life of William F. "Buffalo Bill"

Cody in order to write an epic ballad and biography based on the architect of all things Wild West, I immediately recognized the event of Roy's passing as the metaphorical bookend of a uniquely American cycle.

Embarking on his lengthy movie career, Leonard Slye changed his name to Roy Rogers to honor his boyhood hero, Will Rogers. Originally known as "the Cherokee Kid," Will Rogers began his rise to international fame in South Africa in 1902, doing rope tricks during the twilight of Buffalo Bill's glory days; indeed, the Oklahoma humorist was inspired as a child to perfect a rope act when he saw master trick roper Vincente Oropeza performing in Cody's original Wild West. Coincidentally, the Wild West show in South Africa that put Will Rogers on the path to immortality was organized and headlined by Texas Jack Omohundro Jr., son of the frontier scout who, only thirty years earlier, had costarred with Buffalo Bill and Ned Buntline in the pair's very first theatrical adventure. That initial blundering performance of Buntline's *Scouts of the Plains* gave birth to the beloved art form known around the world as "the western."

Something has always motivated me to connect these kinds of events in history, art, and show business. After researching Buffalo Bill's Wild West in books for most of my professional career, it finally occurred to me in the early 1990s that horses accompanied nearly every important event in Cody's life. I decided I needed fundamental, butt-in-the-saddle experiences with horses in order to write with any authority about the icon. That realization led me to the High Island Ranch, where in nearly a decade of 1800s-period cattle drives, I had accumulated more than a thousand miles in the saddle, and, in doing so, had been presented with just about every experience a man can have with a horse. I had discovered that the Zen of being simultaneously in and out of control with horses, cows, and the elements nourished and tempered my spirit. I learned that twelve to fifteen hours a day in the saddle, breathing dusty, aromatic clouds of cow and horse shit, is a natural antidote to city life in the twenty-first century. In Wyoming, where you can get heatstroke and frostbite in the same afternoon, I had gained respect and appreciation for the constant attitude adjustment required to enthusiastically greet every conceivable quirk of Mother Nature with nothing but a good mount, a slicker, and a bedroll. For many professional, pragmatic, and poetic reasons, I fell deeply in love with the experience of working as a cowboy for two or three weeks a year. Nevertheless, like most who signed up for the annual cattle drives, I grew up on a sugary diet of Gene Autry, Roy Rogers, and countless other Saturday-morning singing cowboys. Of course that saccharine and truly counterfeit cowboy mythology pendulumed into the era of the antihero of the counterculture with Sam Peckinpah and Sergio Leone's slow-motion film orchestrations of the violent brutality of reckless men playing with democracy, guns, and alcohol on the fringes of "civilization." Choreographed blood ballet and western musicals aside, three weeks of getting up at four thirty in the morning bone-weary from the previous full day in the saddle puts the cowboy life in a balanced, *physical* perspective. The old cowboys say if your ass hurts, your stirrups are too long; if your knees hurt, your stirrups are too short. If both your ass and your knees hurt, your stirrups are just right!

So something as simple and exciting as a horse race across the Wyoming prairie had long ago become for me an essential exploration of the landscape of the American West, a detailed perspective that I knew would eventually reappear in verse, song, or prose. Nevertheless, this would be my *last* horse race. At the end of this remuda I intended to leave the cowboy's life to the youngsters.

Fifteen adrenaline-filled miles later, the corrals of the lower lodges of the High Island Ranch appeared on the horizon. Soon we dismounted and unsaddled our lathered horses. As I fed and brushed my pony, it occurred to me that explaining my cowboy adventures would be a relatively simple matter when compared to the rest of my life. I would also find it difficult to explain why I spent nearly a decade ascending the slippery slopes of the record business in Nashville, Hollywood, and Austin only to bolt from the commercial industry and venture into "unexplored territory" with my balladeering. My unusual life had taken so many twists and turns that for decades the hardest questions for me to answer were "What do you do?" and "Where do you live?" In 1982 I had actually come close to an explanation while singing another man's lyrics: as "the Drifter" in Dale Wasserman's groundbreaking western musical comedy, *Shakespeare and the Indians*, I sang:

> Stages, we go through stages
> We don our faces, we heed our calls
> Throughout the ages, we wear disguises
> From the time the curtain rises 'til it falls."[1]

As I stored my tack, the thought occurred to me that I would have to write an autobiography to ever be able to put my unusual career into any kind of personal perspective. But end-of-the-trail festivities soon overtook thoughts of a memoir, and after my first shower in a week, I hurried to prepare for my evening show to celebrate the end of the cattle drive with my fellow wranglers.

At first light the next morning I headed south through the Wind River Canyon, across the high plains, and down the eastern slope of the Rockies to Golden, Colorado, for a visit with my best friend, Vine Deloria Jr. For a quarter of a century it had been a tradition for me to stay with Vine and his wife, Barbara, in Golden on my journeys between Texas and Wyoming. This time, however, Vine had invited two young men from Kentucky to visit while I was scheduled to be there, and he was eager for me to meet his friends. Instead of "hillbillies," Vine affectionately called the Kentuckians "mountain Williams."

In their late thirties, gregarious cousins Jeff Spradling and Russ Ward completely charmed me. A fan of the great Kentucky short-story master Jesse Stuart, I peppered them with questions about the locations and characters of his stories, and they fired back inquiries about Willie Nelson, Lyle Lovett, and other Texas luminaries. As these conversations continued, the "mountain Williams" seemed pleased to discover that I either knew personally or had worked with many of the celebrities that interested them. In the middle of one of these conversations Vine pulled me close and whispered, "You should write an autobiography."

Having known Lakota author/philosopher Vine Deloria Jr. for twenty-six years, I had learned to listen to what he said. But the synchronicity of Vine's spontaneous suggestion of an autobiography also made my memoir musings in the tack barn at High Island Ranch impossible to ignore. Before leaving Vine's I structured an outline and continued to mull it over as I crossed the Llano Estacado, entered the rolling Hill Country of Central Texas, passed through Austin, and continued south. Soon great blue herons, white cranes, flocks of snowy egrets, lush green foliage, and intense humidity welcomed me to the Gulf Coast, and finally, after another glorious summer in Wyoming performing *A Ballad of the West,* I was reunited with my family in Houston.

After Melissa headed to work the next morning, I dropped Gabriel off at school, meandered home, and rushed into the house to answer the ringing phone. It was Melissa, weeping. The Pentagon had been struck by commercial airliners filled with American citizens! Moments later, time stood still as the World Trade Center towers fell. Watching concrete dust clouds rolling like grim gray thunderheads through the canyons of Manhattan on that sparkling September morning, everyone instantly realized the world would never be the same. Like everyone else, I now viewed my life from a different perspective. I eventually began focusing on the historical significance of the period in America between the assassination of President John F. Kennedy and the events of September 11, 2001. I decided that my unique role in the creation of the trilogy *A Ballad of the West*, and the fact that I had *freely* traveled the globe as a balladeer singing a truly American story during these decades, was worthy of documentation and explanation.

In October 1963—a month before the Kennedy assassination—I had begun research that would evolve into *A Ballad of the West*. I started it for the simple reason of wanting to find a folk song about Jim Bridger, but I quickly discovered that no period ballads about the American mountain men existed. This realization eventually led me to John G. Neihardt's five-volume masterpiece, *A Cycle of the West*. But Neihardt's Homeric *Cycle* only kindled deeper curiosity concerning why no historically documented musical interpretations chronicling the nineteenth-century Euro-American "settling" of the American West existed. Of course the great Stephen Foster wrote "Oh! Susanna" in the late 1840s, and it became popular during the California gold rush. By the end of the Civil War era Foster's legacy as America's original songwriter was firmly established. But Foster's lyrics and subjects were essentially a bridge between Appalachia and the Deep South. In 1963, aside from the classic "Shenandoah," affectionately known as "Across the Wide Missouri," and rare gems such as "Sweet Betsy from Pike," "Buffalo Skinners," and "The Sioux Indians," the only known "western" American ballads were in John Lomax's landmark collection *Cowboy Songs and Other Frontier Ballads*. I found it curious that practically 100 percent of Lomax's western ballad collection was post-1870. Moreover, aside from the occasional outlaw/gunfighter ballad, virtually all of the Lomax collection was cowboy. Authentic pre-1850 non-cowboy "western" ballads were nonexistent.

Entering the world of the mountain men through Neihardt, history books, and period paintings, I fell enchanted; I had no idea then that what had begun as romantic fascination with Jim Bridger would expand into a trilogy of historically documented epic-scale ballads that would include Plains Indian culture and "Buffalo Bill" Cody. I also had no notion in 1963 that I would devote most of my artistic career to developing the various talents needed to produce the trilogy as hardcover book, paperback book, four-disc recording, one-man show, full-company musical production, and five-hour DVD presentation. Wandering into the unexplored territory of historical western ballads as a callow teenager inspired me to create the form of the epic ballad simply to write and sing the heroic tale of Jim Bridger's important life. But the creation of this new form of ballad also set me on a path that has taken me on a unique journey into American music, culture, and society.

Even though I completed a rough first draft by late January 2003, work on the autobiography experienced yet another delay when I embarked on a twenty-city tour to promote the publication of *Buffalo Bill and Sitting Bull: Inventing the Wild West*. My tour would begin in Albuquerque, New Mexico, so I recognized a splendid opportunity to contact my friend, painter, author, and screenwriter "Ole Max" Evans. We met for breakfast at his favorite Mexican restaurant, Lorena's. It had been more than two decades since we had last sat alone and chatted, and I had missed my "ole pard." Breakfast drifted into lunch and we continued to talk into the afternoon. After the second meal Ole Max grew serious.

"How long have we known each other, Bobby?" he asked. "Thirty years? Long enough for me to tell you there have been at least three times since I've known you that you came within inches of screwing up your entire life."

"When was that, Max?"

"In thirty years there have been at least three times you nearly became famous."

My laughter turned heads toward our table.

"A man can recover from just about anything," Ole Max continued. "Hell, I've had open-heart surgery. Many have survived cancer. The day will come when we'll whip AIDS. But no one can survive fame; fame destroys every person it touches. If you had become famous you never would have composed this great ballad of yours. Every time fame got close, you avoided it. Congratulations, old pard. Well done."

Ole Max hadn't changed a bit over the years. If anything, he had gotten better with age. And he was right; fame, and the responsibility to maintain and survive it, would have destroyed the balladeer I became. Besides, if I had learned nothing else in forty years in show business and nearly as long digging into the tangled mythology and reality of Buffalo Bill's life and legend, I had learned that celebrity is a ravenous cannibal.

As usual with Max's rare, meaningful appearances in my life, fate quickened with his remarks. I left Albuquerque and began the book-signing tour, traveling throughout the Southwest, the Northern Rockies, and finally out

on the Great Plains. Vivid memories lingered in each region as I returned
to the places where I had lived and worked during my three decades on the
road as a balladeer. As I drove from one bookstore to another, racing ice
storms, blizzards, and rigid schedules across the wintry Great Plains and
Rockies, Max's insight about the disease of fame echoed in my thoughts.
Old friends, familiar haunts, and hideouts reminded me of the unique life
I had enjoyed as a western balladeer, and I realized that my career had been
a lengthy and nimble dance between celebrity and anonymity that I had
performed to my great advantage and artistic survival. So I vigorously
returned to note-taking for the autobiography. Ole Max's comments about
celebrity illuminated my need to clarify the career choices I had made will-
fully, and those I had been forced to make, in order for my epic trilogy to
survive and flourish. His words made me realize that my entire life has
essentially been a journey from one artistic frontier to another. As I completed the tour and started the second draft of this manuscript, new meanings returned with lyrics performed in an earlier role, when as Dale Wasserman's Drifter, I sang:

> Stages, we go through stages,
> We don our faces, we heed our calls
> We look for answers, we find surprises
> From the time the curtain rises 'til it falls.
> From the time the curtain rises, 'til it falls.[2]

ONE

Coyote in the Catbird's Seat

INTENSE DECEMBER LIGHT BLED into a low, angular sunset and bathed the Central Texas Hill Country in sharply defined winter tones. Rolling meadows of silken blond grasses swayed in gentle breezes as I drove west through groves of green cedar and live oak trees and searched for the trapper's compound. He had assured me on the phone that he had the coyote pelts I needed, but I barely had enough time to brain-tan and stitch one into a headdress for my costume. I was scheduled to debut *A Ballad of the West* in less than a month at Austin's Creek Theater, and the costume I was creating for the performance was incomplete without an authentic headdress. Since relocating from Louisiana and the Deep South to the Southwest, I had come to strongly identify with the coyote. The coyote represented survival instinct to me. Several years earlier I had read a newspaper story that described the coyote's ability to adapt and prosper deep in the suburbs of Los Angeles, and I wondered if they weren't more adaptable than I had been in the "city of angels." My song "The Call," recently released on my second album on RCA Records, sang:

> There's a coyote howling down deep in my soul
> Throwing all of his pain at the moon.
> And he sings to the starlight and calls for his mate
> With a lonesome and aching love tune.
> Yes, the coyote sings on the plains of my mind,
> And he howls on my desert at night.

And he calls me to leave this ol' city behind,
'cause the way concrete feels just ain't right,
The way concrete feels just ain't right."[1]

The headdress had to be a coyote.

Four years earlier, in 1970, in Hollywood, the great cowboy actor Slim Pickens had put me in my first coyote headdress. Slim's daughter, Daryle Anne Lindley, starred in a Max Evans film called *The Wheel*, and I sang the movie's theme song, "Circle of Love." Aside from introducing me to Daryle Anne and her famous father, however, Ole Max also acquainted me with the trickster mythology of the coyote.

"The Navajo believe the last sound heard on earth will be the wail of the coyote," Ole Max often said.

"The Call" was written as a portrait of Ole Max while I was living in Hollywood and working on *The Wheel*. But the coyote wandered into my life on yet another level when West Coast RCA Records vice president Joe Reisman's love of "the coyote song" most certainly ensured the release of my second album.

Jovially irascible, Ole Max Evans was at first glance a bowlegged cowboy. A defiant, nonchalant wave of hair curled atop his forehead like a backward question mark, its tip pointing down to the arroyos, cactus, and high desert plains etched and reflected in his mischievous, sparkling eyes and brawl-busted face. But during his tumbleweed youth in the nebulous region where northeastern New Mexico unites with the Texas and Oklahoma panhandles, Max Evans was possessed by a mystical coyote's spirit. Later, in novels, Max dubbed the region "the hi-lo" country, and he forever carried a sense of the place with him. No matter where he happened to be, Ole Max liked to remind folks that something wild was present. When the rogue's spirit so filled him that it had to escape, he would cock his head back and release a splendid yowl.

Having spent his teenage years as a West Texas cowboy, Ole Max entered the military when World War II erupted. After surviving intense combat in Europe, he returned to his beloved hi-lo country after the war. He eventually drifted into Taos and a brief career as a painter before his book on legendary Taos bootlegger Long John Dunn secured his career as a writer. Max realized that few people were writing about the post–World War II West, and he staked an immortal claim on the territory in 1960 when he published the classic modern western *The Rounders*. A hit movie based on his book starred Glenn Ford, Henry Fonda, and Chill Wills. The film's success led to a television series, and suddenly Ole Max Evans was a writer in demand in Hollywood. In the true spirit of his maverick roots, Ole Max turned his back on the established Hollywood studio system and used his success to write, produce, and direct his own "damn little ole movie," *The Wheel*, a terse southwestern drama with only twenty minutes of dialogue in the ninety-minute film. Ole Max hired me to sing the movie's title song, and while working on the film, I performed *Seekers of the Fleece* for Daryle Anne.

"My dad is going to flip when he hears this!" Daryle Anne exclaimed. "He's crazy about mountain men—especially Jim Bridger."

Several months later, preparing to perform *Seekers of the Fleece* for Daryle Anne's dad, I tuned my Martin twelve-string guitar in front of the massive stone fireplace of Slim and Maggie Pickens's Los Angeles home. Seeing the movie star and his wife across the room on a leather couch was surrealistic. Tall and gangly, but with an expanding belly, Slim had lost the leaner implication of his sobriquet long ago. His genuine cowboy person-ality quickly made me feel at ease socially, but performing for him had my nerves on edge. Like the rest of the world, I had loved him in movies for years, and was imprinted with the image of him riding Kubrick's phallic bomb to oblivion in *Dr. Strangelove*.

I got my butterflies flying in formation and started into the narrative verse of *Seekers*. Slim and Maggie seemed to engage with the performance immediately, but when I got to the section depicting mountain man Hugh Glass being mauled by a giant grizzly bear, Slim grew fidgety, suddenly jumped from his seat, and yelled for me to stop. I was paralyzed.

"By golly, this is fantastic!" Slim exclaimed. "But it needs sumthin'."

He grabbed my arm and, flicking lights on as we went, led me down a dark hallway through his spacious house. Soon we entered a large room where every type of western costume imaginable was stored. Guns, hats, shirts, chaps, boots, ropes, spurs, saddles and bridles, war bonnets, spears, bows and arrows, war axes—western accessories of all shapes, sizes, and col-ors filled the room. Slim stopped in front of a striking leather shirt with beadwork down the golden sleeves. Black, red, and green symbolic mark-ings were painted on the shoulders and chest, and coarse black horsehair "scalp-locks" mingled with the abundant fringe spiraling from the sleeves.

"Here, kid," he exclaimed, taking the tunic from the wall and tossing it to me. "Put this-here Sioux war shirt on!"

The shirt smelled like smoked meat.

Next, he took a stunning coyote headdress down from the wall and, with great reverence, placed it on my head.

"Now, by golly." He grinned that famous grin that had been captured in so many movies. "Let's git back to tha fireplace an' start this-here ballad ag'in."

Later that evening I asked Slim to narrate the recording of *Seekers of the Fleece*.

"Shoot, ah planned ta swell up an' pout if ya *didn't* ask me," Slim joked. "It's a one-of-a-kind. By golly, Ole Gabe himself would'a loved it. Ah'll be honored ta be a part of it."

Ole Max's and Slim's enthusiastic support of my work justified my belief that the struggle to record *Seekers of the Fleece* was worth the career sacrifices I was preparing to make. Their endorsement meant more than becoming friends with a famous movie star and a western author; aside from my wife and a few Austin musician friends, Slim and Ole Max were the first two people who appreciated the new form of ballad I had created. Their acknowledgment boosted my courage to continue into unexplored territory as my career in the corporate recording industry was drawing to a close.

Directions to the trapper's compound were simple and I found his house easily. With the sunset, the temperature dropped dramatically and it was shivering cold. I had expected an old coot and was surprised to discover that the trapper was a young man. With his long brown hair and beard, flannel shirt, and boots, he would have easily fit into my circle of hippie musician friends.

"I'm surprised that you are open Christmas Eve," I said, nervously attempting minimal conversation as we walked to the shed behind the man's house. He recognized my feeble attempt to patronize him and chuckled condescendingly before deflecting the implication of my question right back at me. "So, what're you doin' out huntin' ki-yote pelts on Christmas Eve?"

Good question.

We entered the large woodshed and I noticed it was literally wallpapered in fur. Long "green" (fleshed, but untanned) coyote pelts draped the wall, bloody and drying. Fur covered the floor. Other small animal hides dangled from the ceiling. The pungent primal smell of musk and blood filled the air. The strangely pleasant, familiar odor instantly took me back to my childhood and reminded me of hunting with my father. I suddenly became uncomfortable and began to wonder what the hell I was doing in the midst of all that death on Christmas Eve. I quickly picked out two coyote skins and a beaver pelt, paid the man, and left.

As I walked to the car in the crisp, cold night I wondered if I had been wise to turn down Slim's offer to use his coyote headdress for my costume. Nevertheless, I believed it was significant that I create my own headdress; if I was going to wear a coyote it seemed important that I be as personally involved as possible in the process of putting its hide on my head. So I visited the library and gathered formulas for tanning hides the "Indian way"— with animal brains. Following those directions, I also bought calf brains from a local butcher and planned to begin the process as soon as I got home. With two young stepchildren, however, I would have to rush into my role as Santa Claus and set up surprises for Christmas morning before beginning work on the pelts.

"Every animal has enough brains to tan its own hide" is an ancient axiom. American Indians developed this labor-intensive process to its highest, most exemplary standard. If the hair is to be removed from the hide it is usually done with scraping knives. With the hair on or off, all flesh must be scraped from the hide. Before fleshing, however, the hide must be stretched as tight as possible—traditionally on the ground, or between two trees. As soon as the hide is fleshed, it's ready for the brains to be applied. First the brains must be boiled for approximately twenty minutes in just enough water to cover them, with a pinch of salt added. The process creates a thick white paste, not unlike the consistency and color of the paste we all once used in kindergarten. This paste is then evenly spread over the fleshed, stretched hide, and within forty hours the hide is transformed into a glorious, snow-white—albeit rigid—piece of leather. But the work is only half done at this point; the stiff hide must now be kneaded and twisted vigorously until it is softened to malleable suede leather, porous and eager to accept the awl.

When pliant, the leather is ready to be smoked—essentially "cured" like a ham but also to add color. Smoking the snow-white leather creates the golden brown hues associated with traditional Indian clothing. This is usually accomplished by creating a small tipi-like structure of limbs and draping the hide around it. Next, hard and soft woods are used to make a very small fire in the center of the structure. If the woods used are a bit green and difficult to keep burning, smoke will come naturally, but if green wood is not available, water is sprinkled on the fire to accentuate smoking and complete the process. The longer the hide is smoked, the darker the color will be.

Before stretching the green hides, I burned Wyoming sage under them and, as the smoke drifted up to "cleanse and bless" the hides, renewed my pledge to transform their death into art. Then I stretched the green hides— fur down—on a sheet of plywood, tacked them in place, and with dulled knives started scraping and pulling hunks of dead, bloody flesh from them.

The Creek Theater had recently captured Austin's attention with the production of a popular one-man show called *Woody Guthrie, Child of Dust.* My recording engineer friend Jim Inmon suggested that the producers of that show might be interested in my work. I felt that the uniqueness of my epic ballads was in the field of the recording arts rather than in the theater and was initially hesitant to explore Jim's suggestion. But I was also very unhappy with RCA Records and the direction my musical career was heading in Hollywood.

In 1973, twenty-eight years old, with a five-year, multi-album contract with the largest record label in the world, and an equally prestigious contract as a staff writer with one of the world's largest music publishers, I was, to all appearances, in the "catbird seat." But neither my publisher nor my record label would consider allowing me to record my epic ballads. Complicating matters, my support system at the label was crumbling; after an illustrious thirty-five-year career with RCA, the man who signed me to the label, Joe Reisman, had been unceremoniously fired. My first album release had been reasonably successful, but only Reisman's strong support ensured a second release. Now, simultaneously with the release of my second album, he was suddenly gone. Faced with these circumstances, I requested a private meeting with the new West Coast RCA boss to boldly present *Seekers of the Fleece.*

Don Burkheimer laughed when I proposed recording an hour-long historically documented epic ballad about Jim Bridger and the fur trade era. "You're joking, aren't you?" He snickered incredulously. "An hour-long album with no breaks between songs? Something like that will NEVER be played on the radio, Bridger! How the hell can you sell a record you can't get played on the radio?"

Between us, Don Burkheimer was the one in the catbird seat. After signing Canada's the Guess Who, Burkheimer brought John Denver to RCA, and John Denver ruled the record industry and most of pop culture in 1973. As a reward for his signing coups, Burkheimer was named the head of RCA's West Coast operations; RCA Hollywood released nothing that did not first receive his blessing. Soon after Burkheimer's arrival, Joe Reisman departed.

But Burkheimer's response was a double-edged sword. One edge made me painfully aware that my time in the commercial recording industry had come to an end. I loved making commercial records and had hoped to find a way to continue. But I knew now that RCA would not allow me to record my ballads, and I had to separate myself from RCA *and* the commercial record industry for my work to survive. The other edge of Burkheimer's blade severed *self-imposed* illusionary bonds and released a coyote in the catbird seat. Psychically freed, I was certain now that I had created something new and special with *Seekers of the Fleece*, and I prepared to fight for its survival.

To accomplish my goal I knew I had to take control of my life and work. After bolting Nashville, however, only to confront the same narrow-mindedness in Hollywood, I was running out of options as a recording singer/songwriter. Even in open-minded Austin I did not fit into the cosmic cowboy, progressive country mold, but I was lumped into that genre because people didn't know where else to classify me. In an *Austin American-Statesman* preview, written only days before the debut of *A Ballad of the West* at the Creek Theater, freelance music journalist Steve Hogner described me as "an enigmatic misfit in a city full of misfits." True. I had migrated to Austin in 1970 because as a "city full of misfits" it was the very last place in America I could find that could tolerate and nourish my career as a fledgling epic balladeer.

Since my major label debut in Nashville in 1967, I had enjoyed steady success and in three short years had risen to the top of the recording industry—RCA Records. RCA was the label of my father's idol, "the singing brakeman," Jimmie Rodgers, and my own early inspiration, Elvis Presley, and so recording for RCA was literally a dream come true to me. After thinking over my situation with RCA, however, I decided to take Jim Inmon's advice. So the opening of *A Ballad of the West* at the Creek Theater was critical to the continuation of my career.

In truth, fate had already made the decision for me to leave RCA Records. My talk with Don Burkheimer about *Seekers of the Fleece* coincided with the 1973 stillborn release of my second RCA album, *And I Wanted to Sing for the People*. The failure of my sophomore effort was a clear signal that I could no longer expect the label to actively promote my records. But something in me had subconsciously realized that fact going into the project; otherwise I wouldn't have selected such an acerbic, swan-song title. So, confident in my abilities to move forward on my own, I bade them all adieu, returned to Texas, and waited for my contract to expire, or to be dropped from the label. I was convinced that when I became a free agent one of the investors in my debut RCA album, *Merging of Our Minds*, would back me financially to pursue my dream of recording *Seekers of the Fleece*. When I returned his initial *Merging* investment plus a healthy profit, a successful cotton farmer from North Louisiana had indicated that he would like to discuss a more "in-depth" investment. So when negotiations with RCA stalled, I immediately called Joe Mott about his proposal, and he suggested that I come to Louisiana to discuss the matter in detail. I drove home and made my presentation.

While I was in Louisiana for Thanksgiving to meet with Joe Mott, I told my dad what was going on with me in Hollywood. He promptly took me to task for forcing RCA executives to release me from my contract. Smelling those bloody hides at the trapper's compound had reminded me of our recent Thanksgiving confrontation, and my dad's words were still stinging that cold Christmas Eve as I scraped hides to prepare them for tanning.

"You have a college degree, Bobby," he pleaded. "Why don't you go back to teaching?"

"I use my college degree every day, Daddy."

"I'm talking about a *real* job, son!"

"I have a real job, Daddy. It's writing songs and making records."

"Then why didn't you do what they wanted when you had the chance?" he said, his temper rising. "Don't you think they know more about making records than you? I told you to just sing whatever they want you to sing. Then, after you get rich, do what you want. But you forced Monument to release you, and now you're doing the same thing with RCA. People gossip. Now you have a reputation as a troublemaker."

"I know it's hard for you to understand, Daddy, but if I became the person they wanted to make me, I would have always wondered what might have happened to the person I'm supposed to be."

"Well, that's just fancy talk. You are in for a lot of pain, Bobby," he said. "People don't want to hear anyone sing about history. They want simple songs about sex and booze. They want to forget their troubles and lost loves. It's as simple as that."

Austin's now world-famous East Sixth Street was in 1973 a seedy section of town. At Congress Avenue affluent West Austin immediately morphed into slums as the historic street linked downtown with the east-side Mexican barrios. Sad drunks and derelicts littered the sidewalks, decaying buildings, and alleys. Waller Creek intersected Sixth just before the street ducked under I-35.

Literally suspended over Waller Creek, the Creek Theater was the brainchild of a devoted puppeteer and driving force in Austin's avant-garde theater community. As early as 1973 Lynne Alice Carey envisioned a thriving arts scene on Austin's Sixth Street. Lynne Alice hired Austin actor/director Larry Martin, and the pair refurbished a crumbling old café into a hundred-seat theater. The Woody Guthrie play had been their first production—among the very first to attract Austin's art community to Sixth Street. I called the Creek Theater and arranged a meeting with Martin.

Martin's entire bearing offered little to dispel the stereotype of the gay actor; he was so "out" that I doubt he had ever spent much time "in the closet." From tiny Palestine, Texas, Larry had worked in New York and other major theater centers before returning to Austin. He trimmed his dark auburn beard into a precisely satanic Vandyke and was always dressed immaculately, at times in a three-piece suit. Rather than a tie, he wore flamboyant scarves, and he had a habit of using his right hand to effeminately flip them over his shoulder.

"Look at the size of this tiny theater, sweetheart," Larry explained to me immediately. "We don't do company musical productions. Our focus is one-man shows. If you intend to develop your ballad as a one-man show, you've come to the right place. Otherwise, we aren't really interested."

"I would be receptive to the concept of a one-man show," I replied, "but I'm not sure we could find an actor who could both sing and perform the pieces on guitar."

"That would be you, darling!" Larry exclaimed as if questioning my sanity.

"I'm not an actor," I replied with a blush.

"You wrote it, didn't you?"

"Well, yes."

"Then you know how to act it."

"But . . ."

"No buts," Larry interrupted curtly. "If you commit to performing the show, I'll direct and produce it. You go home and think it over tonight. Call me back tomorrow and tell me what you want to do."

After six months of development and rehearsal, *A Ballad of the West* was scheduled to open in a matter of days. I had stitched together a commercially tanned leather shirt and pants and, having taught myself how to bead on a loom, applied bead strips to the shirt. But the headdress was critical to my transformation into a nineteenth-century mountain man. The coyote hide I was fleshing would become that headdress.

I scraped, peeled, and pulled flesh from the hide until my fingers were sore and swelling. I stopped and looked at my bloodied hands. Suddenly, the look and smell of that very primal moment ripped open a scar deep in my subconscious with a painful question: "When are you going to finally kill that deer and wear his hide?"

Instantly, familiar words from *Seekers of the Fleece* ignited like a lightning bolt in my thoughts as new meanings shocked me to my core:

> A good shot would've killed him clean
> Now he's wounded—damn, it's mean
> To be the cause of anything a-dying very slow.

The verse from my epic ballad stunned me with profound new significance and, following in blazing succession, more familiar words struck deep with new meanings.

> Hugh's kinda like a father![2]

I couldn't breathe. Tears of epiphany stung my eyes and opened my heart as I stared at my bloody hands. The surrogate father/song relationship between Hugh Glass and Jim Bridger reflected my relationship with my own father! I instantly realized that *all* of my various poetic and musical characterizations of mountain men were sketches and expressions of childhood perspectives of my father's personality. My subconscious desire to bond with my father had inspired me to seek the incredible history of the mountain men. The sudden awareness of this motivation instantly unleashed an even deeper emotional shock that surged through me: initially intending only to find familial connections in Jim Bridger, I had discovered Hugh Glass. In doing so, I stumbled onto the greatest bear story in American history. But, more important, I discovered the amazing—and true—story of a man and a boy, a surrogate father and son, a mentor and protégé, a story of unimaginable tragedy, against-all-odds survival, herculean endurance, profound compassion, and legendary forgiveness. It began with eighteen-year-old Jim Bridger and forty-year-old Hugh Glass hunting for deer on the Grand River of South Dakota in August 1823. Training as a hunter with Glass when they were members of the historic Ashley-Henry Fur Expedition, Bridger shot and wounded a deer. Aware that dangerous and protective mother grizzly bears frequented such locations at that time of year, Glass stopped the boy from pursuing the deer as it fled bleeding into a plum orchard alongside the river. Instead, the older man himself went into the grove to seek the deer. Within moments Bridger heard Glass's screams as he was attacked by a giant bear. Glass somehow managed to kill the grizzly, but everyone in the expedition believed the mountain man was mortally wounded. Complicating matters, the expedition was being pursued by hostile Indians. Since they expected Glass to live for only a few hours, it was decided that the party had to leave him behind to die. Major Henry asked for volunteers to remain with Glass to give him a proper burial. Jim Bridger and a man named Nat Fitzgerald stepped forward. After waiting several days for the old man to die, however, the pair lost their courage and fled. As nothing of value would be left behind, before deserting Glass, Fitzgerald and Bridger were forced to take his rifle and provisions necessary for survival in order to deflect any suspicious concerns from the other trappers.

Glass did not die. Instead, he crawled across the Dakotas, surviving on his desire for vengeance until love and compassion eventually overcame his hatred; upon finally catching up with Jim Bridger, Hugh Glass forgave him.

Tears dried on my cheeks as I vividly remembered the chilly morning so long ago deep in the ancient forests of North Louisiana with my father.

Daybreak was bitterly cold. We ducked under snarled limbs, vines, and briars as we made our way through the thick forest. Deeply packed beds of brittle leaves crunched under our boots as we struggled through the dense woods to make the clearing before sunrise. Just ahead, the first rays of light had already started to flicker through the trees, creating a silhouetted tapestry of shadow and breaking day. My father suddenly put his arm in front of me, a silent signal for me to stop walking. Speaking softly, with his breath creating tiny puffs of steam in the chilly air, he instructed me to stand in the small grove of hickory trees at the edge of the clearing and wait. With firm sign language, he indicated that a deer might come past and that if a buck appeared I was to shoot him with my twelve-gauge shotgun. Then Daddy vanished deep into the woods, leaving me shivering and uncertain in the cold.

Hunting was Daddy's thing, not mine. But I was a twelve-year-old boy; I craved my father's attention and instinctively understood the importance of the blood ritual he was orchestrating with the deer hunt. Even though I already knew I would never become the hunter he desired, I deeply admired his intimate knowledge of the woods and the ethical stealth he demanded of himself as he sought his prey. A three-pack-a-day smoker, during bow hunting and "still season," in which hunters were allowed to track deer without dogs, he would forsake his Camels and appease his nicotine cravings with roasted peanuts, confident that replacing cigarette smoke with the aromatic nuts would attract deer to him. He hunted deer with bows, arrows, and guns, from strategic perches, and with brave and intelligent bluetick and black and tan hounds, yapping and howling hot on the scent. And my family understood. We did not eat much cow; instead, we ate the seasonal wild game that Daddy killed.

Very soon, true to my father's prediction, a huge trophy buck loped into the clearing and stopped. There, standing beautifully before me, snorting steam, was the perfect shot. I looked at him standing thirty yards away and instantly succumbed to the age-old boyhood syndrome of "buck fever." I could not shoot him. I deliberately shot the tree next to the deer, and he bolted and vanished into the thick woods. Within moments my father hurried into the clearing and asked where the deer fell. I lied and told him the deer had run by so fast that I could not get a good shot. I explained that I had fired just as the buck ran past the tree and the buckshot had hit the tree instead of the deer.

There was no conversation between us as Daddy drove the 1951 Ford pickup back to Columbia. I knew that he had probably watched the whole scene unfold between me and the deer. But his silence indicated it would be one of those things we never discussed again. Silence would shroud much of our relationship for the next few months, but he never made an issue of being disappointed at my failing to kill the deer. He never confronted me with my lie. He remained a loving but distant father. I, however, was a hypersensitive adolescent, and even though he never made an issue of it, I was ashamed that I did not have the nerve to shoot a deer and had foiled his attempt to bond with me. Worse, I felt guilty for lying to my father.

But he had always reached out to me with music, and after the incident with the deer, music became even more important than before. Some of my earliest memories of my father were of him coming in from work exhausted and retreating to the bedroom with his guitar and radio. He would turn off the lights and sit in the dark with his ever-present cigarette glowing as he played his chocolate Gibson and sang to himself or listened to the radio.

Three years before that hunting trip, on an autumn evening in 1954, Daddy called me into his room to ask my opinion about a young man being introduced to sing on the radio on *Louisiana Hayride* in nearby Shreveport.

"I liked him," I said after the singer's performance. "He's different. He sounds like the colored folks in the hills on the other side of the swamp, but kinda hillbilly too."

"They call him 'the hillbilly hepcat.'"

"What's his real name?"

"Elvis Presley."

Nine years old at the time, I realized that music was the way to get my father's attention. So after hearing Elvis, I would creep into Daddy's room and listen to him play his guitar, or just listen to the radio with him. We continued to build communication bridges just chatting about the new form of country music emerging from North Louisiana in those days. *Louisiana Hayride*, broadcast on Shreveport's fifty-thousand-watt KWKH, was already an important venue for many young regional country stars, having played a pivotal role in launching the career of the immortal Hank Williams. After embracing Elvis, however, *Louisiana Hayride* became the shrine of musical rebellion. Shreveport was so close to Texas that the *Hayride*'s largest audience was in the Lone Star State. Because of this, Elvis's first major tours outside of Memphis and the mid-South were to far West Texas. Like a rockabilly bee, Elvis pollinated Buddy Holly in Lubbock, and Roy Orbison in Odessa. As Elvis's career exploded throughout the South and the Southwest, most young singers who had previously fantasized about becoming country music stars now grew their hair and sideburns out and headed to Shreveport. *Louisiana Hayride* became the launching pad for everything rockabilly, and attracted talent that would forever change the direction of American music. Johnny Cash, Webb Pierce, Carl Perkins, George Jones, Johnny Horton, Bob Luman, Faron Young, Ronnie and Dale Hawkins, David Houston, and a host of other now-legendary names first gained attention on "the *Hayride*." Equally significant, the musicians that accompanied these celebrated entertainers would soon become the studio musicians responsible for much of the "California sound" of the 1960s and 1970s, and also the "Nashville cats" that sculpted the sound of modern country music during the same era.

Daddy and I would listen to the latest act and he would ask what I thought. Hungry for his attention, I ate it up. Soon the walls of my room were a crowded battleground as photos of Elvis, Ricky Nelson, Gene Vincent, Johnny Cash, and other, lesser-known emerging stars competed for space. By age ten I was well aware that Elvis's drummer, D. J. Fontana, Webb Pierce, and Floyd Cramer were all from nearby West Monroe, and Ricky Nelson's entire band was composed of Louisiana musicians: Al "Puddler" Harris on piano, Joe Osborn on bass, and James Burton on guitar.

As in nearly every small town in America, however, sports dominated the social fabric of Columbia. Having been an outstanding athlete as a teenager, but with little opportunity to actualize his dreams, my father wished for an athletic son. Recognizing this, I decided if I could not bond with him by killing a deer, then perhaps I could make up for it with sports. He beamed with pride when he learned that I tried out for the junior high football team and was invited to join. As my team started to win games and my teammates' fathers cheered in the bleachers, I ached for Daddy to come watch me play too. But he was so pathologically shy that he would park his car on the side of the highway half a mile away from the stadium and watch the game from afar. It was emotionally confusing to be excited that he was there to see me but embarrassed that he parked out there on the road. Nevertheless, near or far, I had discovered another way to get his attention and that was all I wanted.

My mother filled her days taking care of me and my brothers, Hill and John. She was close to her mother and father, and that relationship brought her great comfort. My mother could not drive a car, so Daddy taught me to drive the two-door 1956 Ford Mainline. Winning my learner's permit at fifteen, I could drive my mother to the grocery store and, on very special occasions, to the nearby "city" of Monroe. As my father's work shifts became increasingly longer, my mother and I became very close. She loved talking about movies and stars. She always had movie magazines around, and I would read them and talk with her about what her favorite stars were doing. Occasionally we went to the movies together, but we would often watch romantic movies and musicals on television. When the string sections would swell and bring lumps to our throats, I discovered that we were both romantics. My mother's love of those musicals exposed me to the great American tunesmiths Irving Berlin, George and Ira Gershwin, Richard

Rodgers, Lorenz Hart, Oscar Hammerstein, Cole Porter, Harold Arlen, Yip Harburg, and Johnny Mercer.

Preferring country music, Daddy believed Hollywood musicals were phony and unrealistic and, jealous of her love of them, would accuse Mama of living in a dream world. But I silently felt the sting of his words. Those great lyricists had made me believe I must be a dreamer myself, because I loved what those songs said and, specifically, *how* they said it. Some of my earliest memories are of looking at the labels on the old 78 recordings and becoming interested in the names of the people who wrote the songs. I was especially fond of Johnny Mercer's songs; his lyrics suggested he was a Southerner. Mercer's "Glow Worm" and scores of early hits had spanned decades all the way to the 1960s with "Days of Wine and Roses" and "Moon River." Within a decade of those childhood days I would sign a five-year contract with E. H. Morris, the publishing company that Johnny Mercer founded in the 1930s with Steve "Buddy" Morris.

As conflict between my parents intensified, their marriage descended into what was essentially a never-ending argument. With our adoring grandparents so near, though, my brothers and I felt the comfort of a family's embrace even as our parents continued their private war. Consequently, we kids spent our days after school with our neighborhood pals generally, frolicking throughout the countryside searching for new adventures. Our barefooted summer days were filled with swimming, fishing, bike riding, and playing board games on the screened porch at our grandparents' house. As I entered junior high, Hill, John, and I grew further apart, though, and I began the long, slow drift away from my family.

TWO

A Painter's Portal

I STARED AT THE LIGHT BLUE COVER of the generic high school theme pamphlet and contemplated the assigned subject: "My Hobby." Tingling with a strange blend of fear and courage, I cracked the little booklet and scribbled the first line of my confession: "I am a painter."

To my surprise, I felt relieved to finally reveal my secret to someone outside my immediate family. My "painting" had actually begun four years earlier, when I received a plastic model airplane as an eleventh-birthday present. In 1956 models based on legendary World War II airplanes were as popular as bubblegum baseball cards. These models came with several tiny bottles of liquid enamel primary colors and a small, cheap brush. I loved applying paint to the airplanes with a brush, but the first time I mixed leftover paint I was hooked. I became fascinated by watching pigment swirl and blend from its singular distinctive brilliance and magically create a completely new color. Though I could not articulate it then, I came to realize I was enchanted by the pure visual aspect of color as an escape from the endless bickering of my parents. Showing either remarkable maturity for a seven-year-old, brilliant survival instincts, or both, my younger brother, Hill, had already fled the constant arguing and retreated to the sanctuary of our nearby grandparents' home. My toddler brother, John, and I shared a bedroom in the tiny five-room wood-frame home. Alone in my room, I escaped into the soundless, visual world of color, which I could control and manipulate into pretty things.

I started requesting more model airplanes as presents and rewards and became obsessed with hoarding enough paint from the models to make the dripped and splashed paintings I was secretly creating with the precious remaining pigment. I knew this wasn't really art and was embarrassed for anyone to see it. Like everyone in my world, I believed "Art" to be idyllic pastoral scenes, the sentimental novelty of Norman Rockwell, Renaissance-influenced biblical illustrations, or Anglophilic portraits of Christ. So as I gradually attempted landscapes, I was painfully aware that no one could appreciate my painting but me, and I deeply wished I could paint what I considered to be "realistic" art. Because of my grandparents' black-and-white Sylvania television and *Life* magazine, Picasso's cubism, Dalí's surrealism, and the work of post–World War II abstract expressionists like Jackson Pollock had come into our world. But caustic phrases like "a monkey could do that" were usually associated with all "modern" art. There was also a lurking, unspeakable social reason I felt my painting should remain a secret: even worse than the brand of "sissy" associated with painting, I didn't want anyone to think I was crazy, like Vincent van Gogh.

Around the time I received those enamel paints in 1956, my mother and I saw Kirk Douglas and Anthony Quinn portray Vincent van Gogh and Paul Gauguin in the Academy Award–winning film based on Irving Stone's novel *Lust for Life*. Looking back, I'm quite certain seeing that film is what inspired me to mix leftover model airplane paint in the first place. Prior to the 1934 publication of Stone's fictional biography based on van Gogh's letters to his brother Theo, however, most Americans knew little about the painter's life. After the huge success of Stone's book, and the subsequent film, Vincent van Gogh was resurrected in middle-class America as the crucified Christ of the art world. The mainstream discovery of the mad Dutchman's tragic life story embedded a sad and cruel implication in our culture concerning painters, as most came to view "painter" and "madman" as synonymous. Even worse, in materialistic America the reason that concerned parents tend to go berserk upon discovering a child's desire to become a painter is the now-accepted social implication of a lifetime of heartbreaking penury, suffering, and rejection, possibly leading to posthumous discovery, success, wealth, and fame.

Living in a cramped house makes it impossible to have a secret about anything for very long, and I was quickly outed as a closet painter. Worried about the van Gogh syndrome, my mother, typically, ran to her mother for child-rearing advice, and soon my grandmother presented my paintings for me to explain. As a young woman, Josephine Sutton Bridger had survived St. Louis encephalitis—sleeping sickness—and the affliction had left her with a permanent palpitating swaying in her right hand. My paintings throbbed to the gentle beat of her palsied arm.

"Are these yours?"

My grandmother was such a force of nature that I was petrified. Large-boned and obese, she was forthright but also utterly honest, detesting any deceitful act, and resolute if crossed. Highly intelligent, she demanded direct answers of children and adults alike with the tact of a courtroom prosecutor.

"Yes, ma'am! I just . . ."

"Don't you ever apologize for being yourself, young man!" she interrupted, bending down to look me in the eye. "We are going to Monroe this weekend to get you a proper set of oil paints."

The following Saturday morning she sang old hymns as her four-door blue and white 1954 Chevy sedan purred through the cotton fields and pecan orchards that graced Highway 165. As we wound our way north to Monroe, I was excited to be on a mission with her. I watched wind from the open windows release strands of her salt-and-pepper hair from the tight bun that usually reined it. Once "Big Mama," as we called her, set her mind to something it was as good as done. Now she had decided that her grandson was an artist, and that meant it was written in the stars.

The little wooden box held six small tubes of oil paints, a bottle of linseed oil, a bottle of turpentine, four brushes of various sizes, and a wooden palette. She also bought me two tablets, each containing fifty sheets of synthetic canvas. All the way home I kept opening the box and peeking at the contents as if they were the keys to the universe.

"All anyone expects of you is to do the best you can," she reminded me as we pulled into the driveway of my parents' home. "If you do that I'm sure you will become a fine young man."

Her gift and support were timely. I had no training, and there was no art department at our school. Yet even if there had been an opportunity to study locally I would have never revealed my artistic interests at this phase of my life. I was bashful and could have never mustered the courage to approach anyone for instructions. In 1956 the town of Columbia launched the Caldwell Parish Art and Folk Festival—destined to become one of Louisiana's most famous and long-lasting celebrations of the arts. I'm sure that the experience of witnessing my entire community uniting around art made a lasting impression on me as a timid eleven-year-old. When I combined that with the impact of seeing hypersensitive painters van Gogh and Gauguin depicted in *Lust for Life* at the same time, my conception as an artist was most certainly complete. Yet even with my grandmother's encouragement and support I had no desire to let anyone in our tiny hamlet know about my hobby. Aside from being crazy, painters were also sissies. Real boys were hunters and athletes.

Daddy tolerated my unusual hobby, but he was proud that I was a fullback and linebacker on the junior high school football team. Now, three years after my trip to Monroe with my grandmother to purchase my first set of oil paints, I was a more confident fifteen-year-old freshman and a letterman athlete. I had also become a secret self-taught "folk artist" painter. So admitting my painting hobby to Mrs. Morris in the essay was an act of liberation.

Francis Morris was Columbia High School's beloved English teacher. In her early forties, she pulled triple duty as the director of the school's plays as well as of such events as the homecoming parade. I was an average student in her class, but the subject she assigned for this theme initiated a life-changing transition for me. When she returned the graded paper, the first thing I saw was her note under my C+: "Please see me after class."

The bell rang and my classmates rose and departed. I remained, squirming nervously at my desk. Without looking up from the papers on her desk, Mrs. Morris finally said, "I was impressed with the subject of your essay, Bobby." Then she looked up and said, "Let's talk about your painting."

I was surprised to learn that her son, Johnny, was a painter. I viewed Johnny Morris, two years older than me, as the "beatnik" of Columbia High School. Exhibiting supreme self-confidence, Johnny remained solitary while everyone else—myself included—struggled to fit into the narrowly defined social rules of adolescence and high school. Johnny was a star on the basketball court, which only emphasized to me that his alienation from the other teenage kids had a self-imposed, romantically courageous, "James Dean" implication. Even though I silently admired his independence, he seemed lonely.

"I think you and Johnny might become friends," Mrs. Morris continued. "Would you like to come over and visit?"

The front room was dark, cozy, and enticing. As in my house, perpetual gossamer planes of blue cigarette smoke floated midair in slow motion. I glanced at the Pall Mall wedged between Mrs. Morris's fingers and realized for the first time that she smoked. Inside, I immediately noticed that the walls were crowded with small, impressionistic-style oil paintings. Still lifes, landscapes, portraits, and animal studies hung beside each other in similar simple wooden frames. Mrs. Morris clicked on a lamp and, awakened with soft under-lighting, the paintings leapt into brighter, vivid focus. She proudly explained that the paintings were Johnny's and led me into the kitchen, where the artist himself sat at the dining table.

Columbia was such a small town that Johnny and I knew each other in passing, but we were not friends per se. As adolescent boys, we were both uncomfortable at first meeting, but communication soon flowed as Johnny explained his different paintings. As we chatted and became more comfortable in each other's company, I heard a sound from the next room. I turned and saw Wooten Morris. Walking with a deeply pronounced limp, he entered the adjoining room and paused for a moment at a waist-high workbench. A large, lean man in his mid-forties, with a shock of dark hair and a neatly trimmed mustache, he reminded me of Clark Gable. Restless strands of straight brown hair escaped his mane and danced in dark arcs over his forehead. A Pall Mall dangled from his lips. The curl of smoke that rose from the cigarette targeted one eye and forced him to squint and peer at me from the other through a pinched grin. Unlike any of the other white men I knew, he wore a bandanna around his neck, and his open shirt revealed a hairy chest. His khaki pants were tucked inside his calf-high black boots. He smiled at me and I smiled back. I accepted the silent invitation in his eyes to shake hands.

The room was obviously his workshop. The floor was covered with sawdust, wood chips, and splintered boards. A shelf containing a variety of chisels and wooden mallets hung on the wall between even more oil paintings. Several black electric hand drills lay among more piles of sawdust and wood chips on the bench. Creative energy danced throughout the small room and stirred something deep inside me. I was afraid of Mr. Morris. He was a mystery. We'd all known that Mrs. Morris had a husband, but no one in my family really knew much about him. He did not work in town like everyone else. I never saw him out on the street, at church or sporting events, or at the barbershop socializing like the rest of the men in Columbia.

"So you've admitted you're an artist," he said, laughing as we shook hands. "That's the hardest part. When you admit you're an artist it scares the hell out of people—most of all *you!*"

He put his cigarette in an ashtray and I noticed the walking cane on the workbench. Leaving four strong corner columns running the entire length of the cane, Mr. Morris had carved the remaining, center section into perfect, tiny, free-moving balls. The curved handle of the cane had been left intact, hand-hewn into a beautiful floral pattern. I had never seen anything like it before. It was a remarkable statement of vision, patience, and artistic craft. He noticed me staring, mouth agape.

"You like the cane?" he asked.

"It's beautiful," I sputtered. "How long did it take you to do that?"

"Oh, a while. You have to be patient and have the right tools," he said. "So, you're a painter."

I told him how I'd started dabbling with the paints that came with my model airplane kits and created designs by dripping the paints together. Then I started trying to make up scenes, or paint scenes I noticed around town.

"I'm not very good at the realistic stuff," I confessed, "but I'm learning."

"That's where I can help," Johnny broke in. "We can start painting together this summer as soon as we get out of school."

Within moments, Johnny and I were making plans to spend the summer painting scenes of the forests, swamps, hills, and prairies around Columbia. Before we could do that, however, Johnny felt I needed some basic lessons with still-life compositions. He produced a graphite pencil and sketch pad for both of us and arranged a still life of fruit at the kitchen table.

"Let's see how we do with this," he instructed. "Sketch!"

We made an unusual pair, stumbling through the Columbia countryside with our paints, brushes, and canvas pads. We spent long summer hours lost in time, pencil-sketching figures from tombstones in the Columbia cemetery. Johnny Morris was a natural impressionist, skilled at capturing essence with a quick, simple pencil or brushstroke. At times he was also a patient teacher, taking great pains to make sure I developed the talent to keep up with him artistically. But he was also harsh when I was lazy or couldn't meet his standards. In the beginning I surrendered to the role of student to his teacher. He set up the subjects we would sketch or paint, and then he evaluated how well we both did capturing the images. He thought nothing of grabbing my pencil or brush and taking over my work to make a point. This usually led to an argument, which ended with me sulking and refusing to talk to him for a few days. When I felt like I had progressed technically with pencil sketching, Johnny made me sketch with my left hand.

"It will teach you to search for the *spirit* of the subject." That was his single cryptic explanation.

Whereas painting initially brought me to their door, nourished, and encouraged me to grow, literature quickly revealed itself as equally important to the Morris family. When Billy Dunn appeared at the kitchen table one afternoon, I discovered there were other students attracted to the Morrises' home. Everyone in Columbia knew "Little Billy" had been submitting poetry to publishers since childhood, and he fit right in with the discussions. Healthy, heated arguments about meanings and metaphors of the classics interrupted equally intense discussions concerning light, shadow, color, and artists. Soon I was trying to keep up and reading classics such as *Huckleberry Finn*, *Moby-Dick*, *The Count of Monte Cristo*, *The Scarlet Letter*, *A Tale of Two Cities*, and with Johnny Morris as a teacher, I had begun to learn to paint.

"Paint what you *see*, not what you *think* you see," he would insist.

He was right. I quickly learned to use brushes to maneuver pigment into landscapes, images of dented beer cans, rusted cars, colorful fruit and floral arrangements, and old, sagging buildings. But as my skills progressed it became clear that Johnny and I had completely different motivations, as well as different artistic styles. Our differences first revealed themselves concerning the exhibition of our work. Perhaps as a result of my grandmother's admonition to never be ashamed of my talent, when I grew more confident with my painting I became more eager to show my paintings to other people. Johnny, on the other hand, believed painting to be an intensely private pursuit and preferred not to exhibit outside his home. He probably should have been a pastel sidewalk artist making pictures destined to vanish with the rain.

"Painting itself is what is important," he once confessed to me. "My family likes to show off my paintings, not me. I don't have the discipline, but I suspect we should probably destroy our completed paintings. The painting only has sentimental value. It is no longer of any use."

We had a major disagreement concerning hanging our work at the Caldwell Parish Art and Folk Festival. I felt we should exhibit and he didn't. So as the October event approached, I spent the late summer painting clumsy cubist crucifixes—Picasso-style rip-offs—on six identical sheets of plywood and prepared for the first exhibition of my work. Paintings were exhibited on chicken wire stretched tight between trees on the grounds of the Caldwell Parish Community Center. I hung my six crucifixes with price tags of ten bucks apiece.

My transition as a commercial artist was complete by the end of the art festival. As the last hour of the weekend event drew near I had sold four of the crucifixes and was preparing to give the remaining paintings to friends when two of Columbia's "grandes dames" (and creators of the art festival), Mrs. Guy Alford and Mrs. O. N. "Mz. Jennie" Reynolds, strolled by my exhibit.

"You must be a religious boy," Mrs. Alford commented dryly as she examined my crucifixes.

"No, ma'am," I stated flatly. "Every home in Columbia has some kind of picture of Jesus hanging on the wall. I figured they would sell. And they did. I've sold four already."

"So you paint for money." Mrs. Alford laughed.

"No, ma'am," I explained. "I just need money to buy more paint."

"We'll be watching you, young man." Mrs. Reynolds winked at Mrs. Alford.

The pair bought my last two paintings. After the Caldwell Parish Art Festival there was no turning back. Only sixteen, with sixty dollars in my pocket from my paintings, I knew then that I was going to be a painter.

It is said that when Columbus arrived on the shores of North America a squirrel could jump tree to tree from the shores of the Atlantic seaboard to the banks of the Mississippi River. A vast primordial hardwood forest spanned the entire eastern half of the continent and was home to countless varieties of plants, birds, and animals. When I was born on March 14, 1945, in a tiny community bearing the famous Italian explorer's name, my home-town, Columbia, was nestled in one of the last remaining stands of the hardwood forests of the Deep South. Since time immemorial, northeastern Louisiana had been home to diverse species of life requiring those Spanish moss-draped swamps and dense forests for survival. For example, the last documented sighting of the rare and reclusive ivory-billed woodpecker— the "Ghost Bird"—was in the 1940s in Columbia's neighboring Tensas River country. North Louisiana in the 1940s was essentially a primeval place, a profuse tangled forest of ancient, vine-draped trees rising from a murky floor strewn with the decaying trunks of their forebears. It was indeed the kind of place where one could see ancient ghosts. In 1997 archaeologists determined the oldest reliably dated man-made structure in North America to be a 5,400-year-old burial mound at Watson Brake, Louisiana. Watson Brake is only a few miles from Columbia's equally renowned 3,500-year-old burial mound, Poverty Point. Named for a nearby plantation, the Poverty Point site revealed evidence of pre-Columbian trade ranging from the Rocky Mountains to Appalachia. The older Watson Brake site, however, revealed that all trade there was local, suggesting that my boyhood home was the region of the oldest known human structures and societies in North America.

North Louisiana in the mid-1940s was indeed still haunted by the spirits of ancient animals, indigenous people, and the more recent antebellum "Old South." No place could ever have been more full of phantoms than Columbia. There, in the heart of the Mississippi Delta, sixty miles due west of Vicksburg, the lushly forested Ouachita (Wash-it-ah) River hills gently descended into sprawling black delta prairies that blossomed annually with endless fields of white cotton. High atop red clay and sandy loam slopes, and also in deeply eroded ravines, kudzu vines intertwined with ancient hickory, oak, poplar, elm, ash, walnut, beech, sycamore, magnolia, sweet gum, pine, and bamboo cane forests, giving birth to a buzzing, whistling, chattering, aromatic tangle of life. Moss-laced cypress trees, palmetto palms, and ferns of all descriptions overwhelmed hardwood and pine foliage as the river bottoms surrendered to mysterious boggy swamps filled with hundreds of species of fish, poisonous snakes, gigantic snapping and soft-shelled turtles, alligators, and countless varieties of insects. Post–World War II Columbia, Louisiana, was an enchanted, honeysuckled Eden—a splendid garden for a boy's imagination.

Among the first wave of America's colonists, the Bridgers arrived in Isle of Wight, Virginia, from Slimbridge, England, in the 1600s. In the 1830s, by way of North Carolina, my limb of the family tree briefly found themselves in Port Gibson, Mississippi, before moving on to northern Louisiana to become a pioneer family of the town of Columbia. My great-great-grandfather Ingadozier Call Bridger settled on the fertile eastern banks and delta prairies of the Ouachita River and helped build the town of Columbia in the hills on the river's western banks. Each day I. C. rowed his dugout canoe across the river from his Bellevue Plantation to the expanding little community. I. C.'s son, Cicero Call, inherited Bellevue Plantation and after prospering in agriculture, went into the mercantile business in Columbia and also succeeded in that endeavor. Before his death Cicero

Bridger started the Bridger Cotton Gin. The third of his three sons, my maternal grandfather, Hartley Call Bridger, ran the cotton gin during the harvest season. His older brother, A. C.—"Archie"—went into banking and founded the Caldwell Bank and Trust Company—still the oldest privately owned bank in the state of Louisiana. The middle brother, Cicero, was a produce buyer and seller. When not running the gin, Hartley also bought and sold produce—pecans, peanuts, sugarcane, peaches, sweet potatoes, watermelons, turtles, etc.—whatever was in season. We called him "Papa."

Papa's wife, Josephine Sutton, was from a similar plantation background in Selma, Alabama. After prospering in agriculture the Suttons became doctors, lawyers, and educators. Trained as a home economics teacher at Judson Women's College in Alabama, "Miss Josephine," as everyone in town called her, came to Columbia to teach school. The old Bridger house, built in more prosperous times, was a dark, three-story, creaky, wood-frame mansion—the kind that frightens children. By the turn of the century the family took in boarders to help with finances. Josephine rented a room in the Bridger family boardinghouse, where she met and soon married my grandfather.

Named after the beloved Confederate general, my mother, Roberta Lee, was born in Columbia on October 19, 1923. True to her namesake and the "Old South," I was ten years old before I discovered that "damn" and "Yankee" were two separate words. Roberta inherited her mother's fiery temper and intellect and her father's immense capacity for dreamy denial, flights of fantasy, and habitual procrastination. But she also inherited her parents' strong sense of place and love of the lingering Old South of her nativity. Roberta had no desire to see the world; the world existed in Columbia. Every type of person, every situation in the human condition, every sin, every salvation was present there in those river hills overlooking the lovely Ouachita. If her family had decided to settle there generations ago, then, by God, it was good enough to provide everything she needed in life.

My father's family, the Durhams, were people of the forest. They arrived in Virginia and the Carolinas from northern England in the early eighteenth century and soon migrated to the Big Thicket of East Texas. Like the Bridgers in North Louisiana, the Durhams had been in Woodville, Texas, since the early nineteenth century.

If possible, the forests of East Texas around Woodville were even more dense than those of North Louisiana, but in a less hilly landscape. The nearby Alabama-Coushatta Indian Reservation was my first awareness of Indians. Unlike the warrior-oriented Comanches, the peaceful Alabama-Coushatta tribes remained safely nestled deep in the bosom of the Big Thicket because of Texas founding father Sam Houston's empathy for Indians. When we visited the Durhams I always hoped I might see an Indian walking along the side of the road.

Whereas the Bridgers were successful planters, merchants, bankers, and community builders, the Durhams lived very simply, pragmatically close to the earth, deep in the woods. The Durham family subsisted by working in the timber business, growing their own food, and playing music. Some of my fondest childhood memories revolve around old-timers in my father's family—particularly my grandfather Hill C. Durham Sr.—playing music. They would sing songs like "Turtle Dove" with ancient "handed-down" British lyrics updated with original Grandpa Durham melodies. And there were always the humorous songs like Grandpa Durham's composition "The German Girl," which everyone knew as "the laughing song":

> Oh, once I had a German girl, her name was Lula Sweet
> Her nose was red and so was her head
> And her shoes were full of feet.
> I took that gal out one night, sat her down to supper.
> She tripped on the jack, and the table cracked,
> When she stuck her nose in the butter.
> Oh, ha, ha, ha, ha, ha, ha,
> Ha, Ha, Ha, Ha, Ha. Ha."[1]

Of course it was impossible not to laugh when everyone around you would sing the chorus as if they were laughing. Later, as an adult, I realized that musical corniness like this helped them to unite and endure hard times, such as the Great Depression. Grandpa Durham would frequently introduce his songs like this: "Here's a song I wrote and another fellow put the words and music to it." Sometimes after singing a song he'd ask, "Want me to do that tune backwards?" Then he would turn his back to the audience and begin singing the song again. One particular favorite moment with him reveals much of his positive nature: once we were walking through the woods and a rabbit ran across the road; he said, "Times must be good. There goes a perfectly good rabbit and no one's chasing him for supper."

Born in 1895, Grandpa Durham was elected and served as Tyler County's judge from time to time, but he was better known for teaching school and playing fiddle at dances throughout the Big Thicket with his older brothers, Levi and Brett. The two of them played guitars, and all three brothers sang and wrote songs. Contemporaries of Huddie Ledbetter, the Durham brothers rode a mule from gig to gig, and they must have traveled the same East Texas circuit as Leadbelly, playing for weekend dances. Whereas my grandfather was a singing judge, however, Leadbelly got himself thrown in prison twice for murder before University of Texas ballad collector John Lomax "discovered" him.

As late as the 1960s many of the Durhams still lived in the traditional homes of frontier Texas, "dogtrot" cabins. A dogtrot house is a slightly elevated structure consisting of long porches that extended along the length of the front and rear of two small cabins, thereby connecting them. One of the cabins had four very small bedrooms, while the other was a family room and kitchen. Another wide porch between the two cabins—the dogtrot—connected the front and back porches while also creating a natural "breezeway." The yards of the dogtrot cabins were mostly sand and were populated with scores of chickens—sand allowing snakes to be easily spotted if they escaped the ever-searching eyes of the chickens. Dog and cats cooled themselves under the house, waiting for any other pests or varmints that might venture toward the house. Beyond the sand yards were woods so thick that you could not see through them. By the time the atomic bomb ended World War II in August 1945, however, most of my father's immediate family had fled the Big Thicket, seeking work in the oil refineries on the Gulf Coast of Texas from Beaumont to Houston.

Born on October 27, 1922, my father, Hill Clinton Durham Jr., was a big man, slightly over six feet tall, lean and blond. Like most of America's young men, my father immediately volunteered for military service after the Japanese attack on Pearl Harbor on December 7, 1941. During World War II young men were allowed to enlist as a team and remain together throughout their time in the service. Daddy and his cousin Everett Durham decided to enlist as a team. Everett wanted them to join the U.S. Navy, but Daddy convinced his cousin they should enlist in the Marine Corps instead. Quite certain that they were headed to the Pacific theater, the cousins shipped out for basic training at the Marines' famous Camp Pendleton in California.

My father was not destined for combat; he had suffered a serious knee injury playing high school football, and he reinjured the knee during the final days of basic training. He was able to hide the injury from his superiors until his platoon arrived in Hawaii. There the knee injury became so aggravated he could no longer walk. Marine doctors examined him and determined that he needed immediate surgery. Everett and his platoon shipped out to fight the Japanese in the islands, and Daddy remained in Honolulu in a Marine hospital for six months, in a cast up to his waist. When Daddy recovered from the knee surgery, he was honorably discharged from the Marines and shipped back to Texas in a state of deep depression and punishing guilt about not being able to fight in the war. Later, Everett was killed on the beaches of Iwo Jima. I don't think my father ever forgave himself for not dying there with Everett.

Life on the streets of war-torn America could not have been easy for him. An able-bodied, unmarried, apparently healthy young man who was not in uniform was presumed to be defective in some dark, unspeakable way. Many people certainly questioned his courage, his patriotism, or—worse—his manhood. He was already hypersensitive and shy, and the situation most certainly accentuated his inherent social paranoia. Throughout his life he never talked with me or anyone else about those years, but even as a little boy I knew it had been a very difficult time for him and I mistrusted the military for hurting my daddy. After returning to Texas from the Marines, however, he immediately found surveying work in the oil fields with Brown and Root Company. In early 1944 an exploratory excursion with that geophysical company brought him to Columbia, where he courted and fell in love with the beautiful raven-haired twenty-one-year-old Roberta "Bobbie" Bridger.

My mother was a reclusively shy, spoiled, and overprotected only child. When I see her favorite springtime blossom, the whimsical wisteria, I always think of her. Her favorite song, Johnny Mercer's "Autumn Leaves," perfectly reveals her melancholy personality. Like most Southern belles of her era, she was totally dependent on stronger individuals' caring for her, but she also inherited her mother's sharp tongue and confrontational personality; she distrusted anyone who wouldn't engage her in a fight—often at the very beginning of the relationship. She believed that once you'd had a good argument—in which she had your undivided attention—you could begin to honestly communicate.

As was often the case during those uncertain days of World War II, love was forced by fate to be "at first sight." Soon after my mother and father started dating, they faced a life-altering decision. Upon completion of his assignment in Columbia, my father was scheduled to travel to Gillette, Wyoming, with his job. So after knowing each other only two weeks, my parents decided to elope. They married on March 12, 1944. After informing her parents of their secret wedding, my father took his bride to Wyoming. At that point in her young life, my mother had been out of Columbia only once before—for a two-week vacation to California with her aunt and uncle. She was terrified simply riding the train to Wyoming to begin their fifty-year marriage. It was not a happy marriage. But they obviously had moments of affection, and there was fire and passion in the relationship— or there would have been no babies.

I was conceived in June 1944 as they began their marriage in Gillette. But my mother was not going to give a thought to having her first baby born in Wyoming; she hated the place. She wanted her comfortable native environment when she gave birth to her first child. Soon after learning that she was pregnant, she started coaxing my father to return to Louisiana.

Convincing Hill Durham to leave Wyoming must have taken some doing. He was in love with the wildness of the place. Unlike his bride, he respected the independent people of Wyoming. Whereas my mother pre-ferred creature comforts, he liked being close to the land and testing him-self with the elements. Until his death at seventy-eight, he spoke fondly of being in Wyoming in the 1940s, when immense numbers of wild game— antelope, mule deer, elk, buffalo—were still plentiful. He was an avid, life-long hunter, and the culture he experienced in untamed Wyoming fit him like a glove. One of his favorite Wyoming stories was the time when he got a Jeep stuck on the rolling prairies far outside of Gillette. Luckily an old sheepherder arrived to assist him, and after freeing the Jeep from the mud, the sheepherder said, "That's probably the first mechanized vehicle to ever touch the ground out here." Nevertheless, my father consented to my mother's wishes, and soon they returned to Columbia for my birth.

Even naming me provoked an argument between my parents. As my father's firstborn it was expected that I would be named Hill Clinton Durham III. It was not to be. My mother's beloved cousin Robert Lee had recently been killed in the famous Battle of the Bulge in the war in Europe, and the family felt that this new baby boy's name should somehow memo-rialize his sacrifice. As a concession to my father's disappointment, my mother named me Robert Clinton, with the promise that the next son would be Hill Clinton Durham III.

My father was able to keep his job with Brown and Root, and soon after I was born he started traveling again. Now it was the three of us traveling the Texas/New Mexico oil patch. From 1945 to 1947 Daddy worked in such towns as Roswell, New Mexico, and Hillsboro and Pecos, Texas, before my homesick mother convinced him to return to Columbia. Daddy quickly found work with the State of Louisiana on a surveying crew, and for the next thirty years he was employed by the Department of Public Works as a supervisor of civil engineering projects. My brother Hill Clinton Durham III was born in 1949, and my brother John Hartley in 1956. My parents never left Columbia again.

Like the rest of the world, Columbia entered the "Atomic Age" in the late 1940s. By the Cold War 1950s, the Soviet Union launched *Sputnik* and thrust the Russians and Americans into a competitive technological and scientific race that continues to this day. Moreover, during this time the South was on the brink of emerging from a one-hundred-year "Reconstruction" era to become the "New South." Real estate agents and loan companies coined the poetic "Sun Belt" concept to replace "Bible Belt" as Yankees—damned or converted—discovered the pleasure of not having to shovel humidity. Dramatic and historic social changes—many born in North Louisiana in the form of early "rock and roll"—were also poised to shock the world into a historic counterculture revolution. But in the late 1940s and throughout the 1950s, Columbia, Louisiana, was sheltered from change by powerful conservative political godfathers still present in full glory. With characters like Governors Jimmie Davis and Earl K. Long, in Columbia we had a front-row seat to witness the blend of show business and grassroots politics that is unique to Louisiana. Each harvest season the first bale of cotton produced at the gin would be ceremoniously placed in front of the Caldwell Bank and Trust Company, and politicians would set up there to speak and perform. They usually brought along a band of musicians, and more often than not, the candidates themselves performed. The composer of "You Are My Sunshine," Governor Jimmie Davis, was a favorite. Davis's mother was a Durham before she married, so we thought we were probably related somewhere down the line. But we also loved his music. Though not a musician, the champion entertainer of them all was Huey P.'s wild kid brother, Earl K. Long. "Uncle Earl" always guaranteed a big crowd and a great show. I still have vivid memories of 1956 when Uncle Earl came campaigning. Several friends and I had climbed to the roof of the Rexall Drug Store for a view of the governor next door at the bank. When the door to

Uncle Earl's shiny white Cadillac opened by the cotton bale, we were stunned to see my kid brother Hill get out of the car before the governor. Governor Long had no children of his own, and he was noted for being fond of kids and giving them nickels at his speeches. Uncle Earl had stopped for gas at a station on the edge of town and overheard nine-year-old Hill holding court and telling some funny jokes. So Uncle Earl invited Hill to ride with him in the limo into town and started his act that day by inviting my brother—still clinging to his fishing pole—to tell the crowd a joke. I was mighty impressed with my kid brother's moment in the spotlight. One of Columbia's own, John J. McKeithen, rose to occupy the governor's office in Baton Rouge throughout the 1960s. Cut from the same fabric as Huey and "Uncle Earl" Long, Governor McKeithen championed the famous "Louisiana Superdome," which was constructed during his administration.

The short walk between Big Mama and Papa's house and ours was about a mile over a well-worn path through friendly backyards and ever-growing fingers of surrounding woods that crept steadily into Columbia's yards. Like many other Southern states, Louisiana planted the Japanese kudzu plant immediately after the war to prevent the constant erosion of the hillsides. Later, Southerners discovered that kudzu is a natural parasite and quickly entangles anything in reach of its tentacles. We lived on a hillside terrace on the northeast edge of town, and as a child I wondered if the Japanese hadn't tricked America into accepting this monster Trojan horse. My parents' house nestled into a sandy hillside that was overrun with kudzu, and one of my first jobs was trimming it back from our yard. It was a never-ending task. Deep in the woods, kudzu vines would grow to the size of an arm and when intertwined with leg-sized bamboo cane forests, they became impenetrable snarls. My playmates and I would sometimes carve tunnels through these impressive tangles of vine and cane and make treehouse-like hideouts high above the ground like Tarzan.

A block north of Lakeview Terrace, separated from the white neighborhood by a long wooden fence, was the Negro section of Columbia. I have no idea how the community got the name Ball Town, but that was how blacks and whites alike referred to the place. Many black families also lived high in the hills rising on the swampy side of the levee system that during annual flooding seasons protected Columbia from the Ouachita River. When the river rose, the black folks from the hills on the backwater side of the levee made their way into town in flat-bottomed boats, canoes, or pirogues. Often at twilight we would hear "race music"—as Negro rhythm and blues music was called in those days—swelling from the hills and wafting over the swamps. On Sunday mornings we could hear the black church in Ball Town—less than half a mile away—gloriously singing God's praises. Daddy would not allow "race" music to be played in the house, but by the time I entered my early teens I was sneaking records by Ray Charles, Little Richard, LaVern Baker, Ivory Joe Hunter (from Monroe, Louisiana), Bobby Blue Bland, Professor Longhair, Ernie K-Doe, Fats Domino, the Coasters, and other black musicians into my collection. My favorites were Jackie Wilson and Sam Cooke. My first awareness of my tenor voice was singing along with Jackie Wilson's "Lonely Teardrops" and "Reet Petite."

My grandfather, a produce buyer in the fertile Mississippi Delta, provided another important window into black culture. Papa's life was a never-ending search to buy something interesting that he could sell later for a profit. He didn't drive automobiles, and that created an interesting connection between him and the Negro community in the waning days of the Jim Crow South. Even though Columbia was profoundly segregated, some of my earliest memories involve running through Ball Town, searching for Papa's friends to drive him on buying expeditions. Traveling throughout the region with him and his black friends was never boring; he certainly had more friends in the Negro community than in the white.

Uncles, aunts, cousins, and family friends were within shouting distance throughout Columbia, and the entire town—black and white—was essentially linked together like a small tribe. Privacy was respected, and gossip paradoxically sealed the bond; children were free to wander unsupervised throughout the town and surrounding hills and woods because everyone knew them and their parents, and anything out of the ordinary was quickly observed. I am certain that one of the most important blessings of my life was a charmed boyhood in a small, post–World War II town in the Deep South. For one thing, the loosely defined community bond most definitely presented a balance between absolute freedom and the consequences of overstepping one's boundaries. More often than not, punishment was the shame of embarrassing your family before the entire community. This social interaction between the immediate family and the extended community family, balanced with keen understanding of the consequences of breaking the rules in such a small town, perfectly defined for me the system and the proper force needed to bend the social mores necessary to blossom within it as an artist.

Obtaining my driver's license at age fifteen brought mobility into my life, and with it a different kind of music and lifestyle. North Louisiana's idiosyncratic blending of black gospel, rhythm and blues, pop, and country music was bubbling and boiling into a gumbo of "blue-eyed soul" long before critics coined the phrase to define the style that the Righteous Brothers would make famous several years later. Big bands like the Rollercoasters, the Carousels, and the Boogie Kings, fronted by lead singers like G. G. Shinn, and Jerry LaCroix, packed the cotton patch roadhouses, honkytonks, and juke joints of the state, playing blues classics like "Honky Tonk," "Matilda," and "Linda Lou." I particularly enjoyed the powerful horn sections—usually two trumpets, a sax, and a trombone—that punched the driving rhythm sections of these dance bands. Now able to drive, I would tell my parents I was going to the movies, then drive to Monroe and sneak into the nightclubs. I made friends with the doormen and bouncers, and if I promised to sit quietly, not drink, and only listen to the music, they would let me into the clubs. I hid deep within the crowds, transfixed in the shadows, smoking and watching the dancers' eternal courting rituals. Lubricated with alcohol, and captivated with the pulsating music, they forgot their troubles and let their emotions run free. My family would have been furious to discover where I was and what I was learning, but I loved being in the nightclubs—particularly watching the musicians and secretly dreaming of one day being onstage like them.

THREE

When the Pupil's Ready, the Teacher Will Appear

I N MAY 1963 MY GREAT-UNCLE ARCHIE BRIDGER invited me in from the humid afternoon for a cool drink after I mowed his yard. Born in 1888 and the founder and president of Caldwell Bank and Trust Company, he was the Bridger family patriarch. Like his brothers, Uncle Archie was bald and pear-shaped. I was always a bit afraid of him. He was friendly enough, but our vast age difference and his standing in our family hierarchy made him seem as ancient and intimidating as Methuselah. His charming wife, Zella, was usually present to buffer our awkwardness with her cheerful understanding of the difference between teenage boys and old men. Alone and uncomfortable that afternoon, however, Uncle Archie and I shared a moment over a glass of cold water in his kitchen. He broke the silence by telling me he had recently come across a story in *Reader's Digest* about a mountain man named Jim Bridger.

"He was one of the first white men to head out west to the Rocky Mountains," Uncle Archie said in his soft, raspy voice. "Why don't you see what you can learn about him? We might be related."

Eighteen years old, a week from high school graduation, and heading to college that fall, I was more interested in painting, girls, and football than an old mountain man—even if he might prove to be a distant relative. My most immediate concern was a summer job that would pay me more than I could make mowing yards. Within days of my chat with Uncle Archie my father walked into my room and surprised me trying to pluck out a tune on his Gibson guitar. "You'll never learn to play that thing," he barked. "I've been trying for twenty years."

By that time I had become so competitive with my father that his negative remark ignited a fierce flame in me. I promptly found a guitar chord book in the school library and vowed to teach myself to play before I left for college in the fall.

During the interim between my conversation with Uncle Archie and my dad discovering me with his guitar, I got a summer job with the Caldwell Parish School Board. After graduation I went immediately to work scrubbing seventy-five filthy brown school buses until they were restored to their original sparkling yellow. But all my spare time was devoted to learning guitar.

Because most of my father's family played guitars and fiddles and sang original songs, it was like folk music had always been there. But now, like most of America during the early 1960s, I was infatuated with folk music. Seemingly overnight it acquired a new, unprecedented importance. I was aware that one of the giants of American folk music, Huddie Ledbetter was from nearby Greenwood, Louisiana. The tale of "Leadbelly" singing his way out of Angola state prison with his immortal "Goodnight Irene" was as legendary throughout Louisiana as our singing governor, Jimmie Davis, and his equally everlasting "You Are My Sunshine." But since the 1920s traditional folk music had been quietly entering the pop charts through pioneers like the Carter Family, Jimmie Rodgers, Carl Sandburg, John Jacob Niles, Oscar Brand, Burl Ives, Harry Belafonte, Pete Seeger, and the Weavers.

Aware of the rising popularity of folk music, by the late 1950s pop conductor and Columbia Records executive Mitch Miller regularly incorporated the form into his hugely popular "follow the bouncing ball" sing-along television productions. Simultaneously, manufactured, sugarcoated, color-coordinated, four-part-harmony acts from the mid-1950s, such as the Four Aces, the Four Coins, the Four Preps, the Freshman Four, etc., kept the matching sweaters but picked up banjos and guitars and, by the 1960s, morphed into the Brothers Four, the Limelighters, the Easy Riders, and the New Christy Minstrels. When the Kingston Trio phenomenon arrived on the international pop charts, the stage was set for what would come to be known throughout America as the "folk explosion." The success of the Kingston Trio could be directly traced to the group's leader, Dave Guard, being inspired by activist/troubadour Pete Seeger. During the McCarthy era Seeger's Puritan beliefs led to his being blacklisted by the House Un-American Activities Committee. But Seeger's blacklisting served only to call broader attention to an already exemplary career, while also proceeding to make American folk music even more popular. Suddenly locked out of the mainstream, Seeger brilliantly exploited his infamy by using his notoriety to draw increasingly large crowds of students to his folk music workshops on university campuses. A modern musical version of Johnny Appleseed, Seeger's workshops planted the seeds that blossomed into the rising popularity of folk music of the early 1960s.

Just as this sanitized "first wave" of commercial folk music was cresting in national popularity, however, Bob Dylan suddenly appeared and made the general public aware of Leadbelly and Pete Seeger's old singing partner, the phenomenal Woody Guthrie. Texan ballad hunter John Lomax's son, Alan, recorded Woody's Depression-era labor union protest songs for the Smithsonian Institution's Folkways label. Guthrie was noted for having the phrase "This machine kills fascists!" printed on his guitar, and that mission melded perfectly with Pete Seeger's egalitarian ideals.

Coincidentally, folk music swept the nation as the youthful John F. Kennedy was elected president. In his inaugural address, Kennedy boldly called for the nation to explore what he termed the "New Frontier," and folk music accepted the challenge. Guthrie's old singing partner, Cisco Houston, Seeger's group, the Weavers, Peter, Paul, and Mary, Bob Gibson, Ramblin' Jack Elliott, Dave Van Ronk, Bob Dylan, Phil Ochs, Joan Baez, Josh White, Odetta, Judy Collins, Tom Paxton, Richie Havens, the Greenbriar Boys, the Dillards, the New Lost City Ramblers, the Smothers Brothers, and the multitude of other acts that followed in their wide wake accepted Kennedy's invitation to "ask what you can do for your country" and began to use their music as a voice of protest and a harbinger of change.

To me the appeal of folk music was honesty. Paradoxically, because of the explosive force created from the morphing of hillbilly and rhythm and blues music into rock and roll in the early 1950s, most of the pop music of the late 1950s had become phony and contrived. Sure, the *Lucky Strike Hit Parade* surrendered to *American Bandstand*, but Buddy Holly, Richie Valens, the Big Bopper, Gene Vincent, Eddie Cochran, and a host of other rock-and-roll innovators were dead. Deeply threatened, reactionary forces in America moved swiftly with a fierce counterattack on the new form and inducted Elvis into the army, banished Jerry Lee Lewis to the "inbred hillbilly file," sentenced Chuck Berry to prison on trumped-up sex charges based on the archaic Mann Act, and sent terrified, swishy Little Richard fleeing to the sanctuary of the ministry. The first major star of the singer/songwriter era, operatic balladeer Roy Orbison, had not yet emerged from the long shadows cast by Sam Phillips's phenomenal "million-dollar quartet" (Elvis, Jerry Lee Lewis, Johnny Cash, and Carl Perkins) at Sun Records. So as conservative America attempted to harness the phenomenal energy of the big bang of rock and roll that was spreading throughout America, the corporate airwaves of the late 1950s and early 1960s were sanitized with the likes of Fabian, Frankie Avalon, Annette Funicello, Connie Francis, Bobby Vee, Bobby Rydell, and Bobby Vinton. Like everyone else, I realized these acts were purely manufactured "rock." Folk music, bubbling below the mainstream, was, if nothing else, honest.

In the days before generic chain stores, or iPod downloads, vinyl records—particularly recordings of folk music—were much more difficult to obtain. I would hover over the radio on Sunday nights to try to pick up Art Roberts's cutting-edge folk music program aired over hundred-thousand-watt WLS-AM out of Chicago. If a new singer, songwriter, or group caught my attention I would save my money, drive thirty miles to the only music store in Monroe, order the record, and anxiously wait for it to arrive.

Once I obtained a recording, I approached music as obsessively as I studied painting. I would spend hours with vinyl records of folk music, repeatedly picking up the arm of the record player, moving it back, and playing the same song over and over until the records were scratched and worn out. After absorbing the lyrics and melody, using visual arts techniques I would break a song's accompaniment down by studying positive and negative space within the instrumentation; very soon I realized that where musicians chose not to play was as important as the places they actually played. Finally, I would analyze the singer's unique approach with each song, searching for influences from previous recordings or other singers. As I deconstructed and reconstructed the recording of songs, I became particularly interested in the way two or three artists interpreted the same song. This tactic was remarkably functional; within a very short time it seemed that everyone was recording Bob Dylan's songs, and this allowed me to study the multitude of styles and techniques used to interpret an individual tune. It also encouraged me to feel free to borrow from other singers, or to interpret a song my own unique way.

Joan Baez's voice put me in a trance. Her flawless vibrato, crystal clarity, and splendid control were to me the embodiment of vocal perfection;

her guitar accompaniment was precise, emotional, and celestial. The classic folk songs that she selected were simultaneously contemporary and time-less. And before Baez I had never heard a singer assume a male or female role in a song depending on the character she wished to portray. I would vanish for hours into Baez's world, and singing along with her records, I awakened the tenor voice I had glimpsed earlier when I sang along with Jackie Wilson's records. Singing in the same registers as Joan Baez taught me that I possessed a very strong, clear tenor voice, and I started to explore the falsetto, vibrato, and contra-tenor ranges of it, while I gravitated to songs that would showcase my ability to hit the high notes.

Since seeing Wooten Morris's sculpted walking cane I had longed to learn to carve with such skill. One afternoon he volunteered to teach me. He carefully marked an oversized test block of wood with a pencil to indicate the shapes he wanted left in the wood and the places he intended to cut away. Then he took out a small electric drill and began to carefully shave curls of wood from the block.

"They say the form is already in the block of wood or stone," he said. "The artist's job is to discover and release it."

The drill's whine made it difficult to talk, but within a few minutes a ball shape was emerging from one side of the block of wood. Once he completed this, he turned the block and started shaping the opposite side of the ball. Before cutting completely through the wood he stopped, leaving the ball shape frozen in the block. Then he turned to me.

"I hear you're quite a drinker," he said.

Surprised by his remark, I had no time to think. I froze in silence.

"Do you know I'm an alcoholic?" he offered nonchalantly, as he started carving again.

"I've never seen you take a drink," I laughed. "You're joking."

"No. I'm serious. I'm an alcoholic. I haven't had a drink in over seven-teen years now, but I'm an alcoholic. If I had a drink now I'd try to drink all the whiskey in Louisiana before sundown."

I stared at the ball shape in the block of wood, embarrassed that he was telling me this, yet afraid to ask why.

"Have you ever wondered why I wear this bandanna? It's to remind me of my drinking days—the dark days when I had the DTs so bad that I couldn't get a drink to my lips without spilling it. I would strap my tie around my wrist, drape it behind my neck, and lever the whiskey glass successfully to my lips."

He couldn't be making this up.

"I just wanted to offer a gentle warning, Bobby," he continued. "You're a good kid and I would hate for you to wake up and discover you have a problem. Do me a personal favor? When you want a drink, have one; when you *need* a drink, stop."

I agreed to take his advice, but knew I would continue drinking with my pals when we headed to college. Drinking was part of our entire social scene and I expected to continue partying in college.

Within an hour Wooten created four corner pillars and a free ball rolling inside the block of wood. He tossed a block to me.

"Try it!"

Summer ended and I prepared to enroll at Northeast Louisiana State College, in nearby Monroe. I had become more confident of my ability to sing and accompany myself on guitar, so I bought a used black Sears guitar from a friend and put nylon strings on it. I started performing regularly for the group of young people that gathered at the Morris home, and my repertoire was growing daily. The flame was now white-hot to play folk music, but I enjoyed performing only for my friends and had no dreams of a career as a singer. On the other hand, I had fantasized about majoring in art in college, but aside from teaching, I could not imagine earning a living as an artist. So I decided to major in sociology and minor in history. Painting and music would remain cherished recreational activities.

Soon after arriving on campus I saw a flyer announcing auditions for the Freshman Talent Show and decided to try out. At the auditions I met a pretty young woman named Sage Redding. She had long, straight, blond hair that she wore in the style of Mary Travers of Peter, Paul, and Mary. She had suffered polio as a child that left her with one leg smaller than the other and a pronounced limp. While we waited for the audition Sage and I started singing together and quickly worked up a duet of the classic "Five Hundred Miles." Careful to avoid duplicating any of the already clichéd versions of the song by famous folk performers, we rapidly found a unique duet voice. By the time of the tryout we decided to audition as a duo rather than as single acts. The director loved our song and invited us to be a part of the talent show. Suddenly I had a singing partner.

Entering the public's eye accentuated a problem I was facing. I would never be able to wear a pompadour hairstyle like my early musical rockabilly heroes. Hartley Bridger genetically disposed me to a bald head, and as early as eighteen the first signs of male pattern baldness appeared. My grandmother warned me of this before she died and suggested I cut my hair in the style known as a Buster Brown: short on the sides with long bangs over the forehead. Big Mama believed bangs would help me disguise my rapidly receding hairline, and she was right. Before the talent show I made sure that my bangs shielded any shiny spots on my forehead.

I peered nervously through the curtain to see the crowd gathering in Brown Auditorium. It would be the largest crowd I had performed for and I was petrified. Once in the warm spotlight, I could nevertheless feel the audience's intensely supportive energy and felt completely at ease sitting on the stool at the bright lip of the stage. I loved singing into a microphone for the first time and hearing my voice soar to the back of the huge theater and come echoing back.

Later that evening I was surprised to hear the announcement that Sage and I had won the second-place award in the contest. Soon the house lights rose and the audience began to mingle in the aisles before departing the theater. Sage left with her mother, and I noticed that my parents were talking with a stranger in a dark suit. Before I could join them to see who he was, I was approached by a very tall man with a wild mop of salt-and-pepper hair and the grin of a mischievous boy in his twinkling brown eyes.

With outstretched hand, Dr. O. Philip James introduced himself and offered congratulations. He dug through the pockets of his tan corduroy jacket and, locating his pipe, struck a kitchen match and soon sent aromatic smoke clouds billowing through the backstage area. A stagehand shouted to him that it was illegal for him to smoke, and though he let the pipe naturally extinguish, he kept it shoved firmly in his mouth. The smell of his pipe reminded me of Grandpa Durham and Wooten Morris and I instantly liked him.

"I want you to go ballad hunting with me in Arkansas!" he said through pipe-clenched teeth.

"I'll have to ask my folks," I said, "but it sounds like fun."

By the time Dr. James and I strolled into the audience, the stranger my parents had been speaking with was gone. Without missing a beat, Dr. James offered his proposal.

"I need a singer to perform examples of folk songs for my lectures," he explained. "I squawk like a blue jay myself. I hope you'll allow Bobby to accompany me to northern Arkansas to learn some of the old-time songs they sing up there."

My parents quickly gave me permission to travel to Arkansas with Dr. James. And when we loaded into the car for the drive home I discovered that the stranger my parents had been speaking with was a talent scout for a Memphis record company. He had offered me an audition for a recording contract and my father turned it down.

I was furious. There was a long silence in the car before Daddy finally spoke.

"There will be other opportunities to make records Bobby," he explained. "I know you don't want to hear it now, but I turned down the record contract because what they offered wasn't right for you. It's more important for you to get an education."

I sat in the backseat of the car and pouted.

In late September 1963 Dr. James and I drove to Mountain View, Arkansas. Soon after we arrived, Dr. James proceeded to cruise town asking about the "old songs." On our second day in the Ozarks we arrived at a small farm nestled deep in a hollow. There, we heard an elderly woman sing old songs in a language Dr. James described as Elizabethan English. Hearing her sing, I was transported back in time and space by the unusual-sounding words and her strident a cappella voice. I tried to memorize the song as she sang, but the language was entirely too difficult for a drawling country boy like me to master in the short time we had there. Instead, I just listened, knowing my life had somehow changed. After we left Mountain View I asked Dr. James why he didn't make a tape recording of her singing.

"This is delicate stuff, Bobby," he said. "Most people are suspicious of making a recording. To begin with, most folks don't like the way they sound when they hear themselves speak or sing on tape for the first time. They also are suspicious of your motives and believe you'll make money and they won't. So you have to move carefully. They have to know they can trust you before they'll consent to a recording. Ask too soon and you'll spook them." As we drove back to Monroe I peppered Dr. James with questions about folk music and ballads. We even discussed his visiting Woodville with me to hear my family's original music.

"Finding original folk music is becoming a thing of the past," he said. "It is increasingly difficult for folklorists to discover an original song actually passed down from one generation to another. More often than not, the songs old-timers play for us these days have been learned from the Grand Ole Opry. People hear songs on the radio now, and those songs have slowly replaced the old songs that for centuries were passed down personally through the family. Ironically, modern recording technology made it possible for collectors like the Lomaxes and my old friend John Quincy Wolf to record folk songs as they teetered at the brink of the abyss in contemporary American society. But that same technology is now creating a new American folk song. Two generations ago folks had to entertain themselves with family versions of traditional songs; now, America has professional folksingers who earn their living as songwriters and recording artists."

Dr. James's remarks made me wonder if there might be any family ballads about that old mountain man Uncle Archie had told me about several months earlier. "Have you ever heard of Jim Bridger?" I asked.

"Of course I've heard of Jim Bridger," Dr. James said incredulously. "He's a legend in American history. In fact, Johnny Horton wrote a splendid folk song about him. It's on the same album with Jimmy Driftwood's 'Battle of New Orleans.' Indeed, that proves my point about technology and folk music; Horton's record was a collection of modern folk songs."

"Then where would a fellow find an old folk song about Jim Bridger?" I asked.

"A period folk song about Jim Bridger?" He puffed his pipe. "That's a very interesting question. When we return to campus we'll initiate a search."

Two months later the only reference to Bridger or the fur trade I had been able to find in American folk music was in John Lomax's definitive *Cowboy Songs and Other Frontier Ballads.* In the Lomax collection I discovered Jim Bridger mentioned in passing in the song "California Joe."[1] Aside from the famous "Shenandoah," I could not find a single song that survived the fur trade era.

"How could this be?" I asked Dr. James. "The mountain men were some of the most flamboyant characters in American history. I've found all these songs about fictional characters like John Henry, Pecos Bill, and Paul Bunyan, but few songs about real, historical people. Also, I've found that most American folk songs and ballads come either from New England, Appalachia, or the Deep South. The only 'western' ballads I've found are cowboy songs, and they are from an era four decades after the fur trade."

"It would appear that you've discovered a void, Bobby," Dr. James said.

"Do you know what to do when you discover a void?"

"No?"

"You leap in!"

On November 22, 1963, I was in my dorm room eating lunch when my roommate, Jim Betts, rushed in to tell me that President Kennedy had been shot in Dallas. We stepped into the hallway and instantly it seemed that people were running in every direction with stunned expressions of disbelief and shock on their faces. Every radio in the dorm was blasting the unimaginable news. A large group gathered in the lobby around the dorm television set, while a long line chattered, waiting for access to the only pay phone. Within an hour we watched Walter Cronkite remove his glasses and announce with a heartbroken sigh that President John F. Kennedy was dead.

Later that afternoon I caught a ride with friends and headed south down Highway 165 to Columbia for the Thanksgiving holidays with my family. The only topic of discussion was the assassination and who did it. Everyone suspected the Russians; only a few months earlier the country had headed for the "fallout shelters" and prayed as Kennedy and Khrushchev played nuclear chess over Cuba. Because of the subsequent Bay of Pigs debacle, everyone suspected that either CIA or KGB subterfuge was behind Kennedy's murder. Like all Americans, my family hovered near the television to watch the president's historic funeral and wept with little "John-John's" final salute. But when we witnessed Jack Ruby murdering Lee Harvey Oswald on live television that Sunday morning we couldn't believe our eyes.

Remarkably, America struggled to return to something that represented normalcy and, as the fallen president was buried, Lyndon Johnson took office. But a sense of paranoia and sadness crept into American life during the 1963 holiday season.

I spent much of the holiday from college trying to sort through my feelings about school. I wasn't happy majoring in sociology. On the other hand, I was absolutely blissful doing research about folk music or painting. But I could not figure out how anyone could earn a living doing either thing. One of Grandpa Durham's sayings was, "Once a fiddler learns to play 'Faded Love' he'll never go hungry." But I also knew that in a welfare state like Louisiana, a social worker would never have to look for a job either.

While I was home for Thanksgiving a friend stopped by to visit. Leeman Stamper had been a classmate throughout my entire life in Columbia. We had become close friends when he was the manager of the high school football team. Leeman told me about a new television program in Monroe named *McCall Comes Calling*. The show was on from 5:00 to 5:30 on Wednesday and Friday afternoons, before the *CBS Evening News with Walter Cronkite*.

"I think you should try out for that show," Leeman said. "I saw you in that talent show up at Northeast several weeks back. I've seen people on that TV show that aren't nearly as good as you. Why don't you give it a shot?"

Leeman's suggestion was timely. Since the talent show I was desperate to perform again. By the time I returned from Arkansas with Dr. James, I was a changed young man unaware of the transformation that had occurred within himself. But the seed of *A Ballad of the West* had been sown earlier that spring in Columbia, germinated during the college talent show, and, after I heard a traditional ballad, sprouted in Arkansas. If *McCall Comes Calling* could help me create more opportunity to sing and perform and continue learning about folk music I was ready to audition.

Jack McCall was a square-jawed man with a thick head of dyed-black slicked-back hair and an eager, buck-toothed smile made more interesting by the gap between his two front teeth. Jack was a great musician who had survived the honky-tonks, nightclubs, and lounges of the "Ark-La-Miss," as the region had become known in early television marketing talk. A natural showman, as well as a master of the Hammond B-3 organ, Jack had the idea to air a thirty-minute regional talk show before the popular *CBS Evening News with Walter Cronkite* show. On *McCall Comes Calling*, Jack focused on upcoming events with community leaders, chatted with garden club presidents and heads of charities, and charmed them all when he grinned and played pop standards on the Hammond B-3. To attract a larger audience, he wisely presented local talent in between the promotional plugs.

Like most Americans in 1963, my family had owned a television set for only a few years. Indeed, I can still remember the night just a decade earlier, in 1953, when my family gathered with the large crowd at a neighbor's house to stare into the snowy screen of the first television set in Columbia. When fuzzy images of humans appeared I remember the old-timers grumbling about the change this would bring, and my parents' sense of awe despite the crude technology. My grandparents got one in 1955, and Dad finally brought one home in 1956. Even with clear black-and-white reception, the medium was still a relatively new national phenomenon in 1963.

Two networks—CBS and NBC—dominated the airways in a constant battle for larger audiences, while upstart ABC nipped at their heels. The local CBS affiliate was KNOE in Monroe, the flagship of the late James A. Noe's chain of radio and television stations throughout the state. Huey P. Long's lieutenant governor during the 1930s, Noe had been a firecracker Louisiana politician before he grew fabulously wealthy in the oil business and parlayed that success into a media empire. The KNOE television station was about five miles from Northeast, and I had no way to get there except on my bicycle. I had learned to balance my guitar case on the bicycle handlebars and pedal around campus, but there was no way to pedal the five miles without arriving sweaty, so I ironed a clean shirt and folded it carefully into my cardboard guitar case. I ran to the bathroom as soon as I arrived, washed my pits, changed shirts, and took my place in line in the dark studio with the other people auditioning.

It was obvious that Jack McCall liked me the minute I completed singing "Old Blue." He peered over his clipboard, and his broad, toothy smile indicated I had won a spot on the show even before he spoke.

"I'll give you one shot," he said professionally. "After that it will be up to the audience. If they write and call to invite you back, then I'll contact you. Can you be on the show this Friday?"

I arrived at the station that Friday thirty minutes before airtime. As soon as I entered the cavernous studio a pleasant, friendly man approached me and introduced himself as the show's director, George Grubbs. We walked through the dark studio to a single stool under a spotlight.

"I'm just going to sit you there and let you sing," he said, pointing to the stool and the two cameras. "The camera with the red light on will be the one broadcasting live. There is also a monitor set for you to see what is being broadcast and adjust your performance. But you should just ignore that and sing like you are alone in your room at the dorm. Sing to all those pretty girls out there in North Louisiana."

I felt completely at home in front of a television camera. It was much less nerve-racking and more intimate than performing in front of a live audience. I learned quickly how to see the red light of the broadcast camera and choose whether to look directly into the camera's eye or ignore it. I followed George's advice, pretended to be singing to a room full of pretty girls, and flirted with the camera. I hit and held all the high notes of "Old Blue" and smiled into the camera while doing it. Jack McCall jumped to his feet when I finished.

"That was Bobby Durham, friends and neighbors! Give us a call or mail us a postcard if you want him to come back on the show and sing again."

After the show was over, McCall came over to me and shook my hand. Again, he was friendly but professional.

"Welcome to the business, kid," he grinned. "You did well. I'm sure you'll get a response to your song. Stay close to the phone."

I had no phone except the one down at the end of the hall in my dorm. But the dorm mothers were always good about getting messages to us, and I trusted that they would certainly respond to a call from KNOE Television. I watched McCall and Grubbs walk away through the television studio and wondered if I would ever see them again.

"By the way, kid—" McCall spun around. "Tell your mother that more people saw you on our show today than the combined total of Eddie Cantor's audience throughout his entire performing career."

As I pedaled my bike back to campus, thoughts of the impact of television were racing through my head. I wondered just how many people besides my mom and dad watched *McCall Comes Calling.*

I got the answer to my question soon. There was a message tacked on my door when I returned to the dorm. All it said was "Call KNOE/George Grubbs."

Over one hundred people called praising my performance that afternoon. In the show's short history they had not had such a positive response to a performer, and they wanted me back as soon as possible. By the end of the week George called again to inform me that nearly eighty pieces of mail had arrived supporting a return performance.

"Don't get your hopes up, Bobby," George said, "but if this keeps up I'm sure Jack will ask you to be a regular on the show. Just keep it under your hat and let him ask you himself."

After my first performance my mother suggested that with my blond hair I looked best in a dark shirt on black-and-white television. So I sang Lefty Frizzell's version of "Long Black Veil" for my encore. I wore a black shirt and dark blue jeans that also fit the mood of Marijohn Wilkin's eerie ballad about an unjustly executed adulterous ghost. Before I left the studio that day Jack McCall asked me to be a regular on the show. Both Jack and George assured me there was no money in the budget to pay me, but promised that as a result of my popularity I would soon be receiving offers to perform all over the region for healthy fees. Within moments a staff photographer came to shoot pictures of me on a stool singing for a camera with the bold white letters "KNOE-TV" painted on its side.

Performing every Wednesday and Friday on *McCall Comes Calling* was a crash course in the fundamentals of show business. I had first picked up a guitar only six months earlier and was suddenly discovering myself artistically and professionally in front of a huge live-television audience. The fact that I was the first folksinger to perform on *McCall Comes Calling* locked me into the show's format and secured my standing in the little community of folk entertainers emerging in the Delta region as the popularity of the genre continued to spread nationally. I was invited to join in the popular "hootenanny" concerts springing up on campus and within a short time developed a substantial fan base in the region. I discovered that I could have a "solo" career based on my television audience while continuing the duet act with Sage Redding. Within the first two months of performing on television I also started receiving offers to make records with various small regional labels. Still a minor, I had to take each contract to my father for his approval. He turned them all down. Each time he rejected a recording contract we would have a fight, but I quickly realized he saved me from more than a few con artists.

During this period I also met a Northeast student from Brooklyn named Steve Rosenberg. Steve could fingerpick a guitar, and soon after our introduction he agreed to meet me twice a week to teach me finger-roll arpeggios, and the classic Merle Travis fingerpicking technique. After my first month with Steve my guitar playing and style improved dramatically.

Meanwhile, I read every letter and postcard that came to me at the station and tried to answer them personally. Soon, as Jack and George predicted, I started receiving offers to come to small towns in the region to perform. I had no concept of what to charge, much less how to go about asking people to pay me in the first place. Complicating matters, with no transportation I had to hire friends with cars to drive me the thirty or forty miles to these little towns. Because of this, more often than not I lost money, since I was performing for practically nothing. Like Hartley Bridger, I was hiring people to drive me to work!

A Lebanese man named Eddie Merege gave me the opportunity to buy my first car. Merege owned a fancy restaurant named the Embers about five miles from the Northeast campus, on the eastern outskirts of Monroe. Merege sent me a fan letter to KNOE with an invitation for a free steak dinner at the Embers to talk over a business proposal. I borrowed a friend's car and drove to the meeting.

Swarthy and mysterious, in his ancestral Arabian lands Merege would have looked normal in robes and turban. Dusky swollen eyelids shrouded his chocolate eyes, and his black hair was slicked straight back, with no part. He wore very expensive shiny suits and smoked little brown Between the Acts cigarettes. Merege sat at my table and spoke directly.

"I can't offer you a salary, but I want you to sing in my restaurant," he said. "You can keep all your tips, and you should do well with that. I see you walking from table to table, like a gypsy violinist, playing for my guests. But this is a classy place and you'll need to dress properly. No more jeans. You'll wear a coat, tie, and slacks. Whadaya think?"

"How many nights a week?"

"As many as you want to work."

"How long will I sing each night?"

"Three hours?"

The first week at the Embers I made nearly six hundred dollars in four nights singing for tips. After my second week there I paid cash for my first car—a used red Triumph Spitfire convertible. I was ready to go on the road. But the road wasn't ready for me. Eighteen-year-old fledgling folksingers should never ever buy used sports cars. The Spitfire nearly died on my first weekend visit to Columbia. My dad noticed symptoms and was able to perform emergency surgery to prevent a cracked head. The following Monday I limped into the Volkswagen dealership, where my Spitfire became a nice down payment for a new white Karmann Ghia. Thankfully, the Embers gig continued to be a financial gusher, and I paid the Karmann Ghia off in a few weeks of singing from table to table two hours each night.

A salesman on an expense account with a date at a four-star restaurant is not likely to part with a twenty-dollar bill for a song about a beloved hunting dog or a hanged murderer like Tom Dooley. At the Embers I learned to play to my audience. I taught myself romantic pop standards like "Unchained Melody," "Ebb Tide," "Stella by Starlight," "Tender Is the Night," etc. Naturally, with only my guitar accompaniment, I interpreted the standards in my unique folk style and again selected songs like "Danny Boy" to showcase my tenor. On five separate occasions at the Embers I received a hundred-dollar tip for singing "Danny Boy."

As might have been expected, my grades suffered dramatically during this lucrative period of my show business education. I brought home average marks for my first semester in college, but the Embers gig came at the end of my first semester, and working every night, I had little time left over for studies. Moreover, what spare time I had was spent either in the library searching for folk songs from the fur trade era or chasing girls.

My increasingly higher profile on television, and on the Northeast campus, definitely brought more women into my life. I had several intense affairs during my first semester in college, but around the time I went to work at the Embers I awoke with a hangover one morning, remembered a promise I had made to my grandmother, and attended the Baptist student center on the Northeast campus. There I met a pretty, petite Polish American girl from Chicago named Diana Glomb. Both sets of Diana's grandparents had fled Poland and immigrated to Chicago after the First World War. The opportunity for a college education prompted her strict Catholic parents to allow Diana to live in Louisiana with Protestant family friends, thereby being able to avoid out-of-state tuition fees and attend Northeast as a resident. After arriving at Northeast, Diana promptly became a Baptist. Her conversion to Protestantism was the major drama in her life when we met.

We quickly became friends and I introduced her to a group of kids from Columbia who met regularly in the student center to play cards between classes. Soon she was a fixture in my extended family of friends from Columbia on campus. It wasn't long before we began dating. More often than not, she was in Columbia with our gang for the marathon weekend poker tournaments at the Morris house.

The psychological "preference test" I took during orientation in the second week of college strongly indicated that I should major in "the arts." My faculty advisor had called me in for a conference to suggest that I consider changing my major, but I didn't pay any attention to him. I already knew I was going to paint for the rest of my life. I was learning how to make good money with my guitar, but majoring in music held no interest for me. I was getting all the music education I needed by performing on television. I had fantasized about teaching art since my teenage years and had actually talked with my Boy Scout leader, Billy Childress, who was also president of the school board, about becoming an art teacher. All of this confusion came to a crashing conclusion, however, when I flunked out of college. I ran to Dr. James, pleading for help.

"Don't worry, my boy," he assured me. "I will help you appeal this. We'll get you a reprieve, but don't you think we need to talk about your priorities?"

After consulting at length with Dr. James, I decided to change my major to art and to focus on painting. He helped me succeed with my appeal, and under the shroud of academic probation, I was allowed to return to school for the fall term in the art department. My father was convinced I had lost my mind.

But Eddie Merege also had a curveball waiting for me. Ever the businessman, he realized I was doing very well financially. Now he wanted half of my tips. He argued that he had given me plenty of time to make a lot of money and, since it had been his idea and it was his restaurant, he was entitled to his share of my increasing prosperity.

I decided that Eddie's demand was a cockeyed way of forcing me to accept the challenge to truly focus and commit to college. I had socked away quite a bit of money and also had a summer job waiting for me in Columbia with the school board, so I decided to let the Embers gig go, thanked Eddie for his help, and we parted as friends.

Summer 1964 was spent with a flooring crew laying the hardwood floor of the new Caldwell Parish High School gymnasium and saving every penny for college. Diana returned from Chicago when school started that fall, and we both got jobs in the campus bookstore. She had decided to not tell her parents about converting to the Protestant church because she believed her father would not allow her to return to Louisiana if he knew what she had done.

I blossomed in the art department. I loved the design, drawing, painting, color theory, and art history classes, and my midterm grades showed it. Brilliant teachers discussed the paintings and techniques of the masters of the Renaissance, Leonardo da Vinci and Michelangelo, the impressionists, Russian constructivists and supremacists, surrealists and cubists, and I devoured it like a starving child suddenly finding himself at a feast. Andy Warhol and the "New Realists" (later known as "pop artists") were the big thing in the early 1960s, but my interest in their style was only perfunctory. Instead, I was enthralled with the "New York School," the abstract expressionists, or "action painters"—specifically Jackson Pollock, Franz Kline, and Willem de Kooning. I was particularly attracted to Kline's simplicity and the bold, masculine, calligraphic action exploding in conflict and resolution in his paintings. The seemingly spontaneous brushstrokes could not disguise the long hours he obviously spent shaping a canvas, and that held a powerful appeal to me. The reconciliation of simple, massive brushstrokes in starkly balanced black and white design held me spellbound for hours. Aside from the action painters' love of controlled yet spontaneous color and movement, I gravitated to their audacious efforts to break with European past masters to create a uniquely American style of painting. My oil painting instructor, Ed Schutz—a gifted abstract painter himself—was fond of emphasizing that painting had been virtually held prisoner by the iconographic dogma of the Catholic Church for centuries and that artists had become free to experiment only after the invention of the camera in the nineteenth century. Schutz stressed that all the various forms of "modern" art had begun to enter the American mainstream only twenty-five years earlier, and he encouraged us to believe we were pioneers creating the future of art.

Most important for me personally was the fact that I finally understood what had attracted me to painting in the first place: as a boy I was instinctively drawn to the simple beauty created by a unique and inimitable visual "accident." Suddenly, the visual accidents of nature occurring all around me became the splendiferous, spontaneous action paintings! Cracks in the sidewalk became stunning asymmetric designs; I could stare at something like a mud-splattered painter's truck for hours. Natural composition revealed itself all around me in the interplay of colorful geometric patterns. The act of painting became more important than creating any illusion of subject matter. Controlling paint while simultaneously surrendering to its natural physical properties and behavior patterns became the ultimate for me; painting became a visual balancing, a dance of serendipity.

This new way of seeing—and *being*—excited and inspired me to surrender to my creative nature, wherever that might lead me. I immersed myself in the art department, where classmates discussed elements of design constantly and encouraged creative experimentation. I sketched constantly—even while taking notes in other classes. When I wasn't playing music, I was listening to the latest folk or jazz musicians while I painted.

With my academic success I was also ready to renew my research into the fur trade era. I proudly took my midterm grades to Dr. James's office to show him I would soon be off academic probation and to ask advice about where I might look next for information on Jim Bridger.

"We've searched the existing American folk music catalog in vain, my boy," he informed me, lighting his ever-present pipe. I had started smoking a pipe with him, so he lit my pipe on the same match. "That Lomax song is the only one that exists. I think you are going to have to turn to history and literature to continue your exploration. Let me snoop around a little for you to see what I can find."

Meanwhile, as I renewed my search into folk music for a song about Jim Bridger, Diana was taking more of my time. She was carrying an enormous amount of guilt about not coming clean with her parents about converting to Protestantism. When she needed a shoulder to cry on, she increasingly turned to mine. She found better-paying jobs for us working in the school cafeteria, so we quit our jobs at the campus bookstore. She worked on the serving line and I worked in the dishwashing room on the cleanup crew with a couple of middle-aged black men and two Persian exchange students. I enjoyed the company of my friends on the crew and the mindlessness of loading the massive dishwashing machine. I could smoke cigarettes and daydream while loading thousands of filthy dishes into the continually moving, rubber-toothed conveyor belt as it disappeared into the tunnel of the gigantic stainless-steel washing machine. There, in that steam room of discarded, half-eaten food, generic white dishes, and brown plastic trays, I escaped into my thoughts for three hours each day. I fantasized about going to Greenwich Village. I had little idea that those dishwashing daydreams of New York were about to become a reality.

Jim Betts had been my roommate throughout my freshman year. From Delaware, Jim had attracted immediate attention in our dorm when Cassius Clay fought Sonny Liston. No one believed the braggart Clay would last a minute in the ring with the bruiser champion Liston, and, against all odds, Jim bet virtually everyone in the dorm that Clay would win the fight. Of course he made out like a bandit and gained the respect of every boy on campus. As Cassius Clay morphed into Muhammad Ali and rose to become one of the most famous men in the world, I always remember Jim Betts when I see the old champion.

I was trying to drink less, while Jim was trying to drink more, so it was inevitable that we went our separate ways. At the beginning of my sophomore year I moved into a dorm room with my old painting companion, Johnny Morris. Johnny had gone "gung ho" in the Reserve Officers Training Corps on campus and was well on his way to a lifetime career in the military. We still argued about art—especially as I increasingly embraced abstraction—but now we also argued about my deeply rooted mistrust of the military. In spite of the arguments, the year we spent as roommates would be the last time in our lives that we would be close friends. Even after

I moved in with Johnny Morris, however, Jim Betts and I remained close, and he offered an intriguing possibility to actually go to New York.

"We can live at my parents' home in Delaware this summer and work for DuPont," Jim explained. "You can make enough money there to head into Manhattan. It's only a few hours' drive from Milford."

In June 1965 we loaded up my Karmann Ghia and headed northeast to the Atlantic Coast. It was my first major road trip. I planned on being in Greenwich Village by September.

FOUR

Like a Rolling Stone

IN JUNE 1965, RADIO AIRWAVES WERE SATURATED with the sugary-pink songs of the Beatles' late bubblegum period. By the time we arrived in Delaware, however, DuPont was no longer hiring, and the Rolling Stones' "I Can't Get No Satisfaction," suddenly ruling the radio, seemed a more appropriate sound track for the adventure. Jim immediately went to work with his dad, and Mr. Betts helped me get a job on a roofing crew.

It was a Sisyphean task, lugging hundred-pound packets of shingles up the ladder to the roof of the house. The unwieldy packets slid from my shoulders so many times during my first day on the job that they scraped off the outer layer of skin. But after several eight-hour days going up and down that ladder, my willpower and my healthy twenty-year-old body rallied and I became stronger. My biggest problem was that the job would last only a couple of weeks; by July I would be out of work again.

One day I noticed a sun-faded sign over a roadside produce stand on the highway from Milford to Rehoboth Beach. I stopped for a chat, did a few quick sketches, and convinced the owner to pay me two hundred dollars to paint her a new sign. After struggling up and down the ladder on the roofing crew every day, I would rush to my painting gig. I enjoyed climbing to the top of the produce stand in the late afternoon to paint. Cool Atlantic breezes arrived in the early evenings while I raced the light painting apples, pears, tomatoes, corn, and the letters of the owner's name. More good luck arrived when a newlywed couple—friends of the Betts family—commissioned me for two hundred fifty dollars to do a large abstract painting for their new home. When I finished all three jobs by early July, I had saved myself a bit of cash and was ready to head to New York. I thanked the Betts family for their hospitality and drove into Manhattan to seek fame and fortune as a folksinger or a painter.

Country life in North Louisiana had not prepared me for New York City. I was shocked to learn that the cost of a single night in a hotel would dramatically diminish my tiny nest egg. Even so, I soldiered on, searching the city for a cheap, safe place to stay. Depressed and in need of a friendly voice, I decided to call Diana in Chicago.

"I can't believe you called," Diana whispered urgently into the phone through her tears. "He's gonna send me to a convent!"

"Whoa," I said. "Who? What?"

"My dad!" She explained, "I told him about leaving the church. He's furious. He says he will never let me return to Louisiana. He's going to enroll me in a convent and force me to return to the Catholic Church. What am I going to do?"

Less than three hours after arriving in New York City, following a quick, perfunctory visit to Greenwich Village and Washington Square, I raced over the Pennsylvania Turnpike, bound for Chicago.

A lovely nineteen-year-old with a lithe figure, Diana had blond hair and, when she wasn't brooding over religious matters, her blue eyes sparkled in an open, happy face. In spite of her spiritual inclinations she enjoyed an off-color joke and a stiff Tom Collins, and like me, she was a chain-smoker and poker player. Our friendship had developed naturally into romance, but I never figured it would progress beyond a college fling. Now, disoriented from "city shock" and lack of sleep, I realized my relationship with Diana had suddenly become much more serious because of my rush to Chicago. Within hours of arriving in the Windy City I drove to Clarendon Hills, a suburban community on the far west side of town, where Diana lived. In the neighboring town of Oak Park, I rented a room in the cellar of a family's home.

Soon after my arrival, Ted Glomb's anger cooled and his talk of enrolling his daughter in a convent proved to be bluster. Still, he was leery at the sudden appearance of his daughter's Protestant friend and kept his eye on her comings and goings.

My first job in Chicago was selling Fuller Brushes door to door. Thinking it might help me make sales, Diana sent me to the "Little Poland" ghetto of Chicago. This proved to be a bad idea: the minute I spoke with my broad Southern accent people would either slam the door in my face or invite me in to laugh at my drawl. When I was able to get in the door, I was so lonely and nervous that I talked too much and didn't know how to close the deal. The effort lasted a week, and by then, having spent half my stash of cash to rent a room for a month, I was running out of money.

I was driving into the city on a job search one day when traffic suddenly came to a complete halt. As cars backed up on the expressway I was made physically aware of the growing influence of Martin Luther King Jr. and the civil rights movement. Dr. King was speaking downtown in the famous Chicago Loop area, and the radio shouted that every expressway in and out of the city was gridlocked for twenty miles. On the Eisenhower Expressway people got out of their vehicles and chatted in the middle of what was normally one of the busiest thoroughfares in the world. My car did not move for three hours.

The murders of three civil rights activists and Medgar Evers, as well as James Meredith's enrollment at the University of Mississippi in Oxford, followed Dr. King's initial demonstrations in Selma, Montgomery, Atlanta, and Memphis. Riots and more protest demonstrations kept the entire South on edge from the days of the landmark integration of Central High in Little Rock in the late 1950s throughout the early 1960s. But Dr. King's literally stopping traffic in America's second-largest city was a clear indication that change—initiated in the Jim Crow South—was now spreading throughout the nation. I heard Bob Dylan's groundbreaking fusion of folk and rock "Like a Rolling Stone" for the first time that afternoon as I sat in Dr. King's traffic jam. Dylan's lyrics perfectly reflected the nation's mood as well as mine.

President Kennedy's assassination dramatically quickened movement in two areas: civil rights and music. Less than three months after the Kennedy assassination, the Beatles' arrival in New York in February 1964 launched the famous "British Invasion" that would precede Dylan's 1965 synthesis of message and rock music. The Reverend Martin Luther King Jr. simultaneously picked up the mantle of change that the slain president had dropped in Dallas, and immediately intensified the civil rights movement. It was as if all the hope of Kennedy's "New Frontier" was suddenly transferred to the civil rights movement and popular music was articulating the hope of transforming the nation. Pete Seeger's "We Shall Overcome" united the diverse strands of the movement.

But while the counterculture and civil rights movements were gathering momentum in 1965, I was stuck in a traffic jam on Eisenhower Expressway without a job. I knew I had to do something fast, and I finally gathered the gumption to visit an employment agency, through which I landed a great job at the GMC Parts Warehouse in Cicero, on the dangerous Southwest Side of Chicago. The dangerous neighborhoods didn't bother me. I was happy to have work. All day long I answered frantic calls from dealerships throughout the country and filled rush orders on parts. I gradually adjusted to life in a big city. Each morning I had another lesson in learning to cope with the massive freeway traffic as I drove into Cicero from Oak Park. I enjoyed my job and coworkers and started to think I should stay out of school for a semester and work instead of returning to Louisiana in August. I loved Chicago—especially my frequent trips to the Art Institute, the Field Museum, and Adler Planetarium. At the Art Institute I was finally able to see the original work of painters and sculptors I admired, and I spent increasingly long hours studying American Indian exhibitions at the Field Museum. With Chicago's museums strategically located on Lakeshore Drive, I could park my car and walk from one to the other and still find time to visit Buckingham Fountain. But one morning a coffee-break chat at the doughnut table put all thoughts of dropping out of school behind me.

"If I were you I'd get back in school quick," a coworker said. "Johnson is dramatically escalating the number of troops in Vietnam and—what are you, twenty? They are preparing to draft thousands of guys your age into the army."

The first time I'd heard about Vietnam was two years earlier. An old childhood friend had just returned from a hitch in the army and we were working together on a gym flooring crew. One day on a lunch break he predicted that Vietnam was going to explode. I didn't even know where the hell Vietnam was. But soon after that morning coffee break in Chicago, the news was filled with reports of President Johnson's sending increasingly large numbers of troops to Southeast Asia. I had to get back into school.

Things were also heating up for Diana and me. Shortly after I arrived in Chicago her father became convinced that since I was a Protestant, I was responsible for her conversion. Diana explained that she had converted to the Baptist Church before she met me, but nothing would change his mind and he refused to let her see me. In spite of his orders, we sneaked phone calls and made secret plans for her to return to Louisiana with me. In early August we schemed for her to slip out of her bedroom window and meet me at 2 a.m. At the appointed hour I parked my car down the street, tip-toed to her bedroom window, and pushed it open. I whispered Diana's name and was startled when her father answered.

Suddenly aware why his daughter was stirring at such a late hour, Mr. Glomb angrily ordered me off his property. I could hear Diana crying as I fled in panic. Two mornings after the fiasco I was at work when I finally received the awaited urgent call from Diana. She sobbed that she had just returned with her father from a preliminary interview at a convent. He was preparing to enroll her the next day! She said her parents had left her alone with her little sister for three hours and if we were going to make a break for it, it had to be now! I told her where to meet me, quit my job on the spot, and hurried to my car. Within an hour I drove down a street a block from her parents' house and Diana ran across the open field behind it, clutching everything she could carry wrapped in a sheet. We pitched it into the Karmann Ghia and sped to my room a suburb away, stuffed my gear into the car, paid my landlord, and raced for the expressway. We assumed that the police would look for us to head straight south on I-55, so I drove east to Indiana before heading south on back roads. We rolled through cornfields in silence for hours, in shock at what we had done. I noticed tears streaming down Diana's cheeks and pulled over.

"Do you want to go back?"

"I can't," she sobbed. "I can't go home and let him force his beliefs on me. No. Let's go to Louisiana."

I pulled back on the road and the silence returned. I clicked on the radio and Bob Dylan whined that new song I'd heard back in July: "How does it feel to be on your own, like a rollin' stone?"

"Just fine, Mr. Dylan," I heard Diana whisper.

Dawn was breaking as we crossed the Mississippi River at Vicksburg. Familiar cotton fields and sharecropper shotgun shanties welcomed us to the Delta. Diana had become close with my old Columbia friends Neil and Barbara Nethery, and we knew they would greet her with open arms. Twenty-six hours after fleeing Chicago we pulled into their driveway.

"You can stay here as long as you like." Barbara smiled and poured dark coffee. "We have plenty of room. School starts again in a couple of weeks and you can either stay here with Neil and me or get a room in the dorm."

My parents were another story. They were furious. Equally enraged, Diana's parents had called them and threatened legal action. My mother could not believe I had spent the night, albeit driving, with a woman I wasn't married to. My father accused me of sullying our family's name and endangering my future with immature behavior. Meanwhile, Diana spoke with her mother and learned she was no longer welcome in her parents' home. Heartbroken, she somehow moved forward with plans to return to college. Our jobs in the cafeteria were secure and that would cover tuition, dorm rooms, etc. I had money saved from my job at the parts warehouse. A few days after returning to school I threw in with some other folksingers and we opened a little coffeehouse in an attic over a popular sandwich shop near campus. Soon we were drawing large crowds each weekend, and after only a couple of weeks my partners and I were dividing nice profits.

Diana and I were now inseparable. As she became increasingly dependent upon me for emotional support I soon learned that the extremely religious are *always* crying. Overcome with sadness at her parents' coldhearted rejection, she would break down regularly and weep. I could offer a shoulder, but one day she suggested I offer more.

"I talked with my mother last night," she said. "She thinks that if we became engaged it might help me win my father's affections again. My father believes we are living in sin, and she thinks if we were engaged she might convince him to forgive and accept us."

My father was against it from the start, but my mother felt the same as Ted Glomb. So a few weeks later I presented Diana with an engagement ring. As her mother predicted, Diana's father warmed to our relationship and agreed to allow her to come home for the Christmas holidays. I drove her to the train station in Little Rock and carried her bags to her berth. She was crying at the window when the train pulled out of the station.

Privately, I was looking forward to having the holidays to myself. After returning to school I had become even more deeply involved with painting. Diana had never understood my devotion to art and was resentful of my affection for my work. So I was happy to have two weeks alone for painting while I was home in Columbia. I had also discovered a tiny lounge in the bowels of the Francis Hotel in Monroe where a torch singer named Joanie Rhodes sang pop standards each night for lonely drinkers. Before the holidays I had started secretly going there each night after Diana's dorm curfew to listen to Joanie. Soon someone recognized me from the Jack McCall show and Joanie asked me to sing a number. I did my dad's favorite Jim Reeves song, "Four Walls," while Joanie accompanied me on piano. Soon after that I became a regular with Joanie at the Francis Hotel lounge.

I enjoyed singing pop standards to Joanie's piano accompaniment; the phrasing was much different from the folk arrangements I used with my guitar. But those standards were so ingrained in the culture they were like a window into the romantic recent past of the twentieth century. Singing in that lounge, I also learned that modern country songs were making a subtle transition into what had been traditional "Tin Pan Alley" territory.

Balancing my jobs, school, playing music, and Diana's religious fragility, I had little time to pursue my quest to discover a period folk song about Jim Bridger and the mountain men. But soon after Diana and I had returned from Chicago and started classes in September 1965 I visited my old friend Dr. James.

"You are going to have to continue your search in history and literature," he reiterated. "Bernard DeVoto's *Across the Wide Missouri* would be a good place to start."

I headed straight to the library for a quick leaf-through of DeVoto's classic. There, aside from the splendid historical account of the Ashley-Henry Fur Expeditions of 1822 and 1823, I discovered the field watercolors of the only artist to capture images of the actual mountain men, Alfred Jacob Miller. There was even a painting of Jim Bridger in a suit of armor! Before the invention of the camera, Scottish lord William Drummond Stewart hired Miller to paint his adventures in the American West as he traveled with the mountain men. Stewart gave Jim Bridger the suit of armor. *Wide Missouri* was the first publication of Miller's paintings. DeVoto's book also introduced me to source material on the hunter of the expedition, forty-something Hugh Glass. Later that important afternoon I learned more about Glass's mentor/protégé relationship with eighteen-year-old Jim Bridger in John Myers Myers's *The Saga of Hugh Glass: Pirate, Pawnee, and Mountain Man*. Armed with this new insight into Bridger and Glass, I decided to search for other books. That September afternoon in the Northeast Louisiana State College library, I discovered a musty antique hardback of *The Song of Hugh Glass* by John G. Neihardt. Published in 1912, here was the story of Jim Bridger and Hugh Glass in breathtaking epic poetry.

I quickly discovered *The Song of Hugh Glass* to be one-fifth of Neihardt's masterpiece, collectively titled *A Cycle of the West*. By the time I put Diana on the train to Chicago for the Christmas holidays I had completed my first reading of *The Song of Hugh Glass* and the four other epic poems, *The Song of Three Friends*, *The Song of Jed Smith*, *The Song of the Indian Wars*, and *The Song of the Messiah*. Neihardt's five-volume feat of epic Homeric verse chronicled the exploration, discovery, and settlement of the American West. With Diana in Chicago for two weeks I would have the solitude to ponder an idea that was coming into increasing clarity with each reading of Neihardt's work: if Neihardt was the Homer of the American West, why couldn't I become an "Alan O'Dale" of the mountain men? But Neihardt's unprecedented work of epic poetry was truly colossal in scale. Even if I were able to write original music to accompany it, the results would take literally six or seven hours to perform. No one would stand—or better, sit—for such a thing.

On a cold December walk over the ancient Copenhagen Prairie overlooking the Ouachita River I came up with a solution: I decided that I would read Neihardt's *Cycle* six times to internalize it. Then perhaps I could condense and structure the essence of it into a completely new, original work. Before Diana returned from Chicago I had completed my second reading of *Cycle*, sculpted a Modigliani-inspired head from a discarded fence post found on my walk on Copenhagen Prairie, and finished a 3' × 3' oil painting. The precious solo time to work opened my creative aperture even wider, and my imagination was on fire with aesthetic visions.

By the fourth reading of Neihardt's *Cycle* I was astounded by his genius—particularly his knowledge of the landscape of the West. I decided that my creative visions were out of scale with my meager abilities to actualize them. Mrs. Morris and other English teachers had stressed that writers should write about what they know. I had no real knowledge of the history of the American West or, more importantly, the region's landscape. I decided that Neihardt had simply led me to the concept of historical epic poetry, and I should write about my own part of the world—the South—with my theme being my own regional history. I began structuring an outline for an epic ballad about "king cotton" and the steamboat era. There would be a song about Memphis, Baton Rouge, and New Orleans as "pivot points," and the tale would be spun around the lives of families living in these three cities and a rambling river rat who linked them all. The concept of a trilogy had taken root, even though I was completely unaware of it then.

Visions of steamboat ballads soon surrendered to painting. By late January 1966 I was spending increasingly long periods of time at the easel and flourishing in the art department. Meanwhile, Diana was communicating regularly with her folks in Chicago and the riff with her father was rapidly mending. This healing brought more emotional security, and Diana was finally beginning to realize that I was totally committed to art. After her father welcomed her back into the fold, she relaxed, we renewed our love affair, and she started talking about setting a wedding date.

During the summer of 1966 friends got me on a crew on the loading docks in West Monroe at one of the largest paper mills in the country, Olin Matheson. It was stinking, nasty work, but the long hours with good pay provided me with the money I needed to prepare for my upcoming marriage. Diana had decided to return to Chicago for the summer to renew bonds with her family and to work. My parents had bought land and built a new home east of the Ouachita River on property that had originally been the ancestral Bridger Bellevue Plantation. My mother and father also owned eighteen acres in the river hills outside of Columbia near Copenhagen Prairie in an area known as Holum. Daddy bought an old crumbling wood-frame house and had it hauled out to the property. There he planted it, scrubbed and painted it, set up a hundred-gallon rainwater cistern, and turned the place into his "deer camp." He had a splendid pack of black and tan hounds penned in the woods behind the camp, and a freezer full of venison. Once the camp was completed, Daddy spent increasingly more time alone there. He took all his vacation time during deer season and just moved to the camp by himself. So I decided to save money and live with my parents in their new home, commuting to West Monroe and work every day. The drive would give me time to think about my riverboat epic. During that period I even wrote the first draft of a song, "Baton Rouge," for the riverboat concept.[1] But the overall concept just wasn't happening. The idea lacked the passion of discovery that led me to the fur trade era. So I kept returning to Neihardt's *Cycle* and rereading it.

Grandpa Durham died in September 1966. His passing made me want to reach out to my father again. As deer season approached in autumn, I stunned both of us at Grandpa Durham's funeral by asking if I could join him on a deer hunt when I came home for the Thanksgiving holiday.

FIVE

Hunters and Farmers

I LEANED AGAINST A TREE, shivered in the dark, and listened to the hounds baying through the brittle, frozen forest. Blending melodiously in harmony while progressively fading, the dogs' echoing voices sang like monks chanting in distant cathedrals. I didn't need to be a skilled hunter to know their chase was several miles in the distance and heading away from me. It occurred to me then that most people are one of two types: hunters or farmers. The farmer is extremely mindful of the elements, but rather than harmonizing with them, ultimately perceives his environment as an enemy to be manipulated into submission. The originator of most all economic "isms," the farmer believes his only defense against starvation is to control and exploit the environment to a degree that will allow him to produce an excess and cache away the surplus.

The hunter, on the other hand, trusting that his environment will provide life's necessities, seeks to blend with the elements; survival depends upon ethical stealth and learning to divine and articulate primal instincts in order to mystically align with the patterns of nature. The hunter honors his environment and the act of taking life to sustain life with ritual and ceremony that reflect spiritual awareness of the necessity of death in the interconnected dance of life.

I realized as a child that I would never be a farmer or a banker like my mother's people. I also realized that I would never become the hunter of my father's expectations. Still, the artist always seemed to me more hunter than farmer. Once I admitted to being an artist, I discovered that by blending with my environment like a hunter, I attracted opportunity. With this realization I began to approach life as an instinctive hunter inspired by the belief that my unique artistic talents would function like a magnet to attract whatever I needed to survive. I believed I was in possession of talent for a purpose and that if I pursued the very simple objective of developing and employing my gifts, the reason for my possession of them would eventually reveal itself.

As morning broke I heard a shot several miles in the distance. Then the dogs stopped barking and running. I took that as a signal to return to camp, and started walking. By the time I arrived at the camp, Daddy and three strangers were skinning a large twelve-point mule deer.

"Bobby, meet the Carters—Fred Carter Sr., Fred Jr., and Reuben," Daddy said, introducing the men. "They're old friends of mine from Winnsboro. Fred Jr. lives in Nashville. Mr. Carter just got himself a trophy buck."

I shook each of the men's bloody hands. They were so friendly I felt an immediate kinship. I tapped out a Pall Mall, lit it, and blew smoke into the frosty air.

"My mother, Miss Tillie, told me about you, Bobby," Fred Jr. said, lighting up his own cigarette. "She's a big fan. She used to watch you on TV out of Monroe. She told me several years ago I should invite you to Nashville to make records."

"Fred Jr.'s one of Nashville's leading studio musicians, Bobby," Daddy explained.

"Hill surveyed a drainage canal through our back pastures and we got to be good friends," the elder Carter interrupted. "We been coming over to Caldwell Parish every deer season for years to hunt with our kinfolks. Your daddy told us we should stop by and hunt with y'all. Glad we did. This here's a nice deer."

"I'll say," I agreed. "That big buck should provide y'all with venison for a long time. Y'all going to mount that head?"

"Hey, Bobby," Fred Jr. interrupted. "I'm producing a country music show in Winnsboro this spring. Why don't you join us and sing a few songs?"

Fred Carter Jr., at thirty-four, was already a legend in the music business. After a hitch in the air force, Fred won a scholarship to attend Centenary College in Shreveport. He arrived in Shreveport at the time that *Louisiana Hayride* was at its peak in popularity. Fred quickly realized that the emerging stars were looking for electric guitar players instead of fiddlers, and he easily made the transition from four to six strings. Soon he was playing guitar for many of the acts that flocked to Shreveport seeking stardom. Fred even backed Elvis on the *Hayride* stage. Later, he described the moment to me as being "blinded by a continuous flashbulb explosion for thirty minutes while struggling to hear over the deafening screams of teenage girls." He said there was not a space on the stage where Elvis didn't dance, swirl, jiggle, or twirl, and the biggest problem was playing deaf and blind while staying out of Elvis's way.

Around this time, Shreveport teenagers James Burton and Dale Hawkins wrote the rock-and-roll anthem "Susie Q." When guitar wizard Burton left Dale's band to join Ricky Nelson's group, Hawkins promptly hired Fred Carter Jr. as a replacement. With a national hit record, Dale Hawkins was suddenly a bigger name than his rockabilly pioneer cousin from Arkansas, Ronnie. But even without a hit record, Ronnie Hawkins was a wild man both on and off the stage, fiercely admired and respected as a prototype by the early rockers.[1]

After touring briefly with Dale Hawkins, Fred and his Arkansas drummer friend, Levon Helm, joined Ronnie Hawkins and the Hawks in 1959. But by then the rockabilly craze was rapidly fading in America. Another Arkansas musician named Harold Jenkins (a.k.a. Conway Twitty) told Ronnie that rockabilly was only beginning to take off in Canada, so Hawkins decided to move his excellent band to the greener pastures of Toronto. Having no desire to move to Canada, Fred decided to leave the band and was recruited to groom young Canadian bassist Robbie Robertson as his replacement. In 1960, after teaching Robbie his way around the neck of a Fender Telecaster, Fred left the Hawks and joined Conway Twitty's Lonely Blue Boys. Within five years the Hawks would gain international fame backing Bob Dylan as the Band.

Meanwhile, playing Nashville recording dates with Conway Twitty led Fred to his future as a session musician. After playing guitar on Roy Orbison's breakthrough hit records, Fred left Conway Twitty and toured with Orbison's road band for a while, but he had seen his future in Music City USA. In 1961 Fred married his lovely wife, Anna, in Winnsboro, Louisiana, and the newlyweds settled in Nashville. Fred immediately started hustling session work and publishing connections for his original tunes. As in Shreveport, his timing could not have been more perfect. Aside from the continual flow of country music stars recording daily in Nashville, the folk music craze was roaring-hot and Fred was a gifted acoustic fingerpicker. Increasingly, more folk acts came to Nashville and Fred soon had more session work than he could handle. Burl Ives, Ian and Sylvia, Joan Baez, the Poso Seco Singers, and scores of major folk acts began to seek Fred out to play guitar on their recordings. Perhaps Fred's greatest work was accompanying Simon and Garfunkel. At the time of our meeting that frigid morning at my father's deer camp he had played guitar on Simon and Garfunkel recordings already considered classics. "Sounds of Silence," "Homeward Bound," "I Am a Rock," etc., had made the duo household names, but they were poised for even greater international acclaim. Before his deer-hunting vacation in Louisiana, Fred played on Simon and Garfunkel's *Bookends* recording sessions. The subsequent release of that album would ensure Simon and Garfunkel's stature in pop music history. Their greatest hits— "Mrs. Robinson" and, particularly, the phenomenal "Bridge Over Troubled Water"—were yet to come. Fred played on both.

No one would believe me at school when I told them I had met Simon and Garfunkel's guitar player. So I quit talking about the meeting. Besides, I wasn't sure that Fred was sincerely interested in me. I let the entire matter fade, and soon painting and sculpture returned to the forefront of my thoughts. But Fred called in March to inform me he was back in North Louisiana producing the country music show he'd mentioned earlier. I accepted the invitation to meet him in Winnsboro.

Before Fred's show in Winnsboro we attended another production in nearby Rayville. The venue was unpretentious—a wagon decorated with bales of hay on the pitcher's mound of a Little League baseball field. The only performer on the bill was sixteen-year-old Hank Williams Jr. Hank Jr.'s entire act in those beginning days of his career was doing dead-on impressions of his father's famous songs. I felt sorry for him because he was a very talented kid. But it appeared that his life was already mapped out to mimic his father rather than to explore his own unique gifts. But young Hank Jr.'s copy act made me aware of something more important: Hank Sr. was an original. If the fundamental requirement of art is originality, how could anyone in my generation of musicians and songwriters escape the long shadows cast by Bob Dylan and the Beatles? Everyone following them would be judged by the standards they set. Half the folksingers I knew were already mimicking Dylan, playing harmonica in metal holders and snarling lyrics, while the rest were growing long hair and singing in phony British accents. Seeing Hank Jr. that night, I decided that if I had to become a copy act to make it in the music business I should remain a visual artist. I also vowed never to accompany myself on harmonica, or to intentionally sing in asymmetric rhythm with a prolonged nasal whine at the end of every phrase.

That said, Dylan's 1965 fusion of folk and rock had a profound influence on me. His apparent random flinging of words seemed the equivalent of verbal action painting; his new form implied that, like action painting, the "process" was often as important as the "result"; indeed, the process often *became* the result. But much more important to me, his fusion of diverse forms indicated that, as in visual art, original aural art could be created by blending forms and seeking new genres.

Fred's country music show was at the football stadium in Winnsboro and was headlined by the great Nashville star Connie Smith. I was one of six or seven acts on the bill, and the audience was there to hear country music rather than folk. A few in the audience remembered me from *McCall Comes Calling* and shouted encouragement, but at the end of the evening I was simply a minor attraction on the Connie Smith show.

After the show the band decided to play an after-hours jam session and asked my dad and me to join them at a local roadhouse. So we followed the musicians on a circuitous journey over a sand road through swampy backwoods and a cotton patch until we finally arrived at the honky-tonk. The walls of the old white wood-frame building literally throbbed with the muffled beat of the music pounding within. Inside, the cacophony of music and shouting was deafening, and the dance floor, backlit by stage lights, was a mass of hundreds of bobbing silhouettes surrounded by diaphanous planes of blue smoke. After a brief chat to decide who would play what instruments, the Nashville cats quickly took the stage and the entire audience became aware that the pros were in the joint. After a few numbers I was invited up to sing. I had never sung with a band before, and they suggested I just put my guitar down and let them back me. When asked what I wanted to sing I picked my dad's favorite, "Four Walls."

"A ballad?!" the bassist shouted. "Ya sure a-that?"

"What key?" the piano player yelled over the crowd.

"I don't know." I shrugged.

"You don't know tha fucking key?!"

"No, sir."

"Let's try C," he said, beginning an intro.

As soon as I finished the old Jim Reeves song the crowd erupted with applause. I could see my dad in the crowd beaming with pride.

"Get this kid to Nashville, Fred," the piano player yelled over the clapping and whistling.

"I intend to," Fred shouted back.

Throughout 1967 America was in a dangerous state of profound historic change. The war in Vietnam was searing and peace demonstrations grew more intense throughout the country in reaction to the massive troop escalations and the slaughter in Southeast Asia. By 1967 the civil rights and anti-war movements consolidated into a larger, more unified force of resistance and transformation now being referred to as the "counterculture revolution." The summer of 1967 was hailed as the "Summer of Love" and "baby boomers" were becoming stereotyped as "hippies," or idealists, with an agenda to change the world. In the two years since Bob Dylan had "gone electric" and introduced John Lennon and the Beatles to marijuana, two popular music forms and two political movements had merged.

I had been able to maintain a 4-F classification in the selective service system because of being enrolled in college. But the classification was good for only one year at a time; one semester of bad grades and I would be heading to Southeast Asia, where increasingly large numbers of young men my age were dying in the war. Since the American Revolution men in my family had fought, bled, and died for the United States. I was all for serving one's country, but I had been deeply distrustful of the military since early childhood because I suspected that the military had wounded my father more than he revealed or I realized. As long as I could remember, I believed that simply being in the military wounded a man for life. Because of this inherent wariness of anything military, I had been against the Vietnam War since the beginning. More pragmatically, however, as no one in Washington could offer a genuine explanation for our involvement in Southeast Asia, I joined the millions of Americans increasingly coming to believe that the entire Vietnam War was a sham. And it is important to note that unlike any previous conflict, the world was watching this war—and its nightly parade of body bags—on television. Aside from all these issues, however, I was a twenty-two-year-old college student with 4-F classifications in the selective service system available and with no intention of volunteering for the draft, and my pragmatic option was to get as many deferments as possible.

In 1967 hair had become so significant that a revolutionary Broadway musical with the simple title *Hair* was just around the corner. Hair increasingly defined one's allegiances as the numbers of young men dying in the war were escalating dramatically and massive antiwar demonstrations spread throughout America and the world. As the beguiling Summer of Love approached, flower children were letting their "freak flags" fly and flocking to San Francisco.

A freak flag meant little to me. Each shower forced me to admit I was losing my hair by the handfuls. When a man starts losing his hair in his early twenties he is compelled to make a simple choice between dignity and vanity. As I was already in entertainment, more than once I had been taken aside by an old showbiz veteran for a confidential conversation about the advantages of a toupee. The dignified choice would have been to simply be proud of my balding crown. As liberated and hair-conscious as we were in the mid-1960s, bald singing stars were few and far between. I got myself a hat.

My attraction to hats actually began a long time before I started losing my golden locks. In nearly every childhood photograph I am seen wearing a hat. Once again, I'm certain it was my father's doing; Hill Durham would never wear a hat. If I had inherited his beautiful, naturally wavy blond locks I probably would not have been attracted to hats either. The glorious mane atop his lean six-foot frame was the summit of a strikingly handsome man. His standard joke with me about my hair was, "Bobby isn't bald; he just has a very wide part." In fact, most men of his generation had abandoned hats. As a child, however, I was attracted to the older men who, like both my grandfathers, always wore a fedora. The way a man wore his hat created a personal style and indicated a unique character under it. So as I started losing my hair it seemed only natural to incorporate a hat into my life the way my grandfather's generation had.

Still, as the pressure of the war and school combined, my dreams of a life as a freewheeling artist were fading. Fred Carter had not called, and even though I was drawing great satisfaction from my courses in the art department, time was forcing me to face some cruel realities. I was eligible for one more 4-F student deferment. Diana was anxious for us to get married, so I began to think it was time for me to put all these art and music fantasies aside and accept whatever fate might be coming my way. Depressed, I enrolled at Northeast for my first summer semester of school and Diana returned to Chicago to work and continue mending her family relationships. As I had done the summer before, I intended to stay at my parents' new home in Columbia and commute to Monroe to save money. In mid-June, however, I received a call from Fred Carter Jr.

"Hey, Bobby," Fred sang cheerfully into the phone. "I thought you wanted to come to Nashville and make some records."

"I didn't think you were serious."

"I'm as serious as a heart attack. When can you get here?"

"I don't know, Fred. I'm in school this summer and I need to talk to my dad about it."

"Well, you do that and let me know as soon as you can. Just get yourself up to Nashville and let's cut some hit records."

My father was enthusiastic for me to make records with Fred Carter. He trusted Fred and his family to treat me right. I would have to drop out of school for the summer, but it wouldn't affect my 4-F classification. I called Fred and told him to expect me in Nashville on July 10.

Bullfrogs and crickets sang to the sweltering summer night as I prepared to leave for Nashville the next morning. There was a knock on my bedroom door.

"I thought you might need a little extra cash," Daddy said, offering me three crisp ten-dollar bills. "I've been saving up a bit and this might help you in Nashville."

Nothing could have meant more to me. I felt I had finally connected with my father and we were working toward a common purpose. Juggling the emotions of my father's blessing and the excitement of the approaching journey, I had trouble getting to sleep that night.

Within two hours of departing Columbia, I drove through the Mississippi Delta on a secret pilgrimage to Tupelo. I found a cheap motel and spent the evening walking the streets of Elvis's hometown and fantasizing what was happening to me in Nashville. The experience was actually calming. Like Columbia, Tupelo was a tiny farming community with southern folks who looked, spoke, and acted much like my own people. The realization that the "hillbilly hepcat's" hometown was similar to mine helped put what was happening in Nashville in perspective. The next morning I left Tupelo with renewed confidence and headed northeast through the rolling hills of northern Mississippi and Tennessee toward Nashville. I clicked on the radio, twirled the dial in search of music, and suddenly tuned in to an ethereal sound that made the hair on my arms stand up like magnetic antenna prepared to receive aesthetic electronic communion. The music sounded like someone learned to play banjo licks on gossamer spiderwebs.

Moreover, the song the instrument accompanied was breathtaking, with lyrics about "sleeping bags rolled behind couches" and "cupped hands around tin cans." I was in a trance, but somehow still heard the DJ say, "That was John Hartford with 'Gentle on My Mind.'" I wanted to hear the otherworldly instrument on that incredible song again and searched the radio in vain for another hour, hoping I might by chance hear it. As Nashville appeared in the east I was still searching the dial for this new singer, his beautiful song, and the sound he draped around it.

Fred's wife, Anna, also from North Louisiana, made me feel comfortable, and the three of us chatted like old friends from our very first meeting. Their young children, Ronnie and Deana, were excited to have a houseguest. Soon after I arrived, Fred and Anna took me on a rubberneck tour of Nashville. They pointed out the home of the Grand Ole Opry, Ryman Auditorium, and the Ernest Tubb Record Shop, Printers Alley, and, finally, the holy heart of "Music City USA"—16th Avenue South.

The recording studios, major and independent record labels, managers' and agents' offices, ASCAP and BMI offices, musicians' union offices, and so forth along 16th Avenue South, or "Music Row," were clustered in quaint 1930s-era wood-frame houses and reconstructed 1950s brick veneer buildings. In evidence of country music's rapidly growing popularity, new buildings were squeezing into every available nook and cranny. As we drove into the parking lot of RCA Studios, Fred specifically pointed to the smaller of the two studio wings.

"RCA-B," he said reverently. "That's where Elvis made his recordings after Sam Phillips sold his Sun contract to RCA.[2] All those great early Presley records were cut there: 'Don't Be Cruel,' 'Heartbreak Hotel'; all the Everly Brothers hits too: 'Wake Up Little Susie,' 'Bye Bye Love.' That's also where you are going to make your first record, next week."

My anxiety returned with a vengeance and I was barely able to disguise the fact that I was paralyzed with fear. The realization that I was going to make my first record in Elvis Presley's studio was something I never could have imagined. Hero worship aside, I had absolutely no knowledge of the workings of a recording studio. When I expressed my fear and confusion, Fred invited me to accompany him to work that evening. He was playing guitar on a session with Billy Grammer. I had sung Grammer's hit "Gotta Travel On" in bars and at hootenannies many times and was nearly as intimidated by him as Elvis. But I was also excited that I might pick up some pointers watching him record. Fred parked in the lot behind the Columbia B Studios, and I helped him carry eight or ten of his guitars from the massive trunk of the Cadillac into the studios.

In 1967, state-of-the art studios were only beginning to incorporate multi-track technology; most were eight-track facilities. The control room of the darkened studio centered around an enormous panel of slider pots and hundreds of blinking lights. In front of the control panel, on the same level as the studio, was a cavernous pit filled with a luxurious leather sofa facing a sheer wall of tilted, smoke-tinted glass that separated the control room from the studio. I took a seat on the leather sofa with some other people who were observing the recording session. All the instruments and studio musicians were sectioned into cubicles by thickly padded colored-burlap oak-framed panels—in studio lingo, "baffling"—set on coaster wheels to allow them to be easily moved and rearranged. An assistant engineer was busy setting microphones as the chief engineer called out instructions into everyone's headsets from behind the board in the control booth. Grammer took a few minutes teaching the musicians his song and then everything seemed to rapidly come together; within moments the tape machines rolled, the musicians began to play, and Grammer sang his song. It was all so very technical, professional—scientific *and* artistic. I wanted to know how to do this.

After the session I helped Fred load the guitars into the trunk of the Caddy. While we were loading the car the great songwriter Roger Miller walked up and started joking with Fred. Meeting the writer of "Dang Me" and "King of the Road," I was most definitely starstruck and would have fumbled my own name if someone had asked me for it at that moment. As we got into the Cadillac and headed toward Fred and Anna's home in nearby Goodlettsville I started to feel so out of my element I could not think of anything to say to Fred. He sensed my confusion and continued my education.

"RCA-B is the place to record, but Columbia B is the place to mix."

"Mix?"

"You know, put the final record together. Remember when you helped your mother bake a cake?"

"Yeah."

"It's the same here. We gather all the ingredients and mix them together. Only here, because of multi-track recording, after we record all the parts we sit at the control board and decide which instruments we want and how much of them we want to include in the final record. It's called mixing."

We pulled into the long uphill driveway to Fred and Anna's two-story Colonial-style home. It was already past midnight, but we poured a cup of coffee, lit a cigarette, and sat and talked about my career aspirations. He asked me to tell him my favorite recording artists and listened patiently as I listed them and told him why I liked their music. I was surprised to learn that he had played guitar on so many of my favorite singers' recordings.

"Have you heard of John Hartford?" I asked.

"John's a good friend."

"Do you think I might meet him?"

"Of course. Why are you interested in Hartford?"

"I heard this song, 'Gentle on My Mind,' on the radio. I loved it. But I also loved the strange-sounding instrument I heard on the song."

"Ah, 'Gentle on My Mind.'" Fred sighed reverently, as if acknowledging a great work of art. "That song is already a classic. Why don't I book John to play on your session? I'll ask him about the instrument and suggest he bring it along."

As the night progressed I learned that Fred had recently resigned as the Nashville head of A&R at ABC-Paramount Records.[3] I also learned that he had a partnership with two other Nashville power players: Bob Montgomery, who was the head of A&R at Liberty Records, and Kelso Hurston, who was head of A&R at Capital Records. Montgomery was a Texan who had been a close friend and writing partner of Buddy Holly's, and Hurston was from Muscle Shoals, Alabama, and had written hits for Brenda Lee. The three men had been able to successfully initiate the careers of budding stars by signing and independently recording them, then brokering them out on short-term contracts with small independent labels. With initial chart success on independent labels, they were able to negotiate sweet deals for the artists with major labels. Fred had left his position at ABC-Paramount, and I would become his first independent production. He had no doubt that he would "find me a home" quickly. Before the evening ended, he had explained the music publishing business to me and gave me a cardboard box full of reel-to-reel quarter-inch tapes.

"Here it is in a nutshell, Bobby," he said. "There are three basic elements in every record: the musicians, the singer, and the song. Of the three, the most important is the *song*; the song is what folks remember—people will sing "You Are My Sunshine" long after they have forgotten Governor Jimmie Davis—or anyone else who happens to sing his song. Next, it's the singer; if the singer is doing his job, he interprets the *magic* in the song and that inspires the musicians. Third is the musical arrangement or the musicians playing the song. Our job is to inspire the singer to interpret the magic in the song. You study these three elements in action now that I've explained them, and you'll see for yourself that what I'm saying is true. For example, all the major labels know how to market a record globally; Columbia Records can promote as well as RCA or Capital. Their marketing muscle alone can literally create a hit song and carry it up to the number three position on the charts. But magic moves a number three song those next critical steps to number one. That magic is in the song itself. The singer can sparkle it up, and we do our best as studio musicians, but it is the magic in the song that takes it to the top. And the song is what makes the publishing business the most important aspect of the entire music industry. Never forget that whoever controls the publishing controls the record business."

"Are these tapes songs for me to consider?"

"Yes. Bob Montgomery, Kelso Hurston—and I own the publishing on all of them. You are going to record songs from our publishing catalogs. Unless . . . do you have any songs of your own?"

I thought a moment before answering Fred's question. I had what I considered feeble attempts at songwriting—basically fragments of my riverboat experiment with historical subject matter. I had copious notes of research into the fur trade era, but nothing musical at that point.

"No," I answered. "I hope to learn to write, but at this point I don't have anything original."

"Well, then, you need to spend a bit of time this weekend going through the tapes in that box. You can use my study. You'll find a reel-to-reel tape machine in there. Make yourself at home and have fun. I want you to pick three songs."

"Okay."

"Now, we need to talk about one more thing. You have been blessed with a beautiful singing voice. You should be able to sustain a very long career and move easily between styles from folk to country or pop. The question is, what kind of singer are you going to be *now*—in the studio . . . next week? We could go folk, but I don't think that direction will sell the number of records we need to sell right now. I think it will be best to introduce you as a country singer and then move slowly into the traditional pop field. Even the Beatles started out doing commercial music. Their early stuff is pure commercial stuff, don't you think? They made their impact with the light material, and now they are beginning to expand into new things. Don't you think you can do that too?"

"Sure."

"Well, then, pick three songs from that big box of tapes." He laughed. "Make sure you pick at least one good country song. But I'll know a lot more about how to record you once you select a range of tunes. We'll start again in the morning. But I think I want you to sign a publishing contract with me as well as a recording contract. I have a feeling that you might develop into a writer."

SIX

Three Chords and the Truth (As Long As It's Cowritten)

"'I Don't Have Sense Enough to Come in out of the Pain.' Take twenty-six . . . rollin'." The voice of Elvis Presley's sound engineer, Al Pachucki, echoed in my earphones. More than a little befuddled, I listened to the pedal steel introduction for my cue to begin the song yet again.

Elvis's ubiquitous presence had splintered my concentration during the previous twenty-five attempts to record the simple song. Recording in "the King's" studio was intimidating, but destroying what was left of my focus, Elvis's original guitarist, Scotty Moore, was Pachucki's recording assistant.

Thankfully, Fred had also booked John Hartford for the session, and we quickly connected when he gave me copies of his first two RCA albums after learning I was a fan. John was a few years older than me, taller and leaner, with short dark hair. I also learned he was from St. Louis and, unlike the other session musicians, came from more of a bluegrass background than from commercial country. He was playing a D-28 Martin on the "Pain" song, but he also brought his Dobro banjo, which was what had enchanted me only days earlier on the radio en route to Nashville. Fred planned for him to play the instrument on "Sharon, Oh Sharon"—if we had time to record another song. Twenty-six takes of "I Don't Have Sense Enough" had eaten up half of our three-hour session.

The musicians had been patient and encouraging throughout my difficult session. Blind piano player Hargus "Pig" Robbins arrived early, on the arm of his ever-present male assistant. One by one, the musicians gathered, joked, and talked sessions and fishing while they tuned various instruments to Pig's piano. Roy Husky, lean and lanky, with a little black cigarette constantly dangling from the corner of his mouth, was on upright bass. Dapper and cool Lloyd Green sat at the pedal steel guitar, alternative-country pioneer Wayne Moss was on lead guitar, and jovial, steady Willie Ackerman was on drums.

In 1967 Nashville's popularity as a recording center was soaring, and it was not unusual for these studio musicians to play fifteen to twenty sessions a week. Led by innovative producers Chet Atkins and Owen Bradley, the famous "Nashville Sound" had been pioneered in the early '60s by such gifted musicians as Grady Martin (who played guitar on Marty Robbins's "El Paso"), Owen's brother, Harold, and Atkins himself on lead guitar. Rounding out the "A" team—as they were called by record producers and artists—were rhythm guitarist Ray Edenton, Henry "Hank" Strzelecki or Bob Moore on bass, Buddy Emmons or Pete Drake on steel guitar, "Boots" Randolph on saxophone, Buddy Harmon on drums, and (from West Monroe, Louisiana) Floyd Cramer on piano. Fred and the musicians on my sessions were referred to as the "B" team. These interchangeable "teams" of musicians, plus a handful of "utility men"—multi-instrumentalists—like Charlie McCoy, were the players responsible for the 1960s "Nashville Sound."

During the late 1950s, Nashville began the steady transition from regional hillbilly recording capital to mainstream pop center as these celebrated musicians helped launch the careers of Elvis, the Everly Brothers, Webb Pierce, Roy Orbison, Marty Robbins, Carl Smith, Eddy Arnold, Brenda Lee, Patsy Cline, Jim Reeves, Don Gibson, Loretta Lynn, and scores of others. Increasingly, traditional Nashville acts "crossed over" between country and pop chart success, while simultaneously folk-rock was becoming more mainstream and many stars in that genre were beginning to come to Nashville to record. Most of the studio musicians working in Nashville during the 1960s started in country, bluegrass, or rockabilly music and were skilled at draping a clean, guitar/fiddle-oriented sound around a pure voice and poetic lyric. Similarly, most of Nashville's studio musicians were from the Deep South or Appalachia region and, like me, had grown up with black music as a constant presence. As demand for the new sound skyrocketed and increasing numbers of hopeful artists inundated Nashville, many early rock-and-roll veterans, like Fred Carter, naturally gravitated to "Music City" and added an electric backbeat and a funky rhythm-and-blues edge to the more traditional bluegrass, or hillbilly, instrumentation.

Fred's voice broke into my headphones: "If you can't cut this little tune, Bobby, you'll never be elected governor of Louisiana."

Everyone laughed and Fred called for a smoke break. Emotionally threadbare, I remained in the isolation booth and waited for my next shot at the tune. As the musicians lit up, Fred offered words of encouragement in my headset, but I could tell he was worried. I let out a deep sigh and took a long look at my situation. The country phrasing "to come in out of" had me flummoxed. I sat on the floor of the sound booth and went over the phrase until the meter and rhythm flowed with the overall line, "and I don't have sense enough to come in out of the pain." Then I decided where to breathe to hit the line in one breath.

Five minutes later I completed take twenty-seven and as the music faded in the headset Fred finally laughed. "Come on in, Bobby. You just nailed it."

We listened to the playback and everyone agreed I had finally recorded a version we could keep. We rushed back into the studio and started the next tune, "Sharon, Oh Sharon." The musicians set up quickly and, inspired by the delicate sound of Hartford's nimble Dobro banjo dancing over Wayne Moss's gut-string guitar line, I nailed the song on the second take. Without even returning to the control room to listen to the "Sharon" playback, we jumped straight into the third song, Bob Montgomery's "Three Squares and a Place to Lay My Head." Four passes with that tune and my first recording session was over.

After the session one of the musicians gave me an income tax form and a document from the Nashville musicians' union. I took the forms to Fred and asked him what I should do. My question sent the room into pandemonium.

"He's not in the union!" the session players began to whisper among themselves. Finally Roy Husky came over and said, "We'll be fined, Fred! Get him signed up quick!"

We loaded Fred's guitars in the trunk, jumped in the Cadillac, and raced to the local musicians' union offices. Within moments, Bobby Durham was a registered member.

"While we're doing this," Fred added, "we should get you registered with the American Federation of Television and Radio Artists."

"Oh . . . ?"

A search through the names registered with AFTRA split my personality in half. Fred broke the confusing news.

"We are going to have to change your name."

"What!?"

"'Bobby Durham' is already taken. The industry can't have several people with the same name releasing recordings. You are going to have to record under a pseudonym."

"That ain't gonna work, Fred. My dad will kill me."

"I'll explain it to Hill," Fred assured me, "but we're taking these rough mixes to MGM Records this afternoon. So you need to come up with another name quick."

When I was getting to know John Hartford earlier in the day, he told me that his given name was actually Harford. RCA had suggested that he add the "t" to create the more recognizable "Hartford." The fact that John and I had discussed name changes earlier certainly made me more receptive to the idea of recording under a pseudonym.

"All I can think of is my mother's maiden name," I said. "They used to call her 'Bobbie Bridger.'"

"That's a fantastic name. Bobby Bridger it is!"

So Bobby Durham was twenty-two years old and on the way to present his first recording to MGM Records on the afternoon of July 17, 1967, when Bobby Bridger was born.[1]

The moment Fred opened the door to the MGM offices he began to hustle our new recordings. He flirted with the receptionist and suggested that she tell her boss that he had discovered a kid down in North Louisiana who could sing as high as Roy Orbison. Fred certainly knew how to get their attention: two years earlier, Orbison had signed an unprecedented deal with MGM worth a reported ten million dollars.

"Always get to know the receptionists and secretaries, Bobby," Fred whispered, and winked as we sat in the waiting area. "They run the show everywhere."

I was still in a state of shock from the recording sessions, and things were moving so fast I didn't have time to even consider the impact of my new name, much less the fact that we had recorded three tunes, registered me with the Nashville musicians' union, completed an AFTRA search, changed and registered my new name, and presented the results to an international record label, all within a five-hour period. If the artist is a hunter, Fred Carter went for the throat.

MGM A&R head Jim Vienneau listened politely to the tapes. After chatting with Fred and praising his production and my singing, Vienneau informed us that MGM was not signing anyone until they recouped a bit of the money they had spent signing Orbison. A year after signing a landmark cash deal with MGM in 1965, the Wink, Texas, singing star had been struck by a series of heartbreaking tragedies. In 1966 his wife, Claudette, was killed in a motorcycle accident. In 1968, attempting to return to routine after Claudette's death, Orbison went on a tour of England. While Roy was in the United Kingdom, his mansion on Old Hickory Lake outside of Henderson, Tennessee, burned, consuming his sons, Anthony and Roy Jr., in the flames. Roy vanished into seclusion.

Fred was undaunted by our rejection at MGM. It seemed only to make him more determined to find a deal for our new recordings. When I told him I needed to get back to Louisiana, Fred assured me that there were many more labels he intended to visit and he didn't need me for the presentations.

"But before you head home, we should go fishing," Fred insisted with a laugh. Many Nashville stars and session players relaxed on overnight weekend fishing trips in the frigid waters of the Center Hill Reservoir northeast of Nashville. In aluminum fishing boats elaborately outfitted for maximum comfort, they would gather at favorite fishing holes, drink spiked and regular coffee, gossip, joke, and cast through the night for fierce smallmouth bass—and lucrative music side deals.

We arrived at the reservoir late in the evening and launched Fred's boat. He cranked the outboard motor and we soon skipped over the water toward the middle of the vast lake. The reservoir had been created by damming the Cumberland River and flooding an expansive range of thickly forested mountains, and in the shadows of midnight one murky hollow of inky water looked the same as another to me. Nevertheless, Fred knew exactly where he was going. He killed the outboard motor and started the quieter trolling motor. It purred like an oversized blender beside the boat, and using an oar as a rudder, Fred aimed the boat down an angular canyon of pitch-black water that was framed by boulders and draped by ancient trees on both banks. A flickering light finally appeared near the craggy shoreline ahead, and as we drew closer I could make out the silhouette of a boat containing two men. Fred pulled alongside the boat, and the light revealed country music star Bobby Bare and the hillbilly comic Stringbean.

With the introductions the first thing I noticed was that Stringbean used a single fly rod, but Bobby Bare had three separate fishing lines in the water. Suddenly Stringbean expertly cast his line deep into the darkness. His line whizzed through the shadows for what seemed like half a minute before it splashed into the water under some trees veiling the shoreline. No words were needed. The grin on his face implied that the cast had landed exactly where he intended.

"A couple of years ago Bare and me were fishing in a canoe," Stringbean announced through pipe-clenched teeth. "Bare flipped the damn thing trying to fish three lines at once. I lost my favorite pipe. We ain't fished in canoes since."

"Ah, String, you needed a bath anyway," Bare joked.

Laughter sang over the water and echoed off the walls of the hollow. I noticed a light had appeared farther out in the lake and was heading slowly toward us. Within moments a gray-haired gentleman floated out of the shadows with a delightfully open Cheshire cat smile. It was the master songwriter Harlan Howard. Soon he purred up alongside the two boats and joined the party. Author of "Pick Me Up on Your Way Down," "A Little Bitty Tear," "Busted," "I Fall to Pieces," "Heartaches by the Number," "Tiger by the Tail," and countless other country classics, Harlan also wrote my favorite Jim Reeves song, "The Blizzard." Harlan was noted for coining the phrase "three chords and the truth" to define a country song.

This had to be a dream.

The feeling that Nashville had been a dream was even more pronounced as I drove through the hot Mississippi Delta. To reassure myself that I had actually cut a record, I repeatedly looked at the brittle black acetate that Fred asked Scotty Moore to cut for me before we left RCA Studio B. Even though Fred cautioned that listening to it too many times would quickly wear down the grooves of the fragile disc, I knew when I got home I would be playing it for anyone who would listen. But I was more worried that the August heat in my unair-conditioned car might warp the shiny black plastic, and so I was careful to keep it out of the direct sun.

Of course my dad's favorite cut was "I Don't Have Sense Enough," while everyone else preferred "Sharon, Oh Sharon." Only my mother preferred the pop-oriented "Three Squares and a Place to Lay My Head." I played the acetate over and over with hopes of reinforcing Daddy's pride in my accomplishment. Meanwhile, I waited, hoping Fred would call and break the news that we had changed my name. When he didn't call, I decided to tell

Daddy myself. He didn't take the news well. After a few days of pouting, however, he announced that even though he did not like it, he understood our reasoning and accepted my new name. I told him I figured the matter of my name was moot anyway, since there was no word from Nashville.

By mid-August I decided that Fred probably had failed to convince a label to buy the record, and I returned all my attention to painting, sculpture, and school. Classes would be starting in a few days, and with the war in the forefront of everything, I knew I had to get back to the primary objective of staying in school and out of Southeast Asia.

But I could not stop thinking about Nashville and making records. When Fred had produced the Connie Smith show earlier that spring I had befriended his piano-player friend from Winnsboro, Al "Puddler" Harris. Working in the Ricky Nelson band, Puddler grew homesick, quit, and returned to Louisiana, where he assembled a makeshift recording studio in Winnsboro. He had encouraged me to come over to see the place, so I decided to drive over for a visit one Saturday. I walked in the door and immediately felt the excitement in the room.

"Hey, Bobby!" Puddler exclaimed. "You need to call Fred Jr. in Nashville. He's got you a deal with Monument Records!"

Legend has it that Roy Orbison was the only person that "King Elvis" feared might steal his crown while he was in the army. Even though Roy also recorded for Sam Phillips's Sun Records, he had not been able to escape the presence of Elvis, Johnny Cash, Carl Perkins, and Jerry Lee Lewis. Roy's career continued to languish while Elvis was in the military but finally exploded in popularity in the early 1960s.

Much of Orbison's success could be attributed to Fred Foster, a North Carolinian who had worked as a field representative for Mercury and ABC-Paramount Records in Washington, D.C. In 1958 Foster decided to invest his life savings in the creation of an independent record label. Foster named his enterprise Monument after the famous obelisk honoring the first president. Billy Grammer's aforementioned "Gotta Travel On" was the label's first hit record, and it set the stage for Orbison's career to ignite. "Running Scared," "Crying," "Love Hurts," "Blue Bayou," "It's Over," "Candy Man," and a host of other hits led to Roy's 1964 masterpiece, "Pretty Woman," and earned both Foster and Orbison their places in music history.[2]

Foster harvested his success with Orbison and developed Monument into a major independent record label by signing a stable of new acts in the country and pop fields. Movie legend Robert Mitchum recorded an album titled *Thunder Road* that sold well for Monument in both country and pop markets. Grandpa Jones introduced a bluegrass audience to the label. A songwriter named Chris Gantry recorded a pop album for the label, and Billy Walker, Jeanne Sealy, and Fred Carter Jr. had country singles set for release. The same month that I was signed to the label a young woman from Pigeon Ridge, Tennessee, named Dolly Parton released her first album on Monument. Several months after my signing, Kris Kristofferson signed with Monument, bringing Billy Joe Shaver to the label as part of the deal.

In the late 1960s, 45 RPM singles were still the standard in country music. It was rare for a label to consider recording an album with an artist until it was proved they could hit the charts with a single and duplicate the success with a second and third effort. Fred Foster and Fred Carter negotiated a deal for me to record three 45 RPM singles. Already under contract to Fred Carter Jr., I had nothing to do with the negotiations.

Fred called to confirm he had signed me to Monument, and soon after that I got a call from "Sheriff Tex" Davis, the publicist at Monument Records. Sheriff Tex said he wanted some biographical information so he could assemble a promotional kit. He also stressed that it was important that I get back to Nashville pronto.

"We love your record, Bobby," Tex said. "If we cover your ticket can you fly up tomorrow?"

I had never flown in an airplane and was nearly as excited about flying as I was to be returning to Nashville. Flying for the first time allowed the reality of my new life to seep into my awareness. As the plane taxied down the tarmac of the Nashville airport, I finally let myself accept the fact that I was now an "official" recording artist. I couldn't wait to get back into the studio.

Fred met me at the baggage area and I told him something in Davis's voice had made me feel instantly comfortable. As we loaded into the Caddy, Fred informed me that "Sheriff Tex" Davis and rockabilly legend Gene Vincent wrote the classic "Be-Bop-a-Lula."

"He would probably be a good manager for you, Bobby. He loves your record and will help get it on the radio. In fact, he's an old radio pro, probably one of the first people to play rockabilly music outside of Elvis's base in Memphis. He booked Elvis in Virginia back in the days when everybody was burning his records and calling them trash. He signed Gene Vincent to Capital when all the labels were scurrying for Elvis copycats. He knows all the big boys—'the Colonel,' Elvis, Ed Sullivan. I'll tell you all about him on the way out to Monument."

We drove out to Hendersonville, Tennessee, and the cozy offices of Monument Records. We entered the front doors as a very pleasant couple was leaving, and Fred introduced me to Nashville's premier songwriting couple, Felice and Boudleaux Bryant. Authors of "Bye Bye Love," "Wake Up Little Susie," "Bird Dog," "Raining in My Heart," "All I Have to Do Is Dream," "Love Hurts," and countless other hits, the pair seemed sewn together at the sleeve. They held hands like teenagers. It was obvious that they were deeply in love as well as creative collaborators. In all these years that have passed, every time I hear one of their songs I remember them fondly as a pair of loving songbirds.

Sheriff Tex Davis was a sweetheart, and Fred Foster was polite, yet distracted. It was apparent that Foster trusted Fred Carter and Sheriff Tex Davis to mastermind whatever future I might have at the label. Unless—as Fred Carter promptly reminded me—unless we cut a hit.

"Everything changes with a hit record," Fred said as we left the Monument offices. "There is nothing as exciting as a hit record. A hit record instantly brings the world to your door. But success makes decisions much more difficult. There are many paths through the forest; not everyone chooses wisely. Success frees some and destroys others."

I was beginning to grasp the enormous social and musical impact of Elvis and the rockabilly buccaneers that followed in his wake in the 1950s. Aside from his landmark music, much cultural history can be defined by the unambiguous, indelible line *before* and *after* Elvis. Threatened by the profound racial and sexual implications of the form when it first appeared, conservative America refused to even acknowledge rockabilly as music. Of course, Elvis bore the violent force of that initial reactionary social venom, and he rose above it to pave the way for the clones that followed. Among hundreds of cultural influences, it is important to note that some music historians argue that prior to Elvis the guitar was primarily recognized as a hillbilly, country, or folk instrument; pop music was made by pianos, big bands, or studio orchestras. But Elvis brought the acoustic rhythm guitar to the forefront of popular music and inspired kids outside the Deep South and Appalachia to want to play the instrument. After the appearance of Elvis in the mid-1950s, the number of guitar players throughout America skyrocketed until the late 1950s and obviously set the stage for the guitar-driven folk revival in the early 1960s, as well as the golden age of rock that followed. Just as significant, much of the songwriting, musical, production, and management talent responsible for those artists that shaped rock and roll immediately after the "big bang" of Elvis enjoyed phenomenal regional success and migrated to Nashville to initiate the new sound and attitude of the recording industry. But the period from 1955 to 1960 had essentially been a major transitional era in the record business in general. Recording technology, primitive and unwieldy by today's standards, simultaneously exploded during this time, making it possible for raw talent like Elvis and Sam Phillips to explore and create new sounds in the studio. Likewise, Les Paul's creation of the electric guitar during this fertile period certainly opened the door for musicians like Scotty Moore. Equally significant, Les Paul, his wife, Mary Ford, and Miss Patti Page were pioneers of multi-track, "overdub" recording in the early 1950s, and this development truly revolutionized record production. Inspired by Les Paul, Atlantic Records engineer Tom Dowd installed the first eight-track studio in Manhattan in the early 1950s. The era of multi-track recording had begun.

Nashville's location between Appalachia, the Deep South, and the Midwest made it a natural place to record the music of those regions. The recording artists, songwriters, and businessmen arriving in Nashville in the late 1950s and early 1960s were all veterans of the rockabilly revolution. Still very young, they had already captured lightning in a bottle and were hooked on hit records. With the rapidly evolving technological advances, they were addicted to the science of making records as well as to the art and business of distributing them.

Fred Carter Jr. was a perfect example. He had strategically positioned himself right in the middle of the creative process as the so-called golden age in American music was exploding. He was poised between old and new country, as well as squarely balanced in old Louisiana rhythm and blues and raw hillbilly rock. He could play a Dean Martin session or pick bluegrass with Lonzo and Oscar. He could write a song in the style of Johnny Mercer, Muddy Waters, or anyone in between, play most of the instruments on the tracks, and produce a master recording in any musical style. Fred intended to ride the studios and publishing companies to the top of Nashville's golden towers and beyond. Fate had somehow hooked me to his star, and I wholeheartedly embraced the fact that I was in for a ride—a crash course in the obsessive pursuit of the almighty hit record and all that that entailed—emotionally, spiritually, and physically. To manifest this dream I had to accomplish two things: stay in school and stay out of Vietnam. Both tasks would require phenomenal amounts of energy and more than a little old-fashioned luck, but I had little choice. To me it was life or death.

After signing my contract in Nashville, I flew home and naively tried to return to my normal routine. But this was no longer possible. My first single was released just as the fall term began at Northeast. The North Louisiana radio stations jumped at the opportunity to play a local kid's music, and my records immediately entered the regional charts. Regional success reinforced radio airplay I was receiving on country music stations throughout the nation, and my career as a professional recording artist officially began. Because of the war and the draft, I was unable to tour America to support the record, but I could perform throughout North Louisiana, Arkansas, and Mississippi, and, as Fred predicted, I was swamped with opportunities that came with a hit record. I rewarded myself with the purchase of my first Martin guitar—a 0021 model. I ordered it sight unseen from the company in Pennsylvania. I didn't need to play it first; if it was a Martin I knew it would be a great guitar. I still treasure it.

I basked in the attention my hit record brought and was somehow able to balance the success with my studies at school. Much of the celebrity clamor was deflected by the fact that all my friends in the art department just laughed, shrugged it off as simply another creative project, and went back to their own painting, sculpture, and pottery and encouraged me to do the same.

Encountering talented songwriters in Nashville made me feel like I would always have access to more commercial songs than I could possibly write. But this is not to say I quit trying to write songs. Exposure to great songwriters only intensified my desire to learn to write better songs. I just became less open to singing my original songs in public—especially in Nashville. I knew that no one in Nashville would want to hear the historical songs I was attempting anyway. As an exercise, I starting trying to write commercial songs like the ones I heard in the box of demos I was given each time I went to Nashville to record. Because I had signed a songwriting contract with Fred, I occasionally went into his study and sang a tune into the reel-to-reel recorder for his publishing company. Soon after "Sharon, Oh Sharon" was released, Fred called to tell me a Canadian artist named Bobbye Kay was recording a song that Billy Dunn and I wrote called "The Fringes of My Life." My self-consciousness about writing songs immediately evaporated.

During the following weeks as extraordinary opportunities increased with my record climbing regional charts, I was introduced to the game of brinkmanship that I would be forced to play for the next two years. My record received enthusiastic reviews in the trade magazines, sold well, and dented the country charts. This ensured my recording career at least through the second and third singles. But this success only made the next records more serious. To capitalize on the success I was enjoying would require intense devotion to career and more than a little luck.

I returned to Nashville in October 1967 for the National Disc Jockey Convention. During this important annual gathering, Nashville's royalty returned from tours and the entire business machinery of the country music industry converged to greet, court, and seduce radio programmers from all over the world. It was at the 1967 DJs convention that I first met Willie Nelson, as well as comic Ray Stevens, country-pop balladeer Ray Price, sweet ol' Grandpa Jones, Little Jimmy Dickens, Jeannie Pruitt, Dolly Parton, Ferlin Husky, and a host of other Nashville luminaries.

The National Disc Jockey Convention offered a clear step-by-step explanation of the pathway to success in country music. With a publishing deal and a decent singing voice, an artist could secure a recording contract. Armed with a publishing and recording contract, the artist was ready to play the game with the suits in the front offices. The first rule of that game required learning how to cowrite a song. Why? Because publishers cut sweet percentage deals with record labels. More significantly, however, so that two publishers can join forces and co-promote for more effective marketing and, equally important, divide the harvest of royalties. With that knowledge, a reasonable amount of brain power, elbow grease, and enough all-night fishing trips to Center Hill to make connections, you could move from publishing company to record company with relative ease and forge a steady, vertical career. Recording and publishing contracts secured, you still needed to coddle radio programmers, trade paper reviewers, and record executives. Generally, a record's fate was determined before it even reached the general public. In other words, if the industry first anointed the record, then the machinery quickly fell into place and went to work to fulfill the prophecy. With the industry's blessing the public would likely follow suit. I completely understood the politics and the process and felt I could negotiate it easily to the top—if I had an unfettered shot. With a war raging, however, a clear shot was impossible for me. The war was intensifying rather than showing any signs of abating and, complicating matters, I only had one more year of eligibility for a student deferment. I figured one way of obtaining a deferment past graduation—albeit remote—might be to secure a job teaching school. So, with a year of college remaining, I changed my major from fine arts to art education. Diana started making wedding plans for March.

I also realized that now that my professional name was Bridger it was imperative for me to learn everything I could about Jim Bridger. Genealogy aside, it became immediately clear to me that as a writer it was not ultimately important if I was in fact related to Jim. What was important to my concept was the fact that of the first one hundred nongovernment explorers to follow Lewis and Clark into the unexplored American West, only Jim lived to be an old man. It was vitally important that he had been an eyewitness to pivotal events in the history of the West—and, more often than not, a participant in those events. Of course, awareness of those important historical aspects of Jim's life made it even more compelling to find out if we were indeed related, but before any genealogical research could begin, I needed to address something equally significant: there was a song being born from the inspiration of what I was learning about Jim Bridger!

Young Jim, at the age of eighteen, was forced to deal with the shame of having robbed and deserted Hugh Glass and left him for dead on the plains of South Dakota in 1823. Jim had to surrender to his circumstances, face his fellow trappers, and admit his guilt. He had to ask for their trust as well as Hugh's forgiveness. Three months after Hugh forgave him for the desertion, Bridger volunteered for the hazardous mission to explore the Bear River in order to prove himself to his fellow trappers and regain their confidence. Jim rode the dangerous rapids of Utah's Bear River into the history books when he discovered the Great Salt Lake. Thinking about his perilous journey riding those rocky rapids started me thinking about the ways water eventually overcomes any obstacle in its path. One of water's greatest strengths is its ability to continuing fighting by surrendering. No matter what the obstacle, if I surrendered to my artistic visions and instincts, like water, I would arrive at the ocean.

> Life is a river and with it you must flow
> Wherever it wants you, it's there that you must go
> We all try to fight it, but deep inside we know
> Life is a river, and with it you must flow
> Life is a river, and with it you must go.[3]

Like Jim, I had to surrender to my circumstances if I intended to make the most of the splendid opportunities that had been presented to me. Fred Carter offered me the unique opportunity to follow my heart's desire—music. Whereas my studies in visual arts remained as an important and completely separate part of my life, with Fred I could actually maintain two artistic careers—one aural, the other visual. But a twist of fate soon presented itself again as my pursuit of the visual arts directed my musical journey off the path into unexplored territory.

When I entered art school in the early 1960s the "action painting" style pioneered in post–World War II New York was escalating in universities throughout America. Since the famous "Armory Show" of 1913 in New York announced the arrival of Picasso's work in this hemisphere, the American mainstream had been slow to embrace "modern" art. President Franklin Roosevelt's Federal Arts Project during the Depression years of the 1930s enabled many of America's more adventurous painters to survive the difficult times, and by the late 1940s a genuine new style of American painting emerged from these efforts. Much of the philosophy of the movement was centered on an artistic vision of Manifest Destiny, or a shifting of the center of focus of the art world from Europe to America, from Paris to New York. The irony that the leader of the so-called New York School, Jackson Pollock, was from Buffalo Bill's town of Cody, Wyoming, did not escape me; the metaphorical masthead of the original concept of Manifest Destiny, Buffalo Bill took the American "Wild West" to the world, and the famous "cowboy drip painter" Pollock brought the "old" world to the American Wild West. That ironic, historic, artistic symmetry was racing in my thoughts one day as I trekked down a dark hall to a boring art history class immediately after a particularly exciting and creative morning in an abstract oil painting class discussing Pollock's impact. As the art history class dragged on, I continued daydreaming about the American West that I was discovering in my research into folk music. I began to wonder what I was doing studying all these ancient European cathedrals and religious dogma paintings instead of the art history of America. I started thinking of Thomas Hart Benton's Americana murals and Grant Wood's heartland scenes. Suddenly I remembered the sketch of Jim Bridger in a suit of armor in Alfred Jacob Miller's work that I had seen in Bernard DeVoto's *Across the Wide Missouri*. After class I ran across campus to the library and located the book. When the janitor's broom swept me from the library late that evening, I had opened a visual window into the past and stepped through.

Hours spent gazing into Alfred Jacob Miller's lush, field watercolor paintings of the mountain men stirred emotions deep inside me. In particular, several of Miller's Rocky Mountain lake scenes and depictions of trappers' rendezvous captured my focus and inspired me to write another song. After four hours of gazing into those scenes I scribbled the lyric:

> At the Rendezvous, White men and the Sioux
> Smoked the pipe, traded hair,
> For the maidens fair.
> To the Rendezvous, men came from St. Lou
> Wanting beaver and mink, bringing whiskey to drink.[4]

When I stumbled onto Neihardt's *A Cycle of the West* in 1965 I calculated that it would take a decade of research and writing to create an original epic piece based upon his structure. Abandoning the concept of a western epic in pursuit of a steamboat piece had come to naught. But the emotional quickening from my success in Nashville, combined with the reality of suddenly being in direct contact with master songwriters and musicians, had triggered renewed interest in an epic inspired by Neihardt's work. Becoming reacquainted with the Miller paintings and the awareness that I could use them like windows to step into the past to hunt for lyrics were the first steps of the long journey toward the creation of my prototype epic ballad, Part One of *A Ballad of the West, Seekers of the Fleece*. With the completion of the first two songs, "Life Is a River" and "Rendezvous," my feet were firmly on that path. From the very beginning, however, I knew the path would be a narrow trail up the side of a rocky cliff.

To begin with, modern audiences were not accustomed to pop songs lasting longer than two and a half minutes. Granted, some of Bob Dylan's masterpieces from the early 1960s stretched far beyond this rigid standard, but they were folk album cuts rather than pop/country aimed at the Top 40 and, given Dylan's astonishing success, he could have done anything he wanted. Besides, like Picasso, Dylan made his own rules from the start. Ultimately, maybe *all* twentieth-century artists—Dylan included—followed Picasso's creative lead; Picasso forever changed our perspective. Like Picasso, Dylan brought a new perspective to songwriting. Dylan himself said it: "Tin Pan Alley is dead; I killed it." The post-camera French impressionists shaped the directions that naturally led to Picasso, the cubists, surrealists, and abstract/expressionists, just as certain as Elvis had made baby boomers aware of the guitar that gave birth to the folk movement. It became obvious to me that those of us who followed in Dylan's wake were expected to write our own songs. The imperative now was to create art that played by our own rules. You create your own target and hit the bull's-eye.

Several brave experimental artists had already succeeded in breaching the time constraints for radio recordings: 1959 disc jockeys referred to Marty Robbins's landmark ballad "El Paso," more than five minutes long, as the "bathroom song"; they could put "El Paso" on, run to the toilet, and make it back before Marty's cowboy died in Fellina's arms. Of course, Dylan's "Like a Rolling Stone" hit the airwaves in 1965, dramatically extending the format of the hit song. Irish actor Richard Harris's record of Jimmy Webb's orchestral opus "MacArthur Park," released on the heels of the Beatles' lengthy "Sgt. Pepper's Lonely Hearts Club Band," had also pushed the radio boundaries of the two-minute-song record well past Dylan's previous five-minute mark, while at the same time announcing the era of the concept album. The Who's "rock opera" *Tommy* would soon appear.

But precisely at the time I rediscovered Alfred Jacob Miller's paintings and wrote "Life Is a River" and "Rendezvous," Canadian folksinger Gordon Lightfoot released his masterpiece, "Canadian Railroad Trilogy." Lightfoot's incredible accomplishment was so similar to my vision it was frightening. Hearing it the first time I knew beyond any doubt that I had to move forward quickly with my idea of historical ballads. But even while it threatened, "Canadian Railroad Trilogy" also affirmed my resolve that I was on target. Lightfoot's song removed all doubt that my idea of a lengthy concept album combining narrative verse and songs—with historical American themes—was inevitable.

By Christmas 1967 I completed the narrative verse that linked "Life Is a River" to "Rendezvous," but other important matters had to be dealt with immediately, before work on the ballads could continue. Fred set up recording sessions for me over the Christmas holidays. This time, rather than returning to the "little Victor" studios, as RCA-B was sometimes called, we were going to record at Roy Orbison's sacred shrine, the old Monument Studios in a hotel downtown. As an added bonus, Fred had booked one of his own idols, Grady Martin, to play lead guitar. Since Grady had a reputation for being a world-class curmudgeon, I was apprehensive, but I trusted Fred's judgment.

As would be the case for the next two years, I hit the ground running in

Nashville. I had to select two very important songs to record. I already had the third picked out. It was an old song of Fred's—a great "story-song" about a guy who worked on the offshore oil rigs out of Morgan City, Louisiana.

Meanwhile, I continued to dig through endless boxes of reel-to-reel tapes of demos of songs, searching for the one that had magic sprinkled on it. Then Fred suddenly delivered the song to me. It was written by Glen Campbell, the man who had turned John Hartford's "Gentle on My Mind" into a mainstream hit. "Glen and I played on some Simon and Garfunkel dates a while back and he sang me a beautiful song he wrote that would be perfect for you, Bobby. It's kind of a hymn. It could easily go pop now that Glen's getting some attention. It's called 'Less of Me.'"

Fred called L.A. and arranged for Glen to record a demo and get it to us in Nashville quickly. I loved the song. The melody was outstanding and the simple message was one of eloquent humility.

"Let's just cut 'Morgan City' and 'Less of Me' for this session, Bobby. We still have 'Three Squares' in the can. If we focus on getting these two right, we'll have our next single for Monument. Meanwhile, let's take a drive out in the country. I want to show you something."

We loaded into the Cadillac and headed north, deep into the beautiful Tennessee hills. After a thirty-minute drive we arrived at a small wood-frame building under a leafless winter stand of elegant sycamore trees. A sparkling brook of clean, clear water lapped at its banks and meandered near the back edges of the building. We stepped into the building and, from the framed records on the walls, I could see that the facility had something to do with country/bluegrass stars Lonzo and Oscar. We walked through a corridor of offices to a heavy double door at the back of the hallway. Fred opened the door and we descended a dark stairway into a basement-level recording studio. When Fred hit the lights, the studio sparkled to life.

"I bought the studios as well as the Nugget Records label. I'm immediately installing a sixteen-track Ampex machine and board and I've ordered EMT echo plates from Germany. We'll be the first studio in town with them. After your Monument deal expires we'll be ready to work here. We can record here, and press and distribute our own records on the Nugget label from here. We'll have much more focus here than any other place in town. I've already signed some other artists, and we're moving forward real quick. But the studio alone will pay for everything. We can experiment here without having to pay the downtown studio prices."

I had no doubt that Fred's new Nugget was just what its logo promised: "Good as gold." I was on the team for the full ride.

The next day was December 20, 1967. We arrived at Monument Studios in downtown Nashville and prepared for my second recording session. I was much less nervous than for my first session, but I was wary of crossing Grady Martin. I had heard horror stories of his temper and lack of patience dealing with artists who failed to meet his high standards. As fate would have it, I walked out to the street for a cigarette just as Grady and his son drove up and started to unload the maestro's guitars from the trunk of their huge white Cadillac. It was freezing cold and snowing, so they left the engine running with the doors open while stacking guitar cases on the sidewalk.

Out of nowhere, a black guy suddenly bolted into the driver's seat of the Cadillac and sped off with the doors and trunk open and flapping like a huge white swan's wings and tail feathers. The strange bird flew through a red light, and within seconds vanished into the snowy canyons of Nashville.

I froze, expecting Grady to explode into a rage. Instead, he just took a long drag off his cigarette, looked at me, broke into an incredulous, ear-to-ear grin, and shrugged his shoulders as he exhaled.

"What are the odds of that?" he laughed. "The son of a bitch just made off with my Cadillac and all my Christmas presents. Merry Fucking Christmas."

I wasn't sure if he was about to go ballistic or if he really was laughing at the absurdity of the moment. I blew a puff of smoke in the frigid air and walked over to him.

"You still have your guitars," I said. "I'm Bobby Bridger. You're here to play on my session today."

"Can you and Fred give me a ride home after the session?" He laughed and offered his hand.

SEVEN

The Sounds of Silence

Billboard Magazine
Spotlight Singles, March 9, 1968
Special Merit Spotlight
Bobby Bridger—"Less of Me" (Beechwood, BMI) (Prod. Fred Carter
Jr./Writer: Glen Campbell)
One of the best of the week's releases was penned by Glen Campbell
and performed to perfection by Bridger. Lyric content must be heard.

Cashbox Magazine
Newcomer Picks, March 9, 1968
Bobby Bridger (Monument 1059)
"Less of Me" (2:34) [Beechwood BMI-Campbell]
Bobby Bridger offers not only a pretty tune, but a strong message that
should apply to all in "Less of Me." Deejays in a wide variety of mar-
kets owe it to themselves to take a listen and try it a few times. May
well go a route similar to "Skip a Rope." Flip: "Morgan City" (2:48)
[Pamper BMI-Carter]

DIANA AND I WERE MARRIED March 29, 1968, in Columbia's
First Baptist Church. Following a weekend honeymoon in
Natchez, Mississippi, my bride and I returned to Monroe to
settle into my two-room apartment in a one-hundred-year-old three-story
wood-frame house on Desiard Street. My student teaching at West Mon-

roe High School was going well and I was enjoying the experience. Diana had graduated and secured a great job as a social worker with the Ouachita Parish Welfare Department. Released two weeks before our wedding ceremony, my second single on Monument Records attracted sterling reviews in the trades and was already selling well. It debuted at number one on the charts in North Louisiana and was breaking out in several other secondary markets around the South. Sheriff Tex called and told me everyone on the Monument team in Nashville was excited by the response and that Fred Foster wanted to sign me to a new contract with Monument and produce me himself. I told him I intended to continue pursuing my musical destiny with Fred Carter Jr. I didn't mention anything about Nugget Records.

Diana and I were unpacking from our honeymoon when we turned on the television to discover the Sunday-night movie interrupted by one of President Lyndon Johnson's increasingly frequent addresses. The weight of history and the toll of death showed in President Johnson's tired, craggy face. As the war worsened and demonstrations protesting the war grew larger and more demanding, Johnson's television addresses had become so routine that everyone in the country did a decent impression of his drawled "Mah fellow 'mari-kins." Democratic senator Eugene McCarthy had recently challenged Johnson in the New Hampshire Democratic presidential primary and proved that Johnson was vulnerable. Suddenly everyone opposed to the war rallied in support of Senator McCarthy. Diana and I assumed that the president was about to fire the opening salvo in what everyone expected to be an intense spate of springtime primaries. We continued our unpacking, half listening to the president's speech until he suddenly stunned the nation with the announcement that he would not seek nor accept the Democratic Party's nomination for a second term.

I naturally wondered what effect Johnson's decision would have on the war and my draft status. Obtaining my undergraduate degree in May would end my eligibility for student deferments. Given Johnson's historic decision, I wondered if perhaps the war might suddenly begin to wind down and the draft board might consider granting me a teacher's deferment if I had a teaching job. I certainly didn't have anything to lose. I was aware that West Monroe's only art teacher, Mary Moore, was inundated with students and the art department truly needed an assistant. Within days I went to the administration of West Monroe High School and asked for a job teaching full-time. With the stern admonition that I was not to bring any of that "Memphis honky-tonk music" into my classroom, Principal Hoyt

Lee hired me to begin teaching in the fall of 1968. I notified my draft board that I had been hired to teach in Louisiana, and requested and received my last year-long deferment from the military draft.

In January 1968, after mixing "Less of Me" and "Morgan City" at CBS Studio B, Fred introduced me to a young songwriter who worked there occasionally as a janitor. Kris Kristofferson was a West Point graduate and a Rhodes scholar who, in the early days of the war, had served as a helicopter pilot in Vietnam. At the time of our meeting, Kris also had a gig in Morgan City, Louisiana, where he flew workers back and forth on helicopters from the offshore oil rigs in the Gulf of Mexico. There was a Ping-Pong table in the concession area at CBS Studios, where musicians held intense matches between sessions. Fred arranged a meeting there with Kris.

"Of course I'll get your record on the air in Morgan City, Fred," Kris growled, his deep-set eyes twinkling in that soon-to-be-famous squint. "I guess my working in Morgan City makes it kinda like karma or something."

For a brief time after that initial meeting Kris and I were label-mates on Monument. He had a reputation as a wild man when he was drinking, but there was little doubt that he was a gifted songwriter. I learned that he wrote for Fred Foster's Combine Music and asked the company manager, Bob Beckham, to help me search through Kris's catalog for songs. Soon I worked his "Jody and the Kid" into my live performances.

Kris took "Morgan City" to the radio stations in Morgan City, Louisiana, and it had a major impact on my career. The Monument promotional machinery was working the single's A-side, "Less of Me," but Kris's action initiated airplay for the B-side, "Morgan City." Like the protagonist in Fred's song, a large percentage of the population of Morgan City, Louisiana, worked as roustabouts on offshore oil rigs—ten-day shifts on the rig, followed by five days off. Also like the character in Fred's song, many of those roustabouts were involved in love triangles revolving around those peculiar work shifts. Fred's character had a lover pragmatically cheating on him in five-day shifts with two other oil-field roustabouts; one cuckold would leave on a ten-day shift in the Gulf just as another returned for his five days off. The terrific melody, the story line, and the witty, carnal mathematics expressed in the double-entendre chorus, "ten days out and five days in," really appealed to me, and I begged Fred to let me record the song.

Following the national hit record of his cover of John Hartford's "Gentle on My Mind," Glen Campbell's career ignited with "By the Time I Get to Phoenix," "Wichita Lineman," "Galveston," and the string of incredible Jimmy Webb tunes that would follow in quick succession and charm the world. Glen and John were already performing each Sunday night on prime-time network television. Of course Monument realized that Glen's celebrity would draw radio programmers to my recording of his song "Less of Me." But after Kristofferson got the record to Morgan City, the B-side started getting as much action on the radio as "Less of Me" on the A-side did. Strong airplay broke out along the "Redneck Riviera" of the Gulf Coast, from Texas to Florida, until the record started playing in the oil patch in California. Next, it broke out in Alaska. Thanks to Kris Kristofferson, Fred Carter's folk ballad of adulterous offshore oil workers had clearly hit a responsive chord and become a "turntable" hit in the world's oil patches.

My delicate draft status and full-time teaching position continued to make it impossible for me to tour in support of my record releases. The immediate result of this was that even though "Sharon, Oh Sharon" had strong radio airplay around the country, Sheriff Tex Davis was forced to limit my personal appearances to North Louisiana. His plan for dealing with this was to hook me up with major acts that played the Monroe Civic Center. The first star Davis booked me to open for was the great George Jones. A folksinger, I had no band. So, rather than letting me proceed as a solo, Davis persuaded me to let "the Jones Boys" accompany me. It seemed a simple enough matter for me to meet George Jones's band at the sound check and teach them two songs for my set. The problem was that Jones arrived drunk. Working desperately to sober "the Possum" up to get him onstage, the promoters and band members had no time to focus on my tunes. The only "rehearsal" between me and the Jones bandleader took place in the backstage gymnasium-style showers, where the star—completely nude and barely conscious—sat on the floor propped against a wall under the shower while I sang my songs a cappella.

Aside from the fact that I believed George Jones was perhaps the most soulful white singer on the planet, I had also wanted very much to visit with him because my Uncle "Tex" Durham may have been one of the very first disc jockeys to play his records and interview him on the radio. From Vidor, Texas, Jones started his career in the Beaumont/Port Arthur/Port Neches area of Texas, known as the Golden Triangle, where my Uncle Tex interviewed him. I had hoped that regional kinship would enable us to have a decent, old-fashioned chat. But by the time Jones appeared to be sobering, I had to take the stage unrehearsed. A hometown roar welcomed me as I stepped into the spotlight and began "Sharon, Oh Sharon" with a couple of the Jones Boys fumbling behind, miserably failing to anticipate any cues about where the song might go next. Humiliated in my hometown spotlight, I stumbled through my two-song set and hurried off the stage to anemic applause. Embarrassment immediately changed to astonishment when I discovered George Jones—now apparently stone sober—standing in the wings, guitar strapped over his shoulder and prepared to stroll into the spotlight. His show was thirty minutes late, but nevertheless would not fall under the category of his other notorious nickname—George "No Show" Jones. Even more surprising, he gave an outstanding performance. I was never able to have a moment alone with him.

I had already stopped serial binge drinking, but as I listened to George Jones sing that afternoon, Wooten Morris's words came immediately to mind: "When you want a drink, have one; when you *need* a drink, stop." In my brief career in the honky-tonks I had already seen many sad drunks, and I realized that in a few years I might very well become one myself. I promised myself that afternoon that I would quit drinking. Aside from the occasional celebratory toast, I've kept that promise for over four decades.

The George Jones debacle was nevertheless an indication of the fundamental dilemma that would eventually force me to leave Nashville. My development as a musician was completely out of scale with the level of professional musicians performing on my records. I couldn't possibly replicate the incredible musical accompaniment on my records in live performance. Of course, if the record was a major hit I could hire musicians to reproduce the recordings onstage. If not, it created a deep chasm between the work I was doing in the studio and what I actually performed in person. But the Jones fiasco indicated there was an even deeper artistic predicament: I didn't write the songs I recorded. I was simply an interpreter. Make no mistake—I loved making commercial records as an interpretive singer. It is truly among the highest art forms to be a professional interpreter of commercial songs. Since I was unable to tour, though, it was impossible for me to sell enough records to hire a pride of Nashville cats to reproduce my studio performances; pragmatically, if I played on the record it would make it easier to perform the song later in person. Nevertheless, it was equally logical that there was no need for me, an inexperienced studio musician, to play guitar in the studio—especially when I had one of America's greatest guitar players producing and playing on my records. In spite of this, I realized that I had to play guitar on my records in order for them to have any credibility whatsoever. Coming to this realization also forced me to see that I never intended to be so removed from direct responsibility for my musical career. So the Possum had unwittingly initiated several important transitions for me. Embarrassing as it was to perform so poorly in front of a hometown audience, the experience had been the sobering slap in the face that would begin to bring me to my artistic senses.

Then, in December 1968, Elvis had a comeback special on television that convinced me beyond any doubt I had to play guitar on my recordings. Elvis had trimmed down, dressed in black leather, and reunited with musicians from his early career. But most importantly, he played guitar. With his rhythm guitar driving the band, Elvis riveted America yet again. A decade later when asked for a comment after Elvis's death, John Lennon said they killed Elvis when they inducted him into the army. But seeing him perform on television that night I realized that even though everyone mocked Elvis as a mediocre musician, his unique rhythm guitar playing was truly the secret behind the phenomenal initial success of his music. That essential element was missing when Colonel Tom Parker took Elvis off guitar and replaced Scotty and Bill. After that, Elvis's performing was limited to terribly contrived movies, unwieldy and overblown Las Vegas orchestras, and life in a velvet rut. And the only difference between a rut and a grave is that the dirt hasn't been tossed over the rut.

I knew the proper time would appear to talk with Fred about playing guitar on my records. But immediately after the George Jones debacle I started a band instead, to attempt to bridge the gap and reproduce the musical accompaniment of my recordings. My brother Hill was a great singer, so I enlisted him for harmony and to share the spotlight. We held auditions and hired fellow Northeast students Sammy Pope on bass, Sherrod Smith on guitar, and Danny Arrington on drums. Hill had heard a stunning young woman named Susan Carter sing in a campus beauty contest, and he'd been impressed with her voice and poise. So we asked her to join the group.

Even with my records playing on the radio there were few venues in the area where we could work, so I started hustling shows in any bar that would book us. After months in seedy honky-tonks in the Delta region, the band slowly came together, and I was eventually able to secure regular gigs at two Monroe nightclubs—a place called the Office and the Fabulous Encore

Lounge at a Ramada Inn motel. Working six nights a week would bring in the money that we needed to function as a band, but working an eight-hour day as a schoolteacher before five of those shows would be physically demanding. It also proved emotionally demanding when my schedule immediately put a severe strain on my young marriage.

Shortly after our wedding Diana told me she did not want me to continue my musical career. She felt I should "grow up" and devote myself to teaching. Worse, my painting also threatened her. My intense teaching and performing schedule left little time for painting, so I set up an easel in the bedroom to paint after coming in from my musical gigs. Painting helped me relax after the fifteen-hour days, and I was determined to keep in touch with brush and canvas even as my musical career unfurled. But Diana would cry through the night and say she wished I would look at her the way I looked at my paintings.

Whereas painting was the fire in my heart, Diana's passion was her religious faith. Several months after our wedding she came to me with a request that made my jaw go slack: she wanted to return to the Catholic Church! After all the drama and heartbreaking family upheaval, she wanted to enlist a priest to begin the process of a second marriage in the Catholic Church.

Awash in guilt and physically exhausted, I acquiesced. Within days we met with a priest she had recruited to reunite her with the Catholic Church. I made it clear to the priest that I had no intention of converting but would agree to whatever Diana needed to return to the church. He agreed, but soon began to proselytize. I became more withdrawn and heard little of what either of them said.

So I was relieved when Fred called and told me to hurry to Nashville to record the third and final single in our contract with Monument. I was anxious to get away from Diana, the priest, teaching school, and the seedy bars. I looked forward to being back in the studio.

Bob Montgomery offered me an incredible country ballad he wrote called "Over You." But there was a songwriter from Pennsylvania named Chris Gantry who interested me and Fred. Chris released an album on Monument that included a song named "Sundown Mary." The first two verses of the song were structured so that the listener would assume "Sundown Mary" was the singer's lover, but the third verse revealed the song was actually about a hobo and his canine hitchhiking companion. That unusual slant on the subject inspired Fred to search Chris's catalog for a song for me to record. Gantry would soon have a monster hit with a Glen Campbell cut of his "Dreams of the Everyday Housewife," but his "Net of Fireflies" was a lyrical tone poem with a melody that would really showcase my vocal range. Fred wanted to experiment with an orchestra, and I agreed that "Fireflies" was a great song for his idea.

While I was creating a band to reproduce my Nashville recordings in live performance, Fred had started gradually directing me from stereotypical country songs to more sophisticated pop songs like "Net of Fireflies." For "Less of Me" and "Morgan City" we overdubbed a small string section after my vocals were completed. Given my range, however, Fred felt I would eventually record with big orchestras. So he booked a sixteen-piece string section to record live with the studio musicians for our "Over You"/"Net of Fireflies" session at CBS Studio A.

Singing Gantry's ethereal song live with a tight Nashville rhythm section *and* an orchestra was an extraordinary experience. But when the orchestra joined me on Montgomery's classic country-pop-two-step, "Over You," everyone in the studio applauded.

When I returned to Louisiana, Tex Davis called to inform me he had booked me at Neville High School in Monroe on a bill with country stars Conway Twitty and Stonewall Jackson. Conway Twitty had a huge pop hit in 1958 with "Only Make Believe" and, reversing the crossover trend of those days, had immediately "gone country." Country fans adored him for the shift toward rather than away from them. Handsome and confident, Twitty and his Lonely Blue Boys provoked normally demure Louisiana women into screaming and tossing love notes and undergarments onto the stage. Stonewall Jackson was still riding the popularity of his crossover pop hit, "Waterloo," and attracted a more traditional country audience.

But Conway Twitty and Stonewall Jackson no longer concerned me. I noticed something during my performance that frightened me: only two songs into our show I became so hoarse I could hardly sing. I had to really push my voice to get through the band's five-song set. Worse, the hoarseness lingered. Subconsciously, I knew I had hurt myself. My everyday routine was teaching from 8 a.m. to 4 p.m., booking shows from 4 p.m. to 6 p.m., singing from 8 p.m. to midnight, and fighting with Diana during the rest of my waking moments. Of course, when I wasn't teaching or singing, the only time I wasn't smoking an unfiltered Pall Mall was when I was puffing my pipe.

Denial swept vocal worries to the side when Fred Carter called immediately after the Conway Twitty and Stonewall Jackson show to invite me to perform on a tour he was producing with one of my idols, the great Marty Robbins. We were scheduled to do three Louisiana shows: West Monroe, Shreveport, and Alexandria.

Even though I tried to deny it, I couldn't ignore the fact that the hoarseness was becoming more serious. Every time I sang, a breathy rasp would shroud my voice sooner and linger longer. Hill started to notice my problem and, having taken vocal lessons, he showed me how to warm up my vocal cords with exercises in which I hummed musical scales. Though the tactics worked to get me through a set, the rasp would still remain for days after I sang. But I decided to postpone any trip to the doctor until after the tour with Marty Robbins. Marty's album *Gunfighter Ballads and Trail Songs* was an important early inspiration for my epic ballads. Aside from his extraordinary songs, Marty was one of my favorite singers. He could sing any type of music. I had followed his career since the late 1950s when my dad brought an album of Hawaiian-influenced country tunes home and wore it out. After that I watched Marty waltz effortlessly from pop to country music and back before finally releasing *Gunfighter Ballads*. That groundbreaking album set him totally apart from the country music stars of the era and announced a new day in western music.

I was pleased to learn that the Marty Robbins tour was scheduled to open in the auditorium of West Monroe High School. That stroke of good fortune turned on me and my embarrassment was doubled when—simultaneously mangling my new name and slighting Marty's talent—a well-meaning journalist friend from college wrote an overenthusiastic review of my part in our first show of the tour. The lead sentence read: "A funny thing happened at the Marty Robbins show in West Monroe Friday night. Bobby Durham 'Brister' stole it."

Marty had a good sense of humor about it all and teased me for the rest of the tour, introducing me as "Bobby Brister." After finishing my set every night of the tour I hurried to a wing of the stage to soak up every radiant moment of Marty's performance. He played with his audience, coaxing them here and there, coddling, cooing, joking, mocking his own lyrics. He had a little 5-18 "Baby Martin" guitar that he played without a strap. Occasionally he played the ukulele-size instrument, but mostly he used it as a prop, pointing it at pretty women in the audience.

I wasn't the only musician coveting Marty's 5-18 Baby Martin: soon after the Marty Robbins tour, Fred Carter Jr. found his own and used it on an important Simon and Garfunkel recording. Played on gut strings on his 5-18 Martin, Fred's nimble cascading run announced the opening of Simon and Garfunkel's immortal song "The Boxer." Fred's trademark style twinkled and danced over Paul's fingerpicking, Charlie McCoy's funky bass harmonica, Joe Osborn's driving bass, and Hal Blaine's drum explosions. "The Boxer" became the first single to emerge from the *Bridge Over Troubled Water* album and set its landmark sales pace.[1]

Opening for artists like George Jones, Conway Twitty, Stonewall Jackson, and Marty Robbins put me in the fast lane for the next phase of my career. "Less of Me" and "Morgan City" were breaking as regional hits and, with my summer break from teaching about to start, the timing was finally perfect for me to actively promote my records. I was walking on clouds. But it was about to rain.

Shortly after the Marty Robbins shows I visited a specialist and learned I had vocal polyps. The doctor urged me to have outpatient surgery as soon as possible to have them removed. After the surgery I would need to remain absolutely silent for six weeks. Rather than making new records, or promoting current ones, I would be using my summer break to recuperate.

Diana arranged a whirlwind trip to Chicago for us to visit her parents before my vocal surgery. After a splendid Arkansas sunset we were crossing into the southeastern toe of Missouri when a newscaster broke into the broadcast to announce that Bobby Kennedy had won the coveted California Democratic presidential primary. Only moments later the regular broadcast was interrupted again with news that Kennedy had been shot. Diana immediately began praying and we drove through the night listening to the radio with hopes he would live, but another Kennedy had been taken by an assassin's bullet. From John Kennedy's assassination forward into the Vietnam era, the 1960s had been a turbulent decade. By 1968, on- and off-campus mayhem, nonviolent civil disobedience, and public demonstration had accelerated into a dangerous, unprecedented period in American history. Beginning with President Johnson's March announcement that he was not going to run for reelection, tragically punctuated by Martin Luther King's April 4 assassination and multiple inner-city riots in the wake of his death, and Robert Kennedy's murder in June, America seemed to be unraveling as the hot summer approached.

Soon after returning to Louisiana from Chicago I had the vocal surgery.

My doctor cautioned that if I uttered a sound in the next six weeks it would scar and permanently damage my voice.

The first two days of silence nearly drove me crazy. Compounding the necessity of summoning profound willpower to suddenly maintain vocal silence, my heavy smoking habit ended with the surgery. Nicotine withdrawal was not helping with the silence or the discipline required to overcome my instinctive desire to speak. After I wrestled with this for three or four days, the nicotine cravings gradually abated and left me brooding silently in my apartment. Telephone answering machines were a decade in the future and my livelihood depended upon the phone ringing. Every time the phone rang I would rush to answer it and then dance in frustration with my hand over the receiver. Worse than that was the awareness that I had done this to myself; increasingly I was forced to admit that my compulsive, frenzied pace had damaged my voice. My obsessive behavior had only intensified after Fred bought Nugget Studio. During this explosive period of creativity, Fred was also recording *Bridge Over Troubled Water* with Simon and Garfunkel. Paul and Artie preferred recording in Manhattan and would fly Fred to New York for a week in the studio experimenting, recording, and overdubbing. Fred would return to Nashville bristling with creative energy and call me to rush to Tennessee to record. So, aside from my regularly hectic schedule teaching school and performing, it was not uncommon for me to get a call from Fred, leave school at three on Friday afternoon, drive to Nashville, and head immediately into the studio. After recording throughout the weekend with only naps to sustain me, I would depart Nashville on Sunday evening and drive all night to get home in time to teach Monday morning. Then the routine of teaching all day, singing in smoky bars all night, and fighting with Diana until the wee hours of the morning would begin anew.

Suddenly ceasing such intense activity felt like being forced kicking and silently screaming into a cell of solitary confinement. Five days into silence made me aware I had to do something to occupy myself or I would certainly go mad. I set up an easel to try to paint. Nothing came. I paced like a wild animal in front of the blank canvas for a full day before I finally took it down. Frustrated and desperate, I remembered the fur trade era watercolors of Alfred Jacob Miller. Miller's lush paintings immediately inspired songs, but my writing technique was based on first singing a melody. How could I write without singing? My way of creating melody was to explore the moods of various chord structures by humming until I discovered a tune and the suggestion of lyrical rhythm that captured my attention. Then I would meticulously lay the rhyme and cadence of lyrics over the inherent meter of the melody and sing the new song repeatedly until the rougher phrasings were polished.

The Miller paintings eased my restlessness, but gazing into them for hours at a time inspired a desire to write songs that soon overwhelmed me. I eventually resorted to playing my guitar and whistling a melody. Soon after a lengthy session with Miller's painting *The Trapper's Bride*, I wrote the wedding song "People Carry On" for *Seekers of the Fleece*. Next, I started writing narrative verse in heroic couplets, reciting it in thought, and tinkering with connecting the three completed songs of the concept and the new verse into a narrative chronological structure. Creatively engaged, I noticed the days again easily flowed into one another. Soon I could just relax and let the phone ring. Within days I returned to Neihardt's *A Cycle of the West* to study the master's techniques and glean a renewed overview of the historical era and a sense of the landscape of the upper Great Plains and Rockies.

With Neihardt as my guide I was also coming into contact with a different American Indian than I had experienced in American history books, Hollywood movies, and television shows. Early on I realized that Jim Bridger spent his entire adult life living with Indian people. Because of that, it was vital that I gain a broad awareness of the tribes of the upper Great Plains and the Rocky Mountain regions. This new knowledge of American Indian history soon became the inspiration for a companion piece that would reflect the American Indian perspective of the nineteenth century as the mountain man piece presented the Euro-American perspective of the same era. This would require finding an Indian man who—like Jim Bridger—was an eyewitness to pivotal events in western history. I didn't have to look any further than Neihardt and Black Elk. Soon, while simultaneously devouring *A Cycle of the West*, I was on a second reading of *Black Elk Speaks*. By the third reading I decided that the holy man's life story would be the subject of my second epic ballad, *Lakota*.

Sometime during the second week of my vocal fast I embraced the quiet. I finally had the time and solitude needed to consolidate my fur trade era research and tinker with the vision that had come to me in 1965 of an epic historically documented musical narrative. Now that research could form the armature on which I could sculpt an epic work. Neihardt's *Cycle* had given me the title:

The trappers and the singing voyageurs
Are comrades now of Jason and his crew
Foregathered in that timeless rendezvous
Where come at last all Seekers of the Fleece.[2]

After six weeks of silence it was difficult speaking again. My reticence was more psychological than physical; my vocal cords had healed up quickly, but I had learned to embrace silence. Hill visited regularly and reiterated the need for me to do vocal warm-ups for the rest of my singing and teaching career. He taught me to hum scales combined with specific vowel sounds that would warm my chest, throat, and facial voices. I would be using my voice in teaching as well as singing, and Hill urged me to warm up each morning before school and to sip water all day long while speaking in class.

In order to keep my band working, I returned to rehearsals. Initially afraid of reinjuring myself, I coddled my wounded voice. The result was an instrument with no emotion. Faced with that, I committed myself to singing with unconditional emotion or not singing at all. When I sang full-voiced, I noticed that the upper registers of my tenor were gone—an effect of the surgery. My new voice was neither as clear nor as high. Naturally this concerned me, but I resolved to accept the reality that I had hurt myself with self-destructive behavior.

When the band returned to our old nightclub circuit my heart wasn't in it anymore. Six weeks of silence had initiated a profound transition in my personality. Aside from the band, I emerged from silence knowing I had to make serious life changes. Most significantly, I was now aware I had to end my marriage. I had not been able to muster the courage to tell Diana that I felt our marriage had been a mistake. Moreover, I absolutely enjoyed teaching art and interacting with kids, but I felt shackled by teaching school to avoid being sent to Vietnam. Each near-success with a record release painfully underscored how chained I was to the war, and how much bigger the success might have been if only I had been free to promote my career. I was seething with anger and resentment that because of the war I could not tour to support my music. Then, in August, as all these forces were coming to the surface in my thoughts, the riots during the Chicago Democratic Convention exploded. Young people like me who were against the Vietnam War were getting their heads busted protesting the war. I realized we were all fighting the Vietnam War, whether we were doing it in the rice paddies of Southeast Asia or the streets of America. I had to change my life.

So I understood that this return to Nashville was a time for reinvention. The expiration of my contract with Monument freed me to record for Fred's Nugget Records, but we were also anxious to record my "new voice" so that we could analyze the full impact of the surgery and recovery. I was also very excited to work creatively with Fred. "Bridge Over Troubled Water" was soaring up the charts and he was hot and in demand. He used the opportunity to launch his label, and started booking his studio in Goodlettsville. On a Sunday evening we sat on his sofa and decided that my first single for Nugget should mark my departure from country music and that we would go after a pop audience. With that thought—and the evening news—in mind, Fred cobbled together a song called "The World Is Turning On." The session went smoothly the next day and we recorded "World" and a terrific B-side tune of Fred's titled "Why Do I Love You?" We also cut another of Fred's songs titled "A Mood I Was In" and a Ralph Welsh song titled "The Shelter of My Mind." Within days "The World Is Turning On" single was shipped to American radio stations, and Fred promptly negotiated a distribution deal in the United Kingdom with London-based EMI subsidiary Beacon Records. Although it immediately floundered in America, the record quickly hit the charts in England. The record's success brought exciting requests for me to come to England to tour in support of the record, but we knew my draft board would not allow it. Still, Fred was eager to break the record in the UK and he came up with a bold plan: if I couldn't physically go to England, then he would send me via videotape. He booked a television studio in Nashville and set up a two-camera shoot: one to tape a lip-synced performance of me singing with the record, the other to pan several easels of photographs of demonstrations, riots, music festivals, and major events of the late 1960s on poster board. This allowed Fred to edit the two cameras into one videotape—essentially creating a crude prototype of what would be known a decade later as a "music video." Within hours of completing the taping, Fred shipped a copy to London. Then, armed with his new "tool," he came up with another tactic: he shipped ten copies of the video to friends who worked at various television stations in small southern cities. Each tape had an accompanying letter that referred to the contents as a "chain video"—the analogy to the "chain-letter obligation" being to air the video once on your station and then send it to a colleague in the television business with a similar challenge.

The scheme was successful. The record continued to climb the charts in England and Fred's tactic also rejuvenated it in several markets in the Deep South even while I was teaching art in North Louisiana. And I was discovering that I loved teaching. Aside from a reputation as an easy class for over-privileged middle-class children, high school art classes are also noted as a last resort for psychologically challenged kids clinging to the school system by a fingernail to avoid entering the ranks of the penal system. I had my share of these types, but my classes were generally filled with kids wanting to study art with the guy they heard singing on the radio. Only twenty-three, I wasn't much older than most of the kids. I enjoyed their company and, having come from such a tiny town myself, I was well aware that I would likely introduce many of them to an aesthetic perspective of life.

My first assignment as an art teacher at West Monroe High School was teaching drawing and calligraphy. In order to differentiate the kids who were sincerely interested in art from the celebrity-curious students enrolling in my class, I assigned each student one hundred drawings a week of any subject matter he or she might choose. The students initially whined at being forced to draw so much, but those who were genuinely interested in art soon found their abilities expanding quickly and were inspired to draw even more. By mid-semester my art classes were humming with creative energy.

Despite the satisfaction I was experiencing in teaching school, the time bomb ticking inside me could not be defused. Writing songs during the vocal fast, and the return of my singing voice, had broken down internal walls. Suddenly tunes were pouring out of me—songs unrelated to western history. It was not unusual for me to write three songs in a day. This creative burst of energy only added to my frustrated feelings of being held captive in an invisible prison. I knew I had to record my own songs to free myself from the dangerous cycle that had nearly cost my voice. Silence had forced me to grapple with internal demons, and wrestling a few of them to the ground had made me aware I had to seek out what imprisoned me and break free.

The greatest of my shackles broke when the government announced the lottery system of selective service. Excluding the most unusual circumstances, there would be no more deferments. Once a year all eligible men would be drafted from 365 numbers, drawn and matched by chance with equally random birth dates. Then, beginning at one and going through 365, the military would draft from the numbers. When the yearly quota of conscription was reached, the draft would end for that year at that number/birthday. If a young man spent a full year in the lottery pool and was not drafted, he was no longer eligible to be drafted—ever. My birthday matched number 353, making it virtually impossible for me to be drafted before the yearly quota was reached.

EIGHT

Scale

SOON AFTER "THE WORLD IS TURNING ON" charted in England, Simon and Garfunkel arrived in Nashville, bringing to Fred Carter a gold record acknowledging his performance on *Bridge Over Troubled Water*. The pair was at the pinnacle of their phenomenal career. Their recordings enjoyed extraordinary sales and international acclaim, but in 1970 *Bridge Over Troubled Water* became the biggest-selling album in the history of charted recordings and made them the major American competitors of the Beatles. To be sure, other legendary American acts also sold millions of records during the so-called Golden Age of Rock, but Simon and Garfunkel were the Beatles' only American rivals as recording scientists, sonic explorers, songwriters, and marketers. Dylan may have introduced John Lennon to marijuana and, in doing so, influenced the songwriting and cultural impact of the Beatles, but Simon and Lennon exchanged lyrical "koo-koo-ka-choos" and "goo-goo-goo-joobs" between "Mrs. Robinson" and "The Walrus."

Everyone who visited Nashville in those days wanted to meet Chet Atkins, and "the boys," as Fred called them, were no different. Aside from Chet, however, Paul and Artie requested a meeting with Mother Maybelle Carter (no relation to Fred), Johnny Cash, and Harlan Howard. Mother Maybelle was a true taproot of American folk music, and her son-in-law Johnny Cash was without a doubt the century's most important link between folk and country music. It was also natural that the boys would want to meet the man that many considered to be the greatest living country songwriter, Harlan Howard. Everyone assumed that Simon and Garfunkel, in requesting an audience with Mother Maybelle Carter, were considering a return to their roots with a project featuring traditional folk or bluegrass music as a follow-up to *Bridge Over Troubled Water*. But the reason for Simon and Garfunkel's being in Nashville was much simpler: they were on vacation. Art's girlfriend and Paul's new wife were both from Tennessee. Artie had already slipped into town with his girlfriend, so Fred asked Chet to accompany us to the airport to greet Paul's flight.

The day would have been magic if only for the opportunity to observe Fred Carter Jr. and Chet Atkins. Both were guitar masters, wizard session musicians, and pioneer recording scientists. Each had razor-sharp intelligence and, like a spirited athlete, possessed a fiercely competitive will. They were both natural psychologists as well, perceptive, shrewd, and deceptively smooth. High-energy Fred brought a driving sexual rock-and-roll and boogie beat to the Nashville session pool, whereas laid-back Chet was rooted in clean country blues, bluegrass, and hillbilly music.

From my very first meeting with Fred Carter I thought his personality was similar to that of a champion athlete in mystical pursuit of a perpetually elusive personal best. Throughout my time in Nashville I accompanied Fred to countless recording sessions. Aside from providing me the opportunity to study his personality, these excursions enabled me to sit in the studio during recording sessions and observe the techniques of session musicians, technicians, and engineers, as well as many of the major country and folk artists of the era. After that first session with Billy Grammer, I was present with Fred at recording sessions of artists such as Tex Ritter, Ferlin Husky, Waylon Jennings, Jessi Colter, John Stewart, Ian and Sylvia, Steve Young, Tammy Wynette, Bobby Bare, George Hamilton IV, Don Williams, Alex Harvey, and Mel Tillis, as well as countless unknowns seeking the brass ring. So I was not surprised that Chet Atkins and Fred Carter possessed similar personality traits. Even so, like me, they were both more than a bit distracted by the arrival of Paul Simon. Chet waited in the Caddy while Fred and I went to the gate to greet the star.

Paul and his bride, Peggy, exited the plane hand in hand. They ignored the small crowd of whispering fans gathering around them at the baggage claim. I knew that Paul was tiny, but was surprised to see he was only five-four or five-five. His receding hairline, like mine, reflected impending baldness. Fred and I took charge of the Simons' bags; Paul signed a few auto-graphs and grabbed his guitars. Soon we loaded into the car. Paul and Peggy joined me in the backseat of the Caddy. Chet turned to face them.

"Welcome to Nashville," he drawled.

"I'm from Tennessee," Peggy drawled back. "I grew up here."

A crooked little smile appeared at the corner of Paul's mouth and his intelligent brown eyes twinkled.

"Why don't you bring this girl home more often, Paul?" Chet teased. "We have a few nice recording studios in town."

Simon's smile broke into a grin that spread over his face. He seemed to prefer to let the conversation focus on Peggy rather than him.

"He's a New York City boy," Peggy laughed, pleasantly deflecting Chet's remark.

The conversation between Peggy, Chet, and Fred drifted toward weath-er, the lovely Tennessee landscape, and fishing before Fred pulled into the parking lot of a restaurant and we all went inside. After a few autographs were signed for fans, we took a table in a dark corner and Chet renewed his interrogations.

"I noticed that you and Art used a producer on your first couple of records and then started producing your records yourself. What provoked that move?"

"Artie and I produced those records," Paul said softly. "Various individ-uals got cigarettes, sandwiches, sleeping cots, and so forth for us. They got producers credit doing those things, but Artie and I produced those records—and our engineer, Roy Halee."

Chet Atkins responded to Paul's answer as an A&R man: "Don't you worry about becoming too close to your material?"

"I mixed 'Mrs. Robinson' so many times that Artie and Roy accused me of turning it into a minor religion. But it was a risk I was willing to take as an artist."

"Have you considered producing other artists?"

"If they need a producer they're not ready to record."

Paul words triggered the hard-won awareness I had gained as a painter. His remarks immediately forced me to take a clear look at the direction I had allowed my musical career to take in Nashville. Fred Carter was my producer; he decided what songs I would record and how we would record them. Dear friends as well as collaborators, we were a superb creative team. Our musical tastes and vision were united, and we rarely disagreed in our approach to making records, or to life in general. Still, Paul's response to Chet forced me to ask myself why I was not as concerned with creative autonomy in the recording studio as I would be when I was standing before an easel.

Nevertheless, from the beginning Fred approached our studio relationship as a teacher collaboratively training me to produce myself. So aside from creative loyalties to him, asking myself about creative autonomy in the recording studio provoked me to address an even deeper problem. Combined with the pressure of the draft finally having been lifted, Paul's responses to Chet forced me to view my life from a different perspective. My marriage, teaching, recording career, and band, my entire life—it was all out of balance. The embarrassing George Jones encounter had made me realize the need to play guitar on my recording sessions, and my bout with vocal polyps made me profoundly aware that spiritual imbalances would eventually lead to health problems. Now, Paul's responses to Chet Atkins's questions suddenly revealed a new importance concerning artistic equilibrium—scale—and its links with my personal life. My thoughts about proportion and balance were running wild when we left Paul and Peggy in the lobby of the King of the Road Hotel and headed for the restaurant to meet Art Garfunkel.

The cavernous dining room was a sea of starched-white-tablecloth-covered, place-set rectangles. Alone, angelic Art Garfunkel sat at the edge of the room's shadows, illuminated in the soft light from a wall of plate-glass windows that overlooked the hotel pool. Artie held a framed gold record under his arm. The record caught flickering light reflected from the pool and ricocheted a rainbow into the shadows on the opposite walls of the dark room. Like Paul, Artie was smaller than I'd expected. About my height, he was taller than his partner, but still short, with a halo of frizzed blond hair surrounding the crown of his balding head. He proved as delightfully eccentric in person as he appeared to be in photographs and movies. We sat at his table and were talking about Nashville architecture when Paul joined us.

When Artie and Paul reunited they momentarily spoke amongst themselves in code as if Fred and I were not there. Then suddenly, with heartfelt words reminiscing about tender or funny moments during various recording sessions and live performances, they shifted the focus to Fred. Artie recalled how their devoted folk audiences sometimes booed Fred and the other musicians—Joe Osborn, Hal Blaine, and Larry Knechtel—when they came onstage after the duo's opening set accompanied only by Paul's guitar.

Fred interrupted Artie, turned to me, and explained, "You have to understand that performing for Simon and Garfunkel's audiences was more like performing in a church service than a concert. During the first act the audiences sang along with Paul and Artie in quiet, reverent tones, aware of minute details in every song. When the musicians came onstage for the second act, it was like an intrusion into that special, private moment for them."

Then Paul explained how either he or Artie would remind the audience that these fellows were the musicians who played on their recordings. After a bit more praise of the band from the boys, the audience would gradually "accept" the other musicians.

Then Artie spoke for the pair and told Fred how important his guitar playing had been to their career and gave him the gold record. Moments later, when the mood shifted again to small talk, Paul asked Artie how his "stroll" was going. I was surprised to learn that Art Garfunkel was literally walking across America. He was fond of walking blue highways, singing to himself while mathematically measuring his stride. Whenever he had a break from touring, recording, moviemaking, or attending graduate school in mathematics and architecture, Art would continue the walk. With peripatetic precision, he returned to the exact location where the previous walk had ended and started walking again. With years of such treks, he was gradually crossing the continent.

Later, when I commented to Fred how Simon and Garfunkel's financial prosperity allowed them such extraordinary freedom, he was quick to remind me that "the boys" had earned their success. He told me that Paul and Artie had been obsessed with musical purity and perfection since childhood. Like me, Paul was first influenced by Elvis, but soon after he and Artie formed their duo they began emulating their idols, the Everly Brothers. Paul and Artie would run home each day from junior high and sit on straight-backed chairs within inches of each other's faces so they could shape their mouths to create precise musical enunciation and harmony. Along the way they gradually developed a fundamental knowledge of early recording technology using crude home tape recorders to teach themselves how to overdub so they could study the blend of their voices. During this time, seeking industry connections, Paul also walked the halls of the songwriting mecca of modern pop music—New York's Brill Building. All that effort paid off; dubbing themselves Tom and Jerry, they cut their first national hit, "Hey, Schoolgirl," as teenagers.

After a while the four of us met Peggy in the lobby of the King of the Road, then climbed into the Cadillac and headed to Goodlettsville. When Paul and Artie saw the basketball goal in Fred's massive driveway, they challenged Fred and me to a game of H.O.R.S.E. These guys seemed to be good at everything; they promptly whipped us.

Unfortunately, neither Mother Maybelle nor her son-in-law, "the Man in Black," could attend the gathering. Nevertheless, Harlan Howard arrived early and immediately engaged Paul and Artie in casual conversation that quickly led to pulling out guitars. Within moments, songs were bouncing around the room. Hearing Paul Simon and Art Garfunkel harmonize in the intimacy of Fred Carter's living room was surely one of the most magic moments of my life. When my turn came, Fred accompanied me and I sang "Morgan City."

The evening flew by. Art declined, but Paul and Peggy accepted Fred's offer of a fishing trip at Center Hill Reservoir. Harlan Howard also agreed to meet us at noon the next day at the lake. I rode with Fred to drive the boys and Peggy back to the King of the Road. On the return trip to Goodlettsville I asked Fred what it was like working on a Simon and Garfunkel recording session.

"I was in the studio for a week on 'The Boxer' alone," Fred replied. "They asked me to play 'The Boxer' as a bluegrass piece, a country piece, a rock-and-roll piece, and so forth. Imagine a week of playing one song over and over and creating a different stylistic approach to the tune each time you play it."

The idea of recording one song in several styles made me start thinking about how many times I had approached a painting with a particular idea in mind that evolved into several others before completion. We were silent for the rest of the drive home, but you could hear wheels turning.

The next morning Paul began to relax and open up a bit as we drove to Center Hill Reservoir. It was particularly educational to listen to the radio with Paul and hear him analyze various records. I was especially impressed with the range of his knowledge of the history of recorded music; his awareness of historical nuance and the influences of the most obscure artists in all genres was outstanding. On the way to Center Hill Fred stopped to give Paul and Peggy a tour of Nugget. I sat with Peggy and Paul on the stairs that descended to the studio while Fred walked around the room explaining his studio design and talking about his plans to build a marble echo chamber.

Paul explained he had no desire to own a recording studio. Instead, he said, he preferred freedom of movement, sampling the diversity of different regional sounds and musicians. Obviously, Fred did not share that opinion. Nugget represented artistic freedom to Fred. He would do his exploration there in the Tennessee hill country.

Fred took a phone call, so I mustered the courage to ask Paul to critique one of my songs. I grabbed a guitar and jumped in, but after I had sung only a few bars of the tune, Paul interrupted and hummed the completion of my melody without the benefit of first hearing it.

"With all respect," he apologized, "your melody is predictable. That works in some cases, but I prefer to be surprised by a melody."

I didn't even bother to ask about lyrics. Paul's criticism of my melody was bull's-eye accurate and, ultimately, kind. His evaluation of my song exposed something I already knew was true. Even though I remained loosely engaged with the conversation in the car, I pondered Paul's critique throughout our drive to Center Hill Reservoir.

As promised, Harlan Howard was waiting for us. When he invited me to join them, I was delighted to learn that I was going to spend the afternoon fishing in the boat with Paul, Peggy, and Harlan. We loaded into Harlan's well-appointed fishing boat, and he pulled the outboard motor to a roar and headed across the huge lake toward his favorite fishing hole. Fred agreed to meet us there in an hour.

As always, Center Hill Reservoir was lovely. Deep forests descended from rolling mountaintops and embraced the rocky, blue-black, serpentine shoreline. The afternoon sun lowered to an angle, and a slight chill greeted us toward the middle of the lake. Harlan killed the outboard motor and started his quieter trolling motor as he approached a deep canyon. Soon we were casting our lines among the rocks along the canyon's banks, fishing for smallmouth bass. Within moments Paul reeled in a nice-size fish. He was as excited as a twelve-year-old boy, and Peggy was nearly as thrilled as her husband. After removing the hooks from the fish's mouth, Paul released it back into the black water. We fished a while longer before Harlan banked the boat at the shoreline and we got out. I started a small fire and we sat and warmed ourselves.

Fred appeared at the entrance to the canyon, and within moments docked his boat beside Harlan's. The two engaged in a conversation, so I gathered my courage and blurted out one last question for Paul:

"What exactly did you mean when you told Chet you are 'un-producible'?"

"Exactly what I said. I'm the only person who knows how to produce my recordings of my songs."

Meeting Simon and Garfunkel made me aware that my musical ambitions were leading away from Nashville, but I was also increasingly aware that my life was changing quickly now. After the completion of a year with a 1-A classification in the selective service lottery pool, I was no longer eligible to be drafted. I decided to quit my teaching job at the end of the school year in order to focus completely on writing and recording my original music. Diana was not happy when I explained I was going to return to Tennessee to spend my holiday break recording rather than driving to Chicago for Christmas with her family.

For the first time since I had arrived in Nashville, the Christmas sessions were specifically for making demonstration recordings of my growing catalog of original tunes. In the past I had made demonstration tapes of my songs one or two tunes at a time. Now, however, songs were pouring out of me so fast I had filled a couple of ring-bound notebooks with lyrics and chord changes.

Even with the dramatic increase in my songwriting productivity I remained perplexed with the structure of the work I was now calling *Seekers of the Fleece*. With the composition of three songs depicting the historical concept, I was beginning to realize that I could use the popular-song structure to my advantage; employing the structure of the three-minute commercial song that I had learned from Fred, I could link the lyrics of the song with the historical context of the narrative epic poetry. Moreover, I could structure the songs so that they could be separated from the historical context of the masterwork to stand by themselves as contemporary compositions. But the matter of the time span of the work was still extremely problematic. Neihardt needed three vast, richly detailed epic poems to chronicle the fur trade. How could I accomplish a similar musical feat without having to ask an audience to sit for several hours while I performed it? The old matter of audience attention span arose again.

One night while I was watching a movie on television the simple thought occurred to me that Americans regularly sat for two-hour films broken into precise sections in order to wedge in advertising. The "destruction" of our attention span wasn't caused by television; instead, it was attributable to the commercials that constantly interrupted our concentration and shifted our focus. Moreover, the two-hour movie wasn't the only part of the television experience that was separated into meticulously timed sections; advertising itself was broken into specifically timed sections—ten seconds, thirty seconds, sixty seconds, and so forth. I began to wonder if perhaps I couldn't incorporate that kind of timing in the narrative flow of my story and make it work for rather than against me. I began to consider creating a shift in the poetic and musical narrative at timed intervals similar to those of the commercials during a television movie. Then I realized I could learn a lot about this art form through a visit to an advertising agency.

Within a few days I walked into the Dave McCormick and Associates advertising agency in Monroe and was surprised to discover that an old buddy from college was the head of the art department. Reggie Geiss was a wild man, but a gifted painter. He was the type who might work for weeks on a painting, become suddenly frustrated, and impulsively take a mat knife and rip it to shreds. But if a painting survived his rage, it would be a fantastic one. Meeting my old friend from art school, now a commercial artist, I wondered if I might not be able to fit in at McCormick and Associates myself.

Dave McCormick was an all-American football player at Louisiana State University before signing a huge contract with the San Francisco 49ers. After the end of his second pro season, he was traded to the New Orleans Saints, and after a single season in the Crescent City he ended his professional football career and returned to his North Louisiana roots. Monroe welcomed Dave and his classy advertising agency with open arms. Everyone was proud that Dave, from nearby Rayville, had done well in the NFL, and within a few weeks he was showered with new business accounts.

Dave was aware of my success with records, and our friendship struck a rich chord the moment I walked into his office. He was a handsome, dapper man with dark brown hair worn over his ears, Elvis-like sideburns, strong jaw and chin, straight nose, and a rich baritone voice. He was also huge—six-foot-six and a lean 275 pounds. A genuinely gregarious person, he was clever, charming, and could sell a beer and a dance card to a Baptist preacher. He was from a dirt-poor family and he'd recognized that football was his ticket. He graduated from Rayville High with a football scholarship to Louisiana State University. From the beginning of his collegiate football career, Dave planned to win offers from the pros. So he majored in business to prepare to capitalize on the opportunities that he hoped would eventually come from the NFL. After a championship 1965 season and an extraordinary performance in the 1966 Sugar Bowl on national television, Dave received the offers that he'd anticipated and negotiated his own lucrative contract. After only three years in the NFL, though, Dave had suffered injuries that left him unable to continue as an athlete, so he retired from professional football with a sizable nest egg and opened his advertising agency.

So we had both returned to our North Louisiana roots after a brief experience with the pros. But the competitive, ambitious fire still burned in our hearts. I told Dave I wanted to learn about advertising.

"Well, you've come to the right place, bro," he laughed. "I've just spent a small fortune so that I can learn about it myself!"

We chatted about football and records for a few moments, and I told him more about my desire to learn about the inner workings of television advertising. Within a few days I received a call from Dave to write my first jingle. It was for Buccaneer Slacks. I wrote the jingle in five minutes and they paid me with twenty colorful pairs of pants. A month later the jingle won a regional ADDY Award.

While I continued teaching school, I was soon hired on a regular basis to write and produce thirty- and sixty-second jingles for McCormick and Associates. Equally important, Dave had established a relationship with an award-winning regional filmmaking firm based in Little Rock. Rodney Dungan and his partner, Willie Allen, produced 16mm film commercials and documentaries, and the successful affiliation that Dave forged between his agency and their team would provide me with the opportunity to learn how to score films—a job exactly in scale with the level of my writing skills. Even more important, writing for film presented a new way to hone my songwriting and editing skills and would certainly help me with the "cinematic" structure of the western piece I was creating.

Over the next few months I was in Little Rock as often as Monroe. Rodney Dungan and I worked so well together that he soon wrote me into his contracts as "inspiration" for location shoots so I could play my guitar and noodle out a song while he rolled film. Once again I found myself hiking through the pastures and river hills of North Louisiana and the Arkansas Ozark Mountains—this time with an eccentric commercial photographer who used my music to awaken his heart and eye. I thoroughly enjoyed the entire process of writing music for films, as it provided the opportunity to explore small regional recording studios—again in perfect scale to my level of skills. Rodney's and Dave's expert salesmanship and their knowledge of the fundamentals of advertising trained my ear and eye to focus on the commercial and artistic solution to creating a piece that would tug the heart-strings of the coldest banker and make him happy to pay for his advertising.

While my exploration of advertising continued, I also started doing some perfunctory research into the Bridger family genealogy and expanded my research into the life of Jim Bridger, the fur trade era, and the American Indian history of the West. After months of research I discovered a genealogical link from Isle of Wight, Virginia, to Ash County, North Carolina, that appeared to connect Jim with my family in North Louisiana. While I was in this phase of the research, however, it occurred to me that Jim Bridger spent his entire adult life living with Indian people; all his wives were Indian, and all his children were half-Indian. Thinking about this, I gradually came to realize that American history is as much an Indian story as it is a Euro-American story; it became increasingly important that I write something from an Indian perspective as well as from a non-Indian perspective.

I returned to the work of John G. Neihardt with renewed obsession. Most of my Neihardt research continued to be focused on *A Cycle of the West*, but now I dug deeper into his larger body of work. The poet's brilliant telling of the life of Sioux holy man Black Elk was well known to aficionados of western literature, but had not yet attained the international acclaim it would reach in only a few short years. After devouring *Black Elk Speaks*, I turned to Neihardt's *When the Tree Flowered*, a book that would become my favorite depiction of American Indian culture. Neihardt's remarkable stories of the way of life of the Sioux before the coming of Europeans opened my eyes to a new perspective of Indian life. In movies and television shows American Indians were depicted two-dimensionally—as noble or savage. After reading *Black Elk Speaks* and *When the Tree Flowered* I would never see Indians or their culture so simply again. Soon after reading *When the Tree Flowered*, however, I found a book by Vine Deloria Jr. with the intriguing title *Custer Died for Your Sins: An Indian Manifesto*. This book simultaneously grabbed me by the heart and throat and brought forth tears, laughter, and anger. These three books initiated a flurry of research into Indian America, and together they served to unite my thoughts around the concept that would soon evolve into my second epic ballad, *Lakota*.

As my research into the history of the American West was blossoming, my marriage was disintegrating. As I disappeared into my increasingly full creative life, Diana retreated into religion. What little time I was home alone with her was spent in either grumpy silence or argument. We decided to find a counselor. I canceled the Christmas demo sessions in Nashville to continue counseling sessions with Diana and to visit her parents in Chicago for the holidays. But after only a few sessions with the counselor we both realized our marriage was over.

Before the marriage counseling sessions began I had become ensnared in Louisiana's first blundering attempt to integrate its school system. In a last-gasp, recalcitrant, "Jim Crow" effort to prevent the races from actually attending classes together, the Louisiana Department of Education swapped teachers from a school of one race with those from a school of another; the art teacher at all-black Richwood High School was assigned my classes at all-white West Monroe High, and I was assigned his class at Richwood.

I enjoyed teaching at Richwood as the only non-black on campus, but I had already decided that as soon as my contract with the Ouachita Parish School Board expired I was going to quit teaching school to devote my full attention to music. The lottery had freed me from the shroud of Vietnam, but my failing marriage was stumbling toward a confusing entanglement with Louisiana's strange French Napoleonic law. Because of the Catholic Church's conservative attitude concerning marriage, Diana and I attempt-ed to divorce and discovered we had to complete a year-long period of legal separation before we could officially end our failed marriage.

So I was trapped in this emotional and legal briar patch when I met Glo-ria Johnson. She was teaching English at Louisiana Tech University in near-by Ruston, and I was ending my teaching career at Richwood High and working for Dave McCormick. Gloria was a stunningly beautiful woman with brains to match her physical charms. She had been "Miss O.U." at the University of Oklahoma before attending Smith College, where she earned her master's degree. Six years older than me, she was married to Dick John-son, a drinking buddy of Dave McCormick's who managed Monroe's Montgomery Ward store. She and Dick had two young children, eight-year-old Jennifer and six-year-old Jeffrey.

Like me, she was snagged on marital thorns. Like my marriage to Diana, her marriage had essentially ended. She and Dick had tried staying togeth-er for the sake of their children, but decided that wasn't working. When the semester at Louisiana Tech ended that spring, Gloria planned to leave Dick and relocate to Austin, Texas, to attend the University of Texas and com-plete her doctorate.

Dave McCormick arranged a springtime camping trip for his staff and some clients. Diana refused to go with me, so I went by myself. The minute

Gloria and I set eyes on each other the fire ignited. But our chemistry first manifested itself through the affinity for literature we shared. Since my first reading of Herman Melville's classic *Moby-Dick* as a teenager, I'd decided to return to it regularly for repeated readings. Coincidentally, I was reading *Moby-Dick* at the time we met, and I was surprised to learn that Gloria's master's thesis was on Melville's recondite masterpiece *Pierre: or, The Ambiguities*. So we spent the entire evening at the campfire talking about literature while the rest of the group drank beer, smoked pot, and howled the night away. Gloria immediately understood my fascination with John Neihardt's epic poetry and my obsession to create a form that would allow me to sing the great story of the migration across the North American continent. I was already in love with her, but I didn't know it yet.

Bridger in first mountain man costume. Los Angeles, circa 1972. Photo by Slim Pickens. Bridger archives.

*Bridger and Slim
Pickens.
Wimberley, Texas,
'73. Photo by
Wally Pryor.
Bridger archives.*

Bridger's father and mother, Hill and Roberta. Gillette, Wyoming, 1944. Bridger archives.

Roberta, Bobby, and Hill. Columbia, Louisiana, 1948. Bridger archives.

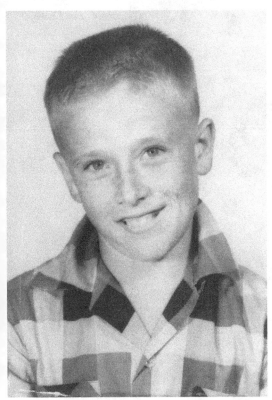

Bobby, 1956. Bridger archives.

Bobby on McCall Comes Calling, *1963. Bridger archives.*

*Bobby and Diana.
Caldwell Parish Art
Festival, Columbia,
Louisiana, 1965.
Bridger archives.*

Fred Carter and Bobby Bridger. Little Rock, Arkansas, 1967. Photo by Jerry Mehl. Bridger archives.

Louisiana Sun, Monroe, Louisiana, 1967. (Bobby's brother Hill is at far right.) Photo by Jerry Mehl. Bridger archives.

English promotion ad, 1969. "The World Is Turning On."

Bobby and Gloria. Willie Nelson's Dripping Springs Reunion, 1972. Photo by Barry Everett. Bridger archives.

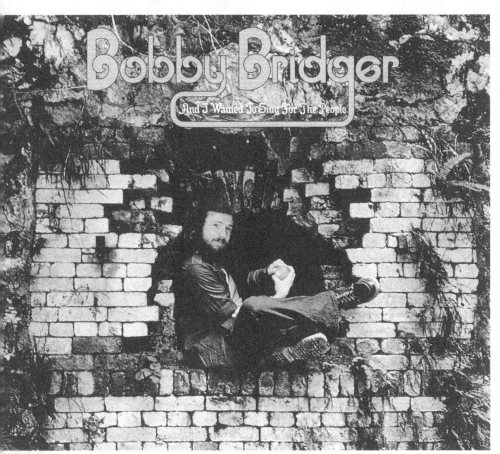

nd I Wanted to Sing for the People *album cover, 1973.*

*Slim Pickens and Timberjack Joe.
Seekers of the Fleece recording
session. Denver, Colorado, 1975.
Photo by Gloria Gannaway.
Bridger archives.*

Timberjack Joe. Wyoming, 1975. Bridger archives.

Bridger, Timberjack Joe, and Vine Deloria Jr. Golden, Colorado, 1976. Photo by Gary P. Nunn. Bridger archives.

Bridger climbing during Desert Dance. Chihuahuan Desert, Mexico, 1978. Photo by Autumn Prebble. Bridger archives.

Bridger in coyote headdress. Austin, circa 1980. Photo by Arianna Vincent. Bridger archives.

Bridger as "the Drifter."
Shakespeare and the Indians.
Omaha, Nebraska, 1982.

Chris Sergel reading from his script Black Elk Speaks. *Wounded Knee, South Dakota, circa 1984. Photo by Bobby Bridger. Bridger archives.*

Bridger, in front of one of his paintings, 1983. Bridger archives.

First cast of A Ballad of the West, *1988. Cody, Wyoming.* Standing, left to right: *Daryl Watson, Wes Studi, Steven Fromholz, Melissa Tatum, and Bobby Bridger.* Kneeling, left to right: *Bill Ginn and Joe Sears. Photo by Jim Bama. Bridger archives.*

ridger and Leonard Marks. First Global Forum of Spiritual and Parliamentary Leaders on Human urvival. Christ Church, Oxford University, Oxford, England, 1988. Photo by Mary Bloom. Bridger rchives.

Pre—Show Mountain Man Demonstrations

Audiences attending **A Ballad of the West** are treated to a special pre-show demonstration of mountain man culture featuring **Dick Fish** and members of the Stinking Water Free Trappers of Cody. A favorite with children, Dick Fish loads and fires a Hawken Rifle, and presents a "close-up" look at a "modern-day" mountain man.

LIVE BAND 15 ACTORS AND SINGERS

(A must-see before or after your trip into Yellowstone.)

Ballad of the West *promo brochure, 1990.*

Melissa, Gabriel, and Bobby. Cody, Wyoming, 1990. Photo by Dewey Vanderhoff. Bridger archives.

Omaha, 1985. 48" × 48". Enamel and oils on plywood. Collection of Billie Lee Mommer.

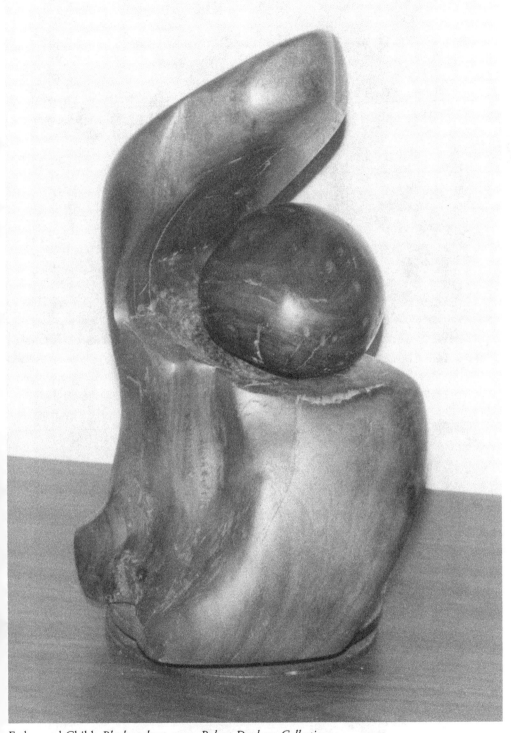

Father and Child. *Black walnut. 1974. Robert Durham Collection.*

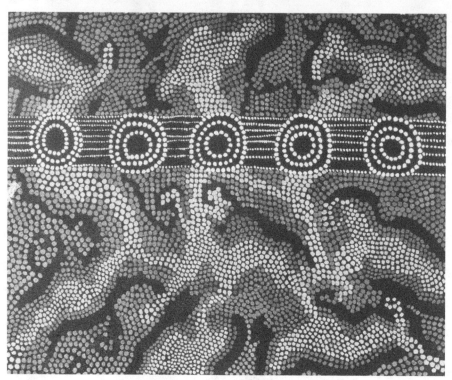

Southern Cross. *24" × 18." Acrylic on canvas. Collection of Leonard Marks.*

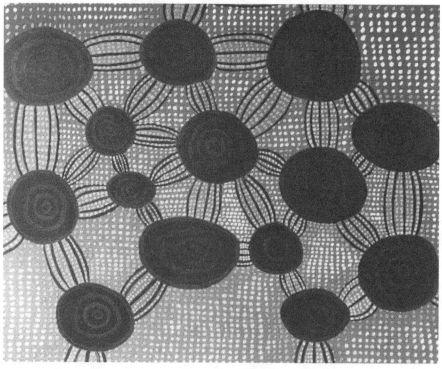

Cactus Dreaming. *24" × 18." Acrylic on canvas. Collection of Billie Lee Mommer.*

NINE

Merging of Our Minds

Billboard Magazine
Special Merit Picks
Bobby Bridger—*Merging of Our Minds*, RCA, LPS 4792
Debut LP for the singer/songwriter is a fine one, displaying a cross
between folk, country, and rock. As well as Bridger's singing and writing capabilities, he shows skill as a producer and fine musicianship is
shown throughout by the likes of Pete Drake. Standouts include the
title cut, "Grandpa," "Sharing's Just Another Word For Love," and
"Sea Chanty," a seven-minute sailor's tale. Bridger is a fine storyteller
and this set should appeal to all music fans.

NOW THAT I WAS FINALLY FREE to pursue music, my path was
most certainly away from North Louisiana and my failed marriage. Gloria suggested that Austin was a progressive college
town and I might find an audience there. I briefly entertained the idea of
moving to Texas with her, but continued to believe my future was in one of
America's major recording centers. We were in love, but also aware that we
had only recently emerged from painful, confining marriages. We struggled
to reconcile our emotions with career aspirations, but both of us pragmatically realized that following our dreams was of primary importance, and
we supported each other's desire to move forward unrestricted.

Toward that end, Gloria continued with her plans to relocate to Austin,
while Dave McCormick introduced me to a group of businessmen eager to

invest in an album project of my original songs. With my financial backing in place, I was soon swept up in the process of producing the recording that I would eventually title *Merging of Our Minds*. I called Fred Carter to make arrangements to record at Nugget in March. From the beginning of our relationship Fred and I had discussed the day when I would take control of my recordings. I don't think either of us expected it to arrive so soon.

"I think it's time I produced my recordings," I said bluntly to Fred over the phone.

"We've talked about this day ever since I bought Nugget," Fred said after a brief silence. "I'll help any way I can. You just produce a great record."

"Can you help me find some young pickers?" I asked. "You know, creative guys with ideas different from the Nashville formula."

"Let's do it!" Fred replied.

To set the record straight, even though major-label politics eventually gave me sole producer's credit on the album jacket, Fred Carter and I coproduced *Merging of Our Minds*. Fred generously realized that the project was my "graduation" exercise in record production and eagerly enlisted a diverse group of musicians and technicians to assist me.

To begin, Fred asked Jesse Tharp to engineer the sessions. Jesse had been the bassist in Roy Orbison's band during Fred's tenure, so I knew I could trust his ears. From Tracy Nelson's funky band, Mother Earth, on drums and keyboards, respectively, Fred enlisted Karl Himmel and Andy McMahon. Bobby Goldsboro's bassist Steve Schafer, guitarist John Pell, keyboardist Dennis Burnside, and his brother, saxophonist Terry "Fatback" Burnside, rounded out the group and formed a tight session band. Aside from Fred, there was only one star Nashville picker on the session—master pedal steel and slide guitar player Pete Drake. Drake was a small, thin man with a slicked-back blond "ducktail" hairdo befitting his name. Early in his career in Atlanta, Drake had formed a band with Jerry Reed, Joe South, Doug Kershaw, Jack Greene, and Roger Miller—each destined to become a major star. It's difficult to believe a group with such talented musicians failed, but it did. After the band imploded, Miller fled to Nashville and Drake soon followed. Before long, all the remaining former "Drake band" members followed Miller and Drake to Music City.

Shortly after arriving in Nashville, Pete began experimenting with the guitar to develop a speaking procedure for people who had lost their vocal cords, and he went on to pioneer the "talking" steel guitar. Pete's technique first appeared on his 1964 release of *For Pete's Sake* and its million-selling

single, "Forever." The recording soared to the top of the pop charts, attract-
ing the attention of Elvis and other major pop stars. When Pete worked on
Dylan's *John Wesley Hardin*, *Nashville Skyline*, and *Self-Portrait* albums in
the late 1960s, the evolution of folk-rock to folk-country-rock began in
earnest.[1] Former Beatle George Harrison discovered Pete's work on the
Dylan albums and flew him to England to play on his deeply spiritual
debut solo album *All Things Must Pass*. My *Merging* sessions were Pete's first
after the stint with Harrison in England.

The *Merging* sessions went well from the start. The two veterans were
inspired by the kids' enthusiasm, and the hungry youngsters were eager to
impress the old pros. The resulting ensemble was united, creatively democratic, and, most important, into my songs. I was also in good voice, so we
recorded most of the album in first and second takes. Several days later I
started early in the morning and recorded vocal harmony overdubs. That
afternoon Fred overdubbed guitar, mandolin, and fiddle parts. Fred suggested that for my song "What I Want for You" I should use a "drum explosion" effect similar to the one Simon and Garfunkel created on "The
Boxer." The effect is achieved by striking a single "thud" beat on a bass
drum in rhythm with the song, double-tracking it to create a second beat—
now "thud-thud." Next, the second "thud"—itself an echo—is "placed" in
an echo chamber submerged in reverb. The result sounds like an explosion
echoing from the first "thud." It took several hours to accomplish the effect,
but the result was well worth the effort. The next morning we overdubbed
horn sections on several songs, and later that evening Don Tweedy came in
with sixteen fiddle players and lyrical string arrangements to overdub
orchestrations. *Merging of Our Minds* was recorded.

I flew home the day after we completed the string session, but the weeks
that followed were a blur of jetting back and forth between Monroe and
Nashville to mix *Merging*, working with Fred and Jesse until we were
exhausted and forced to rest. I had never mixed a record before and I finally understood the humor in Art Garfunkel and Roy Halee's fitting comment that Paul mixed "Mrs. Robinson" until it became a "minor religion."
Now, however, I was making offerings and praying at the altar of the sixteen-track mixing board. Using all ten fingers—plus all of an engineer's—
in a well-coordinated ensemble does indeed create an act of artistic genu-
flection. Adding to the mystical aspect of the experience, while mixing
Merging I learned that pushing myself beyond the point of normal fatigue
introduced a heightened, delightfully lucid, aurally focused dream state. In

early May, we finally had the first mixes of the album ready to present to label A&R men. After a week of presentations, however, every major record label in Nashville passed on *Merging of Our Minds*.

"We knew from the beginning this wasn't a Nashville album, Bobby," Fred said. "But I think Paul Simon's attorney, Michael Tannen, might be able to help you on the West Coast.[2] Give me a couple of weeks to contact him to see what he thinks. Also, it will be expensive, but I think you should make a dub of the sixteen-track master recording. If you make a dub, I'll send it to Roy Halee in San Francisco and ask him to do a mix for you."

In late May Gloria and I said our last good-byes and she left for Austin. After corresponding with Michael Tannen and arranging meetings with record executives, Dave McCormick and I flew to Los Angeles. It was very generous of Paul Simon, as a favor to Fred, to ask Michael Tannen to help me with connections in Los Angeles. It was even nicer for Tannen to help me pro bono. Fred suggested that we stay at the Ramada Inn on Sunset Boulevard because it was close to record label offices, and directly across the street was the Old World Restaurant, a favorite hangout of record people and movie stars. Over a two-day period we made presentations of *Merging* and, in rapid succession, were rejected by Warner Bros., Columbia, and RCA Records. Finally, we found a receptive underling at Capital Records who was interested in signing me, but said it would be several weeks before a new head of A&R assumed office and could evaluate my project. So Dave and I left tapes and promotional materials and returned to Louisiana.

Paul Simon's ability to predict my melody lines led me to reconsider my entire approach to songwriting. When I'd first arrived in Nashville, Fred had taught me several "open" tunings on the guitar. Around the time I met Simon I was beginning to explore tuning my guitar to the open E chord. In other words, instead of the standard E, B, G, D, A, E tuning of the strings, I tuned my guitar to an E chord; without using my left hand to push down strings, I could strum the instrument with my right hand and create the chord of E. Soon after meeting Paul, I tuned my 0021 Martin to E for a songwriting session and when I attempted standard chords and progressions, atypical major, minor, and suspended sounds suddenly chimed and charmed me. Simon's comment about being surprised by a melody was still fresh in my thoughts, and suddenly not knowing what chords I was playing in the new tuning, I was freed to go with any sound that I might discover. Fresh, interesting melodies began to gush forth from these unusual noodlings, and the burst of creative musical energy became the songs of *Merging of Our Minds*. But the new tuning also inspired me to return to the songs I had already composed for *Seekers of the Fleece* in order to use the new approach with them. Within days, the new tunings led me to write the songs that would complete Part One of my epic trilogy. "Free My Spirit, 'Fore My Spirit's Dead" was the first song written in the new tuning for *Seekers*; "Jedediah Smith," "I Had a Vision," "The Crawl," "Blackfeet," and "Free Me Like an Eagle Once Again" followed in rapid succession. Moreover, inspired by the evocative sounds of the open E tuning, I began working on musically underscoring the epic verse and began to link the narrative songs together with poetry in heroic couplets. Suddenly the linear, narrative "flow" of the epic ballad was taking shape.

All of this creative activity indicated that change was imminent. A major transition had already occurred, as Diana and I officially separated when I left for Nashville to record. My new advertising friend and college painting colleague Reggie Geiss leased an old two-story wood-frame house in Monroe, and I moved out of the apartment with Diana and rented a room from him. As soon as the basic *Merging* recording sessions ended in Tennessee I returned to Monroe and moved in.

Spring surrendered to summer, and by June 1971 I sat nervously by the phone waiting for a call from L.A. to determine the fate of my album and my future. By mid-June the call finally came. It wasn't a sure thing, but our contact at Capital Records suggested we fly to Hollywood immediately to discuss a possible contract. Dave and I caught a jet the next day. We were hardly checked into our rooms and unpacked before the bad news arrived: Capital Records had suddenly fired the A&R man who had brought us to L.A. for negotiations. His replacement politely reiterated that it was just "bad timing" and said the firing was an "in-house" matter that had nothing to do with me or my project. We were welcome to resubmit our tapes, but since our contact's firing was only part of a major shake-up in Capital's entire A&R department, he confided that a record deal was a long shot.

Dave McCormick would have headed to the nearest bar whether the news from Capital had been good or bad; now he sprinted to the Ramada Inn lounge. Being a teetotaler, I took a long walk on Sunset Boulevard to let it soak in that this setback probably meant the end of my career.

Three hours later I decided I should go to the lounge to check on Dave. I walked into the dark room from the bright sunshine and was momentarily blinded. When my eyes came into focus I could see there were only three people in the bar. A shapely young bartender was holding her own with her pair of happy patrons. There sat Dave and a stranger, arms linked over shoulders to keep each other from falling off the barstools.

"Bridger-over-troubled-waters!" Dave shouted as I entered the lounge. "Git yer ass over here an' meet mah nu bess fren'."

Dave's drinking buddy slid off the barstool and swayed toward me. Everything about him said "cowboy." He was dressed in a generic blue-plaid western shirt with pearl-snap buttons, jeans, and plain black needle-toed boots. His nose had been broken every way a nose can be broken and still be called a nose. A buoyant wave of brown hair danced over his fore-head like a backward question mark as he stood before me, hand extended in greeting. When I offered my hand in return, he took it in his, reared his head back, and released a loud, very enthusiastic howl.

"Bridger-over-troubled-waters," Dave slurred his introduction as he joined us, "meet Ole Max Evans. Ole Max is a movie director an' he wants ya ta sing in hish nu movie. A movie, bro! That'll show those assholes at Capital Records, huh?"

"Yer pardner tells me you can sing anything," the stranger interrupted. "'S'at true?"

I quickly realized Dave's new friend wasn't as drunk as he appeared. Whereas Dave was genuinely smashed, the stranger, though tipsy, was pre-tending to be more intoxicated than he actually was. This howling cowboy was humoring Big Dave while compassionately taking care of him. Sudden-ly I was quite fond of the stranger. Still, I was skeptical of meeting a film director during happy hour in an empty Sunset Boulevard bar in Holly-wood.

"I'm a singer," I answered coolly.

The stranger's countenance suddenly changed and he became woozy again.

"Well, git yer guitar an' sing us a song, ol' pard."

I figured I didn't have anything to lose. Capital's rejection of *Merging* had pronounced the end of my recording career anyway. There was some-thing poetically neo-noir about ending my career in a lounge on Sunset Boulevard. I spun on my boot heels.

"I'll get my guitar."

"Well, then, you've got tha gig!" Max blurted out. I spun again.

"But you haven't even heard me sing."

"Anyone with the balls to sing for a pair of drunks in the middle of the afternoon in a Hollywood bar can sing in my little ol' movie!"

In my wildest dreams I never would have believed he really was a film producer and director. But Max Evans was indeed a successful screenwriter, producer, and director. At the time of our meeting he had finished the editing of his first independent film and returned to L.A. from his home in Albuquerque, New Mexico, to complete the recording of the movie's theme and score. A famous pop singer had originally been hired by one of Max's associate producers to perform the film's theme song. Upon meeting the crooner, however, Max found the singer's personality insufferable. So he fired him, walked out of the meeting, and headed for the Ramada bar. Dave and I simultaneously stumbled into the same bar in shock from the fiasco at Capital Records and got ourselves involved in a feature film.

First and foremost a writer, Max Evans was the author of scores of novels. He took us to his room at the Ramada Inn and gave us copies of his latest books, *The Mountain of Gold* and a splendid story about an old cow, an ancient coyote, and a worn-out cowboy, titled *One-Eyed Sky*. That evening I read Ole Max's work and realized that fate had introduced me to a new friend who also happened to be a brilliant storyteller.

The following morning Dave and I met Ole Max at the Old World Restaurant. Within moments we'd arranged for me to stay in Los Angeles to work on the film. After breakfast Dave caught a cab to the airport, and Ole Max and I began a friendship that continues to this day.

"Now we've got to teach you this beautiful song 'Circle of Love,'" Ole Max said as Dave's cab sped away. "I'll arrange for you to move in with the composer, Martie Perkins, out in Malibu. She's a great gal an' you two will get along swell."

A talented songwriter, Martie had composed a beautifully lyrical theme for Max's movie. During the next few days I rehearsed "The Circle of Love," and Max regularly brought a cast of character actors by for visits. Within a short period of time I was enjoying hilarious poetic evenings with Max and his friends Denver Pyle and L. G. Jones, actors I had seen in scores of classic western films. I also learned that Max Evans was perhaps Sam Peckinpah's best friend and the legendary director had optioned Max's splendid modern western *The Hi-Lo Country* to develop as a feature film. During this time I also met the female lead in Max's movie, Slim and Maggie Pickens's lovely eldest daughter, Daryle Anne Lindley. The day I met

Daryle Anne I was shocked to learn that her father's real name was Louis Lindley. As a teenager in Northern California, Slim repeatedly sneaked away on weekends against his father's wishes to ride bulls in the rodeo. When he learned of his son's rodeo escapades Slim's father bellowed, "If ya become a bull rider ya might as well change yer name ta 'Slim Pickin's,' 'cause 'at's what you'll be earnin' tha resta yer life."

Slim Pickens quickly rose through the ranks of bull riders to become a champion. His career also took regular downward spirals when, like most bull riders, he was frequently injured. When slowly returning to bull riding, Slim started working as a clown or, as rodeo folks call them, "bullfighters." Bullfighting would become Slim's ticket to the movies. With repeated injuries, he became increasingly famous as a rodeo clown. One of Slim's most "over-the-top" acts involved his trick horse, Dear John. On Slim's command, Dear John would begin to buck and toss him off. Slim's job was to survive a comedic spill without getting hurt. When Stanley Kubrick heard about Slim's horse he couldn't resist the irony; he gave the name "Dear John" to the bomb beside the one that Slim rode to oblivion at the end of *Dr. Strangelove*.

"Why don't you play Daryle Anne that piece about the mountain men you been workin' on, Bobby?" Ole Max suggested.

The large orchestra that I sang with to record "The Circle of Love" dwarfed the orchestra I performed with in Nashville. The regular core ensemble of piano, two guitars, bass, and drums was present for the date, but also on hand were a kettledrum, a harp, an eight-voice choir, a complete brass and woodwind section, sixteen violins, four violas, and two cellos. The session went as smoothly as a summer breeze, and Max accepted my performance after only three passes with the orchestra. I had recorded my first feature film theme.

The day after the session, Ole Max took me out for a Mexican breakfast. Since we were eating alone I expected he wanted to discuss something big.

"I've got a proposal for you, kid. I'm gonna open *The Wheel* either in Denver or Austin. I've got Denver covered, but I need help in Austin. I wanna go after the college kids with this little film, and the University of Texas has more of 'em than just about any place on the damned ol' planet. If I give you five hundred dollars, will you go to Austin for a month or so and check out the scene there for me? You know, find the best place to open the film near the university campus; find out who runs the movie business in Austin? Whaddya think?"

I proceeded to tell him about Gloria and our painful decision to go our separate ways. With her in Austin it was next to impossible to ignore fate at work in my life. Ole Max just laughed and said, "Well, you'll have a place to stay while you're in Texas."

Before I left Malibu, Max also urged me to check out the Texas Film Commission in Austin. He had helped the state of New Mexico create the first film commission in the United States outside of New York and L.A., and he was curious how much the Texas version was patterned after what they had created in New Mexico.

I flew back to Louisiana to update Dave and my family on my impending Texas adventure and to pick up my old Volkswagen Squareback—which joined my 0021 Martin, a guitar amp, a box of oil paints, and two large rolls of canvas as my sole possessions after my divorce. I intended to return to Hollywood after a month in Austin exploring the scene for Ole Max and visiting Gloria.

I was eager to see Gloria, but also a bit afraid that things would not be the same between us after our decision to part. So, in order to delay our reunion a bit to prepare myself emotionally, en route to Austin I made a swing out of my way to Houston to thank an investor in the *Merging* album for his support. It was late August 1970 when I drove up Highway 71 from Houston and saw the famous University of Texas Tower for the first time on the Austin skyline. The image of that tower was indelibly imprinted in America's mind after sniper Charles Whitman's mad rampage. That and the realization that albino blues guitarist Johnny Winter started his career there were about the only things I knew about Austin, Texas. Gloria's apartment was on East Riverside Drive, and she was standing in the parking lot waving for me as I drove down the busy street.

Gloria and I had not come to our decision to part ways lightly, and we were both a bit bewildered by the strange twist of fate that had reunited us. It had been heartrending and traumatic to completely release each other and separately embark upon new lives. Now, seeing each other again and suddenly discovering ourselves somehow magically together again, we surrendered to destiny.

A phantasmagoric migration of monarch butterflies welcomed me to

Austin. The entire town was inundated with magnificent orange-and-black patterns that floated and flitted in phenomenal flocks, draped themselves upon vegetation, buildings, and power lines, and generally enchanted the city. The butterfly migration metaphorically underscored the feeling that kismet had reunited me with Gloria in Austin. We felt that karma had plucked open the chrysalis of our previous existence and, like the butterflies, we were reborn in Austin. Only a couple of hours in this charmed new sphere and I wrote a song titled "Butterfly."

My first few days in Austin also convinced me I had finally found a community on a perfect scale with my talent and ambitions. There were thousands of people my age with similar worldviews. Hippies were everywhere—particularly in an area across from the University of Texas known as "the Drag," where street vendors—craftsmen and artists—sold everything from beads to bread, from beautiful handmade wooden boxes to macramé plant holders. *Lord of the Rings* mythology permeated the university-area shops, with names like the Hobbit Hole and Middle Earth. On the Drag, music and the scents of marijuana and patchouli oil mingled and drifted on the air. Beautiful women and men wore little clothing. I fell enchanted within the open, loving ambience of the town and never wanted to leave.

In spite of all the young bohemians, the first person I met in Austin was a cordial middle-aged Jewish businessman named Earl Podolnick. Mr. Podolnick owned a chain of movie theaters in Central Texas—most significantly, the Texas Theater, strategically located on the Drag across from the university. Mr. Podolnick greeted me warmly in his central Austin offices, and I was delighted to discover that he knew Max Evans from *The Rounders*. Within minutes, pending Max's approval, we negotiated a deal for *The Wheel* to premiere at the Texas Theater. Before I left his offices Mr. Podolnick suggested that I meet his son.

"Down on West Sixth Street my son Jay is refurbishing an old dry-cleaners shop into a recording studio," Mr. Podolnick said. "Who knows? Maybe you will do some recording while you are in town? Why don't you stop in and meet Jay?"

Jay Podolnick and I immediately became friends. The studio was far from being "flight-ready"; indeed, Jay was up to his elbows creating a state-of-the-art twenty-four-track recording studio from the ground up. His engineer, Steve Shields, was an irascible character, more eccentric professor than golden-eared aural scientist. Nevertheless, with my connections in

Nashville and Hollywood, finding a functional recording studio in Austin was not a matter of immediate importance. I had to honor another promise I'd made to Ole Max.

I found the offices of the Texas Film Commission perched on the top floor of the Penthouse Building on Lavaca. The entire Texas Film Commission was *one* person—a very bright young man named Warren Skaaren. A quiet, thoughtful Norwegian from Rochester, Minnesota, Warren had caught the attention of Texas governor Preston Smith when he was the student body president at Rice University in Houston. Inspired by the success of the New Mexico Film Commission that Max Evans had created in Albuquerque, Governor Smith hired young Warren to create and head the Texas Film Commission. Warren and his bride, Helen, soon relocated to West Lake Hills in Austin.

"You're exactly what this commission is all about," Warren said as soon as I explained my purpose in town with *The Wheel.* "My purpose here is to help you."

Yep. Austin was the place I had been looking for since I heard Elvis and picked up my dad's guitar.

TEN

A Hill on the Moon

A FTER THE WORLD PREMIERE of *The Wheel* in Austin, the film's small entourage headed to Denver. Rather than going along for the second gala opening, I decided to remain in Austin. Aside from the twist of fate that had reunited Gloria and me in Texas, I believed Austin was the artistic community I had long sought, and I wanted to continue creative explorations there. Still, I was pleased when Ole Max informed me that my performance of "The Circle of Love" was singled out for praise by Colorado film critics.

Praise was nice, but the money Ole Max paid me to explore Austin was almost gone, and I needed to hustle work. Gloria drew a meager salary from her teaching assistant's job in the Department of English at the University of Texas, and Dick helped her with minimal child support. I knew my experience with songwriting, record production, advertising, and documentary film scoring would help—especially with the tapes of *Merging*, and *The Wheel*'s theme to demonstrate my singing, songwriting, and production abilities. When I went back to Louisiana to inform my parents that I was moving to Austin, Dave McCormick also gave me an antique reel-to-reel tape recorder that I could use to demonstrate my work. It was quite unwieldy, nearly the size of a large fifties-era television set, but it would meet my needs. I searched the Yellow Pages for advertising agencies and film companies in Austin and started making calls.

There were five independent filmmakers in town. Richard Kidd and Fred Miller had production companies, while Gary Pickle, Ron Perryman,

and Tobe Hooper were partners in an outfit they called Motion Picture Productions of Texas. Perryman was a gifted cinematographer who worked regularly with Hooper. In the late 1960s Hooper wrote, produced, directed,
and distributed a splendid art film called *Eggshells*, while Gary Pickle
worked regularly filming athletic events for the University of Texas, and also
as a freelance cinematographer with Fred Miller, a former youth director at
Austin's First Baptist Church. Richard Kidd had major advertising accounts
in Austin, but his business was mostly focused in Dallas.

In the late 1960s Miller hired Hooper, Perryman, and Pickle to produce
a film about the legendary folk trio Peter, Paul, and Mary. Noel "Paul"
Stookey had become a born-again Christian, and as he became increasingly esoteric in his faith, he wished to retreat from the commercial record
business. So the group decided to end a long and influential career in American folk music. After the trio played Austin as part of what was billed as a
"swan song" tour, Stookey convinced his partners to perform an informal,
unpublicized concert for Fred Miller's church youth group. After the show
the enthusiastic youth director—with no previous experience in film—persuaded the trio to allow him to film what remained of the tour for their
archives. Fred also suggested that they market the finished product as a
video. Stunned when the group agreed, Miller brought Pickle, Hooper, and
Perryman in to produce *Peter, Paul and Mary: The Song Is Love*.[1]

I held a preliminary meeting with Miller to negotiate what would
become the first of numerous award-winning documentary films we would
create together over the next five years.[2] Fred never had more than a five-
hundred-dollar budget for music. Needless to say, the costs of the musicians
and studio took most of that and left little for me as the producer, writer,
and performer of the score. But the work was consistent and also important
for establishing a relationship between me, the fledgling film community,
and the recording studios, engineers, and musicians in Austin.

Nevertheless, the first Austin filmmaker to hire me was Richard Kidd.
When Kidd heard my reel-to-reel of "The Circle of Love," he immediately
offered me the score of *Keep Truckin'*. In a wild scheme from its inception,
Kidd had persuaded the owners of Dobie Towers, near the University of
Texas campus, to create an experimental three-screen wraparound theater
in their lobby. Departing from the standard proscenium screen format, the
walls on either side of the theater seats were also screens, on which peripheral perspectives of the film were simultaneously projected, panoramically
linked with scenes visible on the main screen. In other words, the audience

sitting in the theater and viewing *Keep Truckin'* would see the open road rolling ahead under the truck from the perspective of the cab, while concurrently experiencing peripheral views from the side windows.

While I was hustling jingles and film work, I was still focused on my primary objective: securing work. I would worry how I was going to make things happen pragmatically and creatively only after I got the gig. *Keep Truckin'* was no exception. Accepting the offer to score the film would require a recording studio and session players, and in Austin I had access to neither. The five-hundred-dollar fee that Kidd offered would hardly cover a round-trip plane ticket to Nashville, much less session fees, lodging, or meals. So I had no choice except to accept Kidd's suggestion to record the entire score in the theater, cutting tracks directly to the film while carpenters literally constructed the auditorium around us; we would record during their breaks and they could hammer during ours.[3]

The studio situation "resolved," I focused my attention on finding musicians, returned to the Yellow Pages and found a booking agent named Larry Watkins. Waco native Watkins started his management career booking bands for the active fraternity scene at the University of Texas in Austin. His Moon Hill Management was home base for a host of rock-and-roll acts in town—most notably Rusty Weir, the former drummer of a legendary Austin band named the Lavender Hill Express. A flower child, Watkins had shoulder-length blond hair and a quick smile. He told me about a place called the Hill on the Moon.

"It's out on City Park Road, man," Watkins said. "Musicians from several bands share this big house out there. Just give 'em a call, man, tell 'em I sent you, an' arrange a meeting out there an' see who wants to work."

Gloria and I had moved into a two-story apartment nestled into a rocky hillside on East Riverside Drive in the Travis Heights section of South Austin. The apartment faced a lovely live-oak-laced park that gracefully sloped to a clear, limestone-banked creek that meandered between the hills of the neighborhood. In 1971 there were few of the numerous concrete arteries that extend deep into the heart of Austin's overpopulated hill country today. The quickest route from Travis Heights to City Park Road was to zigzag west along Lake Austin Boulevard before twisting and turning, ascending and descending Mount Bonnell Road, to eventually link with FM 2222. Gradually climbing in elevation again, FM 2222 crossed several gurgling streams before arriving at the turn to City Park Road. Then, rising steeply to the top of a high ridge, City Park Road meandered through a vast green scrub oak and cedar forest of prime undeveloped Texas hill country to Hill on the Moon.

Hill on the Moon was a sprawling five-bedroom home of native stone perched high atop the limestone ridge. The house had been built by hand and was owned and maintained by a cheerful six-foot-four, carrot-topped young man named Crady Bond; Crady, his father, and his elder brother had lugged most of the rocks up the hill from the creekbed to construct the house. Grief forced the family to abandon "the Hill" when Crady's father committed suicide soon after moving in. A talented craftsman and carpenter who would become one of the dearest friends of my life, Crady built himself an exquisite A-frame near the mansion. Crady was also a great supporter and lover of music, so he invited musicians to move into the mansion, and he constructed a stage at the bottom of the hill. Every so often, depending on circumstance, a concert would be held at the Hill on the Moon stage and the proceeds would be divided equally among the participants.

A massive fireplace united Hill on the Moon in its center, where a spacious family room had been converted by musicians into a combination dining room/rehearsal space/TV room—often simultaneously sharing those various roles. Wall-sized floor-to-ceiling plate-glass windows offered a spectacular view of unspoiled hill country and the distant Austin skyline before the phenomenal population and development explosion that would begin to escalate dramatically in the mid-1970s.

Hill on the Moon was a true nursery of the Austin music scene, a creative, fluid, musical vortex, where new bands, songs, and careers were being born daily. It was a perfect remote location, where musicians could practice when they wished and play as loud as they wanted—the nearest neighbors were several miles away. Touring musicians often crashed there, but each room belonged to a young journeyman musician who worked in several bands in town to make enough cash to survive. Recording engineer Jim Inmon lived in the master bedroom specifically because of the large bathroom and the fact that its tiled walls created the perfect echo chamber for the makeshift but functional four-track recording studio he set up there.

Jim looked much like a young Orson Welles, and his engineering ears and talents were golden. Most important, in 1971 he had the vision and the aesthetic gumption to create the studio where, among other things, he was experimenting with what he called "soundscapes." Jim's auditory experiments had prepared him to communicate clearly in the aural abstract with me, and I had little difficulty explaining to him that I was constructing a new form by linking epic poetry and long narrative songs into a flowing linear, historically documented ballad. Jim's curiosity was stimulated, and he was ready to get to work with me. Soon we started referring to my new ballad form as "ear movies."

Aside from Jim Inmon, I was particularly attracted to the gifted guitar talents of his brother, John. The sons of an army doctor, the Inmon boys were raised on military bases around the world before their family settled in Temple, Texas, where their dad practiced medicine at the famous Scott and White Hospital.

Also from Temple and living at the Hill was everyone's favorite drummer, the lovable Donnie Dolan. He and the Inmon brothers had been playing music together since junior high school and naturally gravitated to Austin. After Lavender Hill Express broke up, Donnie replaced Rusty Weir as the drummer, and the new group became known as Genesee.

Genesee also introduced to Austin a piano-playing Oklahoma kid with a quick, wide grin and reedy tenor. Gary P. Nunn had been in a Lubbock group called the Sparkles before heading to the University of Texas to study pharmacy. A gifted arranger and songwriter, Gary didn't live at the Hill. Instead, Gary's home was another popular bohemian musicians' hangout on North Lamar Boulevard. Gary called his place Public Domain.

After Genesee dissolved, Rusty Weir's career as a single act didn't last long. He promptly recruited John Inmon and Layton DePenning to form the trio Rusty, Layton, and John. Weir impressed me with his ability to rock a country song. The consummate bar act, he sang original songs like "I Heard You Been Laying My Ole Lady" and Bobby Shehorn's hilarious hippie parody "Acid Makes My Face Break Out." Being a hat man myself, I was mighty impressed with the classy way Rusty styled and wore his, and it seemed important to me that unlike the rest of us, Rusty was a native of Austin. Later, when the progressive country music movement in Austin first attracted Hollywood's attention and they sent John Travolta down to Houston to clone *Saturday Night Fever* as *Urban Cowboy*, Rusty got a fantastic break when his song "Don't It Make You Want to Dance" was central to the sound track. Rusty never got the big break he deserved, but Bonnie Raitt's singing his song on that sound track sure got him close.

Another of Rusty's guitarists, Leonard Arnold, also lived at the Hill. Leonard wrote one of Rusty's best songs, "I Don't Want to Lay This Guitar Down." My budget for the *Keep Truckin'* score was so meager that Leonard Arnold was the only sideman from the Hill that I hired for the sound track.

Since the landmark hippie film *Easy Rider*, folk-country music had worked well in films with counterculture themes, and that's precisely the sound Richard Kidd wanted for *Keep Truckin'*. Since Leonard was the only steel guitar player in town, I felt that definite country sound would work best with the trucking theme of the film.

Like the rest of America during the peak years of the civil rights era and the Vietnam War, conservative Texas had become dramatically—often violently—divided. Still, because of the great number of students at the University of Texas and other colleges in Austin and the politicians entrenched from the progressive social agenda of Lyndon Johnson's presidency, Austin was liberal. While Texas became increasingly conservative, Austin had become a near-idyllic safe haven for hippies and freethinkers; Austin was where Texans came to frolic creatively, to experiment with alternative lifestyles and perspectives. In order to safely blend in outside of Austin, and to lovingly mock the stereotypical image of the Texan, hippies started dressing like cowboys. Hair length defined which side of the fence your political beliefs rested on, but with his freak flag stuffed under a cowboy hat, a long-haired hippie became just another "good ol' boy" when driving through dangerous conservative regions of Texas.

In the early 1970s Austin was brimming with "cosmic cowboys." To set the record straight from my perspective, however, either Leonard Arnold or Bob Livingston was the original "cosmic cowboy." If forced to pick one or the other, I'd have to bet on Livingston, but Leonard Arnold was the first person I heard use the term.

Another Lubbock boy, Bob Livingston was a multitalented strawberry-blond whirlwind who rolled into town from Hollywood playing bass with Mike Murphey. Smitten with mystical Hindu culture and religion, but a good ol' West Texas cowboy, Livingston was known as "Cosmic Bob." Leonard, on the other hand, was a long, lean hippie whose seniority in the Austin band scene gave him the large front bedroom at the Hill. Leonard had been a member of the Austin band Cold Blue Steel, for which Don Henley played drums before he left for L.A. to eventually become a founding member of the Eagles. After Cold Blue Steel, Leonard formed a group called Baby Cakes that worked regularly around Austin. He had brown hair down to the middle of his back and a broad "I-just-screwed-your-girl-friend" grin. Long before I met Mike Murphey, Leonard—who later played guitar on Murphey's "Geronimo's Cadillac"—made a joke, suggesting that I take his photograph and caption it "a cosmic Texas cowboy." Then, with a joint dangling from his lips, Leonard struck a pose in a cowboy hat at his steel guitar with a pack of Camels and a Lone Star beer strategically perched on the instrument. Leonard left Austin in the late 1970s, headed to Nashville, married a woman who was part of the group Sweethearts of the Rodeo, stopped playing music professionally, and became a road manager for country stars like Garth Brooks and Trisha Yearwood. The last time I saw him was in the early 1990s on a package show down on the Texas Gulf Coast. He was road manager for a great young singer named Shelby Lynne. We had a chance to walk down a magnolia-canopied road behind the stage and reminisce about the good ol' days.

These musicians and a small group of others, including former Lavender Hill and Genesee bassist Jess Yaryan, guitarist Craig Hillis, and drummer Michael McGeary, would soon become appropriately known as the Austin Interchangeable Band, the core group of extraordinary musicians who could easily segue from style to style and work with any troubadour who passed through town and needed pickers quick. John Inmon, Bob Livingston, Gary P. Nunn, and Donnie Dolan would soon emerge from the Austin Interchangeable Band to become the Lost Gonzo Band.

Arriving as I did from the corporate record industry towns of Nashville and L.A., I found the Hill on the Moon and Public Domain approach to music strongly appealing. I felt I had finally discovered the peers I had been seeking throughout the early phases of my career. At the Hill, musicians were writing, playing, and recording in a genuinely communal sense, with the song as common denominator. Of course, in Nashville and L.A. everything also revolved around the song, but within the "industry" the song was born from a corporate mentality, written by committee in order to utilize industry connections to ensure success and then to divide the profits among several writers and publishers. With no industry infrastructure in Austin, Hill on the Moon songwriting was motivated by the sheer love of music. A fundamentally important component of the equation was that in Austin young college crowds were eager to hear unknown artists performing original music. In Los Angeles or Nashville there were precious few places to play original music unless you had a record deal or were already a proven star. But in Austin there was a sizable audience even for an experimental artist like me, and there were small clubs where I could perform the songs without the poetic narrative in order to see if they would stand on their own.

Soon after *Keep Truckin'* closed, Tobe Hooper brought me his script of *Texas Chainsaw Massacre* to ask if I would consider writing the score. After reading the script I told Tobe frankly that it freaked me out and I had to pass. But I took him out to the Hill on the Moon and introduced him to Jim Inmon, who agreed to help. He brought Roger Bartlett and Billy Callery of the duo Lusasa Goose to his four-track studio at the Hill and they contributed to the score.[4] When combined with Warren Skaaren's important dual contributions of the provocative title and the fledgling Texas Film Commission's Hollywood connections, the landmark independent film proceeded to earn millions, create the modern "slasher" genre, and put Tobe in the fast lane to direct *Poltergeist* and many other major Hollywood productions.

Merging of Our Minds had been dead in the water since the debacle at Capital Records, my subsequent involvement with *The Wheel,* and my relocation to Austin. But Dave McCormick had never given up on the project, and he played the reel-to-reel tapes for anyone who wandered into his offices in Monroe. On one of these occasions an elderly cotton farmer from Dave's hometown of Rayville, Louisiana, heard *Merging* and exclaimed, "Why, 'at's great. Why ain't it on the radio?" Dave informed the gentleman that we had offered it to everyone in the industry and been turned down. "Well, then," the old gent replied, "it won't hurt for me to give it a try, will it?"

The old farmer had an elderly friend in New Orleans whose career went back to the nickelodeon era. Joy Houck Sr. was one of the pioneer exhibitors of motion pictures in the Deep South. After earning his first fortune exhibiting nickel movies in tent sideshows, Houck developed a chain of more than three hundred movie theaters and drive-ins. Houck built most of the Crescent City's colossal movie palaces, which were the jewels in his crown. Along the way, in the early 1950s, Houck discovered Lash LaRue and developed the actor into a major cowboy matinee star by producing and exhibiting his films throughout his chain of theaters. A noir cowboy, Lash LaRue could have been Humphrey Bogart's twin brother. LaRue did not use a pistol like the other cowboys. Instead, "Lash" was a master with a bullwhip. Significantly, in a day when the good guys wore white, Lash LaRue always wore black and is rumored to have been the star that inspired Johnny Cash to dress similarly.

Dave's farmer friend from Rayville sent a tape of *Merging of Our Minds* to Mr. Houck, who, upon listening to it, explained that he knew nothing about "this modern music." As a favor to his childhood friend, however, Houck agreed to forward the tapes to his son in Hollywood.

Joy Houck Jr. was born late in his father's life. Joy had been producing and directing movies since the age of sixteen. He made low-budget horror films that his family could run in their theater chain until they earned a healthy return on their investment. In his twenties when we met (as was I), Joy Jr. had produced the horror classic *The Legend of Boggy Creek* as a teenager. The younger Houck was also connected to the counterculture. He loved *Merging of Our Minds* and took my tape to a friend named Gary LeMel, who had just taken a job at E. H. Morris.

E. H. "Buddy" Morris's partner was one of the most successful songwriters of the twentieth century. Johnny Mercer's vast catalog of standards, from "Glow Worm," to "Autumn Leaves" and "Moon River," will earn fortunes eternally. Johnny Mercer's catalog was combined with Buddy Morris's four decades of classics such as "The Christmas Song," "Ghost Riders in the Sky," a host of Broadway shows, and the school songs of scores of American universities. With all this and offices in New York, Los Angeles, London, and Sydney, E. H. Morris was arguably the largest music publishing company in the world. (In the 1980s, frustrated by Michael Jackson's purchase of the Beatles catalog of songs, Paul McCartney bought only two music publishing catalogs—Buddy Holly's and E. H. Morris's—the acquisition of which reportedly made McCartney's MPL Productions the largest music publisher in the world.)

In the early 1970s Buddy Morris's son, Steve, decided to revitalize the company. Sidney Goldstein had run the West Coast offices of E. H. Morris for decades, so Steve kept him in charge. But he also hired a young staff, including Gary LeMel, to sign contemporary writers. A gifted crooner of the "Sinatra school," LeMel left his home state of Arizona in legendary jazz singer Anita O'Day's band before being drafted and surviving two tours of Vietnam. After his discharge from the army, he got back into the music business at E. H. Morris.

Upon hearing *Merging of Our Minds*, LeMel contacted Dave McCormick to explore the possibility of signing me to a publishing contract with E. H. Morris. We agreed to meet at McCormick's office in Monroe to discuss the idea.

I agreed to the meeting knowing that ultimately I had no desire to sign my songs away to anyone—not even Fred. My songwriter's contract with

Rondee Music would expire in a few months, and upon reaching that milestone I was certain I would have Fred's blessing to create my own publishing company. I liked Gary LeMel a great deal, and desperately needed a steady salary, but I politely informed him I could make more writing jingles and documentary film scores than the five hundred dollars a month he was offering me to write for E. H. Morris. After several calls to Los Angeles during the meeting, the salary offer was capped at eight hundred a month, which I also declined. Gary was not permitted to offer more, so we ended our talks and said good-bye. I drove back to Austin prepared to hustle film and jingle work. Soon after returning to Austin, however, I received a call from Gary.

"I can't let this go, Bobby," he said. "I love your writing. What do we need to do to make this happen?"

"Sell my album," I said, remembering what Fred had told me years earlier about music publishing controlling the recording industry.

"*Merging.*"

"Yes."

"Let me get back to you?"

Two hours later Gary called me back.

"How does RCA sound to you?"

Held at the close of the 1960s, the Monterey International Pop Festival and Woodstock were twin defining events of the counterculture era. Yet there was another important social and musical template born in the 1960s that would dramatically affect Austin during the following decades: Bill Graham's Fillmore. Whereas Monterey and Woodstock would spawn a very large family of outdoor festivals—such as Texas's long-running Kerrville Folk Festival—"the Fillmore" was born in the Haight-Ashbury hippie nursery in San Francisco, and launched musical acts such as Jefferson Airplane and the Grateful Dead that defined the counterculture lifestyle and era. The Fillmore was certainly an inspiration for a trio of Texas "flower children" during the summer of 1970 to create Armadillo World Headquarters.

Around this time Jerry Jeff Walker moved to town and coined the saying "We don't live in Texas; we live in Austin." Everyone knew Jerry Jeff from his rowdy, rambling ways and his classic "Mr. Bojangles." He had passed through Austin many times over the years, and after his friends Cathy Morgan and Hondo Crouch bought the tiny hill country town of Luckenbach in 1970, finally decided to settle in Central Texas. I had opened for the Nitty Gritty Dirt Band in the spring of 1971 at Louisiana Tech University in Ruston, and when Jimmy Ibbotson told me after the concert that they were headed to Austin I mentioned that Gloria loved the place and was moving there that summer. He told me Jerry Jeff had just moved to Austin.

During the summer of 1970, Texans Eddie Wilson, Jim Franklin, and Mike Tolleson created a concert hall to celebrate southwestern counterculture and offer sanctuary to Texas hippies. Artist Jim Franklin observed resilient similarities between the lowly armadillo and Texas hippies and forged a powerful visual link between them. Suddenly Franklin's ubiquitous armadillo and hippie images, icons that would soon rival the mythical Longhorn cow, were popping up all over Austin. I loved going to the Armadillo World Headquarters with Gloria on Saturday nights to see touring acts, but primarily to see Armadillo master of ceremonies Jim Franklin take the stage in his elaborate, truly outrageous outfits. I thought he was like an Andy Warhol "happening" and was usually more interesting than the main act.

The legal man of the Armadillo trio was Mike Tolleson. He was always working behind the scenes at the Armadillo, but I ran into him around town occasionally and we always had a cordial chat. The third point of the Armadillo World Headquarters triangle was Eddie Wilson, who would later renovate Kenneth Threadgill's old service station into a down-home country restaurant and Austin tradition.

Nevertheless, after Jerry Jeff moved to town in 1970, there was increasing talk of even more singer/songwriters arriving. Like me, many Texas musicians who were also part of the powerful counterculture "rebellion" had been chewed up and spit out by the corporate record industry. The survivors suddenly began to return to Texas, and it was only natural that they would gravitate to liberal Austin. Arriving just after New Yorker Jerry Jeff, I happened to get to Austin right before the Texans started coming home.

My first sense that something major was happening occurred when I was invited to meet Chet Flippo, a *Rolling Stone* journalist who was in town to interview people about the rapid migration of musicians to Austin. I agreed to meet Flippo in the Tarrytown area of Austin and, to my surprise, Doug Sahm was also there for the interview. Sahm, of course, was the famous San Antonio musician also known as Sir Doug, from his early days in the Sir Douglas Quintet. Doug was a delightful, eccentric character, clearly a musician from his perpetually raspy voice down to his Beatles boots. I really enjoyed meeting him. Flippo was a nice fellow, too. He had a disarming smile and a casual and polite manner of getting straight to the point that I admired. I was genuinely flattered by his interest in my work.

Soon after the Flippo interview I started hearing gossip about a Texas songwriter who was returning from L.A.'s songwriting factories. Messianic phrases like "*he'll* be here soon" were whispered with near-religious reverence. Naturally skeptical of messiahs, I was leery of the guy before I ever met him. These days he's known as Michael Martin Murphey, but in the early 1970s everyone called him Mike.

Michael Martin Murphey and I were both born on March 14, 1945. In support of astrology, there are many personality traits that we share, which is probably why we have never been able to become closer friends. We are both fiercely competitive, with epic ambitions, tenor voices, a deep, abiding love of the old and new American West, and we arrived in Austin around the same time. Having worked with us both intimately, Bob Livingston is probably the only person who could objectively articulate our similarities and differences. I have a sincere and deep appreciation of Murphey's original music and his lasting contribution to the national music catalog. During his "post–cosmic cowboy" career he has become a splendid interpreter of classic cowboy songs, as well as a noteworthy purveyor of modern ranching life in the American West. Moreover, because of his rise to fame in Austin in the early 1970s, most of the renewed interest in cowboy poetry and songwriting during the late twentieth century can be directly traced to him. As we have both entered our sixties, now I doff my hat to my fellow Pisces and sincerely wish him "Happy Trails."

While the live music scene exploded at the Armadillo, the Saxon Pub, Castle Creek, and several other venues around town, I realized, like everywhere else in the music business, that sex and booze were driving the engine. As my music focused more on traditional folk styles and was oriented more to the coffeehouse than the fraternity bar scene, I knew my future in Austin depended on a different set of skills, and though I worked in the clubs occasionally, I decided to hustle more jingle and film work rather than attempting to survive the wild bars. Producing film scores and jingles, however, required capable recording studios, so I focused my attention on the facilities in town. My experience in the studio with Fred Carter had also made me aware of the stark differences in recording and performing live music. Because of this I knew it would take many hours in the studio for Austin musicians to develop the art of recording, and we needed working studios to train ourselves. I also realized it was going to be a while before Jay Podolnick's Odyssey Sound Studios were functional and that Jim Inmon's makeshift studio at the Hill on the Moon was fine for demonstration recordings, but not as a master studio.

Deeper exploration led to a four-track studio on Congress Avenue above the KLBJ radio station. The Johnson family owned the station, and LBJ used the little studio to tape his weekly presidential addresses when he was in Austin. I called the studio, made contact with an engineer named Paul Harrison, and discovered he was eager to rent out the studio occasionally.

While I was recording the *Keep Truckin'* score I also succeeded with a presentation for a unique advertising agency led by a strawberry-blond pistol named Roy Spence. Even though Spence appeared to be the head of the organization, AdVantage Agency was essentially a commune of creative students fresh out of the University of Texas advertising school. I was impressed with the way they put all their incoming cash in a jar and at the end of each month doled it out communistically to whoever needed it most. The AdVantage staff sat together and listened to the entire tape of *Merging of Our Minds*, and a few days after my presentation I received a call from Spence. He had secured the senatorial campaign of the champion of Texas's liberal Democrats, Senator Ralph Yarborough. Roy wanted me to write and produce the music for the campaign. A "Yellow Dog" Democrat myself—even before relocating to Texas—I was an admirer of Senator Yarborough and his political efforts to celebrate and preserve the Big Thicket. So I enthusiastically accepted the job. Sadly, it was destined to be the old senator's last campaign. He was defeated in the Democratic primary. But the ad campaign introduced me to Senator Yarborough, and our friendship lasted until his death. He honored me with his presence at the debut of *A Ballad of the West* at the Creek Theater, and years later I was deeply honored when the Yarboroughs asked me to perform at their only son's private memorial services.

In a few years Roy Spence would create the super-agency Gurasich, Spence, Darilek, and McClure—GSD&M—with major national advertising accounts and annual billing totaling in the multimillions. Ever the Democratic campaigner, Spence eventually became a very important player in the rise of the political career of President William J. Clinton. When I was invited to perform "Heal in the Wisdom" for President-elect Clinton and Vice President–elect Gore at Austin's Scholz Garten in January 1992, Roy Spence escorted the pair along with Texas governor Ann Richards and New Mexico governor Bill Richardson into the room. It was the first time we had seen each other since the Yarborough campaign, and he was as surprised to see me as I was to see him.

In early 1972—nine years after first learning about Jim Bridger and having the notion of creating a historically based song-poem chronicling his life—I completed the composition of *Seekers of the Fleece*. Finally, I had my prototype epic ballad.

The first time I performed *Seekers of the Fleece* in its entirety I was alone in Jeff and Jennifer's room in our apartment overlooking a Travis Heights park. When my twelve-string Martin chimed the last chord and faded into silence, my first thoughts were that I would never be able to perform this piece in public. Committing something so lengthy to memory wasn't the problem; the problem was how could I ask an audience to sit for an hour of historic heroic verse?

That evening I performed *Seekers* for Gloria. Her experience in studying and teaching English literature immediately became important to the development of my concept. Like me, upon hearing the ballad performed in its entirety, she was impressed with the work's genuine epic scale. Rather than being intimidated by the scale of the ballad, however, she had a bold suggestion that would make it even more epic in scope.

"You need to write short prose chapters," she said. "You know, vignettes of the history that informed the heroic verse and narrative songs. Keep in mind that no one has sung this history before you! Historical vignettes will inform the audience that you have interpreted history rather than having made up some preposterous, fictitious tale."

Within hours I started writing historical vignettes to accompany the heroic verse and songs. While working on the second vignette I returned to the Miller watercolors for inspiration. Viewing them, it suddenly occurred to me that I could also create a narrative of the entire piece with Miller's paintings properly sequenced with the poetic, musical, historical, and, now, graphic narratives.

The next weeks were a sleepless blur of creative adrenaline and coffee-fueled nights writing historical narratives to accompany the poetic and musical narratives, while simultaneously numbering pages in various art books to create a graphic narrative of *Seekers of the Fleece* with the field watercolors done by Alfred Jacob Miller in the 1830s. I started performing the piece twice a day also and noticed that each time I performed it the hour seemed to pass quicker. Suddenly, while performing *Seekers of the Fleece* and committing it to memory, I started scribbling the opening lines of the companion American Indian piece I had envisioned earlier. It would be a telling of a telling. Lakota holy man Black Elk told it to Neihardt. The poet told it to the world. Now I would sing it.

Willie Nelson and Fred Carter had both been staff writers at Pamper Music in Nashville. I first met Willie in Nashville in October 1967 at the National Disc Jockey Convention, and even though he was already a famous songwriter, I didn't know he was a Texan. I was in Los Angeles recording my second RCA album when Willie arrived in Austin and played the mythic Armadillo World Headquarters show with Mike Murphey—the concert when the hippies and the rednecks smoked dope and danced together and defined Austin as the capital of "progressive country" music. After that milestone Willie was suddenly everywhere; the local alternative country radio station, KOKE, played his music virtually around the clock. In a few short months Willie captured the heart and spirit of the alternative country movement in Austin. Whereas Armadillo World Headquarters was primarily inspired by the Haight-Ashbury hippie counterculture movement, rock, and pop music, Willie was pure outlaw country. Willie was also now the top hippie armadillo. Willie's presence meant that Austin would be considered more an outlaw alternative to Nashville than a psychedelic San Francisco hippie colony.

I was in town when Willie threw his first "picnic" in Dripping Springs. So was most of Austin's music community, as well as many of Nashville's fringe country acts. As the show began, I noticed my old pal Kris Kristofferson racing through the backstage crowd with a throng of reporters and journalists hot on his trail. I had heard the tales of Kris landing a helicopter in Johnny Cash's backyard in Hendersonville to get the attention of the Man in Black. It worked. Now married to Rita Coolidge, Kris was a movie star as well as one of America's most highly regarded singer/songwriters. I wanted to say hello, but from the look on Kris's face as he fled the reporters, I decided the timing wasn't right.

"You have to say hello," Gloria encouraged me. "If he's an old friend, he'll want to see you."

Kris had escaped into a Port-A-Potty, so I waited for him to come out. Soon the door opened and Kris saw me as he exited the outhouse. He recognized me, but you could see the wheels turning as he tried to remember who I was. Then suddenly he grinned and growled, "Bridger?"

We chatted briefly—mostly about Fred Carter and Monument. But the moment to speak with me also allowed the pack of journalists to catch up with him, and he and Rita were soon pushed away in a mob of questions and photographs.

Gloria and I stood alone in the backstage crowd until I noticed a young man standing by the stairs leading up to the main stage. He was a singer/songwriter I had met several years earlier in Nashville when Bobby Bare frequently hired me to sing demos for his publishing company. I sang demonstration recordings for many of Bare's staff writers, but once you met this songwriter you would never forget him—there were three fingers missing from his right hand! That didn't keep him from writing truly poetic songs, though. And the minute you heard the unique language of his lyrics you knew this guy was real. I had sung demos of three or four of Billy Joe Shaver's songs for Bare's publishing company, and he was always there for the sessions to teach me how to sing them correctly.

"Billy Joe," I shouted. "What're you doin' down here in Texas?"

"Hell, Bobby, I'm from Corsicana!" Billy Joe shouted back.

"What the hell are you doing down here, Bobby?" Billy Joe asked. "I heard you moved to L.A. When are you coming back to Nashville?"

"I ain't coming back, Billy Joe. I love it here in Austin," I said. "Say, Fred Carter Jr. told me that Waylon is gonna cut a batch of your songs. Is that true?"

"I had to threaten to whip his ass," Billy Joe said, anger rising in his voice. "But he done a whole album of my songs."

Waylon probably saved his and Billy Joe's life cutting that record. Waylon never lived in Austin, but his album of Billy Joe's songs, *Honky Tonk Heroes*, was the first to wed the so-called outlaw movement from Nashville with the burgeoning progressive country music scene in the Texas Hill Country. Soon Willie, Waylon, Jessi Colter, and Tompall Glaser—all Nashville veterans—would release the first platinum-selling country LP, *Wanted: The Outlaws*. Willie was the only one of the lot who lived in Austin. But because of Willie's rapidly swelling popularity, everyone in the record industry associated the record with the movement in Austin. Those two records changed the course of modern country music. Texas writer Jan Reid soon dubbed it "redneck rock."

ELEVEN

The Big Tent

I N MUSIC BUSINESS TIME, Sidney Goldstein was ancient. He was
tiny, razor-thin, stooped, and sometimes his dentures clicked when
he spoke. His language was sprinkled and spiced with traces of Yid-
dish New York, where he began his career as a song-plugger during the
mythic Big Band era. In those days a song-plugger's success was measured
by his ability to convince a bandleader to arrange a tune for his orchestra or
lead singer. With luck, the song would become part of the band's repertoire
and sheet music sales would soar. Even better, if the bandleader had a popular radio program, the song might earn everyone involved a small fortune.

In the spring of 1971 I flew to Los Angeles and Sidney signed me to
E. H. Morris Publishing Company. Gary LeMel was present for the signing, along with another executive at E. H. Morris named Ron Kramer.
Immediately after I signed the publishing contract, the trio drove me the
short distance to the Hollywood offices of RCA to meet the man who
signed me to the record company. I was delighted to learn that Joe Reisman,
the RCA vice president of West Coast operations, was a native Texan. Jovial
and portly, with dark, slicked-back hair, Reisman left Baylor University in
the 1940s playing sax with big bandleaders such as Bob Crosby, Louis
Prima, and Jack Teagarden. Soon Joe and "Miss" Patti Page joined forces,
and he began arranging her repertoire and produced a string of hits for the
songstress. Selling more than ten million singles in the early 1950s, her phenomenal "Tennessee Waltz" became the official state song of Tennessee, and
today still remains the biggest-selling single by a female artist.[1]

Joe Reisman's talents were discovered as he orchestrated Miss Page's sky-rocketing success, and soon he started producing and arranging music for live television programs such as *The Oldsmobile Hour* and NBC's *Cavalcade of Stars*. In that role, he began working with the popular Ames Brothers quartet, an arrangement that led him to join the A&R staff at RCA's West Coast offices. Upon joining RCA Hollywood, Joe became Henry Mancini's producer, a position he would hold for thirty years. During his lengthy tenure at RCA, Reisman also produced classic recordings for Perry Como, Ed Ames, Julie Andrews, and scores of other gold-standard international artists of the 1950s and 1960s.

Joe was only a couple of years younger than my dad, and from our first meeting he assumed a fatherly role with me. I was deeply impressed that, unlike many so-called A&R men who had passed on *Merging of Our Minds* after only perfunctory hearings, Joe had actually *listened* to my record. He promptly endeared himself to me musically when he started discussing which songs on *Merging of Our Minds* were his favorites and why he liked them. He did, nevertheless, toss me a pair of curveballs when he told me he wanted me to return to L.A. to remix the album yet again in order to familiarize myself with the RCA studios and engineers before we started recording my second album. Learning that I had to remix *Merging of Our Minds* was discouraging enough, but then Joe reminded me of the clause in my contract requiring me to record in an RCA studio. I had hoped I would be allowed to record my second RCA album in Austin with my new musician friends.

"RCA prefers for their artists to record in RCA studios." Joe winked. "Besides," he assured me, "you'll have access to the world's greatest musicians and technicians here, Bobby. Don't worry. I'll personally make sure you are happy."

I trusted Joe. Why shouldn't I? He had just signed me to one of the world's premier recording companies. Aside from producing some of the most memorable artists and songs of the era, he was the producer of classic film scores such as *Days of Wine and Roses* and Blake Edwards's classic *Pink Panther* series.

"I guess this is a good time for me to speak," Ron Kramer said, politely entering the conversation.

Ron explained that even though I had been signed to RCA as a producer as well as a recording artist, E. H. Morris felt "we" needed an experienced producer to shepherd my career to the next level. Ron explained he would be helping me remix *Merging* to prepare the album for fall 1972 release. "We also want to record your next album in quadraphonic sound," Joe continued. "Ron knows quad production and I'm pretty sure you don't want to go to engineering school before you cut your next record." I bristled at the revelation that a stranger would produce my next record. But I had learned to keep a poker face in such important meetings; the right time would come for me to ask questions, and it wasn't during my first meeting with Ron, Sidney, Gary, and Joe.

"You and Ron will remix here in Hollywood with my engineers," Reisman continued. "They've worked with everyone from Julie Andrews to Harry Nilsson. Richie Schmitt will engineer the new album, and Mickey Crawford will remix *Merging* as well as the new album."

Gary, Ron, and Sidney left the meeting, and my new boss invited me to join him at his favorite Italian restaurant to celebrate my signing. We loaded into Reisman's plush Jaguar sedan, and on the way to the restaurant I discovered one of Joe's quirks: having been placed on a very strict diet by his doctor, he could no longer eat anything at his beloved restaurant. So he ordered for me and vicariously enjoyed the meal as I ate. I felt sorry for him, but the food did seem to taste better with him suggesting I try this or that and then describing the finer points of each course of the dinner. It was the first of several delegated meals that I ate for my new boss over the next year.

The next morning Ron Kramer invited me to dinner at his home in Pacific Palisades to meet his family. A songwriter and record producer at E. H. Morris, Ron had a quiet yet commanding presence that was unusual for someone in our ostentatious profession. Centered and focused, he was also a family man, and my instincts were that he would be a steady hand on the wheel. I trusted him, and I believed we could work together. I reasoned that if I was going to be recording in Hollywood it would be best to work with a producer familiar with the L.A. system. Nevertheless, that didn't stop me from complaining to Ron the next morning as he drove me to the airport.

"You did an excellent job with the original mixes of *Merging*," Ron replied. "After all, those mixes got you a major record deal, and you should be proud they accomplished that. Everyone just wants to remix the record to make certain you have a successful debut. Besides, you impress me as a 'hands-on' kind of guy, so I suspect you'll enjoy remixing your album here in L.A. with me and Mickey Crawford. And like Joe said, it'll be great preparation for the next record."

Within minutes I was on a jet to Austin worrying about career "scale," perspective, and balance again. Nevertheless, I reminded myself that I was finally in the big tent at the circus; this was not one of those moments to question good fortune. I relaxed and let the delicious feeling of success spread throughout my being as the jet soared over the southwestern United States toward Texas. Skies were clear and blue.

I was anxious to get home to Gloria. Given the intensity of my career activity in Los Angeles, there had been little time for an important matter we could now finally address. We had more than the RCA deal to celebrate. Now that both our divorces were final, we visited Travis County attorney Ned Granger, and he married us. The money from my contracts with RCA and E. H. Morris provided a much-needed financial boost, and after getting married, we leased a two-story house in the hill country perched over a popular nude swimming hole on Lake Travis known as Hippie Hollow. Even though I had never been to the Mediterranean, the area looked like I imagined Greece—deep green cedar-crested cliffs dramatically plunging into white limestone-scalloped coves of sparkling clear, silvery waters. Sailboats permanently dotted the reservoir and bobbed in distant harbors. After moving into the house on Comanche Trail we were surprised to learn that Mike Murphey, B. W. "Buckwheat" Stevenson, and Armadillo World Headquarters soundman Hank Aldridge, lived a couple of miles down the road.

I had only recently heard of B. W. Stevenson. Soon after signing with RCA I visited the Dallas offices, where I met Merlin Littlefield, who was head of the label's seventeen-state regional distribution center based there. Littlefield proudly informed me that he had personally signed B.W. to RCA about the same time as Reisman signed me to the label. I should have known then that Littlefield would focus most of RCA's regional publicity muscle on B.W., but I was still naive about such things. Still, I figured it was inevitable that I would meet B.W., and soon after I returned to Austin, he played Castle Creek. So I stopped in to introduce myself to him and his sideman, a gifted harmonica player named Mickey Raphael.

I instantly liked B. W. Stevenson. Gnome-like, with a sweet yet booming tenor voice, he was a natural entertainer. His stage patter between songs was hilarious; like fellow Dallas native Ray Wylie Hubbard, I thought Buckwheat, or Chuck, as we sometimes called him, could have been a comedian if he hadn't become a singer. Even more than with his quick-witted sense of humor, I was mighty impressed with Buckwheat's songwriting, picking, and singing, and in spite of all the fawning over Mike Murphey, I felt he was the best songwriter I had met in Texas. Here, as at every other folk club in Austin, the Castle Creek offices doubled as a "green room" for entertainers, and I waited there to meet him after the show. Offstage he was shy and unassuming but still sarcastic and funny. Sadly, I recognized he was also already suffering from a drinking problem. I informed Buckwheat that I was his neighbor as well as his label-mate, and we agreed to meet at Hippie Hollow one day to get to know each other. We remained friends and shared cordial visits whenever we did shows together until his sad passing at an early age while undergoing heart surgery.

With my major label debut in the chute and a house in the country, my new family was finally beginning to bond on Comanche Trail. The record and publishing deal certainly put us on better financial footing and created a peaceful time to get to know Gloria's children and improve my stepparenting skills. The record and publishing deal also helped me establish myself in Austin with my new musician friends and brought more film and jingle work. But my five-year contract called for ten albums of original material, and that meant I would be writing songs constantly. I realized this would put the epic ballads on hold for a while, but that didn't concern me, as songs were flowing out of me now. A favorite was "The Sculpture," down to the "la, la, la" refrain, an homage—indeed, more a blatantly obvious response—to Paul Simon's "The Boxer." Where Simon's boxer sang of a weary, battered spirit departing a hopeless struggle, my sculptor sang of awakening self-realization.

Another song I had completed was a satire of the hippie cowboy characters that were already becoming a parody in Austin. Believing the Austin scene to be taking the persona way too seriously, I wrote "Hopalong Cassidy and Gabby Hayes" to lampoon the fact that our cowboy roots were more in Hollywood than West Texas, and smelled more like marijuana than manure. "Hopalong" offered the tongue-in-cheek suggestion that the herd of singing cowboys gathering in Austin—myself included—was, as real cowboys describe the difference between image and substance, "all hat, no horse." Like the rest of Austin's cosmic cowboys, I had grown up on a steady Saturday-matinee diet of singing celluloid heroes. As post–World War II children we sat spellbound at the end of countless horse operas watching the hero confront the number one bad guy in a perfunctory fistfight. Throughout the entire scuffle, the hero never, ever, lost his hat.

I laid my tune down over a boogie beat hooked with a "doo-wop" refrain, all the while singing about Hoppy never losing his hat no matter what the situation or how atrocious the villain. I was particularly fond of the song's not-so-subtle suggestion that Gabby Hayes was the real star of those hokey westerns.

Soon after returning to Austin from Hollywood, I continued pursuit of work. I had been curious about a company listed as "Rod Kennedy Presents" in the Yellow Pages. When I finally called, Rod Kennedy answered the phone himself and promptly informed me that he was producing a folk festival that would be held in May in Kerrville, Texas.

"I've already booked the acts for the main stage," Mr. Kennedy told me, "but Peter Yarrow suggested we have a concert series called 'New Folk' to showcase emerging songwriting talent. Why don't you send me a tape to review for the New Folk concerts?"

I figured if Peter Yarrow was involved this had to be a top-notch event. I dropped a two-song tape off at Rod Kennedy's North Lamar offices and within days got a call from Ron Kramer to return to California. It was time to remix and shoot more photographs for my first album. But it was also time to get a new manager. As soon as I got out of the cab in Hollywood and checked into the Ramada Inn on Sunset, I noticed the message light blinking in my room.

"'Bridger-over-troubled-waters,'" Dave sang into the phone. "Are you a star yet?"

"That's gonna take a bit longer, bro," I joked. "We've got to mix the album again. What's up?"

"I've been talkin' with Ron Kramer and Sidney Goldstein, bro." Dave grew serious. "They think you need a professional manager, and I completely agree with them."

"You're joking, aren't you?"

"I'm serious, bro."

"No," I argued. "You brought me all this way."

"Listen to me, bro. Seriously, listen." Dave became stern. "I'm way out of my league here. Yeah, I got us this far. But I don't have the skills to take it across the goal line. You need people with connections I don't have. I had my shot with the pros with my football career. You deserve a good clear shot with your music career too, bro."

"But they don't know me, Dave."

"Well," he laughed, "we need help, bro. If you don't want a new manager I'm gonna hire someone myself to take over the job!"

Ron Kramer set up a series of interviews with managers. Most of them represented famous pop recording artists and were only looking for the "next big thing." Finally, we met George "Bullets" Durgom. Marcella, his secretary for decades, greeted us warmly, served us hot tea, and made us comfortable in the unpretentious office. At the time of our meeting I knew nothing of Durgom's celebrated history, but the moment I set eyes on him, I instantly, instinctively, liked him. Of Lebanese heritage, diminutive— barely five feet tall—impish, brassy, and bald, he looked very much like a small, elegant version of my maternal grandfather, Hartley Bridger.

I soon learned that Bullets Durgom was a show business legend. Like Joe Reisman and Sidney Goldstein, he went back to the Big Band era. From New Jersey, Bullets began his career as Tommy Dorsey's "band boy." A grassroots promotion man, the band boy also did the multitude of chores that no one else in the organization would do—a predecessor of rock and roll's "roadie." Throughout the first third of the twentieth century in mainstream popular music, there were few "personal managers" per se; bandleaders like Dorsey were the administrators of the business organization as well as the orchestra's arranger and conductor, and individual singers were under contract to them. During this time the lead singer of the Tommy Dorsey band was a skinny New Jersey kid named Frank Sinatra. "Old Blue Eyes" nicknamed Durgom "Bullets" because, from behind, the shape of his tiny, shiny, prematurely bald head looked like, well, a bullet. When Sinatra left the Dorsey band to embark on his own astonishing career, Bullets briefly became his manager. Bullets would never talk about it, and I have never found any information about what happened between them, but after a brief period together, he and Sinatra split. Shortly thereafter "bobby-soxers" made Frankie an everlasting cultural phenomenon.

Bullets didn't miss a beat. After departing the Dorsey band, he quickly became the manager of another musician bound for immortality. Glenn Miller had been a trombonist in the Dorsey orchestra before Bullets began managing him and nudged him to stardom. After Miller was killed in World War II, Bullets tried his luck in the exciting new medium of television.

Bullets met Jackie Gleason in Hollywood when the Brooklyn-based comedian was cast as a bassist in a B-movie starring the Glenn Miller orchestra. He recognized that Gleason's boisterous, over-the-top style would fit hand in glove with early live-sketch TV. When Bullets convinced executives at CBS television of this, he negotiated for "the Great One" what was in 1954 the largest financial deal in the history of the medium—$11 million for twenty years—and both careers were ensured for life. Able to write his own ticket with *Stage Show*, Gleason preferred filming his popular *Honeymooners* series before a live audience. The comedian, a fan of swing music, pushed Bullets to persuade the ever-feuding Dorsey brothers to host the *Stage Show* part (the live portion) of Gleason's hour-long variety show. The Dorsey brothers, who had a combative relationship as legendary as their music, had ended their partnership twenty years earlier. Nevertheless, Bullets was able to persuade them to reunite for a comeback shot on television. Sadly, they couldn't stay reunited, and *Stage Show* lasted only a couple of years before evolving into the long-running *Jackie Gleason Show*.

After the Gleason/CBS deal, Bullets became the hottest manager in show business. His list of clients became a virtual "who's who" of 1950s stars. At various times his stable included Robert Mitchum, Marilyn Monroe, Doris Day, Natalie Wood, Sammy Davis Jr., Merv Griffin, Lenny Bruce, Mort Sahl, Mel Brooks, Carl Reiner, Allan Sherman, Artie Johnson, Elke Sommer, and many other popular movie stars and comedians at their peak.

After our initial meeting we stepped out of Bullets's Sunset Boulevard offices and walked to a popular nearby café for lunch. We tried to discuss business, but Bullets could hardly chat or eat because of the stars and show-biz types who stopped by our table to say hello and chum up to him. When the flow of visitors finally ebbed, I took the opportunity to break the ice and asked Bullets if he'd ever met Elvis.

"Elvis? I taught him how to eat a banana split!" Bullets cracked. "You laugh? I'm serious! When he came to New York in 1954 he had never eaten a banana split. This was before anyone really knew who Elvis was—hell, he wasn't Elvis himself yet! He was just some hillbilly from down South with a new wiggle. But I liked him. He was a very nice kid, very polite. Like I said, he was just a kid. When he came to New York for the Dorsey show he had one of those corny hand-buzzers that he used on every hand he shook. Everyone thinks his first television appearance was on the Sullivan show, but in 1954 Elvis was on the old Dorsey *Stage Show* program on CBS."

Later I asked the folks in publicity at RCA and learned that Elvis Presley's first national television appearance was indeed on *Stage Show*. Gleason dubbed Presley "Brando with a guitar" and booked the singer for six shows in eight weeks—even allowing his full body to be seen *on* camera, wiggling hips and all. RCA was promoting the single "I Was the One," but Gleason preferred "Heartbreak Hotel" and insisted that Elvis perform that tune. Presley sang the song three times on the show and it became his first national hit record.

We returned to Bullets's offices after lunch and he dug out a contract from his desk and tossed it to me.

"It's my standard agreement." He grinned. "Take time and look it over. But I'll tell you the important part before you read it. I get half!"

"HALF!" I sputtered.

"Keep in mind"—his grin widened and became mischievous—"you'll make three million dollars during the contract's three-year term. The contract is in two stages over three years. If you don't earn a minimum of one hundred thousand during the first eighteen months of the agreement, the contract is void. Don't worry; you'll make the hundred grand. Then, if you don't earn three million during the contract's three-year term, you're free to move on."

I signed the contract without even reading it.

We completed the remixes of *Merging of Our Minds*, and the record was scheduled for an autumn 1972 release. Before I left town I wrote "The Call"—the song that would ensure the release of my second RCA album. Joe Reisman loved "The Call" and wanted it as the centerpiece single for the album. With Reisman's blessing secured, it was simply a matter of scheduling. All the other songs were already written and ready to go.

Or so I thought. Sidney Goldstein didn't like any of the new songs. Sidney and I had experienced problems before the ink was dry on my contract with E. H. Morris. We earnestly attempted to harmonize, but from the beginning of the relationship it was apparent that we were singing from different songbooks. When I played "The Call" for him he sighed sarcastically and said, "Why does every song you write have to have a coyote or a cactus in it? Why can't you just write me a simple love song?"

Sidney's remark hurt. I felt I had delivered him a broad spectrum of subject matter with more than a few love songs.

"What's the problem, Sidney?" I asked, sincerely hoping we would be able to find common ground.

Sidney drew me closer as if to take me into his confidence and, referring to Bob Lind's exquisitely mystical Top 40 hit from the early 1960s, said, "You know, Bobby, a song like 'Elusive Butterfly of Love' comes along once in a blue moon. You tend to write that kind of love song. Either that or one like the song about van Gogh . . ."

"'Vincent,'" I offered. "Those are great songs, Sidney. Don't you want me to try to write great songs?"

All the grandfatherly songwriting empathy disappeared and the bean-counter persona returned. "Just write a simple song for me, Bobby," he said tersely. "A song you know I'll like."

That night I wrote a song for Sidney. The next day I played it for Joe Reisman before I played it for Sidney, and he loved it. It became the title song of my second album, *And I Wanted to Sing for the People*.

> I don't know what made me think they would hear me
> I don't know what made me think they would care
> I don't know what made me think I was different
> From all the people they force to compare.
> Now I'm standin' in the rain.
> Yes, they broke me up again.
> Momma I'll be comin' home
> With a little sadder song.
> And I wanted to sing for the people.
> I just wanted to sing for the people.[2]

In 1973 Slim Pickens was offered a sweet deal on a condominium forty miles west of Austin, at Woodcreek Resort in Wimberley, Texas. So occasionally I was able to run over to Woodcreek, visit with Slim, and update him on the progress of getting *Seekers of the Fleece* recorded.

Unfortunately, there was nothing to report. Joe Reisman informed me that the RCA executives had made it clear I had to strike gold with commercial recordings before they would consider discussing any history projects. I understood this fundamental reality and actually agreed with them. I loved making commercial records with RCA and hoped to continue with the label for the rest of my career. To me, RCA Records was the pinnacle of the commercial recording industry. But I also saw no reason they couldn't record my epic ballads as well as my pop records. A role model, Marty Robbins, had been able to simultaneously record as a pop and country artist before virtually spinning a new, literate western music market out of thin air with his groundbreaking album *Gunfighter Ballads*. I felt I could wait until I scored a commercial hit before pushing the historical material with RCA.

So Slim and I used the Woodcreek visits to get to know each other, have long talks about mountain men, Plains Indians, his life in the rodeo, movies, and our mutual love of Wyoming. Slim also had a cabin in Boulder, Wyoming, and eventually we would meet there in the summer for visits. As these meetings progressed over time, I realized that we had actually become good friends.

Gloria and I made our first journey to Wyoming in June 1972. During this time Gloria was studying with a famous philosopher named Charles Hartshorne at the University of Texas. In his nineties and as frail as parchment paper, Dr. Hartshorne was regarded by many as the global authority on process philosopher and mathematician, Alfred North Whitehead. But Hartshorne preferred to be known simply as the author of a philosophy he called creative synthesis. The main thing I vicariously gathered from Hartshorne via Gloria's interpretation was the concept of "incompatible good." In Hartshorne's creative synthesis, "good" is the natural way of the universe; conversely, "evil" is a social deception perpetuated in our mythology by our continuing empowerment of the illusion and our perception of evil as being the opposite of, and incompatible with, good. My hippie-gonzo pals simply called all that "the mind-trap of duality."

Hartshorne's philosophy was of great interest because I had been studying fairy tales and observed that most were based on conflict between good and evil. The discovery of the same elements of good versus evil in Lakota creation mythology in Neihardt's *When the Tree Flowered* also made me want to learn more about classic mythology, and soon I found Joseph Campbell's groundbreaking *The Hero with a Thousand Faces*. Similarly, Campbell's book made me want to read more about Carl Jung, his concepts of archetypes, the "collective unconscious," and how the concepts of good and evil fit into his theories.

All this reading made me wonder where to look for mythology in modern times. After I considered this question for a few months, it occurred to me that our belief in black holes in space—indeed, most theoretical physics—is increasingly mythological. The black hole seemed to me a perfect theme and location for a modern myth-like fairy tale. So I started studying order and chaos theory while simultaneously returning to Melville's *Moby-Dick*. Knowing of my fascination with *Moby-Dick*, someone suggested I read Dr. John Lilly's *The Mind of the Dolphin*. Lilly's efforts with telepathic interspecies communication with dolphins fascinated me, and I knew from the very first reading of his work that the idea of interspecies communication would become the major theme of my evolving concept of a "modern adult fairy tale."

All these various interests converged in 1972 when I saw Harry Nilsson's *The Point!* Nilsson's stunning cartoon fairy tale pushed me over the edge, and I began structuring what would eventually become a three-hour musical space fantasy that I titled *Aldebaran and the Falling Star.*

Part of my initial exploration with *Aldebaran* was to create techniques to visit "inner space" and regress as far back in memory as I could. Using Jung's *Memories, Dreams, Reflections,* I had concocted a series of meditation exercises to help me search my memories, and I found that my earliest recollection was from when I was around three or four years old, when I spent hours gazing trance-like at my parents' photographs of Wyoming landscapes—particularly the geographic anomaly near their home in Gillette that was known as Devils Tower.[3]

Struggling to find a way to depict Jung's collective unconscious in my third act, I was able to recall a dream from that very early period of my life: that there was an ocean on top of Devils Tower. Later, when I discovered that the Plains Indians considered the monolith they called Mateo's Tipi, or "the bear's lodge" to be a mythical, sacred explanation of the Pleiades constellation, the landmark became metaphorically important to *Aldebaran.* Since one of my primary purposes in creating *Aldebaran* was to wed Lakota philosophy and creation myth into elemental forms of classic Anglo-Saxon storytelling and fairy tales, the Plains Indian mythology associated with Devils Tower became of paramount importance. The ocean atop Devils Tower in my childhood dream would become the "Ocean of One" and serve as the central motif of the Jungian third act of the *Aldebaran* piece.

As I recalled this dream to write that third act, however, the thought did not escape me that it was an important emotional link with my parents and Wyoming. So I was happy that Gloria was willing to join me on a vacation to the Northern Rockies. The Kerrville Folk Festival was approaching, and Gloria and I planned a trip after the festival, to California for the summer, up the coast from L.A. to San Francisco and Oregon. After that we would head east to Wyoming and Yellowstone.

Meanwhile, my career in Austin was becoming increasingly active. My documentary film score work with Fred Miller had become so consistent that it was like a regular job. My jingle business also heated up after I won my second ADDY Award for a wine commercial for a new advertising agency named McClure Feltch.[4] Most important, with *Seekers of the Fleece* completed, the prototype structure for the Lakota ballad was in place. But I felt *Lakota* could truly be a creation in the oral "folk" tradition if it became a "telling of a telling of a telling"—in other words, a genuine oral history. Black Elk told Neihardt his life story; then the poet told the holy man's story to the world. *Lakota* would extend that process in a ballad chronicling the two men coming together to present the history of the Indian wars.

In May 1972 Dick Barrett, Allen Wayne Damron, Segle Fry, Steven Fromholz, Carolyn Hester, Bill and Bonnie Hearne, John Lomax Jr., Mance Lipscomb, Kenneth Threadgill, Michael Murphey, Robert Shaw, and Texas Fever were booked as the main stage acts for the first Kerrville Folk Festival. Ironically, I was the only person on the bill at that first festival who had a contract with a major record label, and I wasn't on the main stage. Instead, I was the first performer on the "New Folk" stage. I had no way of knowing it then, but that first festival was the beginning of a lifetime of performances and near-familial intertwining. What I remember vividly from the first Kerrville Folk Festival is feeling like an outsider. All the acts were native Texans and already legendary in the Lone Star State. Adding to my insecurity, many of the acts were regional, anti-establishment, folk purists who held country and pop "stars" in low regard. For the first time, my career in Nashville and Hollywood seemed to hurt rather than help me.

The person on that bill that I wanted most to meet was Carolyn Hester. I knew she had introduced Columbia Records executive and legendary talent scout John Hammond to Bob Dylan. A major folk artist in the early 1960s, Carolyn booked Dylan to play harmonica on a recording session for Columbia Records, and Hammond discovered him at the session. At the festival I learned that Carolyn had also crossed paths with Buddy Holly, and I was curious about how she had somehow been involved with these two starkly different iconic forces in American music. We somehow failed to connect at the festival, and even though she also would soon sign with RCA Records, it would be years before I got to know her. What a genuine old-fashioned sweetheart she proved to be!

Immediately after the festival Gloria put Jennifer and Jeff on a plane to spend the summer with their father in North Carolina. We traded the old Volkswagen van in on a new Monte Carlo and headed for Los Angeles.

Bullets threw a welcoming party for us at his palace in Beverly Hills. Joe Reisman, Ron Kramer, Gary LeMel, Sidney Goldstein, and a few of Bullets's neighbors stopped by for drinks. The walls of the mansion were covered with candid photographs of him with many of the stars he represented. I was particularly amused to see a picture of Robert Mitchum and Frank Sinatra drunk and passed out on the pool table in Bullets's game room.

The next day I showed Gloria around Hollywood a bit before we headed north up the Pacific coast on Highway 1. After a few magic days camping in Big Sur and a brief visit with my brother in San Francisco, we continued north to Oregon and, finally, east toward Yellowstone National Park and Wyoming.

It was still dark as we raced through Idaho's Swan Valley. When dawn broke, the colossal, jagged silhouette of the Grand Tetons appeared in the east. The enormous shadows of the mountain range dominated the skyline, defied the morning sun, and cast aubergine shadows west of the peaks throughout Idaho. Within moments, daybreak's purple retreated, its departure revealing splatters and swatches of turquoise and periwinkle sprinkled with glorious wildflowers. Finally unveiled in the morning light, rolling green and brown prairies rapidly ascended with the lodgepole pine and aspen tree line to greet the spectacular spine of the Grand Tetons.

We crossed into Wyoming and drove north to the town of Jackson. Like every tourist, the first thing we noticed about Jackson was the town square, with its huge white arches of sun-bleached elk antlers curved over each corner. The town itself was pure Madison Avenue meets faux Old West. We weren't fooled by the boardwalks, "howdy, pardners," and chic catalog outlets; Jackson was a very expensive tourist trap! You got the feeling that the Jackson cemetery would be called Death and Things instead of Boot Hill. We stayed there just long enough to grab a quick cup of coffee, then headed north toward Yellowstone.

The old trappers referred to a vast prairie ringed by mountains as a "hole." North from Jackson we entered Jackson Hole, an expansive prairie at more than seven thousand feet elevation. The Grand Tetons dominate the landscape inside Jackson Hole for more than fifty miles. Dramatically ascending from the immense mountain prairie, the Tetons defiantly face down the smaller Gros Ventre Mountains to the east. The Snake River meanders near the Teton foothills to drink from thousands of cascades that pour from their crags and cliffs.

At that moment driving through Jackson Hole, I decided that if I could somehow return to Wyoming at least once a year, my life and career would be in a positive, healthy place. From that day forward my decision to somehow live part of each year in Wyoming has been the most consistent aspect of my life and career. When my annual pilgrimages to Wyoming became the "prime objective" of my life, important, often intensely emotional and confusing personal and career decisions became easier to make. Explaining my love of Wyoming to folks in Hollywood, however, was another matter completely. The least populated state in the Union didn't have enough people to be important to anyone in the record industry.

Describing Wyoming was a problem that Jim Bridger himself faced. In the 1830s, when Jim first tried to describe Yellowstone's geographic wonders to folks "back east," they thought he was merely a grand raconteur. Jim Bridger was indeed a natural yarn spinner, but anyone who has visited Yellowstone knows how difficult it must have been for him to attempt to explain it to the uninitiated. So when folks refused to believe Jim when he described geysers spewing boiling water more than a hundred feet in the air with clocklike precision, the mountain man exaggerated his stories and added a colorful yarn to underscore the natural wonder that he was struggling to portray. One of my favorite Jim Bridger stories perfectly exemplifies what "flatlanders" surely thought was another of his yarns: In Yellowstone, as a natural occurrence, boiling water overflows from thermal pools and streams into a nearby river's freezing waters. Jim Bridger named the river "Firehole." In describing Firehole River to easterners, Jim said there was a place in Yellowstone where he could enjoy a bath in a hot pool of water while he simultaneously fished in a near-freezing river. Jim said when he caught a fish he could simply pull the fish from the ice-cold water and, without removing it from the fishing line, drop it in yet another nearby pool of boiling water, and cook and eat the fish without ever getting out of his "bath"!

Like most initial visitors to the park, however, Gloria and I had not planned for the time it would take to see everything properly. We had to rush through the park and hurry home. We promised each other that we would to return to Yellowstone the next year, as well as visit Fort Bridger. More important, I now knew Wyoming was the place I would always return to when I needed to renew my spirit.

And I Wanted to Sing for the People

THE RAPIDLY GROWING NUMBERS of singer/songwriters gathering in Austin during the early 1970s initiated a fierce struggle between Jerry Jeff Walker and Mike Murphey over several members of the "Austin Interchangeable Band." Every musician in town knew that Gary P. Nunn, Bob Livingston, and John Inmon had the talent to succeed either as solo artists or united as a band. Most realized that whoever finally captured the gifted musicians would have the best band in Texas. "The Scamp," as Jerry Jeff appropriately referred to himself, eventually won the showdown, and Nunn, Inmon, and Livingston enlisted their favorite drummer, Donnie Dolan, tipped their hats to Hunter S. Thompson, became known as the Lost Gonzo Band, and hit the road with Mr. Bojangles. Murphey soon left town in a huff.

At the time when the Lost Gonzo Band was forming around Jerry Jeff, Frank Zappa recognized Jim Inmon's gifts and hired him to engineer sound for his concert tours. I was happy that my friends' talents were being acknowledged, but touring also made them unavailable for sessions. The studio scene in Texas still left much to be desired anyway, and since there was no recording facility that could meet the standards that RCA expected of me, I was in California as often as Austin.

In spite of my RCA contract's strict studio requirements, I intended to record *Seekers of the Fleece* with the Lost Gonzo Band. I reckoned that while I was trying to either record a hit or persuade RCA to let me record my ballads, the Austin musicians would also need to be prepared to record with me. I believed I needed to teach them the songs as well as explain the musical and historical concept to them. So when the Gonzos weren't on the road with Walker, I became a regular visitor at Hill on the Moon. I was an early-morning person, but the musicians were always courteous when I occasionally arrived at the Hill at 9 a.m. Even when they had been up until the wee hours drinking and playing music, they would politely crawl out of bed, put on coffee, and listen to my ramblings about the history that informed my epics, the techniques I wanted to employ in recording the piece, and the various musical arrangements I wanted to pursue to capture the songs and verse on tape. It's a testament to their naturally cheerful personalities that no one at the Hill punched me out.

Which is more than could be said for Jerry Jeff. Gossip whispered that several of the ultra-mellow Gonzos had cold-cocked Walker several times. Upon learning that the rumors were indeed true, most who knew Jerry Jeff in those days just shrugged. He could be a wild man sometimes. I was backstage the night Jerry Jeff arrived at Castle Creek clad in only a swimsuit, a cowboy hat, and boots, then passed out and fell into the drum kit before completing a single song. But several books have already been written about his "gypsy songman" days, and there is no need for me to add to the legend. My greatest concern was the possibility of losing my friends in a mishap on the road with him. I know that in the years the Gonzos toured with Walker, they landed one of his two aging planes with wings aflame at least twice. As the years rolled into decades, that kind of calamity became the accepted norm of their life on the road with Jerry Jeff. I hope one of the Gonzo survivors will eventually write a book depicting their years with Jerry Jeff. They deserve much more recognition—individually and as a band—than the music industry has given them. Without the Lost Gonzo Band there would have been no "Live Music Capital of the World." Their contribution to Texas and American music will last through the ages. Personally, if not for their friendship and musical talents I would have left Austin after my first month-long experiment and headed back to Hollywood.

On a late-summer day in 1972 I stopped in at French Smith's record store on the Drag. He called me into his office.

"Have you seen the sales catalog for your RCA album?" He grinned through his thick black beard.

French opened the catalog to the page announcing the worldwide release of *Merging of Our Minds*. Even though the photo of the cover was small and the image blurred, seeing the official catalog order numbers suddenly made being an RCA recording artist seem real for the first time. I celebrated that afternoon by buying myself a Martin D-12-28 twelve-string guitar.

I was in Los Angeles in preproduction for *And I Wanted to Sing for the People* when *Merging of Our Minds* was released in September 1972. In spite of the sense of accomplishment upon releasing my first album of self-produced, original songs, I knew I had to sell several truckloads of them to continue recording at a world-class level. Important groundwork had been laid in Louisiana and Arkansas as Dave McCormick and Rodney Dungan put their regional advertising connections to great use promoting the release. As a result, the record was playing on major radio stations throughout the mid-South. In industry terms, a record is referred to as a "turntable hit" if it's getting strong airplay without corresponding sales. My record didn't have a chance at sales because for the first three weeks following the record's release there was no product in the stores. No palms had been greased.

My 1967 release of "Sharon, Oh Sharon" came at the twilight of the era of "open" radio stations in America. Armed with nothing but naïveté and my Monument singles, I was able to create much of my own airplay by visiting cotton-patch and back-alley radio stations and befriending disc jockeys throughout Louisiana, East Texas, Arkansas, and Mississippi. That vital airplay encouraged stations in other regions of the country and in larger markets to play my records until I had the beginnings of a career. By the 1972 release of *Merging of Our Minds,* those innocent days were over in even the most remote regions of America. Unfortunately, the easy access that artists and promo men had to disc jockeys as late as 1967 paradoxically led to the demise of such open contact. When an artist could just walk into a station and get a record on the air, it made disc jockeys easy targets for the bribes that led to the first of many government investigations of the record industry's dark underbelly. Of course, the "payola" scandals of the late 1950s and early 1960s led to the infamous conviction of disc jockey Alan Freed. Freed was convicted of accepting bribes in 1960, forever sullying his fame for reportedly coining the term "rock and roll."[1]

But government scrutiny of the insidious relationship between radio and the record industry only created bigger problems. Radio's rapid evolution into the "Top 40" format during the early rock-and-roll era created a dilemma for disc jockeys as they were inundated with more than two hundred records a month from which they were required to select the increasingly smaller numbers of "hit" records they played. To avoid appearances of impropriety, disc jockeys were forced to become less accessible. This predicament produced the modern broadcasting phenomenon known as the program director, or one all-powerful person who selects what records are played—or not played—on the radio station. This development in programming combined with legislation that arose as a result of the initial payola scandals to give birth to yet another dark period in modern broadcasting and recording: the era of the independent promotion man. Unlike the promotional staff of a single record label, the independent promo man promoted fewer copies of multiple label releases. Superficially, this appeared to confirm the promoter's independence from allegiances to any specific record label, but the result was to render the record label's own promotional staff impotent and grant even more power to the independent promoter. The situation naturally led to a small nationwide network of powerful independent promotion men with "questionable" backgrounds but with vital personal connections to powerful and insulated program directors. Complicating matters further, ambiguous legislation concerning bribes made it easier to offer promotional "gifts" to program directors. It doesn't take a genius to see that the industry was prone to corruption. At the time I signed with RCA in 1971, industry rumors were that it cost roughly $150,000 to $200,000 to "break" an album nationally.

I was well aware of this fundamental truth of the record industry at this point in my career. Still blessedly naive, however, I wrongly assumed that RCA was a much more established international label than those smaller independents of my early career, and I believed that with the label's global corporate logistics now supporting my releases, those days of self-promotion were behind me. But the era of the independent promo man was only beginning. As early as the 1972 release of *Merging of Our Minds* most major record label staff promotion people were already essentially just window dressing, since the only people who could truly break a record nationally were the powerful, and often shady, independent promotion men. By the early 1980s independent promotion men virtually ran the record business.

This truly reprehensible aspect of the corporate record industry is the very reason that I quit playing the game. No matter how clean I tried to keep my hands, somewhere along the line from the divine gift of a song to the receptive heart of another soul, there would always be these types of parasites soiling the karmic purity of it all with their greedy, dirty hands. I refused to play that morally bankrupt game then, now, and forever.

Still, in 1972, though I had neither the cash nor the desire to hire independent promoters, I did have an album that I loved and needed to get to the public as best I could. As a result of relationships I had nourished and harvested with radio stations and program directors before the release, as well as some persuasive and devoted RCA field promotion men and women, *Merging* immediately went on the air on several important hundred-thousand-watt stations in Louisiana, Arkansas, Missouri, Tennessee, New York, Pennsylvania, the Carolinas, Georgia, Arkansas, Mississippi, California, Texas, and hundreds of other smaller stations throughout the country. Dave McCormick and Rodney Dungan redoubled their efforts with media connections in the Ark-La-Miss area to intensify publicity at the taproot of my fan base. After returning to Austin I bought three hundred albums from RCA at my artist discount rate, jumped in my car, and drove nine thousand miles through the American heartland in a month, personally delivering albums to radio and television stations, newspapers, and magazines in major and secondary markets to promote the release. In some rare cases I was even able to get the record on some major-market stations. Moreover, the stations I visited in the smaller markets soon added the record to their playlists, and sales followed in those markets. The record had healthy airplay out of the chute when I returned to Austin to reconnect with the activity there.

It had become nearly impossible to keep up with the music business in Austin. New singers, songwriters, and musicians were moving into town every month. Like me, one of the new guys, Willis Alan Ramsey, had relocated to Austin from the Deep South. From Alabama, Willis recorded a superb self-titled album on superstar Leon Russell's fiercely independent Shelter Records label. Willis Alan became the first Austin-based artist to score a major nationwide mainstream hit when pop act the Captain and Tennille covered his enchanting "Muskrat Love," and their single dominated Top 40 radio for several weeks.

Willis Alan's album was a dazzling one that blended folk-rock, country blues, and playful, intelligent, Texas-oriented lyrics into a strong new regional sound and style. In many ways, I felt, Willis Alan's writing harked back to the tradition of the great songwriter Hoagie Carmichael. Willis Alan was definitely a predecessor of Lyle Lovett. But the first time I heard Willis Alan, and later, Lyle, I immediately thought of the great chanteuse Miss Pearl Bailey; her pinched, lackadaisical, talking-singing, double-entendre lyrics always entranced me, as her style seemed to be simple, bone-bare, country blues while simultaneously sophisticated and urbane. Willis

Alan and, subsequently, Lyle realized that this elegant aspect of country blues had lingered for decades on the fringes of pop culture, and they brilliantly brought it into the mainstream. Since his emergence in the mid-1980s, Lyle has reshaped country blues into an urban style all his own, and I'm quite certain—gentleman that he is—that he would be the first to tell you that he was much inspired by that singular splendiferous Willis Alan Ramsey album. After thirty years of waiting for a second album, it has become apparent that that initial important record is the only major work Willis Alan is going to share with us. Sometimes one is enough.

Willis Alan brought a talented trio of South Carolinians named Uncle Walt's Band to Austin, and they regularly held court at Steve Clark's Waterloo Ice House on Congress Avenue. During the late 1970s I had an arrangement with Steve Clark that whenever Uncle Walt's Band didn't have Waterloo booked for a weekend, I would have first shot at the venue to perform my one-man shows of *Seekers of the Fleece* and *Lakota*.

The tenor and bassist of the trio, David Ball, was the first of them to leave Austin for Nashville, beginning his ascension as a major country music star. Walter Hyatt followed, and with Lyle Lovett's production assistance was on the brink of national success as a solo act when he was killed in a tragic commercial airliner crash in the Everglades. I think Walter's death broke Austin's collective musical heart. If not then, the entire community wept when fiddler Champ Hood later died of cancer. But the legacy of Willis Alan's early '70s arrival in Texas and the impact of his bringing Uncle Walt's Band to Austin most certainly live on today in Lyle Lovett's well-deserved international acclaim.

Jay Podolnick labored away at his Odyssey Sound Studios on Sixth Street while Willis Alan Ramsey, flush with his success from "Muskrat Love," broke ground on his state-of-the-art recording studio in Austin. He enticed Jim Inmon to quit working for Frank Zappa and hired him as the head engineer to help him build the studio, on Twelfth and North Lamar, that he dubbed "Hound Sound."

All of this activity in the recording arts in Austin was the indirect result of the success of another major regional artist, Leon Russell. In the early 1970s, braced with the phenomenal prosperity of his rock career as "the master of time and space" and the success of his financial gamble with the independent Shelter Records label, Russell created the experimental "ShelterVision" wing of the label to seek important regional musical artists and videotape them in concert. Based in Tulsa, Russell dispatched the Shelter-Vision production team to Austin.

Willie Nelson once said, "The early bird gets the worm, but the second mouse gets the cheese." Willie's prescient remark was certainly a poetic synopsis of ShelterVision—and the future of music television, for it would be impossible not to link the birth, short life, and death of ShelterVision with the arrival of *Austin City Limits* only months afterward. As much as it forecast *ACL*, Leon's ShelterVision was perhaps more prophetic of MTV. Ultimately it became the eager mouse that triggered the trap. *Austin City Limits* and MTV got the cheese.

Throughout 1972 and 1973 I became increasingly aware that I had reached what is referred to today as "the glass ceiling." My growing apprehension of the recording industry made me begin to direct my energy away from the pop factory in Los Angeles and focus my creative effort on the avant-garde activity in Austin. I wanted to record in Austin, but even though studios there were steadily developing, they were still substandard. Completing my second album with RCA was my top priority, and we were scheduled to begin recording in February 1973.

In 1972, soon after signing me to E. H. Morris, Gary LeMel left the company to work for up-and-coming film producer Jerry Weintraub. Weintraub lured LeMel away from the Morris company to help with movie sound tracks. Impressed by Gary's work with Weintraub, Barbra Streisand hired him to assist with her directorial debut, a remake of the James Mason/Judy Garland classic *A Star Is Born* featuring the diva and Kris Kristofferson. LeMel promptly introduced Streisand to songwriter Paul Williams, and the pair cowrote "Evergreen" for her film. The song won an Academy Award. Streisand rewarded Gary by hiring him to head the sound-track division of First Artists, a collaborative film production company comprising A-list stars Streisand, Robert Redford, Paul Newman, Steve McQueen, Dustin Hoffman, and Sidney Poitier. When First Artists dissolved, Gary became the head of the Warner Bros. sound-track division, where he literally reshaped the way we experience contemporary film and television scores today.

After Gary's departure Ron Kramer became the closest of my Hollywood associates with either RCA or E. H. Morris. Ron had proved himself a forthright individual and a talented record producer. More important, he had befriended me and made the effort to understand me personally in order to fully appreciate my musical and career aspirations. Ron had helped me find professional management, fed me in his home, and introduced me to his lovely family. Also vitally important was that once preproduction began, Ron included me on each decision as a coproducer; credits didn't matter as much to either of us as results. Since RCA nixed any idea of bringing Austin musicians to Los Angeles to record, Ron asked if I had any special requests for Hollywood musicians.

My "good-luck charm" in the studio was working with various musicians who had recorded with Simon and Garfunkel. Of course, I had already recorded extensively with Fred Carter Jr., but two other players of Paul and Artie's regular ensemble were L.A.'s leading rhythm section: Shreveport native Joe Osborn had left Louisiana in the 1950s, playing bass with Ricky Nelson's band before becoming one of L.A.'s top studio musicians, and Hal Blaine began his career as Patti Page's drummer before settling into the studio scene in Los Angeles. Blaine and Osborn's studio chemistry was nothing short of magic. Playing on countless hit records during the "golden era" of rock—from Johnny Rivers to the Mamas and the Papas, the Carpenters, the Fifth Dimension, and Glen Campbell—the pair had become the bedrock L.A. rhythm section. Blaine and Osborn played on a large percentage of the hits heard on all pop radio from 1965 to 1985.

Ron also brought other important players to the sessions: Richard Bennett was Neil Diamond's guitarist before becoming a session musician. Richard and I connected quickly. I loved his inventive, clean, precise technique and especially his sense of positive and negative space. Mike Anthony helped fatten up my six- and twelve-string rhythm guitars for the basic tracks.

String arranger and conductor Jim Helms was another important addition to the sessions. Red-hot at the time with the score of David Carradine's hit television series *Kung Fu*, Jim had a penchant for tight, lilting string lines with Oriental shades of discord ingeniously balanced in harmony. The result was a hybrid "East meets West" orchestral sound that had worked perfectly with the Carradine series, and I was eager to hear his work with my melody lines and lyrics—especially "The Call" and "The Sculpture."

I was also excited to learn that stellar Muscle Shoals session man Spooner Oldham had relocated to L.A. and that he and noted jazzman Mike Lang would be playing keyboards for my sessions. Spooner would help us get funky when we needed to add some Southern boogie to the stew, and Mike would certainly sparkle things up with touches of jazz.

Ron's major production criticism of *Merging* was that I sang nearly all the background vocals on the album. He wanted to use other background singers for the *People* album to create a different vocal texture, so he hired three splendid women soul singers—Ginger Blake, Julia Tillman, and Maxine Willard—to flesh out my background vocals.

The sessions began in late February 1973 and ran through April. Whereas *Merging* had been a series of first takes, *People* was the opposite. It was recorded in several complex stages, beginning with me and my guitar in an isolation booth singing and playing a "guide" track for the musicians to perform with to record a "basic" band track. Later, I would return to the studio for an overdub session to perform my final guitar and vocal parts to the master tracks recorded earlier with the band. This approach makes recording quite labor-intensive, and *People* was especially so.

One morning during the sessions, I picked up a *Los Angeles Herald* and saw a headline that read like something from *The Twilight Zone:* "Indians Seize South Dakota Church." My breakfast went cold as I devoured the story before hurrying to the studio. American Indian Movement—AIM— activists had become increasingly militant since the late 1960s and now suddenly struck like a lightning bolt on the world stage. Since absorbing John Neihardt's body of work, Vine Deloria's *Custer Died for Your Sins*, and beginning *Lakota* in 1969, I had plowed through nearly forty books and gained a superficial, purely academic overview of the tribes of the upper Great Plains and Rocky Mountains. This extensive research had made me aware of the legal circumstances of the American Indian while also stimulating what would become a lifelong interest in indigenous religion, history, and culture. Gloria and I had visited the Wind River Reservation in Wyoming during the summer of 1972, seeking firsthand knowledge, and we'd been deeply moved by witnessing the poverty and depression there. I vowed I would become actively involved in changing this, and immediately upon my return to Austin I joined a very small group of American Indian student activists at the University of Texas petitioning the university to create and offer scholarships to attract indigenous students. We called ourselves "American Indians Now Texans—AINT." I was the only member of the seven-person group who wasn't a Native American.

So, on February 27, 1973, when Russell Means, Dennis Banks, and more than two hundred other AIM members and supporters seized a church at Wounded Knee on Pine Ridge Reservation, I knew very well that their purpose was to call international attention to human-rights abuses and financial hopelessness in Indian country.

But I had a recording to complete, so I rushed back into the studio. Fortunately, the production was progressing smoothly, and I was pleased to discover how well Ron and I worked together; our production ideas were completely compatible. Richie Schmitt also proved to be an extraordinary recording engineer. He had come into the business cutting classic hits with Jefferson Airplane and never looked back. His list of hit records was growing faster than Pinocchio's nose even while we were in the studio recording my album. His status was such that he even had a pair of intern engineers who ran the twenty-four-track machines at his command, thus allowing Richie to concentrate his energy on precise microphone placement, equalization levels, and capturing any magic that might happen in the studio. With this superb team, the basic tracks for *People* were recorded by mid-March. We promptly began "sweetening," or overdubbing color instruments and background vocals.

Joe, Sidney, and Bullets stopped in regularly to hear the basic tracks and were happy that *People* was shaping up as a much more sophisticated pop record than *Merging of Our Minds*. When Jim Helms conducted the string section's soaring overdub session in early April, even Sidney Goldstein was smiling. But Joe Reisman was elated. He had supported "The Call" from the first time he heard it and fretted like a mother hen over our recording of the song.

"Congratulations," he beamed to Ron and me after the session. "You threaded the needle on the coyote song, boys, but I hear several singles. That Hopalong Cassidy tune is a hoot."

Joe's reaction was music to my ears. So I was supremely confident of my new record as I boarded the jet bound for Austin. Soon after my return to town I got a call from Rod Kennedy that would link me with the Kerrville Folk Festival forever: Navasota bluesman Mance Lipscomb had become too ill to perform on the main stage of the 1973 festival, and Kennedy asked me to replace him. The lineup for the festival now included Dick Barrett, the Bluegrass Ramblers, Allen Wayne Damron, Ewing Street Times, Steven Fromholz, Bill and Bonnie Hearne, Carolyn Hester, Big Bill Moss, Michael Murphey, Willie Nelson, the Royal Light Singers, Sunny Schulman, Robert Shaw, B. W. Stevenson, Kenneth Threadgill, Timberline Rose, Townes Van Zandt, Jerry Jeff Walker, Peter Yarrow—and me.

At the 1973 festival I finally felt more like I fit into the Texas folk scene. But I especially remember B.W. having a screaming fight with Rod after the impresario had his mother evicted from the backstage area because

Kennedy didn't know who she was when he asked for her pass. B.W.'s skirmish with Rod was only a harbinger of things to come later that evening.

The first two Kerrville Folk Festivals were held indoors in the Kerrville Municipal Auditorium rather than at Rod and Nancylee Kennedy's Quiet Valley Ranch. Performers were housed in a local motel featuring 1950s-vintage cottages facing each other across a large courtyard. Immediately following those first two festivals, Rod hosted an after-show outdoor barbecue feast for the performers in the courtyard between the cottages. Even with motel rooms, performers, musicians, tech crews, festival staff, and various entourages often also camped on the motel grounds, and everyone gathered for the after-show feast and picking session. It was the very beginning of the now internationally famous Kerrville after-show campground songfests.

I was putting up our tent when a friend came running to our campsite to alert me that my stepchildren were mixed up in a fight between Jerry Jeff and Rod Kennedy. Flabbergasted, I ran to the food lines, where Jerry Jeff and Rod had just ended their spat and made up. I discovered that Rod had kicked Jennifer and Jeff out of the food lines because they didn't have proper passes. Frightened, they froze and broke into tears. Jerry Jeff quickly stepped in to defend them.

"Those are Bobby Bridger's kids!" someone yelled as Jerry Jeff took Rod to task for his rude treatment of the children.

"I'm sorry," Rod protested. "I didn't know they were Bridger's kids."

"That doesn't matter!" Jerry Jeff shouted. "You don't kick kids out of a food line!"

I was mighty impressed with Jerry Jeff Walker for that moment. Over the years, as the "scamp" often emerged in his personality and people would shake their heads in disbelief at his antics, I remembered the sensitive hero Jerry Jeff was that night defending my stepchildren.

It took Rod several more years to discover the more gracious aspects of his personality. That evening after the ruckus ended peacefully, Gloria told the folk impresario, "Rod, of all the people I don't like, I like you the best." Later, I asked her what she meant by that convolutedly humorous remark. She said: "Think about it. Aside from Rod Kennedy and Allen Damron, do you know any conservative folksingers? 'Folksinger' is the very definition of liberal. Rod's 'redemptive flaw' is his love of music. Essentially, he's a right-wing conservative Republican bomb-the-commies Marine who logically would not be caught dead with left-wing, liberal, folksinging Democrats. Instead, Rod's love of music overcomes his politics and attracts him to liberals. Eventually, this 'crack' in his essence will lead him to become a liberal. That's why I told him, 'Of all the people I don't like, I like you the best.'"

Little did I suspect that evening that in the future Rod Kennedy would become one of my best friends in the music business. As I became more intimately involved with the festival—I joined the board of directors in 1976—our frequent arguments were often resolved with innovations. For example: After judging the "New Folk" contest in 1976 with Townes Van Zandt and Steve Young, I complained to Rod that the contest had become too competitive. This led to a heated discussion between us that inspired the creation of the "Ballad Tree," a gathering at the oak tree on Quiet Valley Ranch's Chapel Hill, where everyone had a chance to sing at least one song for a critical yet appreciative audience.[2] After three decades I have come to regard Rod's unique role in creating the Kerrville Folk Festival with profound respect and appreciation. To elaborate on Gloria's synopsis, have no doubt that without Rod's inflexible "Marine" attitude and authoritarian discipline, the Kerrville Folk Festival would have ended after those first two mythic gatherings. Rod's resolve to make the festival succeed is the single thing that ultimately ensured its survival after many tragic twists of nature and fate that would have withered the willpower of lesser men. Besides, bless his heart, he's the *only* music promoter who booked me regularly for over three decades!

Joe Reisman's voice broke with emotion as he explained his nasty firing; after nearly four decades of major success with RCA he had been given a weekend to clear his office—or have his belongings placed on the curb. The depressing news meant my days with RCA were also numbered, so Gloria and I continued our Wyoming vacation plans with the awareness that major change was imminent. Wyoming had already come to represent spiritual healing to us, and now, more than ever, it felt important to be returning.

As we passed through Colorado, I picked up a copy of the *Denver Post* and discovered a story about a modern-day Wyoming mountain man named Timberjack Joe. I clipped the story, tucked it in my journal, and planned a search for this Timberjack Joe character when time permitted. Now, however, I was on my first trip to Fort Bridger, Wyoming. U.S. 40 climbed west over Berthoud Pass, and upon reaching the spectacular summit, the two-lane blacktop highway continued to rise gradually over high plains and thick groves of lovely quaking aspens that shimmered happy greetings in the sparkling sunlight. The journey west across the ancient mountain ranges of northern Colorado was a rhapsody of breathtaking silence as inadequate words frequently surrendered to the unspoken, eloquent articulation of wonder. We crossed out of Colorado and into the high-altitude desert tip of Utah and suddenly began dramatically rising in elevation again as we approached the Wyoming border in the southwestern corner of the state. Before leaving Utah, we passed through Ashley National Forest, named for the leader of the historic 1822 and 1823 expeditions that brought the fur trade—and Jim Bridger—to the Rocky Mountains. As we drove deep into the magnificent Flaming Gorge area of Utah/Wyoming, I experienced a stunning glimpse into why, with his pick of locations in the Rocky Mountains, Jim Bridger spent most of his life in this region.

A pivotal event in American history occurred in this remote location in 1824. Along the road to Fort Bridger we passed the actual site of the very first "rendezvous" of the fur trade era. Faced with bankruptcy after losing large amounts of money with his failed expeditions into the heart of the Rocky Mountains, General William Ashley asked his partner, Major Andrew Henry, to remain in the mountains through the winter until he could return to St. Louis for more provisions and men. He planned to be back in the spring. Ashley instructed his partner to send the remaining men of the expedition into the mountains in the meantime to explore the region and trap whatever beaver they could. Ashley promised Henry he would rendezvous with him a year later. Over the following year Henry's "exploring" trappers discovered the largest beaver colony in America, and when Ashley returned with provisions, a new system for harvesting and transporting fur was born. The success of the rendezvous concept made Ashley one of the richest men in America and also became the financial toehold that the United States sought in the unexplored Rocky Mountains. Ashley's exploring trappers opened the region to the young American nation.

As we rolled into the tiny village of Fort Bridger, Wyoming, the first thing I noticed was the crude, ignoble, painted plywood characterization of Jim Bridger holding a firecracker. The entire town comprised a small post office, an American Legion hall, a couple of stores, a gas station, a café, a few deserted and collapsing buildings, an elementary school, and the state historical site. The grounds of the site were lovely, well maintained, and blessed with a sense of peace. Gentle breezes rustled through the aspen and cottonwood trees surrounding the parade grounds. The staff at the site, however, seemed bored and uninterested. Sadly, they were unable to answer any of my questions about Jim Bridger. So we spent the morning walking through the old fort and museum, bought a couple of books about the history of the fort, and then got back in the car and headed north toward the Tetons and Yellowstone.

In spite of the inherent tranquillity of Fort Bridger, after all the years of wanting to visit the place, I found it to be an overall disappointment. Fortunately, within a decade the staff at Fort Bridger would change dramatically. Some of that change would begin with the inception of an annual reenactment of the rendezvous of the fur trade era and the event's huge impact in revitalizing strong regional interest in mountain men. The growing popularity of the Fort Bridger Rendezvous convinced the state of Wyoming to employ a staff of younger, educated people and facilitated the creation of a passionate historical association devoted to keeping the spirit and memory of Jim Bridger alive at the historical site.

In fact, by 1973 rendezvous reenactments were beginning to catch on all over the Rocky Mountains. In the Wind River Mountains we stopped for a respite in tiny Daniel, Wyoming. The entire town of Daniel was a single gas station, and I noticed a poster in the gas station window. It was an advertisement for a mountain man rendezvous coming up in five days in nearby Pinedale—just enough time for us to visit the Tetons and Yellowstone and return for the event.

The previous year's visit had made me aware that the only music scene in Wyoming was in Jackson. But Jackson's musical venues seemed more aligned with Nashville than with the region's history, and I would have a difficult time there presenting any kind of music other than alcohol-fueled, belt-buckle-rubbing, soap-opera country. So after a day hike in Yellowstone, Gloria and I returned to Jackson Hole and the Grand Tetons for more investigation into the cultural scene there. During the previous summer we had hiked Cascade Canyon in the Grand Tetons, and we spent most of the time we had in the area hiking there. But our time in northwest Wyoming raced by quickly, and soon we had to head south to Pinedale for the rendezvous.

Nestled in the foothills of the southern slopes of the Wind River Mountains, the Pinedale region was home to six of the twelve known historic rendezvous of the fur trade era. So I assumed that the rendezvous reenactment would be of the top order. To the contrary, it wasn't even a real rendezvous; instead, it was a town pageant. Locals in man-tan makeup and fake buckskins pretended to be mountain men and Indians while an announcer read from a script over a public address system that sounded like it had been borrowed from the Little League park. The text of the script was historically accurate and quite good, but the ludicrous historical pantomime of the citizens of Pinedale—more than a few of them dog-drunk—bordered on embarrassing. Nevertheless, the pageant had enjoyed a long history and was obviously a source of great joy for the audience, so I decided to ask some questions. This led me to the Sublette County Historical Association, where I was introduced to a handsome elderly woman named Alice Harrower. Later, over cookies and milk at her house, Mrs. Harrower told us that she had crossed the Great Plains in a wagon as an infant with her parents. Inherently dignified, she spoke carefully, with a cheerful lilt in her voice. Her body language and movement were as nimble and precise as her speech, and as practical as the style of her clothes. Since Sublette County was the central location of the halcyon days of the fur trade era, Mrs. Harrower and several others from the founding families believed there should be a national museum of the mountain man located there. They had even created an organization to raise the funds to actualize their dream. With great care and respect, she unfolded the architect's blueprint design to proudly explain each minute detail of the proposed museum.

I left Mrs. Harrower a copy of my script and historical vignettes of *Seekers of the Fleece* and told her that I would be delighted to help in any way I could to make their dream a reality. Gloria and I piled back into the Monte Carlo and headed for Texas. Before the journey home we planned one more adventure in Wyoming.

For many years I had pondered how I might go about meeting Indian people. It finally occurred to me that if I wanted to meet white people I would go to church or to a dance. In Jackson I had seen a poster announcing an Arapaho/Shoshone powwow at the rodeo arena in Thermopolis and realized it was the dance I sought. To get to Thermopolis from Pinedale we would have to veer north off course a bit. But it was time to meet some Indians.

THIRTEEN

Juxtapositions

THE TINY TOOTHLESS INDIAN WOMAN shook her ancient brown finger at me and cursed in Arapaho. Stunned, I surrendered to her ambush. I had no idea what she was saying, but she obviously was not pleased that I had joined the colorfully costumed dancers circling with the rhythm of the drum. As the wizened old woman cursed me, the dancers continued, stealing peeks as they passed. A pair of young girls pointed at me, hiding giggles behind fancy bright-colored shawls. Crestfallen, I whirled and fled the small rodeo arena.

I had not envisioned anything like this happening at a powwow. To begin with, Gloria and I were the only non-Indians present. Feeling like intruders, we battled our first impulse, to leave. But we had traveled far to attend a powwow, and the Indian people seemed generally friendly. So we decided to stay long enough to check things out. Recently plowed clods of dirt crushed beneath my boots and released the pungent smell of fresh earth as we walked toward the center of the Thermopolis Rodeo Arena. There, an audience of about a hundred Indian people surrounded a smaller circle of dancers. Some of the dancers were elaborately painted and dressed in sparkling fluorescent-feathered costumes, while others were dressed in street clothes. Every age group was represented, from toddlers to elders. Off to one side of the inner circle a group of six or seven Indian men, dressed in jeans, ribbon shirts, beaded gimme caps, boots, and sneakers, sat in folding chairs around a bass drum that was turned on its side and slightly suspended in a wood and rawhide cradle. They pounded the drum with large leather-tipped mallets and sang high-pitched chants. Painfully out of our element, we joined the audience watching the dancers. After a few awkward minutes, however, my feet started to move instinctively to the rhythm of the drum, and I began to bob up and down, mimicking the dancers. I suddenly became possessed with intense nervous energy, and in what could only be explained as a desperately feeble attempt to explain my presence, bounced out into the circle of dancers. This seemed to amuse several of the dancers, and I was beginning to feel comfortable—until the old woman suddenly attacked me and I fled.

Gloria and I were loading into the car when an Indian man hurried toward us. I recognized him as one of the friendlier faces I had seen on the dance grounds. He appeared only a bit older than me.

"Don't leave with hurt feelings," he said. "You jumped the gun back there. If you had looked carefully you would have noticed only women and little girls were dancing."

His words got our attention, so Gloria and I paused to hear what he had to say. "That ol' grandma was only letting you know you intruded on a woman's dance," he continued. "Soon the leader would have called another dance and invited men to join in."

"I'm sorry," I sighed. "I just wanted to meet some Indian people."

"I'm Lakota/Arapaho," he said, offering his hand with a wide, friendly smile. "Jake White Plume."

I introduced myself and Gloria, offered Jake a Pall Mall, and we leaned against the side of the Monte Carlo and lit up. Jake wasn't dressed in a colorful dance costume with neon-bright feathers and silver bells like some of the other dancers. Instead, like the drummers, he wore jeans, a khaki work shirt, tennis shoes, and a gimme cap. The cap was adorned with a large eagle feather that dangled from the button on the crown, and beadwork sparkled from the rim of the visor. Tightly braided black pigtails, tied off with bright red ribbons, draped over his shoulders down to his stomach.

"So, aside from getting old women mad at you, what brings you to pow-wow?"

I confessed that I was a recording artist, but quickly explained my distant relationship to Jim Bridger and my desire to learn more about his relationship to Indian people. A smile broke over Jake's face when I mentioned Jim Bridger.

"*Ca-sa-py,*" he said.

"*Casapy?*"

"'Blanket Chief.'" Jake grinned. "That is what the Shoshone called Bridger. Of course in those days the Lakota and Arapaho were enemies of the Shoshone, so if we had run into Casapy and his Shoshone friends we would have taken his blankets—and his hair."

I wasn't sure whether Jake was taunting an obtuse white guy or ribbing a naive new friend. But in the decades since that evening in Thermopolis I've discovered mischievous teasing to be a ubiquitous characteristic of every Indian person I've ever encountered; indeed, a trait of American Indian people that most appeals to me is their lighthearted sense of humor and general love of tomfoolery. Years after meeting Jake and forming scores of cherished family relations and friendships in Indian country, I learned to recognize the vital, enduring threads of good-natured pranks and loving mischief uniting all tribes of American Indian people. Jake White Plume's playful teasing that evening proved a perfect introduction.

When I stumbled out into that dance, I had learned much about Indian philosophy and religion—all from books. As intimate personal experiences in Indian country developed, however, I grew to realize that Indian religion most closely reflects my own fundamental beliefs. In its essence, Indian religion represents a sense of environmental harmony and universal interconnectedness. The Lakota refer to this as *mitakuyue oasin*, which translates as "all my relations," or "we are all related." This suggests that every person, animal, plant, stone—everything—has a unique purpose within the intertwined cycle of life. This interconnectedness of everything also implies that ultimately there is no death—only a transition of life forms. This idea perhaps explains another ubiquitous trait that I have observed and admire most in Indian people: they cheerfully embrace life—and death—with a fierce artfulness.

Jake explained that we were certainly welcome at the powwow and that he would stay with us to make sure we understood what was going on. I offered him another smoke as we returned to the powwow grounds and the dance. As Jake field-stripped the butt of his second cigarette and let the paper and remaining tobacco fall to the ground, he told me something about Indian people that I've never forgotten.

"That old woman has seen many curious white folks like you over her lifetime, Bridger. They come out here to Indian country, satisfy their curiosity, go home, and never come back. That's not a very good way to make friends."

After a "kosher" round dance we told Jake good-bye, and the next morning headed south. But White Plume's friendly introduction offered priceless insight into the way to proceed into Indian country and culture. He taught me that patient observation would eventually lead to a graceful, dignified introduction. But Jake's dry wit also made it clear that if I kept my sense of humor intact, and if my intentions were clear and honest, I could make lasting friendships in Indian country. Over time, some of my oldest and most treasured friendships with Indian people were ones that began with my first being willing to assume the role of innocent clown. For example, I have met few Indians who didn't howl with laughter at my Southern drawl fumbling with tribal dialects. That tactic alone has broken the ice with more than one intensely suspicious, taciturn character. My genuine delight at Indians' teasing about my feeble attempts to speak their language allowed my new friends to see that my intention was to learn their language in order to form and maintain lasting relationships. These relationships matured gradually as I eagerly returned summer after summer, ignorant as ever but slightly more aware of their customs, lifestyle, and language. I decided that where Indians were concerned I would always be willing to make a fool of myself if they would allow me to continue learning from them.

Don Burkheimer's negative reaction to *And I Wanted to Sing for the People* dashed any hope of label support. So Bullets suggested I return to L.A. for the August 1973 release of the album and to discuss my future. Understandably, he wanted to start searching for a new record company for me. But I was deeply concerned about his next suggestion: he wanted to book me in Las Vegas.

"My connections are in Vegas," he confessed. "I can get you openings in a couple of small joints there, and we can make some cash. Once I get you started in Vegas I can also get you a couple of shots on network television. Then we can take our pick of record labels."

I was stunned at the Las Vegas prospect, but held my tongue. Nevertheless, when Bullets got me a gig at a small folk club in Greenwich Village to promote the release of *And I Wanted to Sing for the People*, I cheered up. But I also realized Vegas was his power base, and our contract's financial requirements gave him no option other than to sway me toward his strength. Increasingly, we both understood that our goals were divergent and, sadly, our relationship was ultimately dysfunctional.

It was my first time in New York since 1965, when I fled the city in panic after only a few hours, so I savored the success of returning to promote the release of my second RCA album. Some publicity people from the New York office of RCA came to support my performance. They brought a few journalists along, and that generated a tiny buzz in a few national music magazines later. But even though this was the type of gig I wanted, I knew that Bullets was only patronizing me. Even if he wanted to go this route, it would take decades of work in folk clubs for Bullets to bring in the amounts of money detailed in our contract. Furthermore, he had little or no understanding of the counterculture movement, and his idea of folk music was Trini Lopez (yes, another of his clients) singing "If I Had a Hammer." His turf was pure Vegas and television, both anathema to me. In spite of that, we loved each other and kept trying to make the relationship work somehow. Bullets called his old friend Earl Wilson, and the day after my gig the legendary gossip columnist mentioned my show in his daily *New York Post* column, "It Happened Last Night." It was great fun seeing that item in the newspaper as I boarded the flight to Austin, but I realized it ultimately had more to do with Bullets than with me.

We agreed that Bullets would initiate a search for a new record label as soon as he returned to Los Angeles. I flew to Austin excited to reunite with Gloria, but as soon as I picked up my bags she accused me of having an affair on the trip. The ensuing argument lasted nearly two weeks.

On the morning of November 4, 1973, I awoke brooding about John Neihardt. I realized I must have been dreaming about him and was frustrated that I couldn't recall the dream. I hadn't thought about the old poet for some time, so I took it as a sign that I should pull his books from the shelf. As I read from the *Cycle* a grim mood overwhelmed me. After coffee and a smoke I still couldn't stop thinking of Neihardt, and soon my thoughts turned to my own work and my frame of mind became increasingly dark and morbid. I began obsessing that I would soon die, having failed my purpose in life. By midday I rationalized that the gloominess was because of my situation with RCA and my epic ballads. I wanted very much to continue making records within the corporate industry, but I knew my primary artistic obligation now was my new ballad form. I attempted to work through my melancholy by writing yet another letter to Neihardt. Like those before it, the letter sounded too shallow, too pretentious, too audacious, impertinent, etc., and soon was crumpled and tossed. I wrote Dr. Neihardt scores of letters like this one over the years. Sadly, I suffered from such acute "professor worship" that I felt unworthy of his attention and never mailed a single one.

My depression continued until midday, when I drove to Hill on the Moon to ask a bold favor of Jim Inmon: I wanted him to help me record a demo of *Seekers of the Fleece*. I had no money to pay him, but all I needed was a "sketch" that would document its existence. As always, Jim was ready to get to work, and we started that very morning. I was surprised and humbled when, one by one, various musicians living at Hill on the Moon started coming into the bedroom studio to offer their help. Within days, we had a rough four-track demo of *Seekers*. The first glimpse of the epic scale of the piece was finally audible. It was indeed an ear movie.

Several days later I learned that John Neihardt had died on November 3, 1973. Needless to say, this revelation was shocking on many levels. The synchronicity of my grim mood as an unwittingly clairvoyant awareness of Neihardt's passing was simply beyond comprehension. After many long walks along the shoreline of Lake Travis pondering the meaning of all this, I concluded that the entire matter was merely a coincidence and the morbid despair concerning the survival of my ballads the morning after Neihardt's death was at minimum an inexplicable personal omen. I interpreted the coincidence as a "message" for me to redouble efforts to record my epics, because Neihardt's death also marked an awareness that fate was going to require many years of sacrifices if my work was to endure and survive. But that didn't matter anymore; all that mattered now was to continue developing the new ballad form to its most exemplary plane.

This mysterious Neihardt linkage intensified the very next month when I discovered that noted record producers Nik Venet and Bill McIntyre had traveled to Neihardt's home in Columbia, Missouri, only weeks before his death at ninety-two and recorded the epic poet reciting his poetry and talking about his life. Coincidentally, United Artists Records released an elaborate two-disc LP of the work of John G. Neihardt the very month the poet died.

Considering the extraordinary events surrounding Neihardt's passing, it did not surprise me that I had links with Nik Venet. He was a legendary record producer with a pedigree that went all the way back to the Brill Building in Manhattan. Venet had produced Bobby Darin, the Beach Boys, the Stone Poneys, and a host of important transitional folk-rock albums of the 1960s. He was one of the first mainstream producers to incorporate the folk-rock movement into the alternative-pop sounds of Southern California, an action that set the stage for the Byrds, the Eagles, Jackson Browne, Linda Ronstadt, and a host of other acts. In Nashville in the late 1960s, Fred Carter Jr. played a prominent role on an extraordinary John Stewart album called *California Bloodlines* that Venet produced.[1] In fact, Venet incorporated so many of Fred Carter Jr.'s innovative ideas into the fundamental structure of *California Bloodlines* that Stewart eventually hired Fred to produce his recordings. Along with Dylan's late '60s country forays, *Nashville Skyline* and *John Wesley Hardin*, and the Byrds' *Sweethearts of the Rodeo*, *California Bloodlines* became a landmark "progressive country" record. I was excited that a producer of Venet's stature had recognized and recorded Neihardt.

Bullets also knew Venet personally. When Bullets managed Mel Brooks and Carl Reiner, Nik Venet produced their classic comedy album *The 2000 Year Old Man*. So Bullets contacted Venet to discuss my ballads, and he accepted an invitation to an exploratory lunch meeting in Hollywood. Upon learning about my western epics and their Neihardt connection, Venet agreed to help. When he found out that my contract with RCA would expire in less than two years, Venet suggested that we consider simply either waiting for the label to drop me or waiting for my contract to terminate. Then it would be a simple matter to move me to his power base at Capital Records. We agreed, and Venet said he would start laying the groundwork. Bullets urged me not to discuss our plans with anyone at E. H. Morris until we were sure we had a deal at Capital.

Sadly, after all the months of meetings and planning, Nik Venet proved to be a waste of valuable time. Worse, as we devoted energy to Venet's various diversions, RCA released *And I Wanted to Sing for the People*, and it slipped below the surface and vanished before anyone noticed.

Nevertheless, I decided to take Venet's advice and do nothing until either all of my contracts in Los Angeles expired or I was dropped. After the surreptitious behavior with Venet I was too ashamed to talk to Ron Kramer about why I took that action, but ultimately it was once again a matter of scale; three phone calls and Bullets could have me an audience with the president of NBC, but he couldn't book me at Armadillo World Headquarters. I felt I should be working in Austin with my peers who understood and supported my career aspirations. I felt I should be performing in folk clubs, and at universities, for people my age, rather than in some Vegas lounge. Bullets was the least of my problems. RCA and E. H. Morris were another matter. Of my entire West Coast team, only Ron Kramer and Joe Reisman seemed to understand, or care, about my personal career goals. With Joe gone and Burkheimer opposing the records Ron and I produced at every turn, I had little choice but to surrender.

The cost of gas was also suddenly a major factor of our tight budget. As I withdrew from contact with all connections in Hollywood, the nation simultaneously entered what would become the first of many "gas shortages," and the price of fuel—when you could stay in line long enough to get it—escalated. I grew up in an era when gas was twenty-five cents a gallon, and seeing prices suddenly soar to nearly a dollar a gallon was surrealistic.

The financial strain was also affecting my marriage. Gloria and I remained united, but the stress of my career combined with the difficult role of stepparenting, and I was often a less than perfect dad or husband. Unskilled in parenting and suddenly thrust into the role, I was often testy and not very understanding. As pre-adolescents are prone to be, Jennifer was particularly successful at pushing my buttons, which usually led to a fight between Gloria and me.

Another complicating factor was Gloria's terrible jealousy. On the strength of my RCA albums I could hustle up lucrative touring work with little effort, but Gloria was convinced that if I stayed away longer than two weeks I would succumb to the carnal temptations of the road. She absolutely refused to let me book any tour that would require my being out any longer. My film and jingle work in Austin would bring in only a small amount of extra cash, and so, given Gloria's rigid demands that I stay at home, I realized it was time to find a new direction.

That new direction was Wyoming. The previous summer I had visited the Grand Teton Lodge Company, located right in the middle of Jackson Hole. The Rendezvous Lounge in the main lodge seemed to be a place that could serve my purposes. Just as important was the fact that if my plan worked, I could take my jealous wife on the road with me. In January I contacted the Grand Teton Lodge Company and arranged to work there during the summer of 1974.

Administered by the Rockefeller family's Rock Resorts, the Grand Teton Lodge Company is only part of their vast global holdings. Like the southern entrance to Yellowstone National Park, this area too was infested with rampant crass commercialism by the mid-twentieth century. Disgusted by the crude hot dog stands and cheap jewelry vendors that proliferated along the road into Yellowstone, the Rockefeller family secretly bought up vast sections of acreage throughout the famous mountain range until they owned it all. After securing the promise of the U.S. government to protect the region as a national park, the Rockefellers gave it to the American people.

The Grand Teton Lodge Company is in the most spectacular location in the park. The stunning view of the mountain range from the sweeping rear stone terrace of the Grand Teton Lodge Company is ingrained in the perpetual romantic visual imagery of American mythology. To offer universal accommodations for distinct "classes," the lodge company itself is actually composed of three separate facilities. The main lodge caters to mainstream, white-bread America, but Jenny Lake Lodge, nestled at the base of the Grand Tetons on the banks of picturesque Jenny Lake, is where ultra-wealthy folks (such as the late Princess Grace of Monaco) prefer to rough it and make their own beds in tiny, rustic, dirt-floored log cabins. Vagabonds, hippies, park rangers, college kids and retirees working in the park for the summer, migratory rock climbers, and others of their ilk pitch tents or use minimal, cold-water cabins at the Colter Bay Campground.

The Rendezvous Lounge fell victim to a chic clothing store in the late 1980s, but in 1974 it was on the second floor of the Grand Teton Lodge. The room was decorated like the interior of a fort, with real wood pickets jutting up all four walls into a painted, Christmas-light-twinkling, star-studded, indigo evening sky. Rectangular windows were cut into the pickets where, under lights, figures in miniature, dollhouse proportions depicted scenes from the fur trade era. Corny as hell, but with a little luck, a perfect place for me to reinvent myself.

I negotiated a sweet arrangement to perform two days a week at the lounge, two days at the Jenny Lake Lodge, and two days at the Colter Bay Bar. Working six nights a week would whip the piece into fighting shape while also giving Gloria and me the opportunity to hike in the Tetons during the day. Housing and food would be provided, and my salary, though small, was adequate.

Before heading to Wyoming I started daily rehearsals of the epic ballads. One day my rehearsal was interrupted by a phone call from a guy with an East Texas accent. Michael Price informed me that he had worked at *Rolling Stone* magazine before joining forces with *Crawdaddy* magazine publisher Paul Williams to create an alternative music magazine based in New York that they called *Rallying Point*. After returning to Texas to report on Austin for the magazine, Price was considering creating yet another new magazine, based in Austin. I invited him to the debut of my epics that I was planning at the Saxon Pub, and he agreed to meet me there.

Soon after the call from Michael Price, another journalist made contact with me one night after a gig at Castle Creek. A lovely woman named Melinda Wickman introduced herself and asked if I would meet with her partner, Jan Reid, for an interview. The pair were writing a book about the Austin music scene and wanted to interview and photograph me. The next day at the interview at Melinda's home in West Austin I suggested they drive to the Hill on the Moon with me so that Jim Inmon could play our rough draft of *Seekers* for them. After hearing the tapes, Melinda set up dates to photograph me in the Hamilton Pool area west of Austin.

With the sudden interest in my epic ballads by journalists, and to prepare for the summer run in Wyoming, it was time to perform *Seekers* for an audience. The Saxon Pub, on Interstate 35, was the best acoustic room in town, and it would be the perfect place to debut *Seekers of the Fleece*. Gloria arranged for a group of her students and our friends to attend. I called Rod Kennedy and invited him and encouraged him to bring whomever he wished. I hoped Jan Reid and Melinda Wickman, Michael Price, and his brother, Alan, would be there. I figured I would have a decent crowd.

I wasn't too nervous. I had performed the work daily for nearly two months to commit it to memory. A small group gathered, and soon the lights dropped and I started fingerpicking the introductory theme of the piece. I was about halfway through the opening song when I noticed in my peripheral vision a shadowy figure rising from a table in the darkened back section of the audience. Almost erect, the character began a long stumble that continued until he sprawled across the entire back area of the room, taking out several tables in the process. Finally, he collapsed on the floor in a heap of overturned tables, twirling ashtrays, and smashed drink glasses.

It was impossible to continue the performance. Bouncers gathered the man from the floor and escorted him away from the main room, down the Saxon Pub hallway. He shouted something about "herding horses from Montana" as they carried him out. After the room was straightened and calmed, I started over.

The audience seemed to enjoy the performance of *Seekers*, but the response was less than enthusiastic when I completed it. I don't think the lackluster reception was an indictment of a weak performance. Instead, I had the distinct impression that the audience was overwhelmed at the sheer length of the piece.

I was speaking with a small group that gathered at the lip of the stage when the manager of the Saxon Pub, Jess Yaryan, grabbed my arm and informed me there was someone in his office who wanted to speak with me. I excused myself, and we slipped through the small crowd and entered his office. "Okay, Townes," Jess said to the stranger slumped in the office chair.

"I'm so sorry for interrupting your show, man," the stranger slurred. "I didn't mean to fall down in there. Rod invited me to hear your set. I guess I had a little too much to drink."

Which, of course, might have been a fitting epitaph for the late, great songwriter Townes Van Zandt. I was furious and probably would have punched him if he hadn't looked so pathetic slouched in his chair and, though sobering up, still inebriated. His dark brown bloodshot eyes were contrite, so I accepted his sincere apology. We worked together on the Kerrville Folk Festival many times in the ensuing years and, when he was sober, I found him to be boyish, shy, and unassuming. In 1976 Townes, Steve Young, and I judged the New Folk concerts at the Kerrville Festival, and during that time Townes was a compassionate and attentive judge of the musicians who performed for us. Later, I occasionally saw him throwing dice with black musicians around the Clarksville section of Austin, but even though I frequently tried, I don't think I saw him perform sober more than a handful of times. Since his death music journalists and fellow songwriters have canonized Townes as the Vincent van Gogh of American songwriters of the late twentieth century, so there is little I can add to his deification here. But, as a songwriter, I think the best compliment about Townes's songwriting was a bit of insight from John Inmon. Back in the early 1970s, before many people had heard of Townes, John made a remark with which I can certainly agree. John said that Townes's songs just seem to be "waiting" on the guitar strings for someone to play them. "If I Needed You" almost plays itself; it is so simple, beautiful, and "waiting" on the guitar to be fingerpicked.

When Bullets learned I was going to spend my summer in Wyoming, he called and we decided it was best for us to part ways. To this day, I cherish my relationship with Bullets Durgom as one of the most honest of my life. Immediately after the Kerrville Folk Festival in May, however, Gloria and I put the kids on a plane to North Carolina and headed to Wyoming. One of my Austin picker friends, Roger Bartlett, had agreed to join me as a sideman. Bartlett was normally the single member of Jimmy Buffett's original Coral Reefer Band, but Buffett had his first major hit song, "Come Monday," and had flown to Paris to celebrate his success. With time on his hands and needing work, Bartlett heard I was going to Wyoming and suggested I hire him as a sideman. Roger was a dandy picker, and I believed it would be important to have a sideman along to explore various arrangements of the ballads. So I hired him.

My work and play schedule in Wyoming could not have been more perfectly balanced. Performing my ballads each evening and hiking every day in the Tetons was a spiritual tonic. Moreover, we had Sundays off, and that enabled us to explore the broader Yellowstone region. So, as the annual Pinedale Rendezvous pageant approached in July, I looked forward to returning to renew my friendship with Mrs. Alice Harrower and the Sublette County Historical Association.

I immediately recognized him in the "grand entry" of mountain men in the rendezvous. He was that old mountain man I'd read about a year earlier in the *Denver Post*. He was riding an Appaloosa mare around the arena. I couldn't resist the temptation, so I jumped out of the bleachers, ducked under the wooden fencing, and ran into the arena. After catching up with the horse, I was startled to notice a large dog draped across the horse's rump, perfectly blending into the bundle of fur around the saddle.

"And who are you?" His confident voice was musical with hints of laughter. When I told him my name he spun in his saddle and engaged me directly.

"You a-kin a-Jim?"

"Distant."

"But still kin?"

"Pretty sure."

He agreed to meet me after the rendezvous, and I had no trouble locating him. His shabby Winnebago was surrounded by what looked very much like a line of children and parents waiting for an audience with a shopping mall Santa Claus. I took my place in line and noticed a thick plank of wood attached high on the back of the Winnebago on which crudely wood-burned letters read: "Last of the Mountain Man." After a twenty-minute wait, I entered the astonishingly cluttered recreational vehicle and stood before Timberjack Joe. He actually did look like a twinkly, albeit grungy, Santa Claus. But this Santa wore a skunk-skin hat, and bright-red long-handle underwear peeked through holes in well-worn greasy gray-brown buckskins. The smell of hundreds of campfires, various cooked meats, and dogs permeated the Winnebago.

"Didn't you mean to say the 'last of the mountain *men*' on your sign?" I asked, breaking the ice.

"No," he laughed. "When you read that sign on the back of my rig you're seeing the last of *this* mountain man."

It would not be the last time I would fall for one of Timberjack Joe's many routines. Like mountain men vaudevillians, we were destined to become sidekicks. Over the next decade as his devoted companion—and more often than not, his straight man—I would often travel the West with him for months at a time. I had found my mountain man guide.

Timberjack agreed to meet me in Jackson Hole the next week. My friend Slim Pickens owned a cabin in nearby Boulder, Wyoming, so that evening I gave him a call in California on the chance that he might know Timberjack.

"You watch out for that ol' mountain man," Slim warned. "The last time I saw him he was a-living with a skunk!"

"Well," I replied, "he's wearing it now!"

Timberjack Joe was perhaps the first man in modern America to wear a skunk-skin hat. The headdress had indeed formerly been his beloved—de-scented—pet, Rosie. When the skunk died, Timberjack simply skinned her, tanned the hide, and made it into a headdress.

Joseph Lynde was born on March 4, 1911. His sheepherder parents came across the Great Plains in wagons and settled in the Powder River country of Wyoming in the late nineteenth century. Lynde's general explanation was that he became "Timberjack Joe" in the 1930s when he participated in a historical pageant in his hometown of Gillette, and locals grew their beards out and dressed as mountain men. When the pageant ended, Joe just stayed in costume. Nevertheless, there was actually a medical reason behind the "last of the mountain 'man'": As a teenager Joe Lynde discovered that he suffered from lupus. The disease caused his nose and cheeks to regularly form hard, calloused, very painful tumors that would eventually break open as weeping lesions. As he entered adulthood and had more difficulty explaining the sores, he found the "mountain man" role made it easier. When a precocious child might ask, "What's that on your face?" he could respond, "I had a fight with a bobcat last night." Grown-ups bought it too—particularly young females.

On separate occasions, both Timberjack Joe and Slim Pickens stopped by the Grand Teton Lodge Company while I was performing there over the summer of 1974. Overall, however, the summer in the Tetons was a splendid way to isolate myself from Hollywood and the confusion of my various contracts and career restraints. By the time Gloria and I returned to Texas in August 1974, Watergate-weary Richard Nixon had resigned, and I decided it was time for serious changes myself.

Aware of my situation, Jim Inmon suggested that I should approach the Creek Theater in Austin to see if there was any interest in developing either *Seekers* or *Lakota* as a musical. I decided to accept the Creek Theater director's offer to help me mount a one-man show of *Seekers of the Fleece* and *Lakota* in the tiny space on Sixth Street. We rehearsed throughout the late summer and into autumn and winter as I continued waiting for my contracts with RCA and E. H. Morris to expire.

FOURTEEN

Beyond the Fourth Wall

Seekers of the Fleece AND *Lakota* RAN FOR FIFTEEN WEEKS at the Creek Theater, to standing-room-only audiences. Aside from affirming my decision to abandon the corporate record industry and set my own course, the show's success also established my unique professional identity and separated me from the gathering herd of cosmic cowboy singer/songwriters in Austin. Still, I was surprised when that success brought important members of the Austin art colony to performances at the little theater on Waller Creek.

A burly fellow with chocolate eyes came backstage one night after the show. His broad face was topped with thick, tousled hair as black as the huge mustache that draped his lip. When I welcomed him, his eager, toothy smile spread so wide it parted the black curtain of hair above it and lit up the room.

"Bill Arhos," he said, offering his hand and business card. "I'm the executive director of KLRN, the PBS affiliate here in Austin. I'd like to talk with you about an idea I have for a television show on PBS that will highlight local artists."

I told Arhos I wasn't interested in television, but he insisted his idea was different from the way the medium usually treated music. His sincerity persuaded me to agree to stop by his offices so that we could discuss the matter in detail.

Unfettered by advertisers' interruptions, Arhos's concept was deceptively simple: he intended to tape Texas artists performing uninterrupted thirty-minute concerts before a live audience and air them on PBS. Of course Bill's idea was *Austin City Limits*, now, at thirty years and counting, one of the longest-running shows in the history of television. Nevertheless, after seeing my one-man shows, Arhos wanted to seek funding from the Corporation for Public Broadcasting to produce a "special" live television performance of *Seekers of the Fleece* for PBS.

In college I had seen a theatrical production of Edgar Lee Masters's brilliant graveyard poem *Spoon River Anthology*, and I believed that *Seekers* could make a similar transition to the stage. When I arrived at the Creek Theater my concept of a company production of *Seekers* and *Lakota* was totally inspired by that dramatic interpretation of Masters's unique poem. With theatrical aspects of *Seekers* and *Lakota* being explored now in the one-man show, however, I still believed that *Seekers* might be developed into a full-company musical with *Spoon River Anthology* as inspiration. I asked Arhos if we could design the production to include the Lost Gonzo Band. He loved the idea.

As I was now free to record *Seekers* with the Lost Gonzos, Arhos's willingness to include them could not have been more timely. Even so, I could not stop thinking where I might take the one-man show next. Of course, Larry Martin's theatrical concept of what I was now calling *A Ballad of the West* as a one-man show was essentially the same as what Slim Pickens instinctively realized when he dressed me in a mountain man costume to perform *Seekers*. Both men realized that my initial concept of structuring historical characters' eyewitness accounts into epic poetry and songs would spring vividly to life in a one-man show. Performing *Lakota*, however, I was acutely aware that more than a few traditional roles flip-flopped. To begin with, my balladeer was a white man—in Lakota language a *washichu*—singing the history of the Euro-American industrial revolution invasion of the buffalo-and-horse culture of the Plains Indian—from an Indian perspective. I was most definitely venturing into unexplored territory.

As with *Seekers of the Fleece*, I had never intended to perform *Lakota* as a one-man show. Still following the *Spoon River Anthology* model, I envisioned *Lakota* being performed by a troupe of Indian singers and musicians. From my first commitment to Martin to perform the piece as a one-man show I was fully aware that in politically correct modern America both Indian *and* non-Indian people were likely to take offense at a non-Indian singing this story. Conversely, I also believed that most enlightened people would agree that an American Indian should not be forbidden to play

Hamlet just because *she* was not born a Dane. But I had also discovered another void in writing *Lakota*: one of the world's most ancient axioms is that the military victor writes—and sings—history. Collective shame and guilt certainly prevented Euro-American balladeers from singing a history of the blatant theft of North America. Nevertheless, rather than evoking the past, pioneer Indian folksingers like Buffy St. Marie and Floyd Westerman wrote about topical, contemporary issues. In 1971, with the exception of allusions in protest songs, no Indians were writing music about the Indian wars of the nineteenth century. By writing and performing a ballad about Black Elk, Red Cloud, Crazy Horse, Sitting Bull, and other Indian leaders' historical recollections of that terrible chapter in American history, I could sing their story for the very first time. I well understood and respected the fact that the heart of *Black Elk Speaks* was the telling of a holy man's sacred vision to a non-Indian poet. I also understood that to Indian people this meant that Black Elk willingly gave his power to John Neihardt. But another chamber of the heart of that book was that Black Elk gave his power to Neihardt so that he could give his vision to all people. Vitally significant to my purpose, *Black Elk Speaks* was also an eyewitness account of the Indian wars. So from the beginning I decided to present Black Elk's historical perspective of the period and use *Lakota* to suggest to the more spiritually curious that they devote closer attention to *Black Elk Speaks*.

Politics aside, another important insight I gained from the initial theatrical performances of the one-man shows was that from the campfires of antiquity throughout time, humans are genetically hardwired for Homeric couplets and a poet's voice reciting legendary tales in heroic verse to the accompaniment of a harp, lute, or, in my case, twelve-string guitar. Equally important, I discovered that theater's divine blessing of the "suspension of disbelief" accentuates the meticulously structured imagery of poetry, while simultaneously acting as a trigger to set the audience's imagination in motion. Even as I bowed to accept the audience's first warm and lengthy ovation, I knew I was going to take this interpretation of my ballads to the next level—beyond traditional theater's proscenium concept of the "fourth wall."

During rehearsals Larry Martin and I spent many hours discussing the theatrical concept of the fourth wall. Martin taught me how experimental German playwright Bertolt Brecht consciously broke with theater's ancient proscenium format. I learned that prior to Brecht, the actor rarely tinkered with the audience's suspension of disbelief to personally address them over the footlights—the imaginary, invisible fourth wall. Instead, the actor remained in character, involved in the scene unfolding onstage—behind the fourth wall, boxed by the remaining three visible walls of the proscenium.

Midway in the show Martin directed me to discover the neck of my guitar extending over the footlights, thereby "ripping a hole" in the fourth wall. Surprised to discover my audience through the "tear" in the wall, I pantomimed peeking through and pulling at the hole, ripping it wider for a better view. Then I suddenly leapt over the footlights into the audience—usually accompanied by a few surprised gasps. Once within the audience I took a few moments as a puzzled balladeer from a bygone period suddenly aware that he had somehow been magically transported to modern times. Then, more than a little disgusted at what he'd discovered, my balladeer returned through the tear to the stage and his own "time" to complete the performance.

Even though I felt it was a superfluous moment in the show, the concept inspired me to want to permanently leap over the fourth wall to truly become a "time-traveling" balladeer. Consequently, the next goal for me was to take my nineteenth-century balladeer—period costume and all—out of the theater. I wanted to perform these ballads beyond the confines of the proscenium format, out where the audience's suspension of disbelief would be the only "real" wall. There, the audience's last restriction in response to my verse and performance was their imagination.

With the success of the one-man show, the performance of the piece had rapidly evolved from simply singing it as a folk musician. It was now a professionally polished, authentically costumed, and dramatically acted performance piece with none of the accoutrements of modern culture such as microphones, modern electronic enhancements, rear-screen projectors, or any trappings of corporate music. The period costumes alone would nonverbally imply authenticity and theatrical sparkle, while also encouraging the audience to eagerly suspend their disbelief and rely on their imagination to travel through time along my epic balladeer's musical narratives.

While rehearsing *Seekers* and *Lakota* with Martin, I also wrote the first draft of the work I envisioned as the centerpiece of the trilogy. Studying Joseph Campbell's *Hero with a Thousand Faces* for my *Aldebaran and the Falling Star* project returned my attentions to William F. "Buffalo Bill" Cody, and I realized that like Jim Bridger and Black Elk, he met the longevity criteria I required for a protagonist in an epic ballad. Deeper study revealed that Cody lived his life with a foot in both the Indian world and the white man's world, and this led me to conclude that he was the perfect subject for the middle section of *A Ballad of the West*. Since the Lakota people called him Pahaska, or Longhair, years before he was known as Buffalo Bill, I felt that name would serve as a good title.

Following initial research, I explored the theme that movie star John Wayne was Cody's metaphorical grandson. Where Cody was a bona fide hero who became a "star," however, John Wayne was a legitimate star who—through modern media manipulation—became an "illegitimate" hero. The experience of writing *Seekers, Lakota,* and *Aldebaran and the Falling Star* in my epic ballad structure served me well, and the first draft of *Pahaska* was completed in less than two months. Unfortunately, its destiny was my fireplace. Only weeks after finishing *Pahaska*, I was having coffee with a friend at a popular café near the University of Texas campus. When I described *Pahaska* to him, he said my premise sounded very much like a play he had seen in New York by Arthur Kopit called *Indians*. That afternoon I found a copy of Kopit's play and by that evening my first draft of *Pahaska* was ashes. A decade later, in 1983, Arthur Kopit and I were on a symposium panel in Omaha, Nebraska, at Creighton University. Creighton's theater department was producing *Indians*, and the university brought me to campus a week before the show's opening to perform *Lakota* for various classes to "set the stage" for *Indians*. Kopit and I became good friends, and after that I visited him in Connecticut when I was in the East.

Bill Arhos and I started meeting weekly to create budgets and design a company musical production of *Seekers of the Fleece* to propose to the Corporation for Public Broadcasting. John Inmon became the point man for the Gonzos, helping to negotiate fees and coordinate Jerry Jeff's touring schedule with our proposal's timelines. While the PBS proposal was developing, I began urging Joe Mott to come up with the cash for me to record *Seekers of the Fleece*. I argued that with the PBS proposal gathering momentum it would be wise to have a recording to sell when the show aired and we could also capitalize on the rare promotional opportunities that America's bicentennial celebration would provide.

My timing was right on target: Joe's brother-in-law, Bob Warren, was an attorney with a prestigious law firm in Denver. In 1976 the state of Colorado was celebrating its centennial as well as the American bicentennial, and Warren knew several men on the Colorado Centennial-Bicentennial Commission. Warren thought we might be eligible for grant money from that commission if we recorded *Seekers* in Denver.

By the time my one-man show of *A Ballad of the West* closed at the Creek Theater in late April, the Arhos/PBS project was gathering momentum, and Bob Warren found a twenty-four-track studio in Aurora, Colorado, that he wanted me to consider for our production of *Seekers*. Joe Mott and I flew to Denver and visited with the owners of Denver Sound Studios. After we discovered Denver Sound to be a state-of-the-art facility, I called Slim Pickens and asked when he was available. The final piece of the scheduling puzzle fell into place when Slim's open dates matched up with those of the Lost Gonzo Band. We booked the studio for the week of July 18–22, 1975.

In late June Gloria and I loaded the car and headed to Colorado. To pass the time as we drove over the Llano Estacado, Gloria asked me who I would like to meet more than any other person. In previous years I would have immediately answered John G. Neihardt or perhaps Groucho Marx. Since discovering the work of Vine Deloria Jr., however, I had a new hero. Deloria's *Custer Died for Your Sins* had awakened me to a more realistic awareness of Indian people, and *Behind the Trail of Broken Treaties* had done the same from a perspective of their legal history. Only recently I had blazed through Deloria's groundbreaking *God Is Red* and been so impressed with it that notes inspired by the book filled pages in my journals. When Gloria asked her question I was halfway through my second reading of *God Is Red* and, without thinking, I answered, "Vine Deloria Jr." Two nights later I met him.

The "token American Indian" on the Colorado Centennial-Bicentennial Commission, Vine Deloria Jr. gave introductory remarks that shocked his fellow commissioners at the group's initial meeting. The Lakota leader announced his belief that pomp-and-circumstance parades and sentimental television commercials were nothing more than vapid exercises glorifying image over substance. As an alternative, Vine suggested that the commission simply do away with pretense and evenly distribute all its funds to ten poets to chronicle the milestone.

Needless to say, when they eventually realized that Deloria wasn't joking, the investment bankers, lawyers, doctors, and politicians who had been invited to design and implement Colorado's celebration were taken aback by what they viewed as a preposterous idea. Not even fellow commissioner John Denver wanted to abdicate power and bestow name association—and cash—on a pride of poets. So if Vine had not made such a "poetic" proposal we might have never met. Otherwise, Vine most certainly would have never attended a meeting of the commission at a pretentious mansion in the Denver suburbs. Since the purpose of the meeting was to audition "some kind of poet," however, Vine's outrageous suggestion had backed him into a corner.

I had been informed that an Indian commissioner would be present and was stunned to learn that the man smoking cigarettes in the corner was indeed Vine Deloria Jr. He wore a white T-shirt, black walking shoes, and baggy black jeans, frayed at one knee and faded gray on both thighs. Over the T-shirt he wore an untucked, unbuttoned, blue button-down dress shirt, with the sleeves rolled up past his elbows. He was a tad overweight, with a powerful chest, shoulders, and facial features that suggested a still-lean, muscular physique. Black horn-rimmed glasses covered his curious ebony eyes. His straight black hair was cut short.

I made a bold decision. Rather than perform *Seekers of the Fleece* as originally planned for the Anglo-dominated commission, I announced that in honor of Mr. Deloria, I was going to perform *Lakota*. Then, I decided that rather than performing *Lakota* in the theatrical style of my new one-man show, I would simply sing it folk-style.

I looked up occasionally during the performance to notice Vine's stare. It was emotionless, yet seemed somehow to be penetrating deep inside me. After the third time I looked up to try to get a feel for his reaction, I decided not to give it any more attention. I could not risk losing focus, and his commanding presence took me very close to that edge. When I completed the performance Vine came over and introduced himself.

"When you started your song my scalping hand started twitching," he said, "but your sincerity soon won me over. But you really need some work on pronunciation of Sioux words. I'll help you with that. Step outside with me for a smoke?"

"Will you leave your scalping knife at the door?"

"Yeah," he laughed, "but you do look a lot like Custer with those blond curls and that red beard."

We walked out into the chilly Colorado evening. It didn't surprise me that we both smoked Pall Malls.

"Have you ever been to the fort?" he asked.

"I don't think so," I answered, confused.

"William Bent's old fort," he explained. "It's over a hundred years old. It's not too far away. We could head up there now and make it before closing time. How'd you like a buffalo steak? On me."

Vine and I continued to talk at the fort long after finishing dinner. I learned a bit about his illustrious family history, and he told me about a book he was writing titled *The Metaphysics of Modern Existence*. He drove me back to my car, and we exchanged phone numbers and agreed to reconnect in the future.

The next morning I met with the staff at Denver Sound to lock our schedules before Gloria and I headed to Wyoming, where I had planned a retreat in the Tetons to prepare for the recording sessions. By midafternoon we were rolling up Highway 189 toward Jackson Hole. The following morning we arrived at the base of the Grand Tetons, hiked up Cascade Canyon to Lake Solitude, pitched our tent, and camped for three days.

I planned to surprise Slim and the Gonzos with a mini-rendezvous in the mountains, so Timberjack Joe met us in Jackson to caravan to Denver. When we returned to Colorado, Timberjack and I proceeded to a friend's ranch near Sedalia, where we set his tipi up in a lovely meadow in the mountains. With the tipi standing and the studio ready to roll, Timberjack started to cook for our surprise rendezvous, and I raced to Stapleton Airport in a rented station wagon to pick up Slim and the Gonzos.

The Lost Gonzo Band was so overflowing with music that being in their presence was like having your life accompanied by a sound track. A simple walk through an airport terminal with the Gonzos was a concert in motion; they would check their larger gear and carry violins, concertinas, mandolins, pennywhistles, and Jew's harps on airplanes to play throughout the flight for the passengers. I didn't have any trouble finding them at Stapleton. I just followed my ears through the airport to their music.

We were all excited to work with Slim Pickens. He had recently appeared in Sam Peckinpah's film *Pat Garrett and Billy the Kid*. The Peckinpah film featured Slim in a dramatic death scene, accompanied by Dylan's classic, "Knockin' on Heaven's Door." And Slim had also recently starred in Mel Brooks's beloved comedy hit *Blazing Saddles*. Everyone loved Slim from the moment we loaded into the station wagon and he claimed "shotgun" like one of the guys. Soon the vehicle was filled with laughter and music. Behind-the-scenes movie stories and laughter continued as everyone invaded the motel lobby to check in. We agreed to meet in an hour to inspect the studio.

We had only to walk across an empty field to get from the motel to the studio, and Slim fell in with the musicians as we strolled to Denver Sound. Just watching Slim Pickens walk made you think of cowboys. But Slim's unique gait was the result not of horse riding but of a thousand bull rides, often ending in broken bones, torn ligaments, and deep bruises. Slim told me that once he had a physical for a movie role and the doctor thought he must have been in a horrible car accident to have broken so many bones. Slim explained, "Shoot, doc, my biggest accident was being born a bull rider."

After inspecting the studio we loaded everyone back into the station wagon and headed south toward Sedalia. Within two hours we were walking up the mountain to the rendezvous site. Colorado singer/songwriter Big Mike Williams, New York poet Charles John Quarto, Alaskan singer/songwriter Mike Burton, and a dozen Denver music aficionados had joined the swelling entourage by this time, on the way up the mountainside with our crew.

Timberjack's tipi was set up in a remote high mountain meadow. Jim Inmon drove an old Volkswagen van as far up the mountainside as it would go and set up a power generator. Next, he snaked nearly a mile of extension cords up to the rendezvous site so that we could record on a rented state-of-the-art Nigra tape recorder. After that, Jim strategically placed twelve condenser microphones in a ring around the base of the tipi to record our gathering inside. He also set up a string of microphones twenty yards long and had Timberjack ride his horse by them so that we could record the actual sound of a galloping horse as part of the soundscape we were creating to underscore the poetic narratives. After recording a few more ambient sounds, we hurried to partake of the banquet of wild game that Timberjack had prepared. He brought elk, deer, antelope, bear, moose, beaver steaks, and moonshine whiskey.

After Timberjack's feast we gathered around the campfire, where Slim sang some of his original rodeo songs and recited some of the most ear-blistering, bawdy cowboy poetry any of us had ever heard. Slim had not seen Timberjack in many years and the two of them had a great reunion. Timberjack worshipped Slim, and it was one of the few times I ever saw him willingly set aside his own ego and graciously let someone else take center stage. It was easy to put your ego aside for Slim. He had the rare ability to make everyone he met feel important. To thank Slim for his help with my ballads, I tanned a beaver pelt and paid Timberjack's trapper friend, Dave Haggstrum, to make it into a mountain-man hat like one I had seen in a Miller painting. At the right moment I presented the gift to Slim.

I had also brain-tanned a beaver pelt for each of the Gonzos, to symbolize the importance of the animal that had brought us all together in the first place. As I presented the pelts to the musicians, I also mentioned a curious series of coincidences occurring as we started our work together: First, we were beginning our recording sessions holding a mountain man rendezvous in the Rocky Mountains while, above us, American astronauts and Soviet cosmonauts were quite literally completing the very first successful "rendezvous" of explorers in space. Aside from the orbiting rendezvous above, however, the coincidences deepened. On July 17, 1975, we were beginning the recording of Jim Bridger's life story, exactly ninety-three years after his death on July 17, 1881. Coincidentally, on July 17, 1967, I made my first record and was dubbed "Bobby Bridger," exactly eighty-six years after the mountain man's death.

The minute the ceremonies were concluded, Timberjack suggested a toast and broke out a jug of moonshine. Experienced in such situations, Slim took a tiny social sip, bid us all good evening, and caught a ride back to the motel. After carefully touching the tips of our tongues to the moonshine, however, each of us foolishly continued passing the jug around, and the sips became deeper with each cycle. Within moments each of us was gulping the stuff and growing more boisterous as we drained the jug. I will never forget seeing poet Charles John Quarto alone on a hillside that night, silhouetted against the Colorado moon and howling like Ginsberg to an invisible audience. Exhausted within moments of sipping the moonshine, Jim Inmon was given a new name: "Engineer-Who-Passes-Out-And-Falls-Into-The-Campfire."

The next morning the meadow looked more like the location of a plane crash than a rendezvous site. Rag-doll bodies were strewn about, draped over boulders and fallen trees. Reviewing the scene, I wondered how I was going to be able to get everyone back together for the sessions—especially myself, normally a teetotaler. My head was pounding; light and sound were penetrating and painful.

I'd forgotten that the Gonzos were already seasoned veterans of life on the road with Jerry Jeff. They rebounded quickly and were ready and waiting to start the sessions at Denver Sound. Jim had us set up to begin right on time, and Donnie Dolan soon counted down the beat on "Free My Spirit, 'Fore My Spirit's Dead."

After a "live" full-band take of "Free My Spirit" we took a completely different approach to recording the rest of *Seekers of the Fleece*. I decided we should construct each song in simple stages, with me on guitar and John and Donnie playing bass and drums. So I let Bob and Gary P. take a break, and they retreated to the control room to wait for their cue. Then John,

Jim, Donnie, and I started recording basic tracks the same way we constructed the demonstration recording at the Hill on the Moon, and in numerous jingle or film score sessions. By the afternoon Gary P. and Bob gradually entered the sessions as we needed them to add piano, fiddle, dulcimer, mandolin, banjo, autoharp, or whatever. By evening, when we released the band for the day and started recording Slim's narration, we were well on our way to completing the basic tracks for all the songs.

Everyone who saw his movies thought Slim just "played himself," and to a degree that was true. But Slim Pickens was also a very fine actor. Many classic films and television shows were made more realistic by Slim's authentic presence, and he imbued *Seekers of the Fleece* with that same graceful essence.

To create a safety reel, and to have the option of editing from duplicate performances to create a third, edited performance on the twenty-four-track master tape, we recorded Slim's narration on a pair of two-track machines. Slim had committed the script to memory, so we often let him narrate long sections of text when he got on a roll. More often than not, we recorded his narration in short, four-to-eight-line sections. With two master tapes of his narration, we were able to edit from one tape or the other with such precision that we could control Slim's breath, emotional inflection, and phrasing when needed. Of course, with an actor of Slim Pickens's talents, and with his knowledge of the material, there was very little need to manipulate his performance.

As the music sessions began the next morning, we learned we had another illustrious guest: Ramblin' Jack Elliott was passing through town, and when Big Mike Williams informed him of our sessions—particularly Slim Pickens's involvement—the folk legend stopped by to join in and meet one of his own cowboy idols.

The "Brooklyn Cowboy," Jack Elliott Adnopoz, is the musical link between Woody Guthrie and Bob Dylan. The son of a New York physician, Jack became enamored with cowboys, dropped "Adnopoz" and became "Elliott" to mask his Jewish heritage, and to embellish his wandering cowboy image, added the "Ramblin'."[1] While still a teenager, Ramblin' Jack followed Woody Guthrie around Greenwich Village, mimicking the great poet/songwriter's every lick and phrasing. Folk legend has it that Woody Guthrie once remarked, "Ramblin' Jack sounds more like me than I do." Some early folk critics thought Dylan sounded more like Jack Elliott than

Woody Guthrie. Ramblin' Jack fit our motley mountain man ensemble perfectly, soon joining in on the background vocals with the Gonzos and me.

On the evening of the second day of sessions Slim finished his narration. With two complete tapes of it we had enough material to edit whatever version we wished, so Slim flew back to California. Then Jim and I began the process of lacing together Slim's final narration each night at the end of the day's music sessions.

The recording sessions continued smoothly, and we finished all the instrumental underscoring and vocal overdubs within the week that we had budgeted. Finally, Jim, John, and I assembled a rough mix of *Seekers* and planned to return to Denver in the fall to work on final mixes. In the meantime, we planned a party for the ensemble to hear the rough mixes.

Vine Deloria was the only person that I wanted to invite to the "unveiling." I had performed *Lakota* for him with just my guitar accompaniment. I wanted him to hear *Seekers* with the full Gonzo production so that he would understand more about how I wanted to eventually produce *Lakota* with the Lost Gonzos and a quartet of American Indian singers.

I was surprised when Vine accepted my invitation to attend the "first listening." Honored by his presence, when he arrived I offered him the executive producer's chair—squarely between the control room's massive stereo speakers. Jim Inmon sat at the console and rolled the tape. I took a seat on the control room floor with Gloria, the Gonzos, Ramblin' Jack, Big Mike Williams, Timberjack Joe, and Charles John Quarto.

When I heard the completed recording of *Seekers of the Fleece* the first time, it seemed oddly separate from me. I'd had earlier "glimpses" of this feeling, but realized now that the story and the form had been somehow magically blessed with a unique life all its own and had simply used me to get into the world. I looked around the room at the dear artist friends who had joined with me to free this vision. Each of them was reacting to the "birth" of this new form much the same as I was. No one spoke, but every facial expression indicated that we realized we had brought the spirit of those mountain men and their times to life in *Seekers of the Fleece*.

Vine experienced it, too. As soon as the fifty-five-minute "ear movie" faded into silence he asked me what I intended to do with the finished work. I told him I would shop it to major record companies, and he suggested that I meet him in New York in January so he could introduce me to his literary agent and executives at Caedmon Records.

In 1975, a decade before the advent and mass marketing of audiobooks that began with technological advances in cassette tapes, American literary recordings were the exclusive domain of erudite—vinyl LP—Caedmon Records in New York. Actors like Sir Lawrence Olivier or Charlton Heston read from the works of Shakespeare and other noted playwrights. Either that, or celebrity writers like William Faulkner, Dylan Thomas, Robert Frost, Carl Sandburg, or W. H. Auden read their own work. Vine read *Custer Died for Your Sins* for Caedmon, and he thought *Seekers* would be well received there. I told Vine I would meet him in New York in January after we remixed the tapes in the fall.

January was going to be a big month. Bill Arhos contacted me in late winter to suggest that I tape a concert for *Austin City Limits* at the KLRN studios. I was still skeptical of the concept, but Arhos was convincing.

"We'll have a better chance of securing funding for *Seekers* from CPB if I have a video sample of you and your work to send to Washington with the proposal," he said. "Willie's already done the first taping of *Austin City Limits* for us. B. W. is going to do the second, and you will be the third."

FIFTEEN

How to Spell Guru:
Gee-you-are-you!

TV Guide
May 29–June 4, 1976
Austin City Limits—Music
Songwriters Bobby Bridger and B. W. "Buckwheat" Stevenson per-
form. Bridger's songs include "Fompin' Around" and "People Carry
On." Stevenson does his own "Kokomo" and "On My Own" and
other songwriters numbers including "Cold, Cold Winter." (Repeat;
60 min.)

V
INE CALLED ME AT ALL HOURS of the day and night
throughout autumn 1975 to discuss his struggle with *The Metaphysics of Modern Existence.* He had given me autographed
copies of all of his books, and soon FedEx delivered a copy of the first
draft of the unpublished "Metaphysics" manuscript to better facilitate our
conversations.

I had very little grasp of Vine's archaeological and cosmological musings. He was wrestling conundrums so far out on the edge of traditional
logic that I suspected the only reason he needed me was to provide simple-
ton grounding. Nevertheless, we both seemed to draw different strengths
and comforts from the relationship, and, aside from phone calls, our letters
became so frequent that they often passed in the mail. Even though he was
now enthusiastically helping me with *A Ballad of the West,* Vine's friendship
meant more to me than any possible career opportunities his support might

bring. When I turned away from the corporate recording industry and began the process of reinventing myself as an epic balladeer, Vine immediately appeared. His timely entry into my life seemed a powerful affirmation of my decision to surrender myself to *A Ballad of the West*. Moreover, Vine's enthusiastic acceptance of my work spoke silent volumes; aside from his support of *Ballad* as a work of art, Vine's sterling reputation in Indian country predicated his every action, and his endorsement's deeper connotation underscored the credibility of the American Indian themes in my ballads. As previously noted, the evolution of *A Ballad of the West* beyond *Seekers of the Fleece* was motivated by the desire to create a work based on specific historical events from an Indian perspective as well as from a non-Indian viewpoint. This aspect of *Ballad* came into even sharper focus with Vine's blessing. Vitally important, Vine's knowledge of American Indian culture, religion, and legal history would now help define, develop, and actualize my inherent mission with *A Ballad of the West*.

We agreed to meet in early January at Vine's favorite place in New York—the legendary Lion's Head Tavern on Christopher Street in Greenwich Village. Noted journalist/author Pete Hamill once described the Lion's Head as a "glorious mixture of newspapermen, painters, musicians, seamen, ex-communists, priests and nuns, athletes, stockbrokers, politicians and folksingers bound together in the leveling democracy of drink."

Aside from the irony of a teetotaler meeting an Indian in an Irish tavern, a road musician meeting anyone in a bar seemed to me a bit like a mailman going for a walk on his day off. But I was curious to visit the famous Lion's Head Tavern because Bob Dylan sang for the hat there when he first arrived in Manhattan. Regularly holding forth at the Lion's Head, Tommy Makem, the Clancy Brothers, and Frank McCourt kept the flame of Irish folk music and storytelling alive in New York. More than a few literary icons and painters from the 1950s and 1960s continued to gather there. As an added bonus, when I arrived in January 1976, then unknown but future Academy Award–winning actress Jessica Lange was the bartender at the Lion's Head.

Descending the stairs to the basement-level entrance of the Lion's Head, I immediately saw Vine, sitting in the back of the tavern with his agent's husband, author David Markson, and the poet Joel Oppenheimer. Oppenheimer was an alumnus of the famous Black Mountain art colony in Asheville, North Carolina, a legend in the Village, columnist at the *Village Voice*, walking encyclopedia of baseball trivia, and a teacher at NYU. Long and lean, he wore a Buffalo Bill mustache and goatee accompanied by a lion's mane of hair, and was already hacking with the smoker's cough that would take his life in a decade.

After an hour or so talking literature, painting, and the legendary New York folk music scene of the early 1960s with the trio, Vine slipped away to call another old friend. Within minutes an eccentric character arrived at our table. The necklaces of tangled trinkets on his chest—rings, medallions, stone flutes, whistles, lockets, and beads—instantly reminded me of the similar snarl of bear claws, beaver teeth, elk teeth, hawk's talons, and beads—*medicine*—that cluttered Timberjack Joe's broad chest. But unlike the mountain man lingo of Timberjack Joe, this cat spoke beatnik bebop.

"Solid, Pops! David Amram!" he said, shaking my hand and introducing himself. He squinted his eyes tightly shut, tilted his head to one side toward the heavens, and growled like a black bebop jazz musician when he spoke. "Can you dig it, Pops? Here we are with 'Uncle Vine'—the 'Head-Red'! AND the A-number-one poet of the Village, Mr. Oppenheimer. Crazy, Pops! And Daddy-o Dirty Dingus McGee himself, MR. Markson. Outta sight!"

Tall, lean, blue-eyed, and handsome, with a mop of cherubic curls atop his head, Amram obviously knew Markson (the author of *Dirty Dingus McGee*) and Oppenheimer. After he sat with us for a few minutes I was convinced Amram knew *everyone* in the Lion's Head; he attracted people like the Pied Piper. Little did I suspect he was the Pied Piper of Greenwich Village. After an hour of socializing, Amram pulled me close and whispered in a soft jazzman's growl, "Whaddaya say let's split this scene, man? My pad is right here on Christopher; we can walk there and jam. Can you dig it?"

Vine urged me to get to know Amram, and arranged to meet me the next morning for breakfast at our hotel. The beatnik and I stepped out into the cold, snowy night and headed to his loft. As we walked down Christopher Street friendly people greeted Amram as if we were in a small town. I reckoned this guy was important, but I had no idea that David Amram was the very first composer-in-residence of the New York Philharmonic, handpicked by Leonard Bernstein. I didn't know that Amram had been a central figure in the mythic circle of Jack Kerouac, Neal Cassady, Allen Ginsberg, and Larry Rivers, who in the mid-1950s, along with the bebop jazz musicians and abstract painters, established a unique American postwar art scene in Manhattan. David Amram was truly one of the last of the original beatniks; indeed, he had also been an influential player in the alternative bebop movement, playing French horn with such legends as Charlie Parker, Dizzy Gillespie, and Thelonious Monk as they reinvented American jazz. In 1957 Kerouac and Amram performed the first-ever jazz/poetry readings at New York's Circle in the Square Theatre and created the landmark film *Pull My Daisy* two years later. Amram had composed scores for Elia Kazan on Broadway and for Hollywood films such as *The Manchurian Candidate* and *Splendor in the Grass.*

An extension of the scrambled mass of necklaces draped around his neck, Amram's apartment was essentially a disheveled hallway that meandered between sagging and teetering walls of books, manuscripts, and sheet music. Hundreds of exotic musical instruments were hanging on the wall, propped in corners, or balanced on various stands. Diverse sizes and types of drums, flutes, horns, and stringed instruments filled every available space in each of the rooms. Amram's phone was naked: the protective cover had been removed, revealing the internal "guts" of the device itself. It rang constantly, so I know it worked. David just ignored the ringing.

Amram and I swapped old folk songs and corny country ballads until well past midnight. At intervals he would play a lovely instrumental piece, and he must have played fifteen different instruments from various parts of the world over the course of our three-hour jam. I had never heard anyone play two flutes at once—in harmony. He held me spellbound with stories of playing with street musicians in Cuba, Arab Gypsies in the Khyber Pass on the ancient "Silk Road" in Afghanistan, and jazz legends in Paris. I hadn't had so much fun in months.

"You should come to Texas," I said before leaving. "I play a festival down there that would love having you."

"Phan-taz-alisamo," Amram drawled. "I'll lay some press and platters on ya. That would be righteous to score a gig at a Texas folk festival. Would I need a hat like yours?"

He proceeded to pull a book from one of the sagging shelves in his loft—an autobiography. He then went to another shelf and slipped out five or six albums, one being his score to the feature film *The Manchurian Candidate*, another his *Pull My Daisy* score with Kerouac.

Loaded with Amram-abilia, and suddenly aware of his international acclaim, I walked down the stairs to the street and realized I had met an enlightened *meshugah* so enchanted with music that he was genuinely excited and inspired when he engaged anyone musically. Hailing a cab, I recalled

Amram's profound remark earlier in the evening, "It's impossible for people to fight when they're playing music."

The experience with Caedmon Records proved to be a refined, highbrow version of the same corporate mentality I encountered in Nashville and Hollywood. Label executives thought my recording was a compelling yet ultimately confusing hybrid. They appreciated the unusual narrative combination of history, ballads, epic poetry, theater, and literature. They were also very impressed that the man *Time* magazine had recently proclaimed one of the ten most influential religious thinkers of the twentieth century personally brought them my project. They were nevertheless quick to explain that the label's scholarly reputation was built on being the gold standard of recording classic literature and the spoken word; they could never tarnish that prominence by releasing anything with (gasp) music on it—especially the contemporary styling of the music on *Seekers*. They appreciated the avant garde, but explained that their board of directors was very conservative and they were not prepared to release experimental projects.[1]

Aside from arranging the meeting with Caedmon Records, Vine's literary agent, Elaine Markson, booked a series of meetings for us the next day. Elaine sent entertainment lawyer Robert Wachs an advance copy of the *Seekers* demo and my manuscript of historical vignettes and he loved it. Wachs—who would later become comedian Eddie Murphy's manager—forwarded the tapes and script to Arch Lustberg, the producer of the awarding-winning 1973 Broadway hit *Don't Bother Me, I Can't Cope*. Lustberg strongly indicated to Wachs that he was interested in developing *Seekers of the Fleece* as an off-Broadway production.

I boarded the flight to Austin confident that we would have a theatrical production of *Ballad* up and running within a year. As I had agreed to tape a concert for Arhos and his initial *Austin City Limits* productions, however, I didn't have much time to daydream about theatrical productions. I arranged for the Lost Gonzos to join me and we went into rehearsals as soon as I returned from New York. Even with the elaborate set, stage crew, and multi-camera setup, the *Austin City Limits* taping was like doing the old *McCall Comes Calling* show—except this time it was for a live audience. Performing for an audience, we soon lost all awareness of the cameras and crew and let the music take over. We had so much fun at the videotaping that I immediately told Arhos that I wanted to do another taping as soon as possible.

Right after the *Austin City Limits* taping, Joe Mott and I arrived at a crossroads that would kill the theatrical deal in New York and plunge the control of the master tapes of *Seekers of the Fleece* into limbo for the next twelve years. According to our contract, Mott agreed to pay me a salary each month and take care of all our business affairs. Aside from continuing to write and produce music, I agreed to forward my monthly receipts to him. No wonder Mott frequently referred to me as his "racehorse." But Mott had not paid his "racehorse" for six months, and suddenly he informed me that he was not going to pay me any more money. Worse, convinced that the theatrical deal in New York was imminent, he demanded half of my income for the rest of my life.

When Vine learned of my problems, he immediately flew to Austin and took me to meet his old friend Professor Roy Mersky, the director of the Tarlton Law Library at the University of Texas School of Law. Dr. Mersky referred me to an Austin lawyer named Al Smith to deal with Mott. After our meeting with Mersky, Vine and I drove out FM 2222 to my house on Comanche Trail. Along the way Vine wrote me a check for a thousand dollars.

"*Never* tell anyone I gave you this," he sternly instructed me. "This is *not* a loan. Use it to buy food and to pay your lawyer."

The next day, after taking Vine to the airport, I had my first meeting with Al Smith and explained my case. It was worse than Vine anticipated. The contract had been initiated in Louisiana, so any litigation would have to take place there, within the jurisdiction of Louisiana's Napoleonic French law. This would require that Smith and his partners hire Louisiana attorneys, educated in French law, to represent us there. He advised me to negotiate.

"Let Al Smith do all the talking from now on," Vine agreed. "You need to direct your attention on something else or you'll go nuts. Focus on the PBS thing; use that to take your mind off all this stuff with Mott until Al can work something out."

I took Vine's advice and plunged into the Arhos project. Then Vine made a hundred cassette copies of *Seekers* and sent them out to a diverse group of important writers, actors, academicians, universities, and institutions, with an accompanying letter urging them to write the Corporation for Public Broadcasting to endorse Arhos's effort to secure funding for a PBS television special of *Seekers of the Fleece.*

Even with the endorsements of more than sixty prestigious responses to Vine's request, we were denied funding. Deeply chagrined about the blundering bureaucracy, Arhos immediately initiated an appeal.

Undaunted, Vine suggested that I move the project where he had more clout—the Denver PBS affiliate, KRMD. He also felt I needed to immediately "vanish" for a while to force Joe Mott to negotiate with Al Smith rather than try to influence me. When I'd first landed in Hollywood, Ole Max Evans introduced me to the advantage of "vanishing" from time to time, so Vine's advice rang true. Soon I moved the base of the *Ballad* PBS effort to Denver.

So as July 4, 1976—America's bicentennial—approached, Gloria and I made plans to spend the summer in Vine and Barbara's basement. We would become part of their family, living with them and their children, Philip, Daniel, and Jeanne. As soon as we flew Jennifer and Jeff to North Carolina for summer with their dad, we intended to head to Golden.

Before we left, Al Smith reported that he had spoken with Joe Mott personally. He had good news and bad news.

"Don't worry, Bobby," Al assured me. "Mott knows you own the copyright on the material. I've made it abundantly clear he can't legally release anything without your permission. I also let him know that if he damages your master tapes we will sue him. His brother-in-law Bob Warren actually has proxy possession of the tapes now. Warren is a lawyer himself and I've spoken with him and he has agreed to hold the tapes in Denver—in a neutral corner so to speak—until we can resolve this. So, we have a stalemate."

This "stalemate" lasted twelve years. Bob Warren finally returned the master tapes of *Seekers of the Fleece* to me in 1988.

Marlon Brando was one of the people who responded to Vine's request to contact the Corporation for Public Broadcasting on my behalf. The activist/actor sent a two-page mailgram in support of my project to the CPB in Washington. Brando also received one of Vine's cassette copies of *Seekers of the Fleece* and, I later learned, started listening to it regularly.

Brando had become an ardent supporter of American Indian causes in the 1950s. A mutual friend, Wally Heath, introduced Vine and Brando. In 1970 Heath brought the famous actor to visit the Lummi tribe of the northwest Pacific coast to support an experimental aquaculture program the tribe was pioneering. At the time, Vine was a legal consultant to the Lummi concerning their treaty fishing rights. Legend in Indian country was that after Brando met Vine the actor took no action concerning Indians without first consulting him; for example, Vine was the only person who could persuade Brando not to join Russell Means and Dennis Banks during the 1973 Wounded Knee uprising, when everyone but the actor understood that his presence would negatively tip the scales of a dangerous historical event.

Early in their friendship, unaware of the actor's notorious reputation for continually rewriting scripts, Vine allowed himself to be lured by Brando into a screenwriting project. The actor soon had the brainstorming session so completely bewildered that the project was aborted before a single word was written. Unfortunately, Vine had put in a swimming pool before being paid for the project. To remind himself never to be led astray by foolish movie people again, Vine attached a plaque to the patio wall of his house engraved with the words "The Marlon Brando Memorial Pool." So it was probably no coincidence that I was sitting on the patio by the pool when Vine handed me the phone and told me Slim Pickens was on the line.

"Whar tha gol-darn heck you been, kid?" Slim asked. "Ah been a-lookin' all o'er tarnation for you. Took some trackin' ta fine ya, if ah say so mahself. Listen, kid: Marlon Brando called me five times in one day last week! Heck, ah've knowed Marlon since he directed me in *One-Eyed Jacks* fifteen years ago, an' he ain't called me even one time a'fore last week. Says tha Indian writer, Vine Deloria, gave 'im a copy of *Seekers of the Fleece*. He's been a-listenin' to it an' wants ta toss in with us on it."

I had avoided telling Slim anything about the problems with Joe Mott because I hoped they might be resolved without involving him. Nevertheless, I felt better after informing him that Joe Mott had possession of our master tapes. I told Slim I had hired a lawyer and was hiding out at Vine's until things sorted themselves out.

"Wahl, 'ese thangs happen in our bizness, kid," he said, "but they also have ways of a-workin' 'emselves out too. B'sides, ah think Marlon's more interested in a movie than a record; ah think he wants ta play bad military guys. You jest git Vine ta help ya talk ta Marlon. Maybe 'at'll git things a-movin' in tha right direction."

I got off the phone and started jumping up and down on Vine's patio yelling over and over, "Marlon Brando wants to make a movie of *Seekers*."

Vine just sat in his patio chair smoking and looking at me sardonically. Finally he said, "If you think your life has been complicated up to now, you let Marlon Brando get involved in this and they'll take you to the funny farm in a straitjacket in a couple of weeks."

"That's crazy, Vine. He's the biggest movie star in the world. I know you know him and all, but . . ."

"Your work is too important to let Marlon mess it up, Bobby. We'll call him back if you want, but if you get Marlon involved he'll screw it up and drive you crazy doing it."

I was livid. I wondered why the hell Vine had enticed Brando to become involved in the first place if he only intended to reject his involvement. I felt like Vine was playing with both Brando and me and resented him for toying with me like that.

So I jumped in the pool to cool off. Later, when Vine left, I took a drive up Lookout Mountain. Gazing over the expansiveness of the Great Plains from that lofty peak made me start thinking about scale again. Vine's words started making a lot more sense when I remembered how out of balance I had felt in Nashville and Hollywood. The truly colossal scale of Brando's life was vastly out of proportion with mine. Even worse, joining forces with him would put all the focus on Brando, rather than *Seekers of the Fleece.* Try as he might to avoid the syndrome, any project Brando became aligned with was dwarfed by his celebrity.

I never spoke to Marlon Brando. Vine and I wrote Marlon's longtime assistant, Alice Marschak, and asked her to thank Marlon for his interest and support of my work and to please inform him that we weren't interested in a film version of *Seekers of the Fleece.*

The summer at Vine's was a period of reinvention punctuated by the realization that not pursuing Brando's interest in *Seekers of the Fleece* was strangely empowering. As July 1976 arrived I became aware that I had stepped away from something even larger than the scale of Marlon Brando: even though *A Ballad of the West* is absolutely steeped in American history, it was finally clear that it was never supposed to be marketed as part of a sentimental, bureaucratic celebration. Vine and I climbed to the roof of his house in Golden to watch the Fourth of July fireworks over Denver and laughed at the irony that as far as we were concerned, America's bicentennial festivities simply facilitated the beginning of our friendship.

Immediately after the Fourth of July Gloria and I drove up to Wyoming for a couple of weeks of hiking and camping in the high country. After locating Timberjack Joe, we returned to Golden with the mountain man in tow. Vine, Barb, and the Deloria kids loved and welcomed Timberjack, so he parked his Winnebago in their yard and camped for several weeks. Ramblin' Jack Elliott, Jerry Jeff and the Gonzos, and many other musicians also stopped by to visit as they passed through the area with gigs. The summer nights in Golden were full of music, laughter, and great anecdotes centered around Vine's grilled salmon, shipped in fresh daily from Lummi tribal friends on the Pacific Coast. Moreover, the nightclub at Denver's Oxford Hotel had become one of the best acoustic venues in the country and, as the owner, Doug Krug, was a friend, I was able to perform there more often than anywhere in Austin. One morning, however, I received a call from Warren Skaaren. He was finally ready to talk with me about a "feature documentary" that he had been brewing for a year, and he wanted to know when I was returning to Texas.

Since Warren Skaaren and I had met at the Texas Film Commission our friendship had grown steadily. Outside of my circle of musician friends, and some of Gloria's academic associates at the University of Texas, Warren was probably my closest friend in Austin. Warren and his wife, Helen, held an annual New Year's Day soiree at their home in West Lake Hills. Reflecting the Skaarens' pensive personalities, their traditional gathering was a quiet midwinter reunion of artists, a time to sit around the fireplace and discuss various projects and artistic disciplines, or simply to get to know one another. Writers, musicians, painters, sculptors, and many ambitious film artists and technicians met at the Skaarens' winter gathering; in fact, the seeds of the now blossoming Texas film industry had been planted at those New Year's Day events.

Warren left the Texas Film Commission in 1973 and was in the process of building his own production company in Dallas, where, among other things, he created production facilities for the hit television show *Dallas*. He had helped Tobe Hooper with *Texas Chainsaw Massacre* and was beginning to whisper his own desire to write, produce, and direct a project. By the early 1980s, Warren Skaaren would become one of Hollywood's most important "script doctors," or specialists brought in to polish a final draft of a script as it headed into production. At the time melanoma took his life, in the early 1990s, Warren had written the scripts for *Top Gun*, *Days of Thunder*, *Beverly Hills Cop I*, *II*, and *III*, *Beetlejuice*, and the first of the modern *Batman* franchise. While working on *Top Gun* and *Days of Thunder* Warren partnered with Tom Cruise and was in development with the actor on the *Mission: Impossible* franchise when the melanoma was discovered.

In 1974, however, Warren had been away from the Texas Film Commission for only a year and had recently embarked on his career as a producer, writer, and director. I recognized Warren in the audience one night at the Creek Theater, so I was not surprised when he came backstage after the show. A stoic Norwegian, Warren naturally played his cards very close to the chest. So without his saying a word, I knew that his appearance backstage meant something big was brewing. Knowing Warren, I also knew to be patient, that he would reveal more when he was good and ready. I was surprised, however, when he told me that evening that he had a film project in development he wanted to discuss in detail with me later. When Warren tracked me to Vine's basement eighteen months later, I knew his film was ready. As soon as I returned to Austin in September, he wanted me to begin on the score to his directorial debut—the feature documentary film *Breakaway.*

Stress fractures had been appearing in our marriage before the summer at Vine and Barb's. It didn't help that immediately after Gloria and I returned to Austin I entered the studio for an intense nine-month period of scoring *Breakaway.* Though not being paid handsomely for the score, I was getting paid, and I was working on Warren Skaaren's directorial debut. With the ongoing legal fight with Mott, we needed the money, but I also needed the work as an antidote to the legal proceedings. I was working ten to fifteen hours a day in a tiny screening studio, bringing John Inmon and various other musicians in, rolling and rewinding film, weaving guitar riffs and themes into scenes that arranger Bill Ginn could later orchestrate.

The film's theme was reinvention. After a nasty divorce, Austin real-estate developer Walter Yates fled to the wilds of Alaska with an 8mm camera and some crude tools his grandparents used to construct their cabin in Arkansas in the 1920s. Using only his grandparents' tools, Yates built a log cabin completely by himself and filmed the entire process. Then he returned to Texas, searching for someone to edit his footage into a film as a gift for his grandchildren, and found Warren. Envisioning a feature documentary film based on the experience, Warren convinced Yates that he should return to Alaska with a more elaborate camera crew to shoot more footage on 16mm film. Warren was editing footage even as I was recording the sound track.

Gloria and I went into marriage counseling in February while I continued work on *Breakaway* throughout the spring and early summer. In mid-

November 1977 Gloria and I had reservations for a production at Austin's Ritz Theater and were about to take our seats when a young woman paged us with an emergency phone call from Jennifer; Gloria's father had died instantly from a heart attack. We rushed from the theater, picked up the kids, and raced to San Antonio. After two days with Gloria's family making arrangements for her father's burial, I stole away to Austin to check on our house, dog, and cats, and to call my folks to inform them of the death of Gloria's father.

"Where have you been?" my mother cried into the phone. "We've been looking everywhere for you. Your father had a heart attack three days ago. He's alive, but they are sending him to Houston for surgery. I need you to meet me in Houston with Daddy. Please, Bobby. I need you."

As we reconstructed events we were astonished to discover that my father and Gloria's father had had their heart attacks literally within moments of each other. I told my mother I would meet her at St. Luke's Hospital in Houston, called Gloria to inform her of the shocking coincidence, and headed to Houston.

I spent much of my time at Daddy's hospital bedside in Houston looking at his large hands. I studied his long, thick fingers, swollen knuckles, large bones, and veins. We all knew cigarettes had reduced him to heart surgery. Only fifty-five, he was still lean and youthful; even unconscious and hooked up to all those tubes, awaiting the procedure that we hoped would repair his wounded heart, he seemed powerful. Realizing the toll that cigarettes had taken on him reinforced my resolve to stay away from tobacco. After a prolonged struggle, I had quit smoking my pipe and cigarettes a year earlier. I had also been jogging and doing yoga for about a year before meeting a distance runner in Frazier, Colorado, who only months before Daddy's attack introduced me to my first funny-looking pair of running shoes and distance-running techniques. Obsessive compulsiveness quickly kicked in, and within weeks I was running up to three miles a day. The running and yoga had helped free me from nicotine and set the stage for a major diet change: I was now a strict vegetarian and, at thirty-two, in the best shape of my life. Still, looking at my father lying there hooked up to medical technology, I realized I would never be as strong as he had been in his prime; even though he had given me my musical talents, I would never compare to him physically.

Looking at his hands, I remembered my own bloody hands and the Christmas Eve epiphany of 1974 that brought the shocking revelation that much of my motivation for writing *Seekers of the Fleece* had been a subconscious effort to heal an old wound between us. I smiled at the thought that my father's personality traits had become characteristics of the mountain men in my work. Jim Bridger, Jedediah Smith, and Hugh Glass were all facets of my father.

I never spoke to Daddy about what I realized when I was brain-tanning those coyote pelts that Christmas Eve. But it had not escaped me that our relationship seemed to improve after that epiphany. With that revelation, we just seemed to relax and started to actually talk more often, and he remained my worst—and best—critic.

My mother was another story. Seeing her there in the hospital with my father, I realized more than ever how dependent she was on him. Over time I had come to understand that she was a textbook reclusive; her antisocial life as a frightened only child continued into adulthood and, codependently, my father would enable her to remain an "only child" as long as he lived. I realized then that she would probably crumble mentally when he died. Daddy's heart attack was a bell ringing his approaching mortality, but it also tolled my mother's fate: it was now impossible to ignore the fact that my mother's precarious grasp of reality was clinging to my father's strong hands.

So we were lucky when Daddy survived the heart attack, quit cigarettes, and finally went home to Columbia. I loved my parents dearly and would forever remain connected to them as their firstborn son. But the time in the hospital in Houston indicated to me that I was finally my own man. There, in St. Luke's Hospital after Daddy's successful angioplasty, the three of us recalled the day in 1963 before I left home for college when I begged them to seek marriage counseling. Naturally, my pleas fell upon deaf ears then and, as we all realized again in Houston, nothing had changed in the interim. Now, as my second marriage was dissolving and my heart was breaking, I had come to recognize that I was so wounded from the impact of their combat during my tender years that I would probably never find happiness in marriage. I returned to Austin and what would become my last Christmas with Gloria and her children.

SIXTEEN

A Dance in the Desert

CONFETTI FROM 1977'S NEW YEAR'S EVE CELEBRATION was
hardly swept into 1978 before it was apparent that Gloria and I
were headed for divorce. Struggling to save our marriage had
become like thrashing in quicksand. In mid-January I attended a national
collegiate booking conference in New Orleans. To honor Gloria's request
for "space," when the conference ended I stayed with friends in Baton
Rouge for two weeks. When I returned to Austin and attempted reconciliation, Gloria angrily informed me that she and her children got along much
better when I wasn't around. Finally facing reality, I started spending
increasing amounts of time sleeping on friends' couches, in guest rooms,
and occasionally in my car.

This pattern took a dramatic turn at the lip of an Austin stage in March
1978. I finished my set and noticed a guy with a huge grin beaming under
a chest-length copper beard. A hokey straw hat sat stiff and curled farmer-
style atop his head. His blond hair was cropped very short. He looked like
Mr. Green Jeans had joined ZZ Top.

"I want you to go to the desert with me!" he shouted over the noisy
after-show audience gathered at the lip of the stage.

He introduced himself as David Sleeper, founder and leader of an outfit in Terlingua, Texas, called Desert Dance. Sleeper took thirty-day expeditions into the Chihuahuan Desert of northern Mexico to seek unexplored
canyons as "environmental laboratories." These expeditions had the primary objective of aggressively searching out and confronting all forms of

fear as a collective nomadic tribe. To face primal fears from a clear perspective, eliminate sexual game-playing, and because much of the time in the desert was, by necessity, nude, Desert Dancers were required to take vows of celibacy to be part of the expedition; men were encouraged to explore their femininity, women their masculinity. To alleviate codependency issues, couples were not allowed to go on the excursions together, but were encouraged instead to participate in separate Desert Dance expeditions. Aside from the intense social aspects, the month-long experience included technical rock climbing, spelunking, and a series of solos punctuated with water fasting. The number of solos increased over the month-long experience: the first week had a one-day solo/fast, week two brought a two-day solo/fast, and so on.

"I call it a laboratory for creating evolutionary tools," Sleeper explained.

"Well, it all sounds interesting," I said, "but I can't take thirty days off to go live in the desert."

"Thirty days of your own life?" Sleeper countered incredulously. "Weren't you just singing about freedom up there on the stage a minute ago?"

I knew then he had me, but I could not stop clinging to hope that my marriage might somehow be saved. So I asked him to let me think his proposal over before he returned to West Texas. Nevertheless, with my balancing act at home growing increasingly difficult, it didn't take long to arrive at the conclusion that perhaps Desert Dance had come along at the perfect time.

A couple of days after meeting Sleeper I was house-sitting a friend's place. Extremely depressed about the depths to which I had allowed my life, marriage, and career to descend, I noticed a world globe and started absentmindedly spinning it, idly enjoying the colors created by the twirling. When the blue-and-tan swirl visually revealed that most of the world's surface is either ocean or desert, it occurred to me if I could survive in the desert, or on the ocean, I could live anywhere in the world. I figured I'd try the ocean later and called Sleeper to accept his invitation to dance in the desert.

Wyoming presented my next direction. Aside from my interest in Buffalo Bill, I had been attracted to Cody, Wyoming, as the birthplace of the legendary painter Jackson Pollock. Gloria and I visited Cody during our initial trip to Yellowstone, but in 1975 Timberjack Joe introduced me to an amateur archaeologist there named Bob Edgar. Edgar meticulously dismantled historic buildings and cabins from around the region and reconstructed them into a "living" archive two miles west of downtown Cody on the actual site that Buffalo Bill originally surveyed for the location of his town. Buffalo Bill had been unable to convince the railroad to lay the last two miles of rail and, conceding the point, built his community where the line ended.

Indian people were always present at Old Trail Town. Bob Edgar's half-Indian wife, Terry, introduced me to Lakota elders Godfrey and Lucy Broken Rope (full name: Breaks the Rope and Steals the Crow's Horses), who were in their eighties. The Broken Ropes became two of my dearest Indian friends. During the summer months the couple lived in a nylon pup tent near Old Trail Town so Godfrey could paint on the streets of Cody and sell his work to tourists. Ironically, Vine's father, the Reverend Vine Deloria Sr., married Godfrey and Lucy, and to honor the reverend, they named their first son Vine Deloria Broken Rope. Godfrey played Christian hymns on a paint-splattered boom box and had a sign over his easel that read: "I do not speak the white man's lingo unless you want to talk about Jesus Christ or want to buy a painting." He painted only winter, spring, summer, and fall versions of the same mountain lake scene on pre-cut and -framed plywood sheets. He offered them for ten dollars apiece, and probably sold five or ten a day during the peak summer months in Cody.

I looked forward to seeing Godfrey and Lucy each summer when I returned to Cody. One summer afternoon I was sitting on the ground with the two of them in their Sears tent when out of the blue the old man explained my attraction to Indian people. "You know, *kola* [friend]," Godfrey said, "there is a strange *washichu* tribe we Lakotas call *Wannabe* Indians. But you aren't a member of that tribe. You are a Sycamore Indian. Like the sycamore tree, you are white on the outside but red on the inside."

One of the structures Bob Edgar discovered in Meeteetse, Wyoming, was Butch Cassidy and the Sundance Kid's favorite old saloon. Bob reassembled the tiny one-room structure at the head of the north side of the street at Old Trail Town. During my summer sojourns in Wyoming, Timberjack would often meet me in Cody, where, in Butch and Sundance's saloon, Bob would arrange performances of *Ballad*. Bob invited cowboys, aficionados of the West, and artists like Harry Jackson and Jim Bama to my shows in the tiny tavern. A personal favorite of these characters was Margot Belden Todd, the daughter of Charles Belden, co-owner of the legendary Pitchfork Ranch, and the premier photographer of the American cowboy of the early twentieth century; what Ansel Adams is to western landscape photography of that era, Charles Belden is to early cowboy photography.

Because of my lifelong interest in abstract painting I was particularly fond of becoming friends with Harry Jackson. A Chicago native, Harry studied at the Art Institute as a child. His mother ran a café near the Chicago stockyards that was frequented by cowboys who captured Harry's imagination. He ran away to Wyoming in the 1930s and became a teenage cowboy at the Beldens' famous Pitchfork Ranch in Meeteetse. Like my father, after the attack on Pearl Harbor, Harry joined the Marines. Returning from the Pacific theater after World War II with several Purple Hearts, Harry headed to Manhattan, where in the 1950s he became an integral part of the seminal abstract expressionist movement. Because of their connection to Wyoming and Cody, it didn't take long for Harry and Jackson Pollock to become friends. The great regional Americana painter Thomas Hart Benton was Jackson Pollock's mentor, and because of that, Harry once bellowed with characteristic audaciousness, "From the Renaissance to Tom Benton to Jackson to me!"

In the early 1960s Harry was praised as a singer as well as a painter. Alan Lomax recorded an album of Harry singing traditional cowboy songs for the Smithsonian's prestigious Folkways label. Lomax also introduced Harry to Bob Dylan when the singer first arrived in New York City in the early '60s, and Harry did an oil portrait of the fledgling icon. Shortly before Jackson's death in a car crash in 1956, however, Harry and Pollock had a falling-out when Jackson announced he was abandoning abstract painting to return to realism and western sculpture. Not long after the Dylan portrait, Harry relocated to Cody, and a new era in his career blossomed.

In the tradition of Benton and Pollock, Harry possessed an intensely belligerent, confrontational personality. Boisterous, bilious, and pedagogically pugnacious, Harry delighted in being, at moments, physically dangerous. Several times over the years of my relationship with him, when, without a clue of how, or why, we suddenly stood nose to nose, I found myself thinking the spilling of blood would surely be the very next thing to happen. But I cherish those confrontational moments as much as the quiet, elegant ones when I was privileged to tour Harry's studio, alone with a master artist. His impact on the art of the twentieth century is vast and permanent, and being in the presence of an artist of Harry's fecundity is always worth any price that must be paid.

Jim Bama's personality could not have been more different from Harry Jackson's. Before relocating to Cody in the late 1960s, Jim had been a successful illustrator in Manhattan. A photorealist, Bama was destined to become the most prominent contemporary painter of the American West for the next thirty years; indeed, when I met him in 1975 he had already firmly established his reputation, and his remarkable influence on western art was showing in the litters of copycats eating his dust. Each of Jim's paintings sold in the five-digit range, and as early as 1975 his prints already commanded hundreds of dollars. Short, with an athlete's stocky physique, Jim worked out daily in his outdoor boxing gym at his home in the Wapiti Valley. Years later, I posed in costume for Jim Bama on several occasions, but he never completed a painting of me. I also introduced him to the Indian actor Wes Studi, *Greater Tuna* actor Joe Sears, and Black Elk's grandson Clifford DeSersa, and he did portraits of each of them.

Bob Edgar was himself a character destined to loom large in the history of the American West of the late twentieth century; indeed, many of Bama's early western paintings had been of Bob costumed as a menacing gunfighter at Old Trail Town. Bob was in fact a virtuoso with firearms, a master marksman. The citizens of Cody were fond of lining up and taking turns reversing an unlit cigarette in their mouths so that Bob could take careful aim with a .45 pistol and shoot the filter tip off the damn thing from thirty yards away. If that wasn't foolhardy enough, the more daring let him shoot backward, looking through a mirror while holding the pistol upside down and squeezing the trigger with his pinkie finger!

It was for this audience that I continued the evolution of the epic ballad beyond the theater's fourth wall. At Old Trail Town I could perform the ballads for a friendly yet highly critical audience that knew and loved the American West from a broad and diverse scale of artistic perspectives. Their unvarnished criticism helped me locate the minute details of my performance of the work that needed fine-tuning.

During the summer of 1976 the incoming executive director of the Buffalo Bill Historical Center, Peter Hassrick, saw me perform *Lakota* in the Old Trail Town saloon and invited me to perform the ballad as a benefit concert at the museum. Hassrick's purpose with the benefit was to gather major patrons and the boards of trustees and directors to raise money to create an entirely new museum at the center. Hassrick explained that this museum would depict the Indians of the Great Plains and Northern Rockies. Naturally I jumped at the opportunity, and in January 1977 performed for the first time at the museum. After the performance, Hassrick and Mrs. Peg Coe asked me to become the first artist-in-residence of the Buffalo Bill Historical Center. Bob Edgar offered a cabin at Old Trail Town for lodging, and it was decided that I would perform in the museum's two-hundred-seat

Coe Auditorium. I accepted the honor and, after a year of working out the details, the residency was scheduled for the month of July 1978.

So David Sleeper's offer to dance in the desert was an opportunity to break the pattern of moving from sofa to guest room in Austin. I could get out of town for the month of June and then head to Wyoming for my month-long residency at the museum in July.

Fate quickly filled in the blanks of my new direction. I was approaching the conclusion of my set during the 1978 Kerrville Folk Festival and there was time for one more song. Though I hadn't performed the song in years, I spontaneously decided to sing "The Call." I had barely announced the tune when high over the large audience I noticed two turkey buzzards circling. I had no idea why, but I was reminded of John Neihardt and Black Elk. Before beginning the song, I said, "I want to dedicate this song to two of my greatest teachers, Black Elk and John G. Neihardt."

When I walked off the stage after my set, there was a note from the stage manager. Upon hearing John Neihardt's name, two Nebraskans in the audience asked that I meet them at the backstage gate. They introduced themselves as Steve and Bev Preston. Surprised at my mention of Neihardt, the couple approached me because the John Neihardt Center was only a few miles from their farm in Lyons, Nebraska. Steve asked if I had ever met Dr. Neihardt or performed at the center.

I told them that in a dozen years I had written Dr. Neihardt scores of letters but never had the courage to mail any of them. As a result of that pattern, I eventually made a personal promise never to approach the John Neihardt Center seeking their endorsement or support of my work. Instead, I decided to trust that if it was in the stars, that my epic ballads would attract Neihardt's energy to me.

"Then you won't mind me nudging things a bit?" Steve grinned.

As soon as I returned to Austin I received a call from Marie Vogt, executive director of the John Neihardt Center in Bancroft, Nebraska. Mrs. Vogt and I arranged for me to perform in early August as part of the state of Nebraska's annual John Neihardt Day. The governor, Charles Thone, and erudite television star Dick Cavett were also scheduled to attend.

The performance at Neihardt Day would mean that in early June I could depart Austin for Desert Dance, spend July at the residency in Wyoming, and then proceed to Nebraska in August. My tour would put me out of Texas for nearly three months, and Gloria could have the house to herself until we could save enough cash to hire a lawyer and file for divorce.

I hitched a ride to San Antonio with two beautiful young sisters from Austin, Joan and Jeanna Oliver. Joan was a Desert Dance alumnus who was working as a groundskeeper while Sleeper and his companion and partner, Tracy Lynch, were on Desert Dance. In San Antonio, Jeanna returned to Austin and Joan and I caught a train to Marathon, Texas, where we were greeted by Sleeper, Tracy, and their mountain-climbing dog, a Rhodesian ridgeback mix named Wino. Soon the five of us loaded into a pickup truck and headed south to Terlingua. A mile from the Desert Dance headquarters, which were near the Mexican border, Sleeper stopped the truck, walked to a large rock, and shoved it aside. Then, he started scraping sand away with his boot, exposing a heavy sheet of metal. He moved the metal plate and revealed a telephone answering machine buried in a shallow, wood-walled and -floored hole in the ground. The red light was blinking.

"This is as close as we can get with phone service," he explained. The abandoned mining camp of Buena Suerte (Good Luck) is a couple of miles from there.

The next stretch of the trip was at least as interesting as the episode with the buried answering machine. We soon entered a section of desert where the "road" suddenly vanished into two massive boulders that blocked the only route forward. Sleeper had rolled them there before leaving for Austin, a desert-rat burglar-prevention system. I helped move the boulders and we were on our way again.

The day after our arrival at Buena Suerte I was assigned the task of tending to the various racks on which fruits were drying. Aside from raisins and dates, the bananas, apples, apricots, and peaches would be our entire stash of fruit for the expedition, so Tracy urged me to take good care with it. Throughout the day the seven other dancers arrived at Buena Suerte and we started to get to know one another. We were not obligated to tell anything about ourselves other than our names, and that could even be an alias, but everyone was eager to explain their lives. After another day of preparation, we loaded into the pickup truck at twilight and were driven by Joan to a remote location in the desert on the U.S. side of the border very near the Rio Grande. The sun was setting as Joan deposited us in the profound quiet and returned to Buena Suerte. Later that evening Sleeper and Tracy continued our orientation before we bedded down. The next morning at first light we waded across the river into Mexico.

Facing fear indeed. Within an hour we had encountered half a dozen

Mojave rattlesnakes. By midmorning I was convinced I would die from a rattlesnake bite before sunset. Sleeper told us that we should become accustomed to the rattlesnakes, as we would be visitors in their world for the next month. He comforted us with the statistic that more people die from bee stings than snakebites and, in the event of a bite, he and Tracy were the best-trained snakebite experts in the region. After Sleeper's explanation I could see my own doubt reflected in the faces of my companions. Nevertheless, by the end of my month in the desert, after numerous encounters, I would learn that rattlesnakes, unlike aggressive cottonmouth moccasins or copperheads, are indeed actually pretty mellow and, after satisfying their curiosity, want to get away from you as badly as you want to get away from them. Their rattle is essentially a warning of pure, primal honesty: "Stay away from me, I'm dangerous." Perhaps if a few of the people I had met in show business had offered a warning as honest as the rattlesnakes I met in the desert, I never would have been there in the first place.

Soon after crossing into Mexico we entered the mouth of a lovely limestone canyon of white, flash-flood-carved walls that looked remarkably like the sculpture of Henry Moore. Soon we were all frolicking naked in a deep *tinaja*, or pool, naturally created by massive walls of water crashing against porous limestone. During our orientation, we had been warned that in the canyons we were to remain constantly aware that we were vulnerable to instant, deadly flash floods. We were taught that even though the day or night might appear dry, sunny, or starlit, twenty miles away—unbeknownst to us—an enormous thunderstorm could be launching a torrent of water fifteen to twenty feet high that would come raging through the canyon. So when entering the canyons we learned to look first for piles of dried brush caught in plants and rocks to determine the waterline of previous flooding and plan an escape route accordingly.

Naked, Sleeper stood high atop the limestone wall and invited all of us below in the *tinaja* to join him for a spectacular view of the canyon ahead. I eagerly headed up the wall before anyone else, only to quickly find myself stuck halfway, twenty feet above the *tinaja*; I couldn't continue scaling the wall, nor could I find a way down. My strength rapidly failing, I realized it would not be long before I fell back into the *tinaja*. Naked and embarrassed, I noticed my arms were quivering.

"Welcome to the Bruja Traverse," Sleeper announced. "Bobby is about to fall because he is using his strength rather than his balance to scale the wall."

Within seconds of Sleeper's remark, my strength vanished and I fell into the water. Adding insult to injury, striking the water informed me that my ass was terribly sunburned.

Then Tracy Lynch took center stage and we learned the Bruja Traverse was more than a metaphor. She referred to climbing as "vertical yoga," and told us if we failed to ascend the Bruja Traverse without assistance we must go back to the location of our Texas campsite and wait for Joan's return because we would not be able to cope with the dangerous climbing and rappelling that awaited us beyond that point.

Each of us eventually ascended the traverse and embarked upon the next phase of the journey, but not without paying individual tolls of emotional and physical distress. As we rested after the ordeal, dark, silent questions arose as plain as the sunburned noses on our faces. But each of us also realized that now there was no turning back and we had to hold together as a unit to survive the next month.

Only three days after entering the desert with Tracy Lynch and David Sleeper, two psychologists, a Hollywood documentary filmmaker, an ashram cook, a professional photographer, a college professor, a trust-fund kid, and a balladeer ascended a sheer five-hundred-foot wall to a spectacular summit; two days later we were functioning as a skilled canyoneering team, executing complicated technical climbing and rappelling maneuvers. When the inevitable arguments arose, we resolved them nightly around the tribal circle. Our unifying symbol was to compare a dysfunctional tribe to a schizophrenic centipede comically unable to coordinate his feet; without synchronized teamwork in the desert we knew we wouldn't survive. Moreover, the thoughts you have while dangling several hundred feet on the side of a rock wall might be your very last ones, so you learn to keep them high and positive. You become constantly aware that karma is particularly instant and unforgiving in the desert; you rarely get second chances, since there is always something waiting close by to stick, prick, bite, or poison you. Consequently, no matter how passionate the disagreement, we were always mindful that we must remain united and supportive to survive— especially when the group was intensely involved in the process of seeking out each individual's deepest, darkest fear.

The communal dynamic of five men and five women was also well conceived. Given those numbers it was certain that social and sexual dysfunctions would surface and need work. For example: Early into the experience of technical climbing the tribe determined I was always the first to volunteer for dangerous climbs, thereby preventing other tribal members the "opportunity" of being first to face their fear; my companions' witnessing me engaging my fear somehow diminished the uniqueness of first facing their own. So I was diplomatically informed by the tribe that I would now be the last person to attempt a climb or rappel. I was initially furious at being forced to the end of the line, but I eventually began to see that this was exactly what I needed. My nerves were shot and I needed stillness and reflection. But I didn't realize until I found myself at the back of the line that my marriage difficulties had unleashed a subconscious self-destructiveness. While I cooled my heels and watched my comrades deal with issues, the subconscious desire to hurt myself revealed itself and then rapidly diminished as I silently exorcized the monster that had been lurking in my darker corners. At the end of the line I also gained a new perspective on my companions' struggles in dealing with fears that may have seemed trivial to me but through the prism of my newfound compassion were perceived as major breakthroughs for them.

In spite of the bond within the tribe, I was especially fond of the solos and fasts. These solos were usually undertaken at a spot that overlooked a splendid panorama of distant mesas and desert, literally miles from the nearest human. Weakened by the intense heat, lack of food, and the toxins your body was purging from the fast, the solos would sometimes induce lucid, half-asleep/half-awake dream states in which majestic, mystical ideas would appear. Invariably, the crow's larger cousin, the mountain raven, seemed to have a knack for calling to me every time I would become impressed with mystical thoughts. "Caw, caw, caw," he would call out to me like a comic, cosmic laugh—a gentle black clown reminding me not to take myself too seriously. My time out there alone with those dark clowns brought some of the happiest moments of my life.

My last three-day solo was spent perched at the lip of a sheer fifteen-hundred-foot precipice on the Mexican side of the juncture of the Rio Grande's magnificent Santa Elena Canyon and another equally impressive canyon, dubbed Rattlesnake. The canyons were so colossal in scale that they seemed unreal—as if they had been painted by Albert Bierstadt or Thomas Moran. The Rio Grande was so far below me that it looked like a sliver of silver ribbon cutting through jagged brown rock. When I turned my gaze from the canyons and toward the desert herself, I often witnessed gigantic thunderheads clashing in majestic rain and lightning storms that awakened the landscape with sprays of colors I had never before imagined, or accidentally mixed on a palette. Since I had fasted for seventy-two hours, the craving for food had long ago left and been replaced with profound, silent reverence for the antiquity and interconnectedness of the desert and canyons surrounding me.

A most interesting revelation of Desert Dance was a month with no mirrors. The raw-food diet, fasting, and intense daily physical activity of ascending and descending five-hundred-foot walls was like a spiritual boot camp, and soon everyone in the tribe started dramatically trimming and toning; some changes were so rapid they occurred almost overnight! Looking in pools of water revealed only dark shadows and silhouettes. Soon I found myself going to another desert dancer to ask her to describe the ways I was changing physically. I wasn't surprised when she asked me to reflect her changes as well.

When my three-day solo atop Santa Elena Canyon ended I was prepared to live anywhere in the world. Desert Dance taught me how to dramatically simplify my life in order to sustain myself and still function at a high spiritual and physical level. The ascetic tools that I internalized in the desert would enable me to reduce my needs to a minimum whenever I had to endure poverty to continue the pursuit of my dreams. And just as important, the desert discipline could now be applied to my life in general; indeed, I discovered that my perspectives on everything changed in the desert. When I returned from Desert Dance, I brought its austerity with me and incorporated it into my life's "dance." After leaving Chihuahua I gradually expanded the rigorous fasting techniques I had learned and was soon able to live on nothing but lemon water for up to two weeks at a time.

In the desert I had also come to understand that music had overwhelmed my life for several years, and I hardly painted anymore. So I promised myself that as soon as I got back to Austin I would take out my oils and brushes and start stretching canvas.

Two days after returning to Austin from Chihuahua, I learned that the Gonzos were heading to Los Angeles in a rented van. I hitched a ride with them to Albuquerque, where I caught a Greyhound bus to Cody. Sixty miles east of Yellowstone, Cody proved the perfect location for my transition back into contemporary culture. There, the vast Big Horn Basin rose from high desert plains to greet the Wind River, Absaroka, and Big Horn mountain ranges. Originally known as the Bridger Basin, the terrain was in many ways similar to Chihuahua, and the location of Old Trail Town on the edge of town provided just the right measure of remoteness that I needed to read-just. For example, after a month of sleeping outside on the ground, I found it difficult to sleep indoors. At Old Trail Town I could store my few possessions in my cabin and continue sleeping under the stars. In the desert we lived almost exclusively on raw food and various high-protein beans that we sprouted daily in jars. My raw-food diet certainly fit nicely into my routine in Cody. I no longer needed a refrigerator. I could soak sprouting beans in the morning, leave for the day, and have dinner waiting when I returned. My cabin was also about three miles from the Buffalo Bill Historical Center, and I had to walk back and forth to do my shows. Soon, I stored my guitars at the theater and jogged to the museum and back each day.

Coe Auditorium proved to be an excellent venue for my ballads. There was no money to pay for my residency, but the museum allowed me to put an antique beaver-pelt top hat at the exit for "donations." Three times a day the two-hundred-seat auditorium filled with tourists from all over the world en route to nearby Yellowstone. In a month of performing there I earned more than three thousand dollars in nickels, dimes, quarters, and small bills.

Performing in Coe Auditorium was also my first insight into the genius of William F. "Buffalo Bill" Cody's location of his town of Cody at the eastern entrance of Yellowstone National Park; the old boy knew that people would be visiting the world's first national park forever. He also knew that most visitors—domestic and foreign—would be arriving from the east and would have to pass through Cody to get to Yellowstone. I decided if the formula worked for Buffalo Bill, it would certainly work for me and my ballads.

In late July, when Timberjack pulled his Winnebago into Cody, I had fully internalized the Desert Dance ascetic into my daily lifestyle. Shortly after Timberjack arrived, Gloria notified me through an attorney that she had moved out of the house on Comanche Trail, taken an apartment in Austin, and filed for divorce.

Even now I can't explain what happened to Gloria and me, but I guess it was ultimately a familiar divorce story; we initially adored each other, but what appeared to be great strengths in the beginning vanished like smoke when we encountered truly major obstacles.

Because he was boisterous and looked like a display that had come to life and freed itself from a glass museum case, Timberjack Joe had long been banished from the Buffalo Bill Historical Center. But Buffalo Bill was Joe's boyhood hero and his persona non grata status hurt him deeply. I personally escorted him through the museum and tried my best to make him feel like a king. Immediately after my residency at the Buffalo Bill Historical Center ended, we loaded into his dilapidated Winnebago and took off across the Great Plains toward Bancroft, Nebraska. Heading deep into the landscape of Neihardt's inspiration gave the journey the feeling of a sacred pilgrimage.

In three short years Timberjack and I had grown very close. This trip across the Great Plains was the first trip we'd made together; in the past Gloria and I had followed his Winnebago in our car. But we both knew this was only the beginning; indeed, between 1978 and 1983 I would spend as much as four months of the year traveling with Timberjack and his menagerie of animals—much of that time on Indian reservations. We would arrive at powwow and be greeted with throngs of Indian children shouting, "Timberjack Joe!" and running alongside and behind the Winnebago. I soon learned that Indian people considered Joe a trusted babysitter; at powwow they could relax and have fun, knowing their kids were safe with the mountain man. In those moments I was profoundly honored to be his sidekick. I was especially proud to be present when dignified old medicine men would come to Joe's Winnebago during powwow seeking some specific fur, claws, or bones for ceremonies. No matter how exotic or rare their needs were, Timberjack always seemed to have the item on hand, and he would never consider taking any payment in return. Nevertheless, some exquisitely beautiful object, such as a beaded medicine bag or a sash, would always be anonymously placed on the running board of the Winnebago overnight to be discovered the next morning.

My newly acquired Desert Dance skills certainly made it easier for me to travel with the old mountain man. For example, one of Joe's many talents was driving a Caterpillar Cat; the man could move colossal amounts of dirt with the deftness of a brain surgeon. So he could never pass a junkyard without stopping to shop for parts for his various heavy-equipment vehicles, Caterpillars, or trucks. Even on those rare occasions when Joe didn't break the moonshine out for the junkyard owner, I knew he would be staying overnight to barter and palaver. So, after singing them a few songs I would grab my journal, books, and bedroll, and head for the nearest pasture or grove of trees for the evening. Indeed, we were often invited to stay in people's homes, but when a host asked Timberjack to stay inside the house, he would always retire to his beloved Winnebago, explaining that he was like a turtle, and carried his home on his back. Like a turtle, my home was now on my back too; aside from my two Martin guitars, I could get most of my current possessions into a large green backpack.

Before he died, John Neihardt designed a Sioux prayer garden at the site of his boyhood home. There, he planted a flowering fruit tree in the center of a landscaped circle. At the four cardinal points he planted a flower garden that would blossom with the colors white in the north, red in the east, yellow in the south, and blue in the west. This prayer garden would eventually become the site of the John G. Neihardt Center.

Located ninety miles northwest of Omaha and thirty miles west of the Missouri River, Bancroft is a tiny farming hamlet in the middle of rolling prairie. These days they say there are only two cornfields in Nebraska—the one on the right side of the road, and the one on the left. There, you might also find yourself driving down a lovely country road, breathing the sweet aroma of fresh farm air, only to suddenly discover the worst stench known to man invading your olfaction. When Nebraskans smell a pig farm, however, the response is, "Smells like money to me!" Perpetual corn and soybean fields and pig farms surrounded modern-day Bancroft, but in the land's original state, oceans of wild buffalo grass would have grown nearly chin-high over those plains. During Neihardt's childhood vast sections of the region were still untouched. These lands were the source of the horse and buffalo culture of the Lakota, Pawnee, Omaha, and Winnebago Indians. Neihardt understood the "great mood of courage" that still vibrates in that space. Neihardt's epic verse sang with the spirit of the Great Plains and Northern Rockies—the Trans-Missouri.

The first thing I noticed when Timberjack Joe and I arrived in Bancroft was the Sioux prayer garden. The second thing I noticed was that the volunteers who ran the Neihardt Center were rural women of German heritage. Most of them had known the poet in his very last years and were devoted to keeping his poetry alive and prospering. The chief among them, Marie Vogt, took me on a guided tour of the lovely little center. The architect had sensitively selected the motifs of the prayer garden and incorporated the circular design into the building itself. I loved the entire concept of the Neihardt Center and decided to ceremoniously spend the night sleeping in the prayer garden. So that evening, after hanging prayer ribbons in the branches and burning sage offerings, I spent my first night in Bancroft at the trunk of Neihardt and Black Elk's flowering tree, sleeping in one of Timberjack's buffalo robes.

Dawn broke with sounds of increasing pandemonium as the volunteer staff arrived to prepare for the day's events. Larger groups of people started arriving almost as soon as I got the buffalo robe tucked away in Timberjack's motor home.

Occurring annually on the first Sunday in August, Neihardt Day is a statewide holiday in Nebraska. Marie Vogt had warned me that they were expecting the largest audience in the history of the event. She speculated that perhaps as many as five hundred people would be in attendance. I took my guitar to a large cottonwood tree behind the makeshift stage and podium set up for the featured speakers. As I tuned my twelve-string, an Indian couple approached me. The very large man was dressed in a stiffly pressed white shirt, jeans—also starched and ironed with a crease—black boots, and a generic white straw cowboy hat. The tiny woman was dressed in more traditional Indian clothing. A fancy powwow dancer's shawl draped her bony shoulders. The stranger did not mince words.

"Are you Bridger?" the man asked.

"Yes, sir."

"You should not sing here today. Black Elk gave all his power to Neihardt when he told him his great vision. Neihardt put this sacred Lakota symbol in Omaha territory. The Omaha were our enemies, and this sacred prayer garden should not be here."

Stunned, I didn't know which of his issues to address first. To begin with, my performance was scheduled to begin in a few minutes, and this was no time to discuss metaphysics, much less politics. And speaking of politics, even though Dick Cavett had failed to show, the governor of Nebraska was in the audience, as well as more than five hundred people who expected me to sing. But the timing of the Lakota medicine man's appearance so soon after my prayers at the flowering tree could not be ignored. He frightened me.

"Please forgive me, sir. I mean no disrespect. But I have an audience waiting for me to perform, and I must honor them first. If you will wait for me to finish my performance I will be happy to talk with you after my show."

The Indian politely excused himself and escorted his companion to a front-row seat in the audience. As soon as they were seated I began my performance of *Seekers*. I watched the Lakota couple so intently as I performed that it soon seemed as though we were the only people present. About fifteen minutes into the piece the Indian couple simultaneously looked straight up over my head. I couldn't look up without distracting my audience's focus, but the couple were clearly observing something high above.

After the performance they approached me again. Still serious, the man offered me a bouquet of sage.

"Great Spirit sent a sign today during your performance. Today while you sang, six thunderbirds circled the prayer garden. When you finished they flew away."

I didn't dare mention it, but I felt that his sightings of the thunderbirds were perhaps a sign that the prayer garden was a sacred site after all. But other people also saw the birds appear that day. In her introduction to the Neihardt anthology *A Sender of Words*, Marie Vogt wrote that she saw six hawks circling overhead that afternoon as I sang. Timberjack Joe also saw them, as did still another man who was there.

"I loved your show, Bobby," he gushed. "My name is Christopher Sergel. I own the film and theatrical rights to *Black Elk Speaks*. I would like very much to talk with you about a production of *Black Elk Speaks*. Will you be here a while?"

I felt an immediate kinship with Chris Sergel. His inherently sweet disposition easily won my heart. Tall and lean, with old-fashioned New England charm and elegance softened with a clownish giggle, Chris had ginger-colored hair and freckles to match.

That afternoon Chris invited me to join the production team he was assembling to mount a play of *Black Elk Speaks*. Furthermore, he hoped the theatrical play would become a forerunner of the feature film he intended to produce based on Neihardt's book. After seeing my performance, he thought—pending Hilda Neihardt's approval—that I might be the man to play her father, John. And just as important, he wanted me to help him enlist Indian people to train as actors to create the piece from the ground up.

I accepted Chris's offer and took his card. He was a very pleasant man and seemed quite sincere, but I was so wounded from show business that I didn't expect much to ever come from the meeting. I was more interested in traveling back across the plains with Timberjack Joe. Before leaving, I agreed to Marie Vogt's pleas to persuade Vine Deloria to be the principal speaker for Neihardt Day the next summer. Soon Timberjack and I headed west into South Dakota.

As the sun set and the temperature dropped on the Great Plains, heat lightning lit the night in every direction, exposing the great circular hoop of the world. Watching the spectacular electrical show reminded me of Black Elk and the Lakota fascination with the mysterious—and often dangerous—spirits they call Wakinyans, or "Thunder-beings." The Wakinyans dwell in the West and possess the power to "make live or to destroy." Black Elk himself received his name and power from the Wakinyans. When Black Elk was a child, older medicine men viewed his fear of lightning as a sign that he had been visited by the Wakinyans, and they began to ask about his dreams.

The farther west we drove into South Dakota, the more intense the lightning storms and wind shear became. I started saying the old Lakota battle cry "Hoka hey!" each time jagged lightning streaked across the indigo sky and ripped it open with orange and white slashes. As we finally approached the Black Hills, powerful gusts of wind rocked the old Winnebago as they swept across the plains from the south to the north.

Although I had told Joe about my parents' conceiving me in Gillette, I had never mentioned that my earliest memory was an image of Devil's Tower. On the first leg of the journey we had come down the Platte River from Casper en route to Nebraska. We were returning to Cody over the Big Horns, however, and to get there we would travel through the Powder River country. As I had never been to the area before, this journey was becoming more interesting as it unfolded. Increasingly, I felt that I had opened up to something mystical at the flowering tree. As we headed into the Powder River country it occurred to me that landscape was the very heart of my ballads. It felt like a homecoming.

"Play 'Red Cloud,'" Daddy shouted from the audience. It was good to be performing in North Louisiana again. One of my former art students, Doyle Jeter, opened one of the best music venues in the country, Enoch's, A Cafe, in Monroe in the mid-1970s, and I could perform in his club and visit my parents in nearby Columbia. Doyle had been one of my favorite students at West Monroe High. He had continued studying art throughout college and become a fine lithographer and printmaker. He and his wife, Yvette, were also music freaks and fabulous Cajun cooks. Opening the café to nourish their music habit, Doyle and Yvette ended up literally feeding a regular flow of itinerant musicians. The pair not only fed musicians but they demanded that audiences listen reverently to the music; to begin with, they had booked the act because they were fans of the artist and, by God, they intended to hear them play. If someone became overly loud or rowdy, Doyle would interrupt the singer, take the stage himself, and demand that the patron either shut up or take a refund and a free drink and promptly leave the club. Very quickly, audiences understood that only a stranger would get boisterous while a performer was onstage at Enoch's, and soon word was out that Enoch's was a great place to play music.

By the 1980s I played Enoch's twice a year to visit home. My mother's reclusiveness had become so entrenched at this point that she never came to hear me perform, but because of his lecturing work with the Masonic lodge, Daddy became more social as he got older. So he would always come out to hear me perform at Enoch's. Many of my childhood friends would also come out for the show, so Daddy usually had company at his table.

"Red Cloud" was Daddy's favorite of my songs. After performing his request that night, I decided that I would talk with him about "Red Cloud" on the drive home. I had recently returned from the prairies of Wyoming's Powder River country, near Buffalo. I was visiting the site of the Fetterman Massacre—coincidentally, as the crow flies, about sixty miles from Gillette. History walked over those prairies. There, in December 1866, having declared war on everything west of the Mississippi River and after laying siege to Fort Phil Kearny for months, Red Cloud's forces annihilated Captain William J. Fetterman and eighty troops in what was at the time the worst defeat the U.S. military had experienced in a declared war. Luring Fetterman into the trap, Crazy Horse began his rise to immortality in that battle; General Henry Carrington's chief of scouts at Fort Phil Kearny, Jim Bridger, in one of the last endeavors of his long career in the American West, led the expedition to retrieve the frozen corpses of the slain. Red Cloud's victory forced the United States to sign the infamous Fort Laramie Treaty of 1868—the treaty with the poetic "for as long as the grasses grow and the rivers flow" provision.

Only weeks before returning to Louisiana to perform, I had been standing alone in Wyoming enjoying sunset at the memorial that marked the location of the Fetterman conflict. Shadows were rapidly growing longer with the fleeting light, and at the very moment the sun vanished, I heard a chilling scream on the distant horizon. For a moment I became frightened, and as my ears scanned the silence for the source of the shriek, I started to laugh at myself. My imagination was playing tricks on me. The sound was the tires of an eighteen-wheeler whining in the distance on Interstate 25. Then a chilling epiphany echoed the comic aural illusion of a "scream." In the midst of acute energy shortages those whining eighteen-wheelers were hauling coal from the heart of the Powder River country twenty-four hours a day, seven days a week, three hundred sixty-five days a year. Surpassing the effort of the trucks, trains with a hundred overflowing gondolas snaked across the prairie on the same daily timetable. The sacred Powder River country of Red Cloud, Crazy Horse, and Sitting Bull was being ripped apart! Lines from "Red Cloud" suddenly held new meaning:

> On the plains if you will listen close
> You can hear a wailing blue-coat ghost,
> Moaning "I am sorry I was wrong"
> He's crying to the tune of Red Cloud's song
> And the blue-coat ghost cries loud,
> He's remembering the mighty name of Red Cloud.[1]

"Red Cloud" had always been one of my favorite songs too. That's why I felt like it was time to talk to Daddy about it. After my show at Enoch's we climbed into his truck and headed south to Columbia.

"You know, Daddy," I opened, "I've been going to Wyoming now every summer for over a decade."

"Yes," he replied. "I always loved it there too."

"Well, that's what I want to talk with you about. Your requesting 'Red Cloud' got me to thinking about it. Have you ever wondered why you and Mama went to Gillette, Wyoming, for less than a year—long enough to conceive me—and then, when you learned she was pregnant, you returned to Louisiana? I think it's interesting that that brief period of time is the only time Mama has been out of Columbia in her entire life. Don't you?"

"That is interesting. What are you leading to?"

"Don't you think it's curious that I was conceived in the Powder River country—the sacred ancestral lands of the Lakota—and, as an adult, I've written all these songs about them?"

"I wondered about that the first time you came home and played me all those Indian songs, Bobby. But there are mysteries in life we aren't supposed to understand."

"Well, I find it very interesting," I said, "even if I'm in a large group of Indian people from various tribes, I gravitate to the Sioux. My best friend, Vine Deloria, is a Sioux."

Daddy and I could finally talk about such things. Perhaps it was because

I was finally mature enough to realize that he had always been my biggest supporter. Even though he absolutely disagreed with my abandoning the commercial record business, he still came to hear me perform whenever I played in North Louisiana. Each time he sat in the audience we grew closer. He still offered criticism of each performance, but now I understood it as coming from the perspective of a positive, loving father. Now we could sit in the truck in silence, contented in our affectionate bond.

After my Desert Dance experience I had written a batch of new songs that were not specifically linked to an epic ballad. I referred to the songs collectively as "secular hymns." The tunes had proven increasingly popular in live performances, so I decided it was time for me to return to the recording studio and make another album. And from the first notion of returning to the studio, I knew it was time to work with Fred Carter Jr. again.

The project began with a song I wrote in 1979 called "Heal in the Wisdom." Facing the sudden death of two very dear friends in unrelated incidents, I was experiencing profound grief. Then I remembered my own lyrical suggestion of needing "wisdom to heal." The phrase came from a song of mine called "The Hawk." In "The Hawk" I posed the environmental question at the hypothetical moment of a "last" hawk's dying: "What will we do when the Earth needs his *wisdom to heal*?" Almost simultaneously with my recollection of that phrase, my father's remark returned to remind me that there are mysteries in life we aren't meant to understand. Daddy's fatalism made me recall the theme of reassuring hope in the old Baptist hymn that says, "further along we'll understand why." "Further Along" brought to mind Pete Seeger's masterpiece "Turn, Turn, Turn," and its brilliant "to everything there is a season," which, of course, Pete lifted straight from Ecclesiastes. So in the pure folk tradition of Pete Seeger—his classic "We Shall Overcome" was based on Charles Tindley's 1903 spiritual "I'll Overcome Some Day"—I hummed a tune loosely based on "Further Along," but with my own unique chorus melody. The chorus lyrically referred to the Paulinian "seasons" of Seeger's "Turn, Turn, Turn" and the suggestion that there is a higher purpose that we will eventually understand—when we "heal in the wisdom." In the third verse I inserted the core Lakota environmental philosophy of *mitakuye oyasin* to imply that even if we eventually realize the dream of the racial brotherhood of men, we are doomed if we fail to fully comprehend, respect, nourish, and celebrate humankind's interconnected relationship to the earth. The fourth verse reasserted the Lakota theme that we are part of a great cosmic Medicine Wheel moving within the Great Mystery.

I felt that the song needed editing, and was playing it backstage at the 1979 Kerrville Folk Festival for John Inmon and David Amram's critique when festival founder and producer Rod Kennedy raced up to us and asked about it. When he learned it was a new song of mine, he immediately told me he wanted it to be the festival's anthem. I suggested we should play it for the crowd to see how they reacted, but in his enthusiastic introduction Rod proclaimed that "Heal in the Wisdom" was the official anthem of the Kerrville Folk Festival. The minute I began the song, however, it was obvious that Rod knew what he was doing; the audience spontaneously rose, locked arms, and joined in singing the chorus. I had never before—or since—experienced anything quite like the "Kerr-vert Khoir" singing along on "Heal in the Wisdom" with me. "Heavenly" is perhaps the best word to describe it.

"Heal in the Wisdom" was actually the last in a series of new songs I had written over a six-month period. These songs were united in concept, a cycle of birth, death, and rebirth—spiritual reinvention. Songs like "Something in the Words" obviously reflected the end of my second marriage, and highlighted the lyrical tones of the album, but songs like "Lighten Up and Let It Go" and "Arrows of Light" mirrored my Desert Dance experience and the spiritual awakening it brought to my life. In retrospect, I wish I had titled the album *Secular Hymns*; the word "secular" in the title—especially when juxtaposed with "hymns"—might have clarified any religious ambiguity, and also could have deflected attention from the song "Heal in the Wisdom" to place the focus where I intended—on the album as a whole. The popularity of the song "Heal in the Wisdom" overshadowed the public's overall perspective of the album as a united concept. More significant, the lyrics of the album, with titles like "Eternally New" and "Rise and Shine," confused many who thought I had—heaven forbid—become a "born again" Christian. Bob Dylan was experimenting with Christianity about a year before "Heal in the Wisdom" was released, and many nasal-singing, xeroxed lemmings were discovering Christ during this time, so I should have anticipated the confusion. The album's opening song, "Eternally New," was, however, indeed inspired by Dylan's "Forever Young"; when I heard "Forever Young" I thought: "I'd rather grow old and remain eternally new." Unfortunately, because of its Christian connotations, I learned that poets should use the word "eternally" only with the greatest caution. Likewise, "rise and shine."

Fred Carter Jr. certainly understood the concept of my "secular hymns." When I had signed with E. H. Morris a decade earlier in order to secure the RCA contract, I immediately went to Nashville to personally explain to Fred what had happened in Hollywood. Fred was not happy that I had signed with another publisher when our contract expired. He had expected me to create my own publishing company and employ his help in the administration of it. Moments after I told Fred about E. H. Morris, he called Sidney Goldstein and, while I sat in the office, accused him of "stealing his writer."

Fred veiled whatever anger he had toward me over the situation. After all, he had presented *Merging of Our Minds* to every label in Nashville and it had been rejected. I had presented it to every label in Los Angeles and New York and it had been rejected. The businessman in him naturally understood that the deal with RCA was too good for me to pass up. Because of the tension between him and E. H. Morris, I was afraid of creating trouble if I insisted that Fred be brought to Hollywood to work with me on *And I Wanted to Sing for the People*, and that only further estranged me from my mentor. Nevertheless, when I contacted him ten years later, Fred quickly agreed to coproduce the record with me. Once he heard the songs of *Heal in the Wisdom* we didn't need to discuss the matter any further; he understood my purpose in coming back to work with him.

The first thing I noticed when we reunited was that Fred had aged dramatically. He explained he had developed Nugget Records and Studio to the point that he threatened the "big boys" on Music Row and they drove him out of business. In spite of the battle scars, he remained as positive and creative as the day we'd met all those years ago in Louisiana—and even more in possession of the heart of a champion. He fully appreciated that we had come full circle as friends and artists.

Aside from the aspect of spiritually mending with Fred, returning to Nashville was pragmatic; I knew I could make a world-class record there. The Nashville "assembly-line" formula for record production was simple: record three tunes in a three-hour session. I figured if I focused on recording one song in a three-hour session in Nashville I could spin that structure on its ear and use it to my advantage to get the most out of the great session musicians there. A bonus: bassist Joe Osborn had moved from L.A. to

Nashville, and with him and Fred on the record I could continue my super-stitious "charm" of having various musicians from Simon and Garfunkel's recording and concert band—Fred, Joe, and Hal Blaine—on all my "non-ballad" albums. After getting the rhythm tracks done in Nashville, Fred and I decided we would return to Texas and dive into the deep Austin talent pool for sweetening and color.

But there was more spice for the stew. His name was Bill Ginn. When I moved to Austin in 1970, a neighbor had boldly suggested to me that I needed an arranger and suggested a friend attending the University of Texas. Realizing that I would indeed need an arranger if I intended to keep doing film scores and jingles in Austin, I sought Bill out and found him in graduate school at UT. From Lexington, Mississippi, he was a graduate of the prestigious Eastman School of Music in New York and eager to get into the commercial recording business rather than teach school. As our boy-hood homes were in the Mississippi Delta region of the country and we had relocated to Texas, Bill and I fit like a hand in a glove, and quickly became friends as well as colleagues. We worked on countless jingles and documen-tary film tracks in the early 1970s, leading to Bill's arranging and conduct-ing the orchestral score of *Breakaway* with me in 1976. After that film pre-miered and I "vanished" into the desert and began living in the back of a pickup truck as a wandering balladeer, Bill founded a jazz-fusion group called Passenger that quickly became a favorite in Austin. While playing a gig in L.A. the group contacted Henry Levy, an engineer/producer who had worked on some early Joni Mitchell recordings. Levy was engineering ses-sions for Leonard Cohen's album *Recent Songs*, and he invited the band to visit the sessions. Cohen immediately hired Bill and some members of the band. Oscar-nominated vocalist Jennifer Warnes often sang background vocals for Leonard Cohen, and that relationship linked her with various members of the Passenger group. Bill would eventually win a Grammy nomination for his arrangements of *Famous Blue Raincoat: The Songs of Leonard Cohen*, performed by Warnes, and also become the music director for my full-company production of *Seekers of the Fleece* and my coproduc-er/arranger for my musical *Aldebaran and the Falling Star*. In 1986 Jennifer Warnes sang the role of the Dolphin in a demonstration recording that Bill Ginn and I produced of *Aldebaran and the Falling Star*. Also, for about a year in the late 1980s, Bill and I were the front-runners to compose the score for *Dances with Wolves*—then known as "Kevin's Gate"—a derogatory phrase alluding to Michael Cimino's financially disastrous 1980 western,

Heaven's Gate, and star/director/producer Kevin Costner's three-hour "Indian movie" with Lakota dialogue and English subtitles.

With Bill on keyboards and involved with the basic arrangements for the Nashville *Heal* sessions I knew we would steer clear of any stereotypical country sounds, and his jazz and classical sensibilities would challenge and inspire Fred and Joe and spice up the basic rhythm tracks. Later, Bill could work his magic and conduct his orchestral arrangements with firsthand knowledge of the album's basic tracks.

The basic tracks to *Heal* went smoothly in Nashville, and soon Fred and I flew to Austin. There, I brought in the Lost Gonzo Band to sing and play, as well as a host of Austin vocalists, including Layton DePenning, Julie Christensen, Tina Marsh, Andy Murphy, Ray Benson, Natalie Zoe, and Cactus Pryor, to stack the background vocals into choruses.

We returned to Nashville to mix and manufacture and had the record ready to release in time for the 1981 Kerrville Folk Festival. As always, after the festival I headed straight to Wyoming to join Timberjack Joe for the summer powwow and rendezvous season. After the summer, however, I planned to go to New York City to try to sell *Heal in the Wisdom* to a major label.

SEVENTEEN

The Medicine Wheel

I AWOKE TO DISCOVER A GOLDEN EAGLE SOARING, perfectly silent, ten feet above me. The magnificent bird's great wings were opened wide, suspending it motionless on the powerful thermals rising sharply at the lip of the thousand-foot precipice. I remained still as death in my bedroll, peeking through squinted eyes, hoping the eagle would not notice I was awake—or alive. After several moments of satisfying its curiosity, the eagle turned its head, banked, and without flapping its wings, glided west along the edge of the cliffs. Minutes later, it vanished on the cobalt horizon.

After Gloria and I divorced in 1978 I continued to return each year to the Medicine Wheel. There, at ten thousand feet in the Big Horn Mountains, I would pitch my bedroll on the Medicine Wheel cliffs, fast, and gaze over the Big Horn Basin. From that lofty perch I could easily see a hundred miles south, where gentle dunes rose from the high-altitude prairies of the Red Desert before ascending to embrace the Big Horns. Each moment at that promontory was an ever-changing light and shadow action painting, splashing violets, lavenders, purples, yellows, ochers, reds, greens, and browns on the muted sandy canvas of the Big Horn Basin's sensual, rolling foothills.

The ancient and mysterious Big Horn Medicine Wheel lay forty yards behind my roost at the cliff's edge. Straddling the border of eastern Montana and central Wyoming, the Medicine Wheel is on ancestral Crow Indian land. Yet in spite of this, Crow tribal elders and oral historians maintain that it pre-dates their recorded history. The Medicine Wheel is an asymmetrical disk approximately eighty feet across—now encircled by a protective cyclone fence topped with barbed wire to discourage vandals and thieves. From a large central circular stone cairn, or "hub," smaller stones create twenty-eight spokes, or triangular sections, gradually opening from the hub to form the shape of the wheel. Six larger stone cairns are strategically positioned around the perimeter of the wheel. In the mid-1970s ethno-astrologists and archaeologists discovered that the relic can be used to align stars and accurately predict the arrival of the summer solstice. This led them to conclude that the Medicine Wheel was originally a celestial timepiece ecumenically shared by medicine men from several Plains Indian tribes to calculate the arrival of the longest day of the year—the traditional time for beginning the annual Sun Dance ceremony on the Great Plains.

My first pilgrimage to the Medicine Wheel was in the summer of 1976. Gloria and I had been living in the Delorias' basement for about a month and felt they needed a respite from our intrusion. We had also recently been surprised to learn that Aldebaran was one of two stars that the Medicine Wheel aligned to predict the summer solstice, so we were very curious about this site. In 1976 we were also among a mere handful of annual visitors to the relic. Few people dared to exit U.S. Highway 16 and brave the dangerously cratered road to ascend to the Medicine Wheel.

My 1987 solo at the Medicine Wheel was especially important. A few hours after that golden eagle disappeared on the southwestern horizon, I broke a four-day fast and drove to the airport in Billings, Montana, to greet Melissa Tatum for a tour of the Yellowstone country. We both hoped the time together in the majestic backcountry would help determine whether or not our relationship was going to survive the delicate stage of evolving into something more committed. Melissa wanted to get married and I avoided even discussing the notion. After two failed marriages, I was terrified of the very concept.

My friend and attorney Len Marks knew that Melissa and I were at an impasse, and he generously suggested that I retreat to his summer home in East Hampton, New York, to meditate about the future of our relationship. I had met Leonard Marks a decade earlier, during the summer of 1977, after I persuaded a ski lodge in Winter Park, Colorado, to let me offer a course on western history during the afternoon and perform each night for the guests. Summer traffic was slow, and by the second day I was ready to toss in the towel when a mysterious dark-skinned man dressed in fine white linen clothing came to the terrace where I offered my class. My visitor introduced himself as Chitrabhanu. He told me he was on a western retreat with a group of people from an interfaith organization based in Manhattan. I played a few songs for him, and he promised he would bring many more people for my class the next day.

The next morning the terrace was crowded with devotees of Hindu guru Dev Chitrabhanu. Most were from New York City and many were also members of an international interfaith organization called the Temple of Understanding. My audience was suddenly composed of people from the United Nations, the Margaret Mead Institute, the Omega Institute, Esalen Institute, and many other prestigious organizations. I also learned that Chitrabhanu was a Jain monk who held a chair at Harvard Divinity School and, along with the Dalai Lama, Mother Teresa, the archbishop of Canterbury, and a host of other spiritual leaders, was on the board of directors of the Temple of Understanding.

Chitrabhanu introduced me to Leonard Marks. As we chatted, I learned that Leonard was also a member of the Temple of Understanding board and the organization's vice president. Leonard offered his card, emphasized that he represented major recording artists, and suggested that if I needed help in the music business I should give him a call. My marriage was already in deep trouble at this point, however, and Gloria and I had agreed to focus all our energies on saving our relationship. Sadly, by the time we returned to Austin late that summer the disintegration began in earnest and I had little emotional energy to spend on trying to get back into the recording industry. But I kept Leonard's card.

After the divorce and my first Desert Dance, I decided to return to the Chihuahuan Desert in June 1979. I joined a group of Desert Dance alumni and we went into the desert for thirty days. While in Chihuahua I began a twenty-one-day fast that continued after I left Mexico and caught a train to Tucson to spend some time with Vine and Barbara Deloria. During that long reflective period I reached the conclusion that I had lost my nerve in show business; dancing in the desert made it clear that I had to overcome my fear of the spotlight. So my return to the studio in spring of 1981 with Fred Carter to produce *Heal in the Wisdom* was indeed a healing. To capitalize on the popularity of the song at the Kerrville Folk Festival, I decided to act on a notion I had been pondering: to create my own record label to release *Heal in the Wisdom* in time for the May 1981 event. I believed mythology's "golden egg" to be an androgynous symbol of economic and spiritual portent, so I chose it for the symbol of my record label. The next phase of my recuperation was to try to actually secure a distribution deal with a major label. So I called Len Marks and arranged to meet him in Manhattan in January 1982.

Lean, with light brown hair and an eager, enchanting laugh, Leonard Marks was a tough Jewish kid from the Bronx. A graduate of New York's City College and Yale Law School, he found his first success as a Watergate prosecutor during the waning months of the Nixon era. He was also a serious student of meditation, taught yoga to stressed-out New York lawyers, and had traveled throughout India with Chitrabhanu. In the mid-1970s Leonard won a landmark copyright case for the legendary songwriting team Leiber and Stoller, composers of such seminal rock classics as "Hound Dog," "Searchin'," "Young Blood," "Jailhouse Rock," and "Get a Job." After the Leiber/Stoller case, Leonard's reputation in the music industry began a steady rise to the pinnacle. When he won a similar copyright case for the Bee Gees, his stable of clients grew until it included such luminaries as Grace Jones, David Bowie, Eddie Murphy, Billy Joel, Madonna, Andrew Lloyd Webber, and the estate of Tennessee Williams. By the early 1980s, whenever titans in the record industry waged war Leonard usually represented one of the combatants. Len's crowning achievement, however, was representing the Beatles' Apple Corps. Beginning in 1980, aside from such things as preventing trademark violations by an upstart computer company with the same name, Leonard litigated the Beatles' grievances with Capital Records. Despite a gag order by the judge's ruling in the 1988 case, Leonard won what the *Wall Street Journal* and *Rolling Stone* magazine leaked as the largest settlement in the history of the record industry—more than $300 million. More important, Leonard's win returned ownership of their classic master recordings to the Beatles. With the world waiting for the Beatles catalog to be released on compact disc, the group itself was able to reap that incredible financial harvest.

In spite of—or perhaps *because* of—his status in the industry, Leonard was unable to find a label for *Heal in the Wisdom.* He initially explained that music business executives were intimidated by his reputation as a litigator, but he eventually confessed that he believed it was because his heart was never truly into connecting me and my work to an industry run by crooks.

After *Heal in the Wisdom* was rejected by the kings of the industry's gate-keepers, Leonard took me on a walk through Central Park and told me he was actually happy that everyone had passed on my album.

"From the very beginning, the entire structure of the record business was designed to allow unethical businessmen to take advantage of idealistic, talented kids," he said. "If a record company can screw the Beatles out of millions of dollars over a period of twenty years of unprecedented global fame—and get away with it—imagine what they do with unknown artists like you."

As we continued our walk in Central Park that afternoon, Leonard told me that he felt my future was in the spiritual realm of music anyway. "Not religious—*spiritual*!" he emphasized. "I think you've had so many disappointments in the record business because your music is spiritual. But I can open doors for you with spiritually motivated people, people who are trying to make a difference in the world."

And Leonard was as good as his word; he represented me pro bono, arranged important bookings for me with prominent individuals, institutions, and organizations in the interfaith community, and offered his home in the Hamptons and his apartment in Manhattan for my occasional visits to the East Coast. Immediately before my 1987 Medicine Wheel solo I spent three weeks at Len's home on Louse Point in the Hamptons. While driving out to the house, Len stopped at the memorial that Jackson Pollock's widow, Lee Krasner, had placed at the spot where the painter died in a car wreck in 1956. Knowing my interest in painting, Len reminded me that Jackson Pollock created his immortal drip paintings in nearby Springs. Len also reminded me that his house was only a few miles from Willem de Kooning's home and studio, where the old master, defying an Alzheimer's haze, was painting the last works of his long, prolific career.

Lee Eastman, the father of Len Marks's friend and mentor entertainment lawyer John Eastman, had represented de Kooning since the 1950s.[1] Knowing that I would be interested, Len told me that the abstract expressionist frequently pedaled a bike through the neighborhood, riding to Louse Point. With the remote chance of encountering de Kooning and the immediate intent to ponder the light on water that inspired so many de Kooning and Pollock works, I borrowed a neighbor's bicycle for daily rides to the beach at Louse Point. I was never fortunate enough to see de Kooning, but the long bike rides gave me time to consider my relationship with Melissa. Pedaling from Louse Point to Len's one afternoon I decided I should open myself to a more committed relationship. I contacted Melissa and she agreed to meet me in Wyoming in late August.

I first noticed Melissa at the Kerrville Folk Festival in the late 1970s. Lovely brown hair caressed the sharp, delicate features of her face and draped over her shoulders down to the middle of her back. Willowy, with a beguiling kiss of melancholy in her gregarious hazel eyes, Melissa could have been Modigliani's model. A provocative eighteen-year-old, she would sit on the front row during my set at the festival and mouth the words, "I'm going to marry you." That most certainly got my attention.

When Melissa entered her early twenties she got a job on the folk festival's volunteer staff that allowed her access to the backstage area. There she would greet me each year as I exited the stage after my set. Even though her directness enchanted me from the beginning, I continued to skillfully deflect her romantic overtures. Still, Melissa's "country-girl" guilelessness inspired reciprocal honesty, and I had a sincere respect for the sixteen-year difference in our ages. A typical backstage interaction between us during those years usually ended with me advising her to find someone her own age, get married, and have kids. Privately, Melissa's overt reference to marriage scared the hell out of me; experience proved I should devote myself to art because I was truly dangerous to commitment-minded women. So my relationship with Melissa remained strictly platonic from the late 1970s until May 1983, when we continued talking one night long after the festival ended and spent the night together. The following morning I left on a three-month tour.

My time in Austin was becoming increasingly rare. It was not unusual during the 1980s for me to be on the road six months at a time. As Melissa was a beautiful young woman in freewheeling Austin and exploring life herself, the uncommitted relationship worked well for both of us. She occasionally fell in love and got her heart broken, but always turned to me for advice and comfort.

But *all* my relationships had become part-time. Since my 1978 divorce from Gloria I had been in constant motion. Fleeting relationships were the only kind I could have. By '79 I had literally moved into the back of a Mazda pickup truck and begun to crisscross America with my one-man show of *A Ballad of the West*, making the trip so many times that I eventually lost count. Moreover, by the early '80s the range of my travel was expanding as I received the first offers to perform in England and Europe. But an exciting new literary career was opening for me as well: after visit-

ing Nebraska as the featured speaker for Neihardt Day in 1979, Vine Deloria edited the anthology *A Sender of Words*, spotlighting fifteen noted western authors celebrating the poet's contributions to western literature. Vine
invited me to join the effort, and I contributed an essay titled "The Enduring Presence of John Neihardt." Also in 1981 a world-class western art magazine, *Four Winds*, published a striking two-part presentation of the text of
Seekers of the Fleece, illustrated with the watercolors of Alfred Jacob Miller
and featuring introductions by Vine and legendary western author Frank
Waters. This publication attracted the attention of Wiyaka Press and led to
the publication of a slipcased hardback limited edition of two hundred fifty
copies of *Seekers of the Fleece* and *Lakota*. The book sold for $150, and I was
pleasantly surprised when all the copies sold in less than six months.

Golden Egg Records was established with the release of *Heal in the Wisdom* in May 1981, so I made another important business decision. Rather
than surrendering control of my career to managers or agents, I created my
own production/management company and hired two full-time employees
to coordinate my increasingly complicated business dealings and tour
schedules. In keeping with the ancient notion of an "artistic manifesto," I
also began publishing a quarterly newspaper called *Hoka Hey!* To scratch
my "outdoor" itch, I started a business called Earth Journeys to book excursions with small groups accompanying me and other artists to perform concerts in remote historic locations in the American West. A vitally important
aspect of all this was that having the staff at Bridger Productions enabled
me to devote my precious remaining personal time to painting, and I had
completed more than twenty major new mural-scale acrylic paintings. In
fact, aside from the input of a handful of investors, much of the initial
income of the production company came from the sale of my paintings.

Capping these endeavors, a flurry of professional theatrical activity
began for me when I met Christopher Sergel at Neihardt Day in 1978.
Chris's connections in the international theatrical community were old,
deep, and vast. The Dramatic Publishing Company, created by his great-
grandfather in the early nineteenth century, was the very first theatrical
publishing house in America. By the time I returned to Nebraska with Vine
for Neihardt Day 1979, Chris was ready for me to take a more active role
with the *Black Elk Speaks* production team. He had completed script revi-
sions and, because of the large Indian populations in Denver, Tulsa, and
Phoenix, targeted those areas as possible locations for a production. When

Vine and I left Bancroft, I had promised to stay in touch with Chris as I continued wandering around the West.

I had not kept my promise. So when I went to New York in January 1982 to meet Len Marks to try to place *Heal in the Wisdom* with a major label, I called Chris to reconnect and apologize and he asked me to meet him at the Lone Star Cafe the next day. After briefing me on the progress of the *Black Elk Speaks* project, Chris asked, "Have you ever heard of Dale Wasserman?"

"No."

"Well, you've certainly heard of *Man of La Mancha* and *One Flew Over the Cuckoo's Nest*," Chris went on. "Dale wrote those plays. He also wrote a drama called *Elijah and the Long Knives* for *Playhouse 90* back in the '50s. After *La Mancha* he returned to *Elijah* and developed it into a musical about mountain men. Now he's searching for a balladeer who sings about mountain men. Do you know where we can find one?"

Though physically different, from our first meeting Dale Wasserman reminded me of Wooten Morris. Their innate elegance and locution seemed to stem from a similar bemused perspective of art and life. They shared worldviews formed during the era of the Great Depression, and both were highly intelligent and against-all-odds self-educated. An orphan from Wisconsin, Dale ran away from a foster home at age twelve and spent his teenage years riding the rails throughout America. He traveled throughout the country, "borrowing" two or three books from a library in one town and exchanging them for two or three more in the next. For years I have begged Dale to write a musical based on his life as a teenage hobo during the Great Depression. He once held me spellbound for hours with stories from the era. Since he was in his sixties when we met, his youthful escapades were long behind him, but the survival instincts of the hobo still lingered in his personality in spite of his unprecedented success in the theater and movies. Among scores of screenplays featuring major stars of the 1940s and 1950s, Dale wrote *The Vikings*, starring Kirk Douglas and Tony Curtis. He also wrote the screenplay for what was in the 1960s the biggest-budget film in history—*Cleopatra*, starring Elizabeth Taylor and Richard Burton. Atop its lofty windmill, *Man of La Mancha* was the box office champion of Broadway for decades. Featuring one of the most heroic songs ever composed, "The Impossible Dream," *Man of La Mancha* will live forever. When I asked how many productions of *Man of La Mancha* were up and running in 1982, Dale responded with a question: "In America or globally?" "Globally." "Perhaps three hundred." He was quick to say that that number was an estimate of "legitimate" productions, adding that there were probably scores of pirate productions.

Dale's career in show business began in his twenties when he drifted into work as a lighting artist. One thing led to another and, as would become his lifelong habit, he kept changing careers. After Hollywood success writing screenplays, in the 1950s he became a playwright during the so-called Golden Age of television, when the shows were live and the scripts were fresh out of the typewriter. A generation of great American actors and writers began their careers working on those live dramatic black-and-white television programs.

Dale's success with *La Mancha* in the mid-1960s brought him full circle, and he resurrected *Elijah* as *Shakespeare and the Indians* and based it on a historical footnote in the life of illiterate mountain man Jim Bridger. In his late thirties, deeply ashamed that he couldn't read or write, Jim Bridger hired a young man to read the works of William Shakespeare to him. Bridger memorized long passages of Shakespeare and was known for wearing a suit of armor—given to him by Scottish lord William Drummond Stewart—and riding a white mule through the Wind River Mountains of Wyoming as he quoted long soliloquies from his favorites of the bard's plays—*King Lear* and *Macbeth*. Wasserman's musical revolves around a shell-shocked survivor of the Civil War, still haunted by the horror of the conflict, who instinctively sought healing in the Rocky Mountains of his youth. The audience soon learns that this "drifter" was orphaned after an Indian raid on a wagon train in which his family was killed. The boy was rescued by three colorful mountain men and raised from childhood reading Shakespeare to them. Over the course of the musical comedy the drifter conjures the ghosts of the mountain men, as well as the spirits of Shakespeare's characters, in his quest to heal and reinvent himself.

It was my great good fortune that Dale Wasserman hired me for the *Shakespeare and the Indians* initial two-week workshop at the Eugene O'Neill Theater Center. A graduate of the Yale School of Drama once told me that a post-performance note session with Dale Wasserman was comparable to a year of study at the prestigious university. I believed him; on several occasions I had witnessed thick-skinned professional actors departing a Wasserman note session in tears.

Days after he received my press kit, Wasserman called me, and for once

I was home to answer the phone. A few days after Dale's call, I was on a plane to New York and, from there, a train to New London, Connecticut. A winsome young woman named Gayle Ritchie met me at the station and we drove down a rocky coastline to Waterford and the Eugene O'Neill Theater Center.[2] Over the next five years I would spend two months of each year at the intensely creative theatrical laboratory on Long Island Sound.

Upon my arrival at "the O'Neill" I was immediately escorted to a sparse set in a barn theater on the campus. There I was introduced to a cast of New York actors who had trampled everyone else in the cattle call for twin plums of America's most prestigious theatrical laboratory and a Dale Wasserman musical on their résumé. After the first day among such prodigious and ambitious talent, I feared I had gotten myself into something way beyond my abilities. Nevertheless, the workshop's director, George C. White—who was also the founder and executive director of the Eugene O'Neill Theater Center—seemed impressed that I was a genuine balladeer, and his friendliness made me feel less intimidated and encouraged me to keep growing. Thankfully, we were in a workshop production with minimal blocking and with scripts in hand throughout the production. Even with tiny victories, however, I was barely able to mask my increasing panic, as each day I became more uncertain of my footing in this new territory.

At this point in the evolution of my one-man shows of *A Ballad of the West* the acting was minimal; my focus had been to develop the pieces in the style of a balladeer. But the cast in this workshop had trained their entire lives to get to Broadway, and each of them was a triple-threat performer, able to act, dance, and sing simultaneously. I was humbled in their presence.

Halfway through the two-week workshop Dale asked me to come to the main mansion for a talk with him and George C. White. Expecting to be fired, I gathered my courage, prepared for the worst, and went to George's office. I was greatly relieved to find that Dale had no intention of firing me. He needed my help.

"Could I impose upon you to perform your one-man show for our company?" Dale asked. "Most of our cast is from Ivy League drama schools. They have no idea how a mountain man talks, and know even less about his attitude. I hope your show can provide a crash course in the history of the fur trade, particularly the vernacular of the mountain man's perspective of the American West."

"And we could have a party!" George White chimed in.

Seeing Cliff Robertson and Dina Merrill on the front row in the audience at the O'Neill barn intensified my fear. I realized that major Broadway producers and critics attending the National Composers and Librettists Conference were also in the audience, and even with fellow cast members' encouraging thumbs-up signals, I was petrified. This would certainly be one of the most important performances of *Seekers* that I would ever give. As usual, once into the show, I became blessedly lost in the material. So the two-minute standing ovation I received upon concluding my performance was pure and sweet. I'd earned it. Aside from winning the role of the drifter that evening, however, I also won an audience with one of America's top movie stars.

"You have to do this show for Redford," George White announced, shaking my hand. "He will love this!"

Robert Redford had released his film about mountain man Jeremiah "Liver-Eating" Johnson in the mid-1970s, around the same time that I opened *Ballad* at the Creek Theater. I was aware that the year before I arrived in Cody, Redford had come to Old Trail Town because of a controversy swirling around the physical remains of the real Jeremiah Johnson.

After seeing Redford's movie, a middle school class in Los Angeles did a research project on Johnson. They discovered that the mountain man died in a Veterans Administration nursing home in L.A. and, against his final wishes to be laid to rest in Montana, had been buried in California. The children raised money to have Johnson's body exhumed and reburied in Montana. Alas, the governor of Montana believed the reburial was a promotional stunt by Warner Bros. Studios and refused to accept Johnson's bones. That was when Redford stepped in and with an entourage of modern-day mountain men led by Timberjack Joe, joined forces with Bob Edgar and reburied Jeremiah Johnson at Old Trail Town.

Redford had also been profoundly moved by the concept of the Eugene O'Neill Theater Center and its efforts to create a laboratory environment for people to hone their craft in the theatrical arts. The actor asked O'Neill founder and president George C. White to assist with the design and creation of a similar laboratory for film. The result was the Sundance Institute in Utah. George C. White became the first chairman of the Sundance board.

Three weeks after my performance of *Seekers of the Fleece* at the Eugene O'Neill Theater Center, I arrived at the Sundance Institute. I was originally scheduled to perform *Seekers* for Redford in his home, but plans changed at the last minute and I was asked to do my show in a cafeteria on the Sundance campus.

I waited ten minutes for Redford to arrive before being instructed by a Sundance official to begin without him. When Redford finally came in, I was five minutes into the piece, so he quietly took a chair offstage behind me, away from the audience. Consequently, from that point forward it was comical the way all the eyes in my audience were focused on the movie star while I performed.

Aside from being upstaged by Redford, I was wishing for a fourth wall for once. My audience consisted of thirty jaded Hollywood studio executives, at best amused at the novel prospect of a singing mountain man and present only because Redford was there and my show offered an opportunity to grab his ear. Compounding matters, the cafeteria setting was a nightmare. Acoustics were terrible and the large plate-glass window behind the audience was a constant distraction of gawking passersby. Worse, insensitive busboys regularly clamored between me and my audience, shattering any rapport I might have been able to establish. Completing my bow at the end of the hour-long performance, I was nevertheless greeted with the funniest response I've ever had to singing an epic ballad: one of the ladies in the audience stood, raised her hand over her head, and shouted, "One more time!" Redford shook a few hands, kissed a few cheeks, and graciously asked me to step into the cafeteria offices to talk. Once there, he suggested that I sit in the office's only chair while he perched on the edge of the desk. He sincerely apologized for arriving late and for sitting to one side and upstaging me, explaining that there had been no other option.

In the twenty minutes I spent alone with him, I was mighty impressed with Robert Redford. I felt privileged to meet a man instead of a celebrity. With more fame than most could deal with in several lifetimes, he remained sensitive enough to apologize to an unknown balladeer and take time for a brief visit. As we continued our talk, he revealed his profound love and knowledge of the people, history, and landscape of the American West. I was delighted to learn that we had visited many of the same remote places, such as the Medicine Wheel, and we shared stories of an intimate awareness of more than a few cherished sacred grounds. Most of all, I was pleased to discover that he had started his career as a painter. When reminded I was from Austin, he told me that he had spent many happy hours with relatives there as a boy and recalled swimming at Barton Springs.

My conversation with Redford that June afternoon in Utah in 1982 also led to a 1983 meeting in Manhattan with his literary representative, Barbara Maltby, on behalf of Chris Sergel and *Black Elk Speaks*. Chris wanted Redford to direct *Black Elk Speaks*, and he asked me to contact his Sundance representatives to arrange a meeting. Redford was too busy to attend the meeting in New York, but Sundance business manager John Lear made it clear that Barbara Maltby spoke for him. Ms. Maltby informed us that Redford was well aware of *Black Elk Speaks* and was honored to even be considered to direct such an important work. After his Academy Award–winning directorial success with *Ordinary People*, however, Redford's calendar was booked for seven consecutive years. She said that Redford encouraged us to look elsewhere, but if we decided to wait that long, he would consider directing *Black Elk Speaks*.

No longer a young man, Chris Sergel was already looking mortality in the eye. He couldn't wait seven years. He respectfully thanked Redford and moved quickly to the director of the Oscar-nominated *Never Cry Wolf*, Carroll Ballard. David Carradine and Ballard promptly argued and the director bolted. It should be noted here that David's participation in any play or film of *Black Elk Speaks* was sacrosanct, as he had been personally selected by Black Elk's grandchildren to play their grandfather. They had loved watching David on his old *Kung Fu* television series and often remarked how much he looked like their grandfather. When Chris Sergel asked who they wanted to portray Black Elk in a film they immediately requested David.

Chris Sergel moved quickly to Leonard Nimoy. Chris had published Nimoy's one-man play about Vincent van Gogh when the actor was so stereotyped from *Star Trek* fame as Mr. Spock that he couldn't get arrested. Chris's "favor" kept Nimoy in work through some very lean years before fate shifted with his astonishing success with directing several *Star Trek* feature films. So Chris asked his old friend to direct *Black Elk Speaks*. Nimoy took the project to the Disney Company, but they were interested only in filming the sections of the script dealing with Black Elk's horse visions for Disneyland IMAX. Of course Chris declined. At the time of his death in 1992 Chris was still searching for the right people to produce his screenplay of *Black Elk Speaks*. Sadly, even though Chris Sergel's theatrical adaptation of *Black Elk Speaks* continues to enjoy successful productions around the country, his screenplay vision of "the American Gandhi" has yet to be developed into a movie.

By the time of our 1983 presentation to Robert Redford, I was becoming more deeply involved in *Black Elk Speaks*. Ironically, much of this increased activity with the Black Elk project sprang from my evolving friendship with Dale Wasserman. After becoming closer to Dale, I discovered he despised New York and Broadway. He believed Broadway productions had become so expensive that it extinguished the desire to risk anything bold or provocative in New York. Instead, Dale considered regional theater companies the last important venues for original drama, and he was growing increasingly devoted to writing plays for daring regional companies.

More personally significant, I had also come to realize that when Dale's show went to Broadway the producers would demand a star of John Denver's galaxy in the role of the drifter. When I asked Dale about this directly, he replied, "You are an astute young man. Follow your instincts."

So after *Shakespeare and the Indians* closed in Omaha I told Dale I was going to focus my energy on *Black Elk Speaks*. He smiled and said he would be there on opening night. He kept his promise. His friendship remains one of the most cherished of my life.

Meanwhile, as my touring continued, I was named the first (and, so far, the only) "balladeer-in-residence" of the Eugene O'Neill Theater Center and the John Neihardt Center. The work at the Eugene O'Neill expanded my theatrical career dramatically, and now in possession of an Equity card, I had performed for months at a time in several regions of the country in nearly two hundred productions of *Shakespeare and the Indians*. Also, for several years running, I was frequently in Tulsa, Oklahoma, where, as a member of the board of directors of the American Indian Theater Company, I helped to assemble and train the cast for a major production of *Black Elk Speaks*. In 1984 I costarred with David Carradine and Will Sampson in a thirty-six-person, all Native American (except for David, me, and three others) production of *Black Elk Speaks*. During this time of developing the play, I often camped on the Pine Ridge Reservation at the home of Black Elk's grandchildren in Manderson and became close with the family. While all this was taking place, I was jetting back to the Eugene O'Neill in Connecticut to supervise the design and direction of two major workshops of my space fantasy musical, *Aldebaran and the Falling Star*, by the National Theater Institute.

The growing British influence on American theater throughout the 1960s had become prevalent by the 1970s. Reacting to this, in 1982 George C. White hired Lynn Britt to head the O'Neill's National Theater Institute (NTI) program. The director of more than fifty productions at the Bristol and London Old Vic theaters, Ms. Britt was also the "movement master" at those regal English institutions. Her first task at NTI was to plow through a five-foot stack of scripts submitted for workshop development. There she discovered my *Aldebaran and the Falling Star* script. Unaware that I was the "balladeer-in-residence" of the O'Neill and was also developing my western ballads there, Ms. Britt selected *Aldebaran* for the 1983 spring NTI musical workshop. She felt the script called for pantomime and puppetry arts, and she hired a young man whose reputation in those schools was rising rapidly in New York.

Having begun his career as a street mime, Peter Lobdell was trained in Japanese Kabuki, as well as mime and puppetry, and it was only natural that his gifts eventually found a home in the theater. After designing the innovative horses for Richard Burton's Broadway debut of Peter Shaffer's disturbing drama *Equus*, Peter joined the NTI faculty at the O'Neill. Soon thereafter, he became an integral part of the creative team developing my *Aldebaran* show. We became close friends after he brilliantly designed and choreographed the central and essential stage illusion of a clipper ship taking flight in *Aldebaran*, and also solved many other daunting staging conundrums that were inherent in the piece. At orientation for the initial spring 1983 workshop Ms. Britt said while introducing the play to the cast that she believed my *Aldebaran and the Falling Star* script required all the theater arts to produce, and, as such, it was an ideal workshop piece for students. She believed this so strongly that she broke with NTI precedent to bring *Aldebaran* back for a second consecutive workshop in spring 1984.

Because of the multiple new careers simultaneously opening for me with theatrical productions and literary publications, and because of my predilection for remote places, much of the period between 1979 and 1988 was spent dancing on the tip of lofty promontories such as the Medicine Wheel or on the lip of a theatrical stage. Time spent in glass-and-steel canyons was usually followed by the need for an equal amount of time in ones made of stone. The space between these extremely diverse locations is a blur of baggage claims, airline terminals, soaring through the clouds in silver bullets, driving on the wrong side of the road in foreign lands, and endless hours burning hot with white-line fever in my little red truck on America's blue highways. I was increasingly uprooted, roaming, and alone.

My return from an unprecedented twelve-week tour of the outback of Australia marked the completion of a series of tours extending over nearly eighteen months. Aside from having performed my ballads in one of the most isolated regions on the planet in central Australia, I was crispy road-fried and in desperate need of a very long rest. But I was also burning to write an account of my Australian experience while it was still fresh in my mind, though I also yearned to return to painting. Before departing on the series of tours that had culminated in Australia, I had finally hit my stride with a synthesis of abstract styles that I was exploring in my painting, but now fueling my fierce need to paint was the unique Aboriginal Papunya Tula style of "dot painting" that I had seen in some of the galleries and homes in Australia. I was anxious to explore the technique myself.

But something else happened to me in Australia. The deeper I traveled into the profound intensity and unimaginable space of the deserts of central Australia, the more my longing for Melissa grew. Aussies call central Australia "the space," or "the dead red heart," but the refreshing, unjaded people I encountered there reminded me of the America of my 1950s childhood. Meeting and living with the cheerful family folks in the extreme remoteness of the Australian outback forced me to come to terms with the loneliness of my vagabond life of perpetual movement; encountering profoundly isolated yet lovingly connected people in that immense space illuminated the fact that humans are not meant to be alone. I saw in them that it is fundamentally important for us to mate, bond, and create families. During a much-needed meditation about the emotional detachment of my nomadic lifestyle, it occurred to me that my global wanderings might be masking painful childhood wounds that affected my ability to form normal familial bonds. Whatever grand adventure in whatever exotic locations I could imagine could never heal the psychic wounds and scars I was skillfully avoiding with constant movement. Melissa suddenly became a very clear mirror reflecting my fear of allowing intimacy into my life. Her love for me had always been innocent, honest, and vulnerable. But I was denying my feelings for her. Before I departed for Australia, Leonard Marks had arranged for me to perform on Pete Seeger's *Clearwater* sloop during ceremonies celebrating the relighting of the Statue of Liberty on her centennial. In New York Harbor on the *Clearwater* Len confronted me about my denial with respect to Melissa.

"Why are you running away from that sweet, beautiful girl?" he joked. "Does she have a sister?"

Len had no idea that his remarks echoed those of another close friend, made only weeks before. Billie Lee Mommer, an Omaha art collector who would soon purchase thirty-four of my paintings, called me to task about

Melissa. Billie Lee and I had met while I was in Omaha performing *Shakespeare and the Indians* and, bonded in our love of art, we remained close friends and business associates.

"Why are you avoiding that delightful girl, Bobby?" she asked upon meeting Melissa. "You're afraid of her strength, aren't you?"

This was not the first time Billie Lee had offered psychological observations about my behavior. An analytical architect and successful businesswoman, she was an expert at details. When we met she had recently amassed such a comprehensive collection of American primitive antiques that merely storing it required four whole floors of the eight-story Reilly Building in downtown Omaha, which she owned. On her first visit to Austin she saw my paintings and bought a couple of small pieces. I had no idea that the purchase of those two works would eventually lead to her buying nearly every painting I had.

"I'm considering purchasing your entire collection," she announced. "But I've noticed something odd. These early paintings from the 1960s are all signed 'B. Durham,' but the paintings from the 1970s forward have no signature. I assume this is because of your music business pseudonym, but my question is: Did 'B. Durham' or 'Bobby Bridger' create the unsigned paintings?"

This was truly an "aha" moment for me. No question: Robert "Bobby" Durham was the painter.

"Well," Billie Lee grinned, "I want Robert Durham to sign the paintings I buy. Furthermore, Mr. Bridger, I think it is high time that you acknowledge Robert Durham."

The series of paintings I had done before embarking on the tours that led to Australia had already subconsciously initiated the healing process that Billie Lee articulated. Since childhood I had been attracted to the exquisite visual resolution of conflict in abstract expressionist paintings. In college, however, I found myself equally drawn to the antithetical techniques and orderly grids and planes of constructivism, cubism, and geometric abstraction. Before leaving on tour I was deep into a series of paintings attempting to synthesize the two forms. It was beginning to occur to me that perhaps these new paintings were an intuitive effort to comprehend and placate old emotional wounds, but Billie Lee's insight concerning "authorship" shifted my focus from the process of painting to the completed work instead and suggested the necessity of a creative psychic reconciliation between Bobby Durham and Bobby Bridger. I signed all of the paintings "Robert Durham" and Billie Lee bought them. Still, Billie Lee's perceptiveness of the creative conflict between my two artistic selves set the wheels turning as I hit the road for a year and a half. By the time I arrived in Australia I was beginning to realize more about my dual personalities and was determined to unite them into one whole, creatively healthy individual. But the reasons I was running from Melissa were also beginning to come into sharper focus. In the "dead red heart" of Australia I arrived at the realization that my tender formative years were spent avoiding the intense confrontations of my ever-combative parents, and that led me to avoid emotional confrontation—especially with myself! I escaped emotional conflict through art. But I had faith that my evolution as an artist also meant becoming emotionally healthy personally, while remaining passionately creative and artistically productive. It was in this frame of mind that the people and landscape of outback Australia brought me to the realization that "emotionally healthy" meant being willing to confront my subconscious terror of intimacy. Deep in Australia's "space" I realized that I had to open up my "dead red heart" and let Melissa inside. I flew from Sydney in September 1986 and as soon as the plane landed in L.A. I called Melissa and asked her to meet my flight when it arrived in Austin.

Old habits die hard. After a week with Melissa, I retreated into my familiar cocoon and began a twenty-hour-a-day routine of writing and painting. In the past I had followed a strict exercise regimen, but even that routine fell by the wayside as painting and writing consumed every waking moment. I would rise at 5 a.m., write on a legal pad until noon, and then paint until I collapsed around midnight. After I vanished for ten days, Melissa called and tearfully confronted me about my absence. She told me that she could no longer continue a relationship with me if we were going to see each other only once every couple of months. I realized that she was serious and offered a desperate and terribly unromantic invitation.

"Maybe you could come over and watch me paint sometime?"

She accepted. She started coming over to my house in Hyde Park and sitting by the fireplace and smoking cigarettes while I painted. After a few weeks she developed a sixth sense for knowing the precise moment when my eyes were tiring, and she would sneak up behind me and, with her knee, gently tap behind mine and whisper in my ear that it was time to stop.

So, after a year of living together, an unpublished manuscript called *Coyote Dreamtime*, and more than fifty new Papunya Tula–influenced paintings, we had reached a crossroad. Melissa wanted to get married and I

refused to even discuss it. Worn down by my resistance, Melissa had finally given up on me and was beginning to drift away. Realizing this, I suggested that she meet me in Wyoming for a romantic vacation so that we
could work on our relationship before I headed off on a tour of the Soviet
Union in the fall of 1987.

During the time of my solo at the Medicine Wheel to prepare to meet
Melissa, there was much media hoopla concerning the theory of the Harmonic Convergence. On the basis of prophecies from an ancient Maya calendar, Colorado University professor and Maya scholar Jose Arguelles suggested that people should gather at power spots around the planet during
the "stellar alignment" for spiritual reunification ceremonies with Mother
Earth. As we would be in the Yellowstone country when the actual Harmonic Convergence occurred, I planned to meet Melissa's plane in Billings
and then return to the Medicine Wheel for the Harmonic Convergence. At
the Medicine Wheel I intended to reveal to Melissa that I was open to a
more committed relationship.

Melissa and I arrived at the Medicine Wheel two days before the celebrated stellar alignment. Unfortunately, a flock of more than a hundred
New Agers had descended and were roosting in Gore-Tex tents and bags all
over the sacred site.[3]

Shocked by the numbers of people at the Medicine Wheel for the Harmonic Convergence, I decided to take Melissa directly to Yellowstone.
Another of my favorite "medicine" spots was—and remains—Yellowstone's
Grand Prismatic Pool. There, elongated diaphanous steam spirals swirl to
heaven, escaping thermal pools of unimaginable temperatures bubbling up
from deep within the volcanic bowels of Mother Earth. The temperature
from the pool's deep, hot core cools as it approaches the banks, allowing
various intrepid forms of living algae to defy the heat and flourish in rich,
deliciously intense colors. Creating a steamy aurora borealis as a visual celebration of their bold survival, the algae pools mirror the heavens while
simultaneously casting a ghostly reflection of their own translucent pastel
hues into the spiraling vapor clouds. From my first visit, the Grand Prismatic Pool seemed to me the perfect mystical metaphor of a human: light
shining through vapors, creating rainbow prisms of color.

Melissa and I arrived at the entrance to Yellowstone well before sunrise
and, much to our surprise, discovered we had the park virtually to ourselves.
At the very moment when the sun was rising we parked at the trailhead of
the Grand Prismatic Pool. We bundled up and headed toward the main pool

on the long, wet boardwalk over the colorful fields of delicate algae. Warm mist from smaller thermal pools soaked us as we walked. Then, rays of sunlight suddenly slashed through the sheets of hot steam, revealing millions of sparkling microscopic droplets of water stuck to every minute fiber and hair on our bodies. In an instant we realized that the sheets of hot vapor spinning around us were infinitesimal prisms of water—each exploding into rainbows with light. At that moment, without a word being uttered, we knew we were going to spend the rest of our lives together.

Luminescence

IT WAS SO DRY YOU COULD SPIT AND SPARK A FIRE. The brutal drought that punished the Rocky Mountains in June 1988 was only in the intermediate stages of its relentless cycle, but old-timers were already prophesying catastrophe. Preceding the drought, biblical legions of pine beetles mounted cancerous offensives that consumed vast sections of healthy green alpine forests, leaving colossal swaths of expanding brown blight in their rapacious wake. A malevolent heat wave crept behind the beetles and drought, shriveling the Yellowstone region in a grim, evaporative shroud. Parched brittle and thirsty for fire, the forest floor was a tinderbox of fallen, decaying trees.

During a "wet" season fourteen years earlier I had witnessed an immense forest fire in the Grand Tetons and was surprised to discover park rangers calmly monitoring the conflagration from the side of the road. Like everyone else in America, I had been raised with "Smokey Bear" and his Advertising Council admonition, "Only you can prevent forest fires." Confused, I pulled over to join the flock of tourists demanding answers from the rangers and received instead a fundamental course in naturalist philosophy. First we were informed that the lodgepole pine has an extremely shallow root system that makes it prone to uprooting. Next the rangers explained how earlier that year a powerful windstorm swept down from the peaks of the Tetons and slapped down broad sections of the lodgepole pine forest like pickup sticks. The fire we were currently observing was naturally cleansing fallen timber from the windswept forest. When asked about the healthy trees that would be destroyed in the process, the rangers expressed the essence of the naturalist's philosophy: since the fire had been started by a lightning strike, they would not extinguish it; rangers attack and subdue a fire only when it is determined to have been started—accidentally or intentionally—by a human. Otherwise, as environmental scientists, they observe rather than interfere, even if the "natural fire" burns a healthy forest. If the fire threatens human populations they are prepared to intervene; otherwise, they take the view that fire is part of the intrinsic pattern of nature, a cycle often completed by fire itself, as evidenced by the lodgepole pine. The cones of the lodgepole pine are naturally inclined to pop during the extreme heat of a forest fire, flinging seeds of the future into the nourishing ashes of their antecedents. The rangers said if we returned the next year we would discover a resplendent field of wildflowers amid charcoaled stumps where fire now raged. They explained that within three years a nursery of thousands of lodgepole pine sprouts would be flourishing from the nutritious remains of their parents; in twenty years a healthy lodgepole pine forest would have replaced the conflagration we were witnessing.

I had been reminded of that simple yet profound environmental lesson in 1986 in Australia, where nomadic Aboriginals are noted for intentionally setting fires to burn the landscape in their wake as they follow songlines over ancient ancestral "Dreamtime" routes. There, as in the American West, entire ecosystems depend upon fire to cleanse and initiate the cycle of rebirth. When visiting Aboriginal tribal people in Australia, I had no idea how the ancient cycle of fire, purification, and rejuvenation would soon affect me in Cody, Wyoming.

In 1988, after five years of development, including several intense personal workshops with George White at the Eugene O'Neill Theater Center, *Seekers of the Fleece* was ready to be mounted as a full-company musical production. When reminded of the phenomenal flow of tourists through Cody each summer en route to Yellowstone, professionals at the O'Neill advised me to forget New York and focus my energy instead on developing a summer perennial at the eastern entrance to the national park. So in June 1988 I took an entourage of sixteen actors, singers, musicians, technicians, and business associates to Cody, Wyoming, for the world premiere of *Seekers*. I had assembled a star-studded cast featuring Joe Sears, Steven Fromholz, Wes Studi, Bill Ginn, Daryl Watson, and Melissa Tatum. Melissa did double duty as stage manager and as the "Indian maiden" of the cast. We also had a company manager, a lighting director, and six other company members. One of our producers came directly from the O'Neill.

Working together creatively in workshops at the Eugene O'Neill Theater Center, Peter Lobdell and I had become friends. In 1987 he moved to Austin to continue work at Bridger Productions as a coproducer on the *Aldebaran* project. As the *Seekers* production gathered momentum, Peter joined the team. Soon he and Austin character actor Tim Mateer went to Cody to locate a space for us to rent and build a theater from the ground up. Billie Lee Mommer, the Omaha architect/art collector who had bought thirty-four of my paintings, joined Peter and Tim, and the trio found a failed gymnasium languishing over a flower shop on Twelfth Street in downtown Cody. By the time the company arrived, Peter, Tim, and Billie Lee had gutted the gym and reconstructed the room into a small theater with bench seating.

While creating the theater the advance team also searched Cody for housing for the company. As Cody is a "tourist town" economically dependent upon Yellowstone traffic, available rent housing is scarce and rates soar to the stratosphere during the peak summer season. Our jaws fell when we realized how much we would have to pay for minimal housing for our company. Moreover, as we were depicting mountain men in the very heart of mountain man country, the costumes had to be meticulously detailed and authentic—in other words, expensive. I hired professional fur trade reenactors to measure the cast and assemble the wardrobe, and the final costs of costumes alone were staggering. Capping all these expenses, Joe Sears, Wes Studi, and I were all members of Actors' Equity, and the production had to be sanctioned by the stringent contractual fees required by our labor union. Ultimately, the production was an expensive, Broadway-style, roll-the-dice gamble in a very conservative western town.

You could practically trip over the irony surrounding the production. To begin with, the town of Cody, Wyoming, literally came into being as a result of Buffalo Bill's phenomenal success at creating from the ether much of what we now recognize as American "show business." And the coincidence of debuting *Seekers of the Fleece* in Buffalo Bill's and Jackson Pollock's hometown had never escaped my notice. If for no other reason than artistic/historical symmetry, my uniquely "American" work almost had to be born there. After all, it had to do with "enterprise."

In 1822 Jim Bridger answered an advertisement for "one-hundred enterprising young men." Heeding that call led Jim and the very first "enterprising Americans" to the Yellowstone. Buffalo Bill and mankind followed the mountain men's trail. Though most western towns arose and grew along railroad lines, William F. Cody and his wealthy and influential eastern business associates realized that the world would beat a path to Yellowstone forever. They focused the scout's international fame and wealth on creating a community that represented American entrepreneurship; indeed, they named their town's newspaper the *Cody Enterprise.*

Whereas Buffalo Bill showcased and exported much of America's fundamental historical mythology, Jackson Pollock shocked and transformed global visual iconography when he escaped Picasso's shadow, threw painting down from the easeled elitism of the Renaissance, extracted demons from his tortured subconscious, flung, splashed, and dripped exquisite color and nearly single-handedly proclaimed America's "Manifest Destiny" as the new center of the art universe. So whether another soul realized it or not, the delicious irony of debuting *Seekers of the Fleece* in Cody was multifaceted for me. I laughed out loud when I realized that the financial key that started the engine of the theatrical production of my ballads was the sale of my paintings—the harvest of a career that had begun thirty-three years earlier with Pollock-like color doodling. But all the money from the sales of my paintings, as well as many thousands more from investors, was riding on success in Cody. Further complicating matters was the fact that even with investors backing the production, I needed to keep Bridger Productions operating smoothly in Austin while we set up second offices and production facilities in Cody. To accomplish this I secured a large bank loan. Betting on the cards to fall in my favor with the production, I anted up everything I owned and pushed it all into the pot.

Even though the production was building a head of steam with workshops at the O'Neill before Joe Sears became involved in 1985, he agreed to direct the full-company musical debut of *Seekers of the Fleece.* Joe and I had met when I enrolled in one of his comedy character acting classes as a result of a quirk in the 1984 production of *Black Elk Speaks* in Tulsa. Aside from my featured role in *Black Elk Speaks* as William Bent, I was unexpectedly cast in a second part a week before the show's opening. Director Tom Brennan pulled me aside to explain that the actor originally cast in the role of reporter John Finnerty had suddenly bowed out of the production. As directors are apt to do, Tom didn't give me an option; he told me I was taking the part. I argued with him, pleading that I wasn't skilled enough to master Finnerty's Irish brogue in a week. He had little patience; he was in over his head with an enormous, unruly cast of Indian actors, most in their first theatrical roles. He brusquely informed me that he was counting on the "pros" in the company to take up the slack.

"Just make him funny," Tom bellowed.

Desperate, Tom realized that I knew John Finnerty's history and that familiarity would allow me to get to his character's essence quickly. A Chicago newspaper reporter, Finnerty was an Irishman fascinated with General George Armstrong Custer. Long before the concept of "embedding" reporters with military expeditions, Finnerty personally followed Custer throughout his various military campaigns during the Indian wars and, through his heroic newspaper columns praising Custer, contributed greatly to the impetuous general's legend. Chris Sergel had written Finnerty almost like a modern play-by-play broadcaster at a football game. Vitally important as a theatrical device, the character narrated Custer's final stand—and fall—at Little Big Horn. The dissolution of Finnerty's arrogance as he comments on the battle from the sidelines in disbelief metaphorically reflects the physical disintegration of the Seventh Cavalry.

I went into "horse rehearsals" distracted with how to deal with the challenge of creating something comedic in Finnerty's big scene. "Horse rehearsals" were, however, comedic in themselves. Julie Taymor, the master puppeteer and set designer who would in fifteen years dazzle Broadway with her Tony Award–winning direction of Disney's *The Lion King*, and be nominated for an Academy Award in directing for her work in *Frida*, was the set designer for *Black Elk Speaks*. Creating the illusion of the Indian Wars of the 1860s depended upon resolving the dilemma of presenting horses onstage, and Julie came up with an ingenious solution: she designed stick horses with padded leather heads. Rather than dime-store versions, though, Julie's stick horses looked exactly like the classic authentic "wintertale" images painted on buffalo robes depicting battle scenes from the Indian wars. The horses looked fantastic, but in spite of this everyone in the cast still felt ridiculous riding a stick horse while acting in very serious high drama. At first impression the *Black Elk Speaks* actors looked like the Monty Python boys with coconuts in their King Arthur spoof—yet, instead of imaginary horses like the Brits, they were even sillier on stick horses re-creating a profound historical tragedy. Each day the cast had a short class, ostensibly to learn how to ride stick horses in pantomime but, in truth, to help them overcome embarrassment and fully commit to the seriousness of the prop. The stick horse had to become "real" before we could expect the audience to suspend disbelief.

Fortunately, only days before arriving in Tulsa for *Black Elk Speaks* rehearsals, I had been in workshop production with *Aldebaran and the Falling Star* at the O'Neill with Peter Lobdell. Much of Peter's design of the *Aldebaran* production had included mime and puppets, so I had recent hands-on experience with the magic that those art forms brought to my own play. Having already overcome the awkwardness of riding a puppet in *Aldebaran*, in stick-horse class I immediately started to experiment with a "greenhorn" Finnerty who was unable to ride his horse. Soon I had my hapless reporter grabbing his saddle-sore ass and pulling or chasing his recalcitrant runaway stick horse over the prairie even as he watched his hero fall in mortal defeat. Tom loved it. Even more important, our opening night audience was 95 percent American Indian, and they howled with laughter as my Finnerty was dragged, pitched, and bucked by the stick horse. They applauded as the stick horse finally ran away with me at the precise moment when Crazy Horse seized the stage and the Battle of Little Big Horn.

I had never attempted comedy onstage before, and I was smitten with the audience's reaction. As soon as the *Black Elk Speaks* production ended, I returned to Austin and discovered that Joe Sears was conducting a two-week comedy "character" workshop. I immediately signed up.

Joe and his partner, Jaston Williams, had spun gold with their comic masterpiece, *Greater Tuna*. Ironically, I had played a small role in the launching of that famous show. More accurately, I was simply part of a chain of coincidental events involving *Greater Tuna* that, for me, began with legendary blacklisted Texas folklorist John Henry Faulk.

Since the 1970s John Henry and his wife, Elizabeth, had been on the front row for many of my Austin performances of *A Ballad of the West*. I always loved seeing them, so when I received a call from John Henry in January 1982, I promptly accepted his invitation to drive out to West Lake Hills for a visit. I soon learned that my old friend needed a favor.

"Mah eighty ye-ah ole mutha-in-lah is he-ah from England visitin' 'lizabeth, Yohan, an' me," John Henry explained. "Wouldn'tcha know it, honeychild, hat tha same time, a couple a strangahs are comin' ta Austin from Nu Yawk 'pectin' me ta show 'em 'round town. Ah've nevah met these he-ah folks; all ah know is dey hav sumthin' ta do wid tha the-a-tah. But dey are associates of tha oldest frinds ah hav in Nu Yawk—angels who heped me when ah sued CBS aftah dey fired me 'cause ah was blacklisted. But dese folks want ta git baptized in tha Austin music scene, honey, and since ah can't vera well go club-hoppin' wid mah eighty-ye-ah-old mutha-in-lah, ah figured you would be a sweetheart an' hep me."

I explained to John Henry that I could entertain his guests on Friday and Saturday, but on Sunday I was flying to New York myself.[1] Nevertheless, as all we knew was that John Henry's guests had a theatrical background, an idea for Sunday's entertainment immediately came to me, and I assured him that I could entertain his "guests" for their entire time in Austin.

I didn't know Joe Sears at the time, but had recently seen his and Jaston Williams's two-person show, *Greater Tuna*, at TransAct Theatre on Sixth Street and loved it. I learned from the playbill that Joe was from Oklahoma, so on a lark I called Gary P. Nunn and asked him to contact Joe as a fellow Oklahoman and beg him for tickets for John Henry Faulk's surprise guests for the Sunday matinee. Gary P. knew Joe and was more than happy to help, but there was one small problem: the show had closed. Gary P. asked Joe and Jaston to remount the show for a Sunday matinee and the pair agreed.

The following Thursday I greeted Dick Humbler and Marilyn Stasio at Robert Mueller Airport and was stunned to learn that Dick was the New York editor of *Variety* magazine and Marilyn was a theater critic for the *New York Post* as well as many major magazines.[2] Marilyn brusquely informed me that they had absolutely no desire to see any theatrical productions; they came to town to hear music. They specifically wanted to hear "this guy Butch Hancock." Fortunately, Butch was playing at Emmajoe's, so I could arrange for them to hear and meet him. Unfortunately, I explained, after learning of their theatrical connections I had already made arrangements for them to see a show on Sunday. Marilyn initially protested, but after I promised her two absolutely chock-full nights of avant-garde Austin music and the author of "London Homesick Blues" as a theatrical "tour guide," she acquiesced and agreed to attend a Sunday-afternoon matinee. So with the New Yorkers deposited safely in Gary P.'s custody, I caught an early flight to New York on Sunday morning.

Dick and Marilyn fell in love with *Greater Tuna* and immediately connected Joe and Jaston with agents at the William Morris Agency in New York. They booked *Greater Tuna* in Atlanta, and soon Joe and Jaston owned the town. Next, the show moved to Hartford, Connecticut, where it was an even bigger hit. Then it ran at the Circle in the Square in New York for over a year and has been running ever since. *A Tuna Christmas*, *Red, White, and Tuna*, and *Tuna Does Vegas* followed, and Joe and Jaston continue tickling

America's funny bone. They have become true national treasures, helping us lovingly laugh at the antics of our conservative rural kinfolks.

Legendary oral historian Studs Terkel often said that John Henry Faulk's suit against the CBS network was the singular act of courage that broke the powerful grip of the McCarthy era in American history. Given his history with the McCarthy investigations and his successful twenty-year legal fight against blacklisting, destiny seems to have had a hand in the linkage of rural folklorist/humorist John Henry Faulk and a satirical play of the so-called Moral Majority like *Greater Tuna*. But karma definitely was directing the connection between me and Joe Sears. At the moment when all these connections were coming together in Austin between *Greater Tuna*, Humbler, and Stasio, I was in New York and Chris Sergel was hooking me up with Dale Wasserman. As previously mentioned, my relationship with Wasserman led me from the Eugene O'Neill to *Black Elk Speaks* and, by 1985, back to Austin and Joe Sears. Given Joe's extensive theatrical training, he was the perfect choice to direct the debut of *Seekers of the Fleece*. And as an added bonus, he agreed to play Jedediah Smith.

Fate definitely brought a colorful cast of characters together for my production of *Seekers* in Cody, Wyoming, during the summer of 1988. My old friend Bill Ginn was fresh off a Grammy nomination for his work with Jennifer Warnes, and Steven Fromholz had blossomed into one of the best actors/singers in America. I had hired an Indian kid I had worked with in *Black Elk* to create the Blackfeet Indian role, but at the very last minute he dropped out. In desperation, I contacted another "Black Elk" alumnus, Wes Studi, and he accepted the role. Immediately after the production ended Wes headed for Hollywood, where he soon won leading roles in *Dances with Wolves*, *Last of the Mohicans*, *Geronimo*, and other feature films.

Our embarrassingly small audiences reflected the effects of the drought, heat wave, and increasing numbers of fires on tourism. The first of the fires broke out even before we arrived in Cody, but seasonal fires in the region, although dangerous, were nothing out of the ordinary. Like the beetle invasion that preceded the drought, the heat wave was only a harbinger of tragedy yet to come. Six weeks after we opened *Seekers of the Fleece*, major fires were raging in Yellowstone. And more were breaking out daily, encircling the entire region. When the clear mountain air filled with suffocating smoke and white ash began falling like the snow of a nuclear winter, the town drained of tourists and filled with firefighters and news crews. Cody merchants and businessmen joined the cacophony of coffee shop pundits at Buffalo Bill's Irma Hotel, who ratcheted their daily conservative political grumblings into chest-thumping talk of lynching parties heading into Yellowstone for "them goddamn naturalists and their let-burn theories." I tried to argue the naturalist philosophy even as it quickly became apparent that the fires were burning everything I had.

A couple of producer friends of Joe's flew up from Austin. They agreed to help if I would close the show in Cody and return immediately to Texas. Austin's Live Oak Theatre was contacted and booked. In just two weeks we closed the Cody production, dismantled the theater, moved the entire company to Austin, reblocked and relit the show, wrote and introduced two new scenes, bookended them at the opening and closing of the show, did a publicity blitz, and opened in Austin. The show did well in Austin, but the damage had already been done.

After the production at Live Oak Theatre closed, I called for an emergency meeting of the Bridger Productions limited partnership. Lawyers and accountants in the partnership offered one option: file for bankruptcy. When I asked for an explanation I got no further than their telling me that bankruptcy would cost me ownership of my copyrights. I refused that option and requested an alternative. They informed me that as general partner the only other option was for me to dissolve the Bridger Productions limited partnership and assume the entire debt. I decided to take that path, and suddenly I became the sole owner of Bridger Productions, responsible for all its debt.

Within days of the dissolution of the Bridger Productions partnership, the wolves weren't simply howling at the door—they were foraging through the closets, pantry, and file cabinets. Five months after assuming the debt—just as the full impact of my decision was overwhelming me—Melissa informed me that we were expecting a baby. Soon the room that had been the middle office of my operations at Bridger Productions was converted into a nursery. As the ultimate sign that an era had ended, even my freewheeling artist "friends" began to gradually drift away when we announced our baby news.

Survival required stark simplicity, so I returned to the rigorous discipline of Desert Dance. I went directly to my creditors and explained my situation. After enduring more than a few serious legal threats and humiliating verbal assaults, I was able to convince my creditors that, even though it would probably take years to pay them, I was not running from my obligations. My desperate tactic proved successful. In most cases, once a creditor realized I was confronting my debt rather than writing it off to bankruptcy, I was able to actually negotiate a lower debt, coupled with an empathetic payment plan. Once again my paintings came to the rescue; the sale of nearly seventy-five paintings over a five-year period had established a paper trail of prices, cash flow, and "financial value" that appealed to bankers as a real asset. The major bank note I had signed was renegotiated as a promissory note, with twenty-three of my paintings as collateral. After we inked the deal the banker wryly commented that my paintings were paying for my "folk music habit."

With a baby on the way it was time to plan a wedding. Since so much of our history was tied to the Kerrville Folk Festival, that seemed the most appropriate place for an official ceremony. We married on June 4, 1989, on Chapel Hill at the festival. Melissa's Uncle Buddy Weeks and Aunt Willie Sowell—well into their eighties—sang a couple of lovely songs that were rivaled only by the mockingbirds.

Immediately after our wedding Melissa and I took off on tour for Wyoming. She was six months pregnant, and living in the back of a Ford 150 pickup truck would not be easy, but we needed any work we could get, so we had no choice. I had gigs in Taos and Rapid City, and after that we would hit the rendezvous circuit in Montana and Wyoming for a few weeks before arriving in Cody, where the senior curator at the Buffalo Bill Historical Center, Dr. Paul Fees, had helped me rent the Robbie Powwow Garden at the center to perform my one-man show for the summer.

After playing the Kit Carson Museum and visiting Indian friends at the Taos Pueblo, we headed for the Paha Sapa (Black Hills) Festival in Rapid City to benefit KELI radio station on the Pine Ridge Reservation. With headline acts Willie Nelson, Neil Young, Jackson Browne, John Denver, Kris Kristofferson, Bruce Cockburn, John Trudell, Timbuk 3, Floyd "Red Crow" Westerman, and a host of others on the bill, the Paha Sapa Festival was going to be the Woodstock of Indian country. In a last-minute ambush attempt, however, local conservatives evoked archaic city laws and forced the festival—originally to be held outdoors—into the Rapid City Civic Center. Inside, the event was under tighter government control and subject to closer scrutiny and union restrictions. Moving the show inside also restricted the number of people who could attend and how long the show could run. With such an incredible cast of headliners, the Rapid City Civic Center quickly filled to capacity. Within hours a crowd of several thousand Indians gathered in a growing tipi community outside the civic center, and a stage was set up to entertain them simultaneously with the shows inside.

I was scheduled to perform *Lakota* on the main stage with the premier traditional Lakota singing and drumming group, the Porcupine Singers. Soon after arriving in Rapid City I met with the leader of the Porcupines, Severt Young Bear Sr. and started rehearsals with the group. The Porcupines sang and chanted traditional songs as underscoring for my verse and sat silent while I performed songs from *Lakota*. During rehearsals we learned about the change of venue, and the large gathering of Indian people outside the civic center, so Severt and I went to the promoters and requested that they move our shows to the outside stage.

After rehearsals with the Porcupine Singers we raced to the plush Alex Johnson Hotel for the pre-show press conference. Melissa was thrilled at the prospect of meeting her favorite artist, Bruce Cockburn, and was flabbergasted as soon as we arrived at the press conference when, as if on cue, he walked straight up to us and introduced himself. We spent most of our time at the festival with the Canadian folksinger and his lovely twelve-year-old daughter, Jenny. Later, at the outdoor stage, Melissa, Bruce, and Jenny Cockburn were the only *washicus* in the audience as I performed *Lakota* with the accompaniment of the Porcupine Singers. After the show I promised Severt that if I ever recorded *Lakota* I would hire the Porcupine Singers to perform on the recording. Sadly, by the time I was finally able to record it, in 2000, all the original Porcupine Singers had journeyed to the spirit world. So I licensed their recordings and laced them into the recording of *Lakota*.

The morning after the Paha Sapa Festival Melissa and I headed west into the Powder River country. After a picnic lunch at the base of Devils Tower, we ascended the Big Horns and entered the high plains of Montana for an enchanted two-week journey performing for a series of mountain man rendezvous. Nestled in picturesque summer mountain meadows at the "vous," I was performing *Seekers* in large tipi villages that were meticulously replicating the trade fairs of the Rocky Mountains in the 1820s and 1830s. In this environment everyday dress was buckskins, and we were often lodged in an authentic tipi provided by our hosts. As Melissa was pregnant, the women all gathered around and made her comfortable, talking about babies and sharing natural child-birthing experiences. By the time we arrived in Pinedale for the town's annual rendezvous pageant, however, we had an urgent message to call Joe Sears.

Joe knew I had booked the Robbie Powwow Garden at the Buffalo Bill Historical Center from mid-July through the end of August. Acting on that information, Joe persuaded his *Greater Tuna* producer, Charles Duggan, to join him as coproducer for a bare-bones production of *Seekers of the Fleece*. When Duggan agreed to put up a small amount of cash for housing and to pay Bob Livingston's fee to join the cast, Joe contacted C. H. Parker, his theatrical mentor, at Northeast Oklahoma University in Tahlequah and persuaded him to direct the new production. With C. H. on board, Joe caught Bob Livingston in Paris en route to India and persuaded him to return to America and join us in Cody. With Bob as Hugh Glass and himself as Jedediah Smith, Joe next persuaded our technical assistant, James Gonzales, to play the Blackfeet warrior, and we had a minimal but workable cast. My wardrobe and props from the first season would easily costume the production. By the time I returned Joe's call, he had all the elements in place to begin the second season of *Ballad* in Cody. He had even dealt with the fact that by moving the show outside we could claim workshop status to silence any Equity grumblings. All I had to do was agree to play Jim Bridger and become a coproducer of the new production.

A veteran director of the acclaimed Cherokee outdoor drama *Trail of Tears*, C. H. Parker quickly adapted *Seekers* as an outdoor production. One of his changes directly affected Melissa, who had already agreed to reprise her role as the Indian maiden that Jim Bridger marries in the second act of the show. But C. H. had another idea for my pregnant bride. Aware of her training in theater, he asked her to become an "Eagle Dancer," unseen by the actors but a metaphorical, omnipresent representative of the "natural" world, posing behind and alongside them throughout the production to punctuate specific verse and scenes. To facilitate this, C. H. had some old feathered "wings" and a headdress he brought up from Oklahoma for her to try out.

We thought C. H. was joking. When we realized he was serious, Melissa reminded him that she was seven months pregnant.

"I don't think anyone wants to see a pregnant eagle dancer," Melissa laughed. "Besides, we wouldn't want to hatch an egg onstage."

C. H. was persistent. He calmly assured her that he would design a dress from trade cloth so that no one would know she was pregnant. More to the point, he assured her that if she ever became uncomfortable or concerned for the baby's health she could simply step out of the scene and no one would know the difference.

Ever the trouper, Melissa became our eagle dancer and our Indian maiden. When the show's run ended in late August Melissa was so close to her due date that the airlines refused to let her fly. She drove home to Texas with Joe and James while I headed to the Fort Bridger Rendezvous to complete the tour I had originally booked. Finally, in mid-September, I raced home and arrived in time for one Lamaze training class; on October 7, 1989—barely a month after exiting her stage role in Cody—Melissa gave birth to a healthy boy. We gave him Jim Bridger's mountain man nickname—Gabriel. Assisting with the birth of my son removed any doubt that the ancient need for shedding blood in puberty manhood rituals has finally begun to recede into the mythology of the past.

At the end of the summer 1989 run of *Seekers of the Fleece* in Cody we made a tiny profit, and that was the start of a seasonal run in the Robbie Powwow Garden that would continue for the next five summers. By Wyoming's centennial in 1990, I was able to secure major grants that matched Joe and Charles Duggan's investments and allowed our company to expand to twenty-six actors, singers, musicians, dancers, and technicians. That year—now with our infant son, Gabriel, as part of the company—*Seekers of the Fleece* was the featured attraction at Wyoming's Centennial Rendezvous in Jackson Hole, and we became the very first professional theatrical troupe to tour Yellowstone and Grand Teton national parks.

I was so emotionally and financially involved with mere survival at the time that it took years to fully comprehend the meaning of it all, but the "heat" from those monumental blazes during the summer of 1988 popped seeds in me as surely as in the lodgepole pinecones. Those seeds fell into the ashes of my former life. Fields of wildflowers would eventually spring from the enriched soil to herald the birth of a new cycle. Three years after the historic conflagration, my wife, Melissa, and our toddler son, Gabriel, stood like seedlings in the charcoal and wildflower landscape of Yellowstone National Park, beginning our lives together as a family.

EPILOGUE

Digital Balladeers

ARCH 17, 2005, was Jim Bridger's two-hundred-and-first birthday. Having turned sixty only three days earlier myself, I was in a pensive mood that intensified as I crossed the Sabine River and drove into Louisiana. Upon visiting the location of my childhood so soon after beginning my seventh decade, it was only natural for me to become reflective. Still, I was happy to finally be heading to Kentucky. Since meeting Jeff Spradling and Russ Ward at Vine Deloria's four days before 9/11, I had remained in regular communication with the cousins, and they even had me proclaimed a "Kentucky Colonel." But there was more to celebrate: in addition to a ten-day tour of rural regions of the state, Jeff arranged what was truly a highlight of my entire career—a performance of *Seekers of the Fleece* at the John Jacob Niles Center for American Music at the University of Kentucky in Lexington.

When I began research for *A Ballad of the West* in 1963, one of the first collections of folk songs I explored was that of Kentucky balladeer John Jacob Niles. Based on personal compilations of folktales and intimate observations of the language of Appalachian people, Niles composed "Black Is the Color of My True Love's Hair," "I Wonder as I Wander," "Go Away from My Window," "Hangman," and scores of other classic folk songs. In four decades of performing folk music, I had come to regard Niles and his contemporaries A. P. Carter, Carl Sandburg, and Woody Guthrie as vital transitional figures in the history of American ballads. Each rose to prominence as rapidly evolving recording technology forever affected oral history and ballads. During the first third of the twentieth century folk-lorists like A. P. Carter and John and Alan Lomax collected ballads. But when the Carter Family became internationally famous recording artists, and Leadbelly and Woody Guthrie accompanied John and Alan Lomax to the halls of academia for live performances, the era of the folk "star" was born. Indicative of this change, Carter, Sandburg, and Niles collected—but also composed—unique folk material and became famous intermediary figures bridging the days of pure oral tradition and the multiple stages of rapid advancement in recording technology that began in the mid-twentieth century. Of course, Woody Guthrie wrote all his material, but he had no reluctance at "borrowing" melodies from whomever, or wherever, he pleased. Woody remarked on occasion that he preferred a melody that had been around for a while and had proved popular. Since time immemorial that has been referred to as the "folk process," but as Woody would no doubt agree, all art is hybrid. Thinking about the Carter Family, Guthrie, Sandburg, John Jacob Niles, the folk ballad process, and the advances that I personally witnessed in recording technology over a forty-year career of writing, performing, and producing *A Ballad of the West* reminded me that the ways we create and distribute art were radically—permanently—transformed with the creation of the World Wide Web. In 1963, when I began synthesizing ancient storytelling arts to create an "epic" western ballad, the only technical arts available for me to capture and record my concept were labor-intensive and prohibitively costly options. Complicating matters, since the form itself did not exist except in my head and my personal performances, it was difficult to persuade anyone to finance the creation of a prototype that did not fit accepted distribution procedures that would allow the investor to recoup the investment. Addressing that problem head-on, I took the epic ballad to the stage in 1974 to develop it as a performance piece. In 1975, with the help of dedicated, talented musicians and technicians, I recorded my prototype, *Seekers of the Fleece*. Continuing throughout the 1970s, however, no comprehensive, affordable technology existed to fully synthesize the new form I envisioned.

But everything turned on its ear when the digital age arrived. Seemingly overnight, anyone could cheaply construct a digital state-of-art studio, then record and distribute music without ever leaving home. This development certainly vanquished many gatekeepers, hobbled the recording industry, and exposed the ironic inability of its infrastructure to incorporate the profound technological changes that occurred during the last quarter of the twentieth century. Failing to cope with file downloading, the recording industry began to implode, while at the same time biblical legends of singer/songwriters advancing their careers on the Internet exploded. Moreover, driven by connections cultivated over the Internet, intimate singer/songwriter "house concerts" simultaneously began popping up with increasing frequency all over America. Clearly, digital balladeers are already reinventing themselves on the fringes of the electronic frontier the same way their predecessors did in cozy parlors, on front porches, at family reunions, and eventually on concert stages and in the recording industry.

I was fantasizing about the possibilities of producing a Web cam performance of *A Ballad of the West* as I rolled into my hometown. I had planned my route and schedule so that I could stop by the Columbia cemetery to double-check birth and death dates on grandparents' and great-grandparents' tombstones for this manuscript, and I was also going to visit my mother in West Monroe. After my father's death in 2000, my mother's mental and physical health rapidly declined until my brothers and I had no choice except to surrender her to full-time medical care in a nursing home. My regular visits with her became increasingly heartrending as her body ceased to function. Her mental capacities jumbled, twirled, and reshaped into the vivid illusions and fantasies of a child. Even though she took me down some confusing emotional trails, it became important to talk to her as often as possible, whether she was lucid or not.

As I entered Columbia and drove past the Caldwell Bank and Trust Company, it occurred to me that our long family history in the community was drawing to a close. Even so, the bank that Uncle Archie had founded at the turn of the twentieth century would remain a cornerstone of Columbia. Archie's eighty-six-year-old daughter, Dorothy Bridger Eglin, and his grandson, Bridger Eglin, remained on the bank's board of directors. Nevertheless, Dorothy had not lived in Columbia since childhood, and now that my mother no longer lived there, the last remaining link of the Bridger family was my kid brother John. Shy and introverted, John is a bachelor who will likely remain so for the rest of his days—which he will also likely spend in Columbia. But, as significant as the passing of the Bridger family connection to Columbia, when my mother and Aunt Dorothy die, the last branches of our limb on the Bridger tree will pass with them. Throughout my professional career I always believed that reality alone was reason enough for assuming the pseudonym "Bobby Bridger."

Trekking through the steep hills of the Columbia cemetery reminded

me of my childhood there and that my friend Johnny Morris had died of a
massive coronary two months earlier. Being in the Bridger graveyard in the
Columbia cemetery and recalling my youth there sketching tombstone
angels with Johnny also brought to mind all the people mentioned in this
book who have made the journey to the spirit world: Wooten and Francis
Morris, Dr. O. Philip James, Jack McCall, Slim Pickens, Marty Robbins,
Marlon Brando, Dave McCormick, Rodney Dungan, Warren Skaaren,
John Hartford, Chet Atkins, Pete Drake, Harlan Howard, Stringbean,
Conway Twitty, Roy Orbison, Waylon Jennings, Grady Martin, Bullets
Durgom, Joe Reisman, Sidney Goldstein, Harry Nilsson, Nik Venet, Tim-
berjack Joe and Tuffy, Severt Young Bear, Godfrey and Lucy Broken Rope,
Terry Edgar, Billy Childress, Alice Harrower, John Henry Faulk, Alan
Lomax, Joel Oppenheimer, Crady Bond, Bill Ginn, Chris Sergel, Will
Sampson, Hilda and Enid Neihardt, John Denver, Walter Hyatt, Champ
Hood, B. W. Stevenson, Doug Sahm, Townes Van Zandt. So many now
dwell with the Great Mystery.

I sat in the cemetery with ghosts and memories for a while, but I had a
tour schedule to maintain and the time had come to move on. Before
departing for Kentucky I contacted my alma mater, Northeast Louisiana
State College—now the University of Louisiana/Monroe—and booked an
afternoon show in the new on-campus coffeehouse.

Massive new high-rise buildings towered over what remained of the
1960s campus. I located the offices of the coordinator of student events and
we headed across the campus. I was surprised to learn that the college's old
library had been converted into a bookstore and campus coffeehouse. But
I had to laugh at the irony when I discovered that the coffeehouse was in
the precise location where four decades earlier I had sat at long wooden
tables, hovered over musty books, and first explored the ballad collections
of Niles, Sandburg, Child, and the Lomaxes. In that library I also discovered and fell in love with the work of historian Bernard DeVoto, the paintings of Alfred Jacob Miller, the epic poetry of John G. Neihardt, and the
father of all epic poets and balladeers, Homer.

I completed my show and within moments was back on the road. Even
as I mused over the paradox of the old Northeast library becoming a coffeehouse, I realized I was probably going to be reminiscing throughout my
entire tour, as driving to Kentucky would retrace even more trails of my
past. I rolled through northern Mississippi to Memphis for the first time in
decades and headed to Nashville.

Over the years I had stayed in contact with Fred Carter Jr. and his family. In 1994 Fred's kidneys failed and he spent five days in a coma. Ever the fighter, he rebounded, eventually had a kidney transplant, and now well into his seventies, continues to write songs and record them in his home studio. I had visited Nashville as recently as February 2005 to videotape an interview with Fred for a documentary film based on my life and work that a British company produced. After we filmed his interview, Fred warned me that I would hardly recognize Music Row today.

"Thieves took it all," he lamented. "In the past when hucksters came to town they harvested the crop, but had the good sense to leave seeds. The recent waves of crooks just took it all. There's little regard for the future or the past. It's hardly even about music anymore."

My trip down memory lane on Nashville's Music Row was an affirmation of Fred's words. "Music Row" still beckoned with bright, catchy shingles and neon lights advertising wares and chart successes up and down Sixteenth and Seventeenth avenues. Now, however, it looked much more like a quaint California interpretation of "country"; all of Nashville's rich hillbilly heritage seemed hidden away, like some hayseed cousin brought out in public only for sentimental "roots" celebrations or flag-waving. Texas journalist Jan Reid truly prophesied the future of country music when he coined the term "Redneck Rock."

I headed north on Interstate 65 and entered the "Bluegrass State." Turning east toward Lexington on Highway 64, I passed Abraham Lincoln's birthplace and the location of *My Old Kentucky Home*, the outdoor drama based on the life of Stephen Foster. Passing the site reminded me of years of affiliation with the National Outdoor Drama Association and the full-company outdoor musical productions of *Seekers of the Fleece* in Wyoming—six years as the only outdoor, non-Shakespearean production performed in verse in America. But passing the location of the Stephen Foster outdoor musical also reminded me that I was entering the cradle of American ballads. Here, ancient Anglo-Saxon lyrics, reels, and jigs crossed the Appalachian Mountains and descended on the Ohio River en route to a melodious wedding with African, French, and Spanish influences on the Mississippi. I was entering hallowed musical ground.

Still, I thought, what about the West? Asking myself that question made me proud once again that I had devoted my career to filling the void in American folk music that I had realized as a kid when I stumbled across the fact that no ballads had survived the fur trade era. The simple desire to fill that emptiness with verse and songs that authentically depicted the people of that historical era, and the events that shaped their lives, took me into a world previously charted only by the epic poet Neihardt. The trail of my own that I subsequently forged into that time period, into that enchanted, catastrophic landscape, into those extraordinary heroic lives, forever changed me. Over the years, as I repeatedly reinvented myself during my explorations into the mountains, deserts, high plains and prairies, history, indigenous religion, and mythology of the region, I came to believe—as many before me—that the West is the sacred place Americans will always return to as a nation to reinvent ourselves.

So, embracing sixty and on the road to perform *A Ballad of the West* at the holy shrine of American ballads, I smiled to recall lyrics that I wrote decades earlier describing eighteen-year-old Jim Bridger's emotions in 1822 as he embarked into the unknown territory of the Great American West. New meanings whispered:

> I want to open my window, let the sun shine in;
> I've got to kick down my fences, let my freedom begin;
> Don't want nothing but blue sky up above my head,
> I've got to free my spirit, 'fore my spirit's dead.
> I want to do something that I ain't never done
> And see how far it gets me—maybe to the sun
> And find that place where heaven and earth are wed
> I've got to free my spirit 'fore my spirit's dead.
> I want to see something no man has ever seen,
> Go somewhere no man has ever been
> Find myself alive with every breath
> So I will know life when I meet my death.
> The Rocky Mountains are as high as you go
> And everything is up there that I want to know
> Nothing but heaven up above my head
> I've got to free my spirit, 'fore my spirit's dead.[1]

Notes

PROLOGUE

1. "Stages," lyrics by Rob Preston and Rita Briggs, music by Alan Jay Friedman. From the musical *Shakespeare and the Indians* by Dale Wasserman. © Dale Wasserman.
2. Ibid.

ONE

1. "The Call" by Bobby Bridger. © Edwin H. Morris Company, ASCAP, a division of MPL Communications, Inc.
2. *A Ballad of the West/Seekers of the Fleece.* © Bobby Bridger, White Coyote Music, ASCAP.

TWO

1. "The German Girl" by Hill C. Durham Sr. © Bobby Bridger, White Coyote Music, ASCAP.

THREE

1. "California Joe" was George A. Custer's chief of scouts and perished with him at Little Big Horn.

FOUR

1. "Baton Rouge" was eventually recorded by three different acts, including the immortal Hank Williams's favorite opening act, Texan Claude Gray. It won an ASCAP Chartbuster Award.

FIVE

1. At the peak of his fame in late 1969, John Lennon went to Toronto seeking Ronnie Hawkins—a decade past his prime—to play music and to listen to the master's stories of the birth of rock and roll. In the late 1970s, Lennon recorded a rock-and-roll tribute album with some Ronnie Hawkins tunes on it. Some might wish to view Martin Scorsese's biopic of the Band, *The Last Waltz*, for another perspective of Ronnie Hawkins.

2. Sam Phillips sold Presley's contract to RCA in 1956 for $35,000 plus a $5,000 signing bonus.

3. Originally "arrangement and repertoire," A&R men (very few were women) were executives responsible for signing artists to recording labels, arranging the songs artists recorded, and supervising recording sessions. By the 1960s the "arrangement" part of the title had become "artist."

SIX

1. Imagine my surprise two years later when it dawned on me that Jim Bridger had died on July 17, 1881.

2. Fred Carter Jr. played lead guitar on most of Orbison's recording sessions as well as in his band.

3. "Life Is a River" by Bobby Bridger. © White Coyote Music, ASCAP.

4. "Rendezvous" by Bobby Bridger. © White Coyote Music, ASCAP.

SEVEN

1. Only weeks after "The Boxer" went gold in 1969, someone stole all of Fred's guitars from the trunk of his Cadillac. The police recovered all of the guitars *except* 5-18 "Baby" Martin. In 1977 I bought a 5-18 Martin in Denver. I gave it to Fred in 1980 when we recorded *Heal in the Wisdom*; he gave it back to me in 1986 when I played Nashville as part of the Texas Sesquicentennial Tour.

2. John G. Neihardt, *A Cycle of the West* (Lincoln: University of Nebraska Press, 1963).

NINE

1. Jan Reid coined the term "redneck rock" to define the progressive country movement of the late 1960s and early 1970s. As modern country truly has become "redneck rock," the neo-folk/country/rock movement has become categorized as "Americana."

2. Michael Tannen's father, Nat Tannen, structured the Acuff-Rose publishing company for Roy Acuff and Wesley Rose. Aside from Paul Simon, at various times Michael represented the Rolling Stones, John Lennon, Billy Joel, Merle Haggard, and others.

TEN

1. Peter, Paul, and Mary have performed numerous "reunion tours" since their first "breakup."

2. Several of Fred Miller's films that I scored won second prize to oceanographer/environmentalist Jacques Cousteau's consistent first prize in the New York Documentary Film Festival.

3. After *Keep Truckin'* opened and closed within a month, the Dobie Towers remodeled the room into a normal movie theater that, after several other massive makeovers, continues screening art films today.

4. Roger Bartlett was destined to soon become the first, and for several years the *only*, member of Jimmy Buffett's Coral Reefer Band.

ELEVEN

1. Patti Page was also the first person to sing in harmony with herself through the then-revolutionary recording technique of multi-track overdubbing.

2. *And I Wanted to Sing for the People* by Bobby Bridger. © Edwin H. Morris Company, a division of MPL Communications, Inc.

3. In 1973 I used Devils Tower as a major motif and metaphor in *Aldebaran and the Falling Star*, and the work was copyrighted four years before *Close Encounters of the Third Kind* appeared in movie theaters.

4. Tim McClure and Frank Feltch. McClure would later become the "M" in Roy Spence's superagency, GSD&M. McClure coined the phrase "Don't Mess with Texas," nominated in 2006 as the best advertising phrase ever.

TWELVE

1. There is substantial evidence that legendary record producer and co-owner of Atlantic Records Jerry Wexler actually coined the term "rock and roll" when he was a cub reporter for *Billboard* magazine. Wexler definitely coined "rhythm and blues" to replace the term "race music."

2. Sadly, lightning struck the Ballad Tree in the mid-1990s and it no longer stands on Chapel Hill.

THIRTEEN

1. John Stewart was Dave Guard's replacement in the Kingston Trio before embarking on a solo career as a singer/songwriter when the group disbanded in 1966.

FOURTEEN

1. The legend is that a black woman actually dubbed him "Ramblin'" because he talked so much. She said, "That boy do ramble on."

FIFTEEN

1. Caedmon's resistance to change is perhaps why after so many years of dominating the niche, it rapidly faded in prominence as cassette tape technology exploded and audiobooks suddenly swamped the market in the 1980s. Nevertheless, as pioneers in the genre Caedmon recorded the rich and deep catalog of the best literary figures of the twentieth century reading their original work.

SIXTEEN

1. "Red Cloud" by Bobby Bridger. © White Coyote Music, ASCAP.

SEVENTEEN

1. Lee Eastman is the grandfather of Linda, the late wife of Sir Paul McCartney.
2. Within a decade I would introduce Gayle Ritchie to Chris Sergel, and she would become his fourth wife.
3. It would be thirteen years before I would return to the Big Horn Medicine Wheel. Sadly, the Harmonic Convergence led to the sudden "discovery" of the Medicine Wheel by the mainstream public, which ignited passionate arguments between various Indian tribes, environmental activists, scientists, hippies, and state governments. When I returned in 2000 with my son, Gabriel, a state law required us to stay on a specific sidewalk around the "relic." We were forbidden to even walk over to my old campsite at the edge of the cliff.

EIGHTEEN

1. The January 1982 trip to see Leonard Marks to present *Heal in the Wisdom*.
2. For many years Marilyn Stasio has also written crime novel reviews for the *New York Times Book Review*.

EPILOGUE

1. *Free My Spirit, 'fore My Spirit's Dead* by Bobby Bridger. © White Coyote Music, ASCAP.

Index

Robert Redford at Sundance Institute, 262–263; performs for Slim Pickens, 11–12; performs title song for feature film *The Wheel*, 10, 137-138, 142–143; signs contract with E. H. Morris Publishing Company, 158; signs contract with legendary manager George "Bullets" Durgom, 164–166; signs contract with RCA Records, 158; studies art, 26–31, 46–47, 57–59; has surgery for vocal polyps, 111–114; teaches art, 103–105, 116; tours Australia, 266–267, 269; tours with Marty Robbins, 110–111; works as cowboy, 1–4; writes *Coyote Dreamtime*, 269

Bridger, Cicero Call, 32–33
Bridger, Hartley Call, 33, 48, 55, 164
Bridger, Ingadozier Call, 32
Bridger, James (Jim), 6–7, 11, 14, 18–19, 42, 50, 59–60, 68, 96, 113, 128, 155, 172, 185–186, 189–190, 205, 211, 227, 274, 283–285
Bridger, Josephine Sutton, 26, 33
Bridger, Roberta Lee (Bobbie), 33, 36–37, 87, 227, 287
Bridger, Zella, 42
Bridger Productions, 258, 274–275, 280
Brill Building, 122, 193
Britt, Lynn, 265–266
Broken Rope, Godfrey, 230, 288
Broken Rope, Lucy, 230, 288
Brooks, Garth, 148
Brooks, Mel, 165, 194, 209
Brothers Four, the, 43
Browne, Jackson, 194, 281
Bruce, Lenny, 165
Bryant, Boudleaux, 92
Bryant, Felice, 92
Buffalo Bill Historical Center, 232, 239–240, 282–283
"Buffalo Skinners," 6
Buffett, Jimmy, 198
Buntline, Ned, 3
Bunyan, Paul, 50
Burkheimer, Don, 14–15, 191, 195
Burnside, Dennis, 132
Burnside, Terry "Fatback," 132
Burton, James, 22, 73
Burton, Michael, 210
Burton, Richard, 259–266

"Busted," 89
"Bye Bye Love," 79, 92
Byrds, the, 194
"By the Time I Get to Phoenix," 105

Caldwell Bank and Trust Company, 33, 38, 42, 287
Caldwell Parish Art and Folk Festival, 26, 30–31
California Bloodlines, 194
"California Joe," 50
"Call, The," 9, 166, 180, 182
Campbell, Glenn, 100, 102–103, 105, 109, 180
"Canadian Railroad Trilogy," 99
"Candy Man," 90
Cantor, Eddie, 54
Captain and Tennille, 177
Carmichael, Hoagie, 177
Carousels, the, 41
Carpenters, the, 180
Carradine, David, 180, 265
Carrington, Henry, 245
Carry, Lynne Alice, 17
Carter, Anna, 73, 79, 81
Carter, A. P., 285–286
Carter, Deana, 79
Carter, Fred Jr., 72, 77–84, 81, 86–94, 97, 99–101, 103–105, 108–112, 115–116, 118–125, 132–134, 151, 156–157, 180, 194, 247, 249–251, 289
Carter, Fred Sr., 72
Carter, Mother Maybelle, 118–119, 123
Carter, Reuben, 72
Carter, Ronnie Dale, 79
Carter, Susan, 107
Carter, Tillie, 72
Carter Family, 43
Cash, Johnny, 21–22, 45, 90, 118, 149, 156
Cashbox Magazine, 102
Cassady, Neal, 217
Cassidy, Hopalong, 162, 182
Castle Creek, 153, 161, 174
Cavalcade of Stars, 159
Cavett, Dick, 233, 242
CBS Evening News with Walter Cronkite, 52
Charles, Ray, 40
Childress, Billy, 57, 288
Chitrabhannu, Guru Dev, 253–254

Walker, Jerry Jeff, 151–152, 173–174, 182–183,
206, 211, 224
Wall Street Journal, The, 255
Wanted: The Outlaws, 157
Ward, Russ, 5, 285
Warhol, Andy, 152
Warnes, Jennifer, 250, 279
Warren, Bob, 206–207, 221
Wasserman, Dale, 4, 8, 259–261, 265, 279
"Waterloo," 109
Waters, Frank, 258
Waters, "Muddy," 93
Watkins, Larry, 144
Watson, Daryl, 273
Wayne, John, 206
Weavers, the, 43–44
Webb, Jimmy, 99, 105
Webber, Andrew Lloyd, 255
Weeks, "Buddy," 281
Weintraub, Jerry, 179
Weir, Rusty, 144, 146
Welles, Orson, 145
"We Shall Overcome," 64, 247
Westerman, Floyd Red Crow, 204, 281,
What I Want for You, 133
Wheel, The, 10–11, 138, 140–142, 149
When the Tree Flowered, 128, 168
White, George C., 261–262, 265, 273
White, Josh, 44
Whitehead, Alfred North, 168
Whiteplume, Jake, 189–191
Whitman, Charles, 139
Who, the, 99
"Why Do I Love You?," 115
"Wichita Lineman," 105
Wickman, Melinda, 197
Wilkins, Marijohn, 54
Willard, Maxine, 181
William Morris Agency, 278

Williams, Don, 119
Williams, Hank Jr., 74
Williams, Hank Sr., 21, 74
Williams, Jaston, 277–278
Williams, Mike, 210, 212–213
Williams, Paul, 179
Williams, Tennessee, 255
Wills, Chill, 11
Wilson, Earl, 192
Wilson, Eddie, 152
Wilson, Jackie, 40, 46
Wind River Indian Reservation, 2, 181
Winter, Johnny, 139
Wood, Grant, 97
Woods, Natalie, 165
Woodstock, 151
Woody Guthrie, Child of Dust, 14
"World Is Turning On, The," 115, 118
Wynette, Tammy, 119
Wyoming's Centennial Rendezvous, 284

Yarborough, Ralph, 154–155
Yarrow, Peter, 44, 77, 143, 163, 182. *See also* Peter, Paul, and Mary
Yaryan, Jess, 148, 197
Yates, Walter, 225
Yearwood, Trisha, 148
Yellowstone National Park, 169, 172, 186, 195, 238–239, 270, 273–275, 275, 279, 284
"You Are My Sunshine," 43, 82
Young, Faron, 21
Young, Neil, 281
Young, Steve, 119, 184
Youngbear, Severt, Sr., 282–288
"Young Blood," 255

Zappa, Frank, 173, 178
Zoe, Natalie, 251
Z. Z. Top, 228